ABNORMAL PSYCHOLOGY IN CONTEXT

ABNORMAL PSYCHOLOGY IN CONTEXT

Voices and Perspectives

David N. Sattler
College of Charleston

Virginia Shabatay
Palomar College

Geoffrey P. Kramer
Grand Valley State University

HOUGHTON MIFFLIN COMPANY   Boston   New York

Sponsoring Editor: David C. Lee
Senior Associate Editor: Jane Knetzger
Editorial Assistant: Lou Gum
Project Editor: Anne Holm
Associate Production Coordinator: Deborah Frydman
Senior Manufacturing Coordinator: Marie Barnes
Marketing Manager: Pamela J. Laskey

Cover design: Harold Burch, Harold Burch Design, NYC
Cover photographs: © Wilhelm Scholz (top left); © Jenny Lynn (top right); "Man in Empty
Room" by Nancy R. Cohen (bottom left); © Shigeru Otsuki (bottom right)

Printed in the U.S.A.

Library of Congress Catalog Card Number: 97-72432

ISBN: 0-395-87451-3

9-MP-08 07

To my wife, Sudie,
especially with love and for shared dreams and journeys
and
to my father, Jerome M. Sattler,
with deep respect and love
DAVID N. SATTLER

To my family,
with love and admiration
VIRGINIA SHABATAY

To Michelle,
my love, my partner, my pal
GEOFFREY P. KRAMER

Brief Contents

Contents

2

DISSOCIATIVE DISORDERS   26

3

SOMATOFORM DISORDERS AND FACTITIOUS DISORDERS 45

4

MOOD DISORDERS 65

5

SUICIDE   81

6

PSYCHOLOGICAL FACTORS AND MEDICAL CONDITIONS

9

SUBSTANCE-RELATED DISORDERS   165

10

SEXUAL DYSFUNCTIONS AND DISORDERS   186

11

COGNITIVE DISORDERS   202

12

DISORDERS OF CHILDHOOD AND ADOLESCENCE, MENTAL RETARDATION, AND EATING DISORDERS   226

13

INDIVIDUAL AND GROUP THERAPY   247

Creating an Ethical Position in Family Therapy 266

Ivan B. Inger and Jeri Inger

Psychological Concepts: family therapy, collaboration by cotherapists

A family therapy team interviews a family whose gifted son has been labelled severely emotionally disturbed by school officials; the therapists, however, meet a very different boy.

Preface

Abnormal Psychology in Context: Voices and Perspectives is a unique collection of first-person accounts and narratives written by individuals who live with a psychological disorder and by therapists, relatives, and others who have direct experience with someone suffering from a psychological disorder. These individuals describe in touching, informative, and poignant ways their experiences with the disorder and how it has affected their lives. The narratives illustrate psychological disorders and issues covered in most abnormal psychology textbooks. This book is appropriate for abnormal psychology courses, and undergraduate and graduate courses in counseling, clinical psychology, psychotherapy, and social work.

Our goals for the book are the following:

- To promote students' understanding and retention of the origins, symptoms, and treatment of psychological disorders by presenting first-person accounts written by individuals who have direct experience with a psychological disorder.

- To present individuals with a psychological disorder as persons to be respected and not simply as diagnostic examples.

- To broaden students' knowledge and understanding about the use of mental health services and the effects of psychological disorders on social relationships.

- To stimulate critical thinking about gender, multicultural, ethical, theoretical, and research issues.

The First-Person Approach to Teaching Abnormal Psychology

We believe that the issues in abnormal psychology are learned best when they are presented in conjunction with personal and interpersonal experiences. Many instructors who teach abnormal psychology became experts by working in applied settings, listening to clients describe—in ways that no textbook ever could—what it is like to have a disorder, and by trying to help clients overcome their symptoms and improve their lives. For these persons, clinical knowledge became vivid and understandable in large part because of the people they met. Symptoms became poignant and memorable, and questions about etiology and treatment became compelling. One of the challenges for instructors of abnormal psychology is to convey the richness of such personal experiences to students. This book can help instructors meet that challenge.

The authors whose narratives are included in this book have an intimate knowledge of psychological problems, and they represent a highly articulate and insightful group of people suffering from psychological disorders. Their stories provide insight and capture nuances of the disorder, and we gain new appreciation for their experiences and how the condition has affected their lives. With this information, we can empathize and develop a more complete understanding of psychological disorders. Many of these authors have been helped through months or years of treatment. Their discussion of treatments that worked or did not work for them can broaden our understanding of treatment approaches.

Of course, these authors face the same biases and limitations of self-knowledge that we all face. For example, they might advance more biological explanations and fewer psychological explanations for their disorder because biological explanations seem to invite less reproach. They might appear pessimistic because sufferers are usually acutely aware of their pain or the memory of it. Sometimes they may not understand fully the etiology of their problem or the reasons they received a particular type of treatment. Despite any limitations or biases, however, there is great value in first-person accounts.

Some authors preferred to change their name and/or the names of others in order to protect their privacy or the privacy of those whose stories they tell. All are courageous people who persevered in the face of confusion, pain, and anxiety. We are grateful to them for sharing their experiences.

Criteria for Selecting the Readings

We used several criteria for selecting the readings. First, the selections had to illustrate psychological disorders covered in most abnormal psychology textbooks. They had to provide clear descriptions of psychological symptoms and information about etiology or treatment. This information is important for understanding various theoretical perspectives and treatments, and for critical thinking. Second, because psychological disorders affect more than just the sufferer, we also sought narratives that convey something of the social and interpersonal consequences of having a disorder. Third, each narrative had to be provocative: it had to arouse us, hold our attention, and stir us with questions. Fourth, we favored selections that would broaden students' perspectives on gender, ethnic, and cultural influences related to psychopathology. Finally, the selections had to be long enough for readers to become absorbed in the writer's experiences but short enough for instructors to assign them as supplemental readings.

Chapter Organization

The chapters correspond to the categories of major psychological disorders presented in most abnormal psychology textbooks. Each chapter contains between two and four narratives, and each narrative covers a different disorder from the category or a different aspect of the disorder.

An introduction precedes each chapter and each selection. The introductions orient the reader, introduce the major issues encountered, and may provide brief biographical information about the author. Two types of pedagogical questions follow each chapter:

- *Response and Analysis* questions ask students (a) to connect material in the readings with material presented in lecture or their primary textbook; and (b) to examine their reactions to the reading. Some questions may ask about etiology, symptomatology, differential diagnoses, treatment, or ethical issues. Other questions ask students about their reactions. Students often experience a wide range of reactions to the descriptions of psychological disorders. For example, sometimes their reactions are complex and informed. They may recognize that disorders can have multiple causes, that symptoms can be powerful and varied, and that effective treatment can involve several obstacles. Other times, however, they may believe that certain behaviors are just "too strange," wonder why somebody doesn't "do something about it," or think that a person ought to "get a grip." These reactions vary from person to person and, even within the same person, from disorder to disorder. It is important that students recognize and think about their reactions to the various disorders. Doing so will help them better understand both the disorders and themselves.

- *Research* questions ask students to think about how research can advance our understanding of abnormal behavior. They present methodological issues appropriate for students who have not had a course in research methods. The questions ask students to try to solve problems or test alternative hypotheses. They cover basic methodological concepts, such as identifying and measuring variables, constructing simple research designs, controlling for extraneous variables, and applying ethical research principles. These questions highlight the importance of empirical research in understanding and treating psychological disorders.

Suggestions for the Instructor: How to Use This Book

Abnormal Psychology in Context: Voices and Perspectives can be used in a variety of ways in small and large classes. Instructors may assign the readings to illustrate and amplify material presented in their lectures. The readings also provide a valuable resource for class discussions, writing assignments, research projects, or other individual or group projects.

Class Discussion

Students enjoy discussing their reactions to the readings in class.

1. The Response and Analysis questions and the Research questions following each reading stimulate active class discussion and reinforce students' understanding of the psychological disorders. Students can be asked to answer the questions prior to class or to share their responses during class. This can serve as an excellent way to introduce a topic in class.

   The Research questions serve as a good foundation for discussing research methodology. The questions teach basic concepts and principles and also show students the role of methodology and statistics in understanding and treating disorders.

2. Students often enjoy a class debate. Many of the issues raised by the readings and the questions following each reading serve well for critical thinking and illustrate opposing viewpoints. For example, in her essay, *I Am Not Afraid*, Barbara Harrison tells about her husband's rejection of her panic attack on an escalator. His injunction, "grow up," is full of assumptions about willpower and the degree of control one has (or can have) over symptoms. It also raises questions about the role of social support. Debates about the appropriate treatment of persons with a disorder who commit crimes or who are homeless and mentally ill can be lively. Further debates may center on evidence for and against competing theoretical perspectives, how best to treat a particular disorder, and how friends and family members might best handle a situation in which someone is suffering from a psychological disorder.

Research Projects

The readings can be used to generate interesting research ideas and projects.

1. Students can work alone or in groups to design a research proposal based on an idea raised by a Response and Analysis question or a Research question. The proposal might include: (a) a statement of the problem or question and why it is interesting or important; (b) a summary of previous research about the problem or question; (c) a statement indicating the relevant variables and the hypothesis; and (d) a description of the relevant method (e.g., participants, materials, procedures, controls, ethical safeguards). Such an assignment might require students to focus on methodological issues by addressing the recruitment of participants, informed consent, random assignment, counterbalancing, ethical treatment, and reporting the results.

2. Students can work alone or in groups to write a term paper based on one of the readings and its questions. The term paper might explore the current state of knowledge about or controversy over various psychological disorders. The paper, which might include an introduction, literature review, and discussion, could be turned in during the term or presented in class in a ten- to fifteen-minute presentation.

3. Advanced or honor students can investigate one question or author in detail. For instance, a student could read one or two books or articles by an author whose selection is included herein. They could learn more about the political, social, and economic forces that might have affected the author and his or her experience living with the disorder. The students could submit a written research report or make an oral presentation to the class.

Writing Assignments

Writing assignments are a valuable way for students to focus on academic material, to engage in critical thinking, to analyze, question, and give personal responses to what they have read, and to develop writing skills. Instructors may require students to answer some or all of the Response and Analysis questions and Research questions at the end of each chapter.

The readings and questions can serve as a basis for journals or response papers. Instructors might allow students to develop ideas that occur to them after reading the narratives and questions. The writing assignments might be turned in weekly or only a few times during the course, depending on class size and time available to read and grade them. Instructors can assign grades, satisfactory or unsatisfactory credit, or extra credit as appropriate.

Individual and Group Projects

The readings can be used to generate engaging individual and group projects.

1. Students can be divided into groups to compare responses to the questions. It is often useful to provide a rough agenda, time limits, and to select a person or persons to serve as group facilitator, recorder, and reporter. Each group could compile and summarize its responses and note similarities, differences, and any trends. The reporter could give a synopsis to the class at the end of the exercise. The variability of responses both within and among groups is often instructive.

2. Students can work alone or in groups to compare the diagnostic criteria listed in their textbook or DSM-IV with the symptoms described in the readings. This exercise should help students better understand the disorders and some of the problems associated with diagnostic classification.

3. Students can make individual presentations on a disorder. They might incorporate a variety of materials, including academic readings and other sources like artwork, music, or drama. For instance, the suicide of a rock star might be discussed in light of the progression of his or her problems, the social environment, and the music.

4. One instructor we know has a day in which students role-play various disorders, either presenting themselves individually to the class or mingling in class with other in-character role-players. Of course, caution must be exercised that disorders are not stereotyped or treated as sources of humor (just as caution is taken that students should not diagnose friends or family members). But if this exercise is conducted toward the end of the course, after students have been exposed to a range of information and humanizing readings, it is usually done with respect, and post-role-playing discussion is lively and educational.

Extending the Borders: A Final Note

In his remarkable book *An Anthropologist on Mars*, Oliver Sacks reports that what he has found most effective in understanding both his patients and their illnesses is to get out of his office and into their lives, making "house calls at the far borders of human experience." In this way he comes to know them and their conditions from within, as persons, and not merely as patients who have been handed a diagnosis. It is our conviction that students, too, will better understand the issues in psychology whenever they extend the borders of the theoretical into the world of human experience. Such is the aim of this book.

Acknowledgments

It is a special pleasure to express our appreciation to the many talented and dedicated people who provided creative ideas and suggestions for this book. We wish to thank Douglas A. Bernstein for his continual enthusiasm and excellent feedback, and the following individuals for reading various portions of the manuscript and offering constructive criticism.

Angela O. Ballantyne, University of California—San Diego

Beth Benoit, University of Massachusetts—Lowell, and Middlesex Community College

Peggy R. Brooks, North Adams State College

Deborah Carlin, Washington University

Craig R. Cowden, Northern Virginia Community College

Roy Darby, University of South Carolina—Beaufort

David R. Harrington, Sheldon Jackson College

Ronald W. Jacques, Ricks College

Ricki E. Kantrowitz, Westfield State College

Christopher Murphy, University of Maryland Baltimore County

Patricia Owen, St. Mary's University

Ralph G. Pifer, Sauk Valley Community College

John L. Romanek, Jefferson Community College

Sudie Back Sattler, Medical University of South Carolina

Raymond L. Scott, Whittier College

Robert Sommer, University of California—Davis

We have enjoyed working with the outstanding staff at Houghton Mifflin Company. David Lee, Sponsoring Editor, has provided invaluable advice and support. He has been a strong advocate of this project and the *Psychology in Context* series. Jane Knetzger, Senior Associate Editor, has offered sharp and helpful suggestions on the structure of the book and on pedagogy. We thank them both for their professionalism and encouragement. We thank Anne Holm, Production Editor, for her excellence in overseeing the production of the book, Craig Mertens for helping us secure permissions, and George Lang of Books By Design for his assistance with production. We are grateful to Pamela Laskey, Marketing Manager, Beth Foohey, Marketing Coordinator, and Karen Pund-Hutto, Senior Sales Representative, for their excitement about the book and creative ideas in promoting it.

We are indebted to Michael Phillips and the staff of the College of Charleston Interlibrary Loan Department and the staff of the Mason County Library in Ludington, Michigan, for helping us obtain books and other materials. Thanks also go to the staff of Palomar College campus in Escondido, California, and especially to Marsha Booth, whose gracious, invaluable help was given with great patience and a wonderful sense of humor. Thanks to The Write People in Ludington, Michigan, for encouraging writers. We thank David Gentry, Conrad Festa, Samuel Hines,

Stacy Clark, and the College of Charleston Psychology Department faculty for their support.

We particularly wish to thank Sudie Back Sattler, Yehuda Shabatay, and Michelle King-Kramer for their steadfast enthusiasm toward this work, their ardent support, thorough reading of the manuscript, and their always valuable suggestions. We are indebted to Jerome M. Sattler for his wise counsel and unwavering support. Finally, we thank other family members: Heidi, Walter, Nicole, and Justin Philips; Bonnie and Keith Sattler; Debbie Hendrix; Harry, Bonnie, Tony, and Beverly Back; Elizabeth, Tom, and Phoenix Voorhies; Deborah and Eli Knaan; Michael Shabatay; and Rachael and Evan Kramer.

David N. Sattler
College of Charleston
Department of Psychology
Charleston, South Carolina 29424
E-mail: sattlerd@cofc.edu

Virginia Shabatay
Palomar College
Department of English
1140 W. Mission Road
San Marcos, California 92069

Geoffrey P. Kramer
Grand Valley State University
Department of Psychology
Allendale, Michigan 49401

About the Authors

David N. Sattler received his B.A. in psychology with a minor in Spanish from San Diego State University and his M.A. and Ph.D. in psychology from Michigan State University. He teaches at the College of Charleston, a four-year, medium-sized liberal arts college. David has held academic positions at the University of California—San Diego, San Diego State University, and Scripps College of the Claremont colleges. His research examines responses to extreme psychological trauma (e.g., coping, social support, and posttraumatic stress disorder in the wake of natural disasters) and behavior in social dilemma situations. He has published in numerous journals, including *Journal of Personality and Social Psychology, International Journal of Stress Management, Journal of Psychological Practice*, and *Teaching of Psychology*. David is coauthor (with Virginia Shabatay) of *Psychology in Context: Voices and Perspectives* (Houghton Mifflin Company, 1997) for the introductory psychology course. He is an avid photographer and backpacker.

Virginia Shabatay has a Ph.D. in Humanities. She teaches at Palomar College in San Marcos, California, and has held academic positions at San Diego State University, Portland State University, Lewis and Clark College, and Grossmont College. She has served as editorial consultant on numerous books, including *Martin Buber's Life and Work* by Maurice Friedman, and has contributed essays to several books. Her most recent publications are "Martin Buber and Sisela Bok: Against the Generation of the Lie," in *Martin Buber and the Human Sciences*, and "The Stranger: Who Calls? Who Answers?" in *Stories Lives Tell: Narrative and Dialogue in Education*. Virginia is coauthor (with David Sattler) of *Psychology in Context: Voices and Perspectives* (Houghton Mifflin Company, 1997). In her leisure, she likes to read, travel, swim, and take long walks on the beach.

Geoffrey P. Kramer received his M.A. in clinical psychology with a minor in philosophy from Central Michigan University and his Ph.D. in psychology from Michigan State University. He teaches at Grand Valley State University and is a writer. Geoff previously held an academic position at Indiana University—Kokomo. He served as a clinician for several years at the State Prison of Southern Michigan, and also worked in private practice. His research interests and publications are primarily in the area of psychology and the law. In his leisure time, he enjoys his family, biking, tennis, reading, fishing, and music.

_____*chapter* *1*

ANXIETY DISORDERS

I have a new philosophy.
I'm only going to dread one day at a time.

CHARLES SCHULZ

When does anxiety become disruptive in our lives, interfering with our activities or incapacitating us? Most of us are able to live with our fears and even profit from them. Mild anxiety can improve performance in certain situations, and strong anxiety can help us avoid dangerous situations. But for persons with anxiety disorders, responses are seriously out of proportion to the objective situation. For them, mild apprehension, the type everyone feels, can start a chain reaction of catastrophic thoughts and physiological reactions: muscle tenseness, dry mouth, increased perspiration, heart palpitations. Sufferers might feel distracted and unable to control their tension and dread. Although they often recognize the irrationality of their behavior, they resort to avoidance of anxiety-inducing situations or to repetition of behavioral or cognitive rituals.

Extreme anxieties can limit our choices, affect our social and professional lives, and hold us hostage. In the first selection, writer Barbara Grizzutti Harrison tells how her anxiety evolved into panic attacks that would come without warning and leave her breathless, nauseated, and weak. She could be in a restaurant with friends and suddenly become terrified, unable to carry on a conversation and barely able to breathe or walk. At such moments, she was overwhelmed by the danger she felt. As a result, Harrison often avoided places where she feared she might have an attack.

Although some anxiety disorders can be precipitated by a broad range of situations, phobias are triggered by a single object. The second selection tells of Sam, who developed a fear of snakes. Sam had to check every spot to make certain no snakes were in his bedcovers, shoes, drawers, or any corners of his apartment. He ventured out very little. On one occasion, his terror was so intense that he admitted himself into a hospital because he believed it was a snake-free environment.

Obsessive-compulsive disorders are characterized by repeated intrusions of unwanted thoughts (i.e., obsessions) or behaviors (i.e., compulsions). If you were at work and suddenly wondered whether you had locked your house, unplugged the iron, or turned off the oven, would you drive back home to find out? Once you determined that you had indeed safeguarded your house, would you then feel compelled to return, say, twenty minutes later to check once again? People who suffer from obsessive-compulsive disorder (OCD) may do just that. They are unable to turn their attention away from a particular thought, and, overcome with anxiety, they perform some ritual or dwell on some special thought to pacify their concerns. In the next reading, Dr. S. tells of his frustration with having to meet the demands of OCD. For instance, on one occasion, he had to check repeatedly to see if he had run over someone with his car. Eventually worn down by this disorder, he sought help. Interestingly, he recognized signs of his disorder not only in his young son but in his grandfather, father, and brothers.

Another form of anxiety disorder, posttraumatic stress disorder, can develop after an extremely traumatic, life-threatening experience. Posttraumatic stress disorder includes symptoms such as recurring painful memories of the experience; emotional withdrawal; avoiding people, places, or events that are associated with the traumatic event; and heightened arousal. We conclude with the story of a Vietnam veteran who for the past twenty years has suffered from this disorder. In this interview, he makes it clear why some forms of stress may be difficult to overcome. His story shows the transformation he underwent to survive in Vietnam. That transformation, however, left him shattered after the war.

Anxiety disorders are among the most common psychological disorders and account for a large portion of the costs of mental illness. The lifetime prevalence of panic disorder is between 2% and 5%, and for obsessive-compulsive disorder it is between 2% and 3%. The prevalence of some phobias is as high as 15%. The prevalence of posttraumatic stress disorder, which can result from traumatic events such as war, natural disasters, or criminal violence, varies depending on the population sampled.

I AM NOT AFRAID

Barbara Grizzutti Harrison

Psychological Concept
panic disorder

Barbara Grizzutti Harrison, recipient of the O. Henry Prize for Short Fiction, suffers from anxiety and panic attacks. Harrison has traveled worldwide, interviewed the first lady at the White House, and visited countries on the brink of civil war. Yet she is so terrorized by stairs that one time when an elevator was out of order, she sat on the nearest stair and bumped her way down ten flights. She is nearly paralyzed by the prospect of taking an escalator, crossing a street, or being overwhelmed by panic. At such moments, she may suffer chest pains, have difficulty breathing, and believe that she is having a heart attack. Therapy, antidepressant medication, and courage have enabled Harrison to live a creative life in spite of this disorder.

Sometimes I feel a vague foreboding, a slight dislocation, as if the world had swung almost imperceptibly off its appointed axis, before the quicksilver onset of a panic attack. I am speaking of terror brought on by no recognizable stress or trouble or sadness, terror that strikes like an assassin on a sunny day. I am in the middle of a panic attack before I know it or can pronounce its name. The neurons of my brain are doing a lunatic dance, thrashing and colliding and nattering in an unknown tongue. An attack may last seconds or minutes but seems to have lasted for hours, and it leaves a kind of hangover—an anticipatory fear of the next attack that lasts for days and weeks.

This is what it's like: I am at MacDowell, an artists' retreat in New Hampshire. It's the bright end of a glorious autumn day and I have worked intensely and with good results. I am contented. I am sitting at dinner with my fellow residents—amusing, some of them, irritating, some of them, and most of them kind and work-obsessed. The conversation is desultory; the food is good. Suddenly and without warning my limbs turn to jelly; my jaw tightens until my teeth hurt. I cannot breathe. The pain in my chest presents itself to me as the harbinger of a heart attack.

My dinner companions are unaware of my altered state. I am exhibiting no outward symptoms; I feel detached from them and indeed from all outward reality. I am living inside my fear. When I stand to leave, the ground does not quite rise to meet my feet. It's perhaps 15 yards from the dining hall to the residence where my pretty room awaits me—the fire in its fireplace, white curtains stirring slightly in the autumn breezes, faded bunchy pink roses decorating old white wallpaper, a big brass bed. I cannot bring myself to walk the familiar path. My legs are not the servant of my will. Something terrible will happen if I walk to my room. And something terrible will happen—is happening—if I continue to stand here.

Later, I am able to see that what I have experienced (and would not wish my worst enemy to suffer) corresponds, in a general way, to the criteria for panic attacks established by the *Diagnostic and Statistical Manual of Mental Disorders IV:* "The attack has a sudden onset and builds to a peak rapidly (usually in ten minutes or less) and is often accompanied by a sense of imminent danger or impending doom and an urge to escape. . . . Symptoms are palpitations, sweating, trembling or shaking, sensations of shortness of breath or smothering, feeling of choking, chest pain or discomfort, nausea or abdominal stress, dizziness or lightheadedness . . . fear of losing control or 'going crazy.'" An estimated 3 million Americans suffer from panic disorder, meaning they have four or five attacks a month. Women are twice as likely to develop the disorder.

I suffered crippling panic attacks on and off for more than a decade before I went for help. Now I am ever so much better, though I am not cured. Panic—and the fear of panic that leads to phobias—will always be my unwelcome companion. Still, I have learned something from my experience that I feel impelled to share with you.

I am skipping backward in time, back before I was diagnosed: I have left the tenth-floor office of a psychiatrist I do not like. The elevator is not working. Nor am I. I bump down ten flights of stairs on my rear end. I am afraid of stairs, and my erstwhile "healer" is the last person in the world to whom I'd apply for help.

I am also afraid of escalators: One day, at Lexington and 53rd Street, my husband grabs my arm at the top of the escalator, the longest subway escalator in New York City, and says, with a smile containing a world of soured gratitude and contempt, "Grow up." Halfway down the escalator, drenched with sweat, I know I will divorce him.

I cannot cross avenue streets.

I cannot swim with my head in the water.

I used to be able to cross broad avenue streets, and then my father died, and I couldn't anymore. I remember looking up at the windows of the apartment my children and I shared and thinking, I will never get to them. I called my son from the street-corner telephone. He could see me from the window, stuck as if in some kind of existential glue.

I used to float in the water—there is a pool on the roof of my building that gave me enormous pleasure—and then an old lover came into my life. Desire and stimulation of a new and remembered kind came into my life, and all of a sudden I was afraid of the water, afraid of suffocating.

Today, there are times when my world shrinks. More accurately, I shrink the world around me and cocoon myself. I spend the greater part of days—not unhappily—in bed. I tell social lies. I break dates, disturbing and in some cases forfeiting friendships. I lie in bed with a heating pad on occasions when I could be having a glam (and maybe even a good) time. I regard the changing sky and the skyline. I can see the Empire State Building and the Chrysler Building from my bed. I rearrange the thousands of silk swatches I am making into collages. I listen to Johnny Cash, Bach's Mass in B Minor, my honeybunch Mr. Sinatra. I pledge allegiance to the TV remote control. I am safe.

I am not safe.

Anywhere, any time, even in this bedroom arranged entirely to suit me, panic may intrude.

I am not a coward. I write for a living. I entertain. My kids, now grown, come to commune and play and so do my friends. I make love, I go to the movies. I live. But I live with the echo and the shadow of experienced terror.

I had courage enough, when I was 22 and wholly innocent of the world, to extricate myself from the religious cult that had been my life. I was nine years old when I was indoctrinated into a religious organization that preached its message door to door—by my mother, who was the group's leader. When I left the group, I did so in the face of my mother's icy disapproval and the loss of the only friends I had.

Courage also enabled me to give rein to the love and passion I felt for a man of a different race, at a place and time—Brooklyn in the fifties—when intimacy between races was literally life-threatening. And later I had courage enough to leave a moribund marriage with no financial resources and two small children and no plans except to survive and keep my babies joyfully alive.

I have, in the course of my work, visited countries on the brink of civil war. I have come nose to nose (as it were) with snakes, wild dogs, and murderers. I have interviewed the first lady over lunch at the White House. In the interests of journalism (and my need to make a living), I have reported on the ravings of cult leaders from their claustrophobic confines in border towns.

My courage is a source of vanity to me, and from it I draw self-love. And, because it is a gift from God, I am immensely grateful for such courage as I have.

You would think, would you not, that courage and bravery were inseparable. No such buoyancy for me. Not only can I not cross avenue streets, easily climb down steps, or submerge my face in the swimming pool, I take a shower (feeling myself to be on the threshold of suffocation) only because my funk demands it. There are days when I can't walk from my house to the post office.

I have not always had panic attacks. I used to have mere anxiety attacks (I called them the shakes) almost daily after working hard. I would find myself in the middle of preparing dinner, unable to control a feeling of diffuse unease (trembling in a minor key). The Victorians called this the vapors, a tenseness accompanied by an exhausted sadness. It was disturbing and uncomfortable, and I would retire to bed, leaving the final assembly of dinner to my children.

With anxiety, I almost always saw the light at the end of the tunnel. I met anxiety on its own grounds, and for many years it did not escalate.

A panic attack has the force of an oncoming train. Panic is anxiety severely, grotesquely heightened. When you think of anxiety, think of Woody Allen; when you think of panic, think of the Last Judgment. While sometimes an attack may be triggered by a stressful situation, often it comes completely out of the blue. The nervous system mounts a fight-or-flight response normally reserved for life-threatening emergencies. It is hard not to believe that you are about to die. Not unnaturally, you go to great lengths to avoid a recurrence.

This is where phobias—especially agoraphobia—come in. One-third of panic sufferers go on to develop agoraphobia. Patients are not so much afraid of open spaces—the classic definition of agoraphobia—as fearful of suffering an attack in public. They progressively constrict their activities until they are no longer able to travel alone for fear of being suddenly rendered helpless, says Donald Klein, a psychiatrist at Columbia University who has written extensively on panic disorder. "The condition is episodic, with exacerbations and remissions," he says. "Complaints of depression and apathy are frequent. But patients are often lively, popular, and friendly when not anxious."

I am interested in Klein's account both for the ways it validates my own experience and for the ways my experience tends to contradict it. Patients are often popular and friendly? I am overaccommodating. I apologize excessively. I sing for my supper. I am gregarious enough to entertain and amuse a small nation-state. I overcompensate when I am not anxious to make up for those times when I am anxious. In either mode, I risk becoming a bloody bore.

On the other hand, my experience of traveling differs from what Klein describes. I am often more at ease in India, Italy, Hungary—where I reinvent myself by writing about a world that is new every day to me. I escape from myself and find myself in the innocence of the new, away from the scene of earlier emotional crimes. In a world of strangers, who is there to betray or reproach me?

I say I am more at ease. I mean I am less apt to suffer anxiety. I am *more* apt to suffer the Big Bang of panic: Two years ago, my confidence bolstered because I have not had an attack for some time, I fly to Italy. At night the moon illuminates my bedroom in the old farmhouse where I'm staying. The shadow-tracery of leaves on the roof beams mingles with the smell of brown water from the source of the Arno river and the exotic smell of ripe peaches. I am as happy as if the world were totally good and known to me to be good (and deserved).

A few hours after I wake up, I am calling my doctor in New York, convinced I am having a heart attack. He sends me to the nearest hospital. When it is all over—the trip over bumpy roads, the prodding, the mangling of two languages, the battery of tests—I realize I have been heedless and overconfident.

In a matter of days, I have another attack. Memory is erased: I forget I was not having an embolism the last time. Memory is also enlarged: The terror is so strong that I go the hospital again.

What causes it? Medical treatises can give us at best the rough outline of the braiding of mind and body that go into the making of inappropriate panic. Most scientists now believe that changes in the brain are partly responsible, that panic is a biological disorder owing to neurochemical abnormalities. Early childhood trauma also seems to play a role. Klein believes that panic is prompted not by fear but by a defect in the way the brain warns against oxygen deprivation. Normally, when levels of carbon dioxide in the blood get too high, the brain sounds an alarm. In panic patients, Klein says, the alarm is tripped too easily: A slight increase in carbon dioxide may trigger a false suffocation alarm. "Just before the attack, the victims are overwhelmed by feelings of suffocation and try to compensate by breathing deeply," he says. "When they still can't catch their breath, they panic." This, I am not happy to say, rings true for me.

My father tried to kill me when I was a child, by strangulation. I derive no pleasure from such self-revelation. But I want you to profit from my example: Trumpet your pain. Panic does not yield to stoicism. I was stoic for years, and consequently cranky for years, congenitally out of sorts. I am much better now. Sometimes screaming is more dignified than whining or grumbling. It is certainly more therapeutic. That's my advice. *You do not die of panic. You can find help.*

Like most panic-prone patients, I had been averse to talk therapy. It's common for people with panic disorder to consider their affliction unrelated to their emotional relationships. The experience is so physical that psychotherapy seems irrelevant.

Then, two years ago, a long and winding road of successes and failures, heart's ease and heartbreak brought me to my current therapist's office, where he proposed talk therapy, together with the antidepressant Prozac. It is the closest I have felt to having recovered. I now have far fewer panic attacks, but I still have them. I had one two nights ago.

Appropriate treatment reduces panic attacks in 70 to 90 percent of cases. The National Institute of Mental Health is currently engaged in a study to determine which treatment works best: behavioral therapy, antidepressants, or a combination of the two. (The results won't be in for another two years.)

In behavioral or cognitive therapy, patients are taught to confront fearful situations and develop what professionals call coping skills; they are conditioned to recognize that their bodies are having a false alarm. Antidepressants regulate the amount of the neurochemical serotonin, which may be involved in flipping the switch that causes panic. And talk therapy, given the multiple influences that are likely involved, can't hurt. In the right hands, psychotherapy is poetry; it is intuition and art. I am lucky enough to have a psychiatrist who believes in both—and in Prozac.

The more I write about panic the more apocalyptic it sounds, which is why many sufferers take drugs or booze. Life is hard; perhaps you've noticed. It is wonderful, too—a human comedy. All our lives are in some way circumscribed—by temperament, luck, class, opportunity. And our lives are a struggle to transcend circumstance and enter a realm of freedom where we can be our truest, best selves. Today, my life is circumscribed by panic attacks, by the siren call of agoraphobia. I struggle. What is amazing to me is not the amount of pain that lurks in the shadows, but the amount of joy that can be seized from the pain.

Response and Analysis

1. Barbara Grizzutti Harrison describes her husband's reaction to her fear of getting on an escalator: "Grow up," he tells her. What thoughts and feelings might have produced his reaction? What does the reaction imply about beliefs that persons with this disorder can control their responses?

2. How does anxiety affect Harrison's social and professional life? In what ways are her experiences typical? Atypical?

3. What physiological symptoms associated with anxiety does Harrison experience?

4. Harrison suggests that there is a relationship between panic and other anxiety disorders. What is this relationship? How might you distinguish between panic disorder and panic that occurs with other disorders?

5. What treatment has Harrison found helpful? How does she deal with her anxiety after receiving treatment?

Research

Suppose you suspect that persons with panic disorder are more sensitive to physiological arousal than are persons without panic disorder, and that this heightened sensitivity is a cause of their panic. Heightened physiological arousal is called *biological sensitivity*. To examine this idea, you design a study and recruit one hundred participants of whom some have and some have not been diagnosed with panic disorder. To create physiological arousal, you have the participants hyperventilate. You hypothesize that individuals with panic disorder will show more symptoms associated with panic attacks than will individuals without panic disorder. Suppose your results reveal that 70% of individuals with panic disorder displayed symptoms associated with panic attacks but only 10% of individuals without panic disorder showed these symptoms. Do the results support your hypothesis? What alternate interpretations could explain why individuals with panic disorder reacted as they did to being physiologically aroused? Does a finding that physiological arousal produces higher rates of panic attacks among panic sufferers rule out the role of cognitive appraisal of the arousal? Why or why not?

A FEAR OF SNAKES

Raeann Dumont

Psychological Concept
specific phobia

When Sam was in his late thirties, he sought help for his fear of snakes. He was so incapacitated by this fear that often he could not leave his apartment, and he checked every cranny for snakes. Sam insisted that his therapist treat him at home because he feared snakes might be on buses, taxis, or subways. The snakes did not have to be real to send terror through him; even pictures or thoughts of them could upset him. Yet Sam, his therapist writes, was one of her brightest, most creative clients, and eventually he was able to master many of his fears, continue working productively, and get married. What are some of the techniques the therapist used that helped Sam?

Sam dated the onset of his problem from 9:12 A.M., September 16, 1981. The day started out like every other. His alarm went off at 5:30 A.M. Then he began a long ritual of checking for snakes. He got out of bed and immediately stripped the bed of the blankets and sheets, shook them out, folded them neatly, and put them in a tightly covered cedar chest along with the pillows. He took his large flashlight and looked in the closet, starting from the ceiling on the left, carefully checking all the corners and crevices, working his way carefully past the shelf and the clothes down to the floor, where he kept his shoes. He did the same meticulous checking in the bedroom, living room, and kitchen. An hour and a half had passed before he started on the bathroom, where he checked each corner of the room, behind the toilet, and under the sink. He poured drain opener down the bathtub drain, let it fizz for a while, ran water down the drain for exactly seven minutes, stopped up the drain, and ran water in the tub for his bath. By then it was about 7:30.

He bathed quickly, drying off with a towel he had taken from a metal container, and returned to his bedroom to dress. He picked up his undershorts and shook them vigorously, checked the front and the back, the inside and the outside, then put them on. He repeated this action with each article of clothing.

At 8:30 he left his apartment for the walk to work. During the walk he kept his eyes focused on the sidewalk, stopping only at the same deli he stopped at every morning for a container of black coffee and a plain bagel with cream cheese.

When he arrived at his office building he waited outside the elevator. He entered, pushed the button for the seventeenth floor, and concentrated on the light panel above the elevator door until it indicated that he had arrived. Once in his office, he began a similar ritual of checking.

Sam had two terrible years before September 16, 1981, and the time he called me. He was hospitalized at his own insistence, saying that he had had a nervous breakdown and that the hospital was the only safe place (safe from snakes, that is). Somewhere along the line he was diagnosed as psychotic and medicated to the point of not being able to get out of bed. (He still had terrible fears of snakes but wasn't as wild and verbal about expressing them.) Later he was put in an implosion therapy program where for several hours each day he was required to sit in a small, unfurnished room with images of snakes projected onto the ceiling and walls.

Immediately Sam told me that if I were the kind of therapist who would force him to come in contact with snakes, he would not be interested in seeing me. Also, because he was fearful of snakes curled up under the seats in buses or taxis, or in the dark corners of subway stations, he insisted he could not come to see me; I would have to work with him in his apartment. He lived on the Upper West Side of Manhattan before it became as fashionable as it is now. Just down the street from his building was a small square on 73rd and Broadway called Needle Park. I was not enthusiastic about working in the area, but I made an appointment to see him, expecting the problem to be relatively uncomplicated.

Sam's apartment was a walk-up on the third floor of a small old building. A few minutes after I rang the bell the door opened about two inches, restrained by a chain on the inside. His eye peered out at me.

"Hi, Sam. I'm Raeann Dumont; we have an appointment."

He eyed me slowly from my head to my feet, then back up to my head again.

"Take your coat off and shake it out," Sam said. I put my bag on the floor and took my coat off and gave it two good shakes.

"Now fold it up inside out, leave it on the floor across the hall, and come in."

I looked around the hall at the peeling paint and the broken banister and said, "It's twenty degrees outside and I don't feel like going home this afternoon without a coat. If you want an appointment with me you'll have to accept my coat as well."

"What's in your bag? Why is it so big?"

"Because I like big bags. Sam, I'm not crazy about snakes either. I don't have a snake in my bag."

"I thought the theory was that I have to encounter the fear in order to get over it."

"We'll work up to it gradually. I promise Sam, no snakes."

Sam was a very tall, very thin man in his late thirties. He smiled grimly and gestured for me to come in. His apartment was brightly lit by many long fluorescent bulbs and spotlights shining into all the corners. Everything was white: the ceiling, the walls, the floors. The furniture was all unupholstered white wood. I could tell right away that Sam's phobia was more complicated than I had anticipated.

Although Sam dated the beginning of his problem to two years prior to contacting me, our interview indicated that Sam had had problems most of his life. As a little boy he compulsively counted his toys and lined them up on the floor in a very specific way. If his mother inadvertently rearranged them while cleaning, he would become very upset. At meals, even in the school cafeteria, he insisted on having a separate plate and fork for everything. If his mother was serving peas, potatoes, and meat, she would have to serve it on three small plates along with three forks. . . .

Although Sam's history clearly indicated problems with OCD at a very early age, snakes didn't become a problem until his late twenties. On an early spring evening he was hanging out with some friends in a bar after work. One of the guys was talking about the company softball game that had taken place on the previous weekend. The man described how he was standing in the outfield while the pitcher and the umpire were arguing over a foul ball: It was a cool day. He stood in the sun with his arms wrapped around himself to keep warm when he felt something funny on his right leg. He looked down and saw a snake curled up around his leg from his ankle to the knee. He stamped his foot and swatted at it with his glove, but the snake clung fast. Then he ran over to one of his teammates to ask for help, but the teammate ran away laughing. He continued to stamp and kick and yell for help. The rest of the guys came running over, teasing him about what a snaky guy he was, and so on, but none of them helped get rid of the snake. While Sam's friend was telling the story he was chagrined that he had panicked because it was a harmless garden snake, but he was also irritated that his teammates hadn't responded a little more sympathetically.

Sam, who had gone to summer camp as a kid, had certainly seen snakes, but he had never thought of the possibility that a snake might get on him. As his friend told the story, Sam found himself getting sick to his stomach. He was afraid to look at his leg and felt impelled to leave. That night he dreamed of snakes wrapping themselves around him.

The next morning when he got up he checked his apartment for snakes. The thought of snakes wrapping themselves around him continued to occur throughout the day. Every time, he violently shook his leg and stamped his foot; he couldn't control the reaction. He left work early that day and went home. He felt so exhausted he just wanted to go to sleep but was afraid that he'd dream of snakes again. To reassure himself that he wouldn't have snakes crawl all over him as he slept, he checked his apartment again. He started in the kitchen, got halfway through and couldn't remember if he had checked under the sink, so he started over. Again when he had almost finished, he felt a nagging doubt that he hadn't checked behind the stove. Sam spent the entire night checking, his kitchen for snakes over and over and over again. The next morning Sam called his mother and said that he had had a nervous breakdown and wanted her to take him to a hospital. His mother called his old psychiatrist, who prescribed tranquilizers, rest, and resuming psychotherapy.

For the next six years Sam managed by avoiding, checking, and taking heavy doses of tranquilizers. Until, as he told me, September 16, 1981, when he opened his desk drawer and found a snake in it.

"Sam," I asked, "have you given any thought as to how the snake got into your desk drawer?"

"Sure I have," he said. "That's a part of what makes me so crazy. It was put there by someone who worked with me. That means I can't be safe anywhere; people will torment me with snakes."

"How did they get the snake into the building? Someone walking into a building on Madison Avenue with a snake around their neck would be noticeable. Desk drawers aren't the natural habitat for snakes. Once they got it into your drawer, how did they get the snake to stay?"

"Well…"

"What?"

"Real."

"Real what?"

"The snake."

"Sam, do you mean that the snake in your desk drawer wasn't a real snake?"

"Uh, yeah, that's about it."

"What was it? Was it like a rubber snake?"

"No, uh, it was more like a picture of a snake."

"Why did you lead me to believe that it was a real snake?"

"I didn't think you'd take me seriously if you knew it was a picture of a snake. You'd think I was just a nut."

The picture in Sam's desk drawer was a very realistic image of a snake prepared to strike, taken from a nature magazine. Sam responded with the same amount of passion to the picture of the snake as he would have to a real live snake. He had been able to manage his fear of snakes (with many limitations and much time-consuming checking) while it remained a fear of real snakes, but when it became a fear of pictures, images, and thoughts of snakes Sam's life became immensely complicated. Magazines and by extension newsstands became danger-ous. Store windows became dangerous; not just pet shops and fish stores, but also jewelry store windows because of bracelets, pins, and necklaces in the form of snakes, and toy stores, which often have rubber or plastic snakes in their windows. The possibility of seeing a snake in some form or fashion was overwhelming. Sam felt so bombarded by snakes that every expedition outside his carefully inspected and controlled apartment was formidable.

Most days Sam felt unable to leave his apartment due to his fears. He took a leave of absence from his job, but his work was so highly valued that his boss arranged for him to work at home two or three days a week. He never returned to the office where he had found the picture of the snake in his desk drawer. On the rare occasions he went to the office building, his boss let him use a small room that had been painted white and furnished only with a drawing table and a chair; there were no cabinets, drawers, or low furniture in which snakes could hide.

Sam made good money while he was working, but he hadn't worked full-time for more than two years. When I started working with him he was under financial pressure because the money he had saved while he was working was beginning to run out, and his boss was pressuring him to either return to work full-time or to quit. On the one hand, Sam felt he had to get rid of his fear of snakes immediately, and on the other, he felt powerless to deal with the fears and wanted to be hospi-talized. I was constantly trying to mediate between the two aspects of Sam. . . .

Here is Sam's hierarchy of fearful objects or situations:

1.   Having a snake on me
2.   Touching a snake
3.   Seeing a snake
4.   Being somewhere I might see a snake
5.   Thinking of snakes. . . .

Our exposure and reality testing started by seeing if snakes would actually appear if we thought or talked about them. Sam didn't want to say or hear the word "snake." He referred to them as "the S thing." Every time Sam thought of "the S thing" he silently repeated seven times:

Fire and flame,
singe and simmer,
scorch and burn,
blaze and inflame,
cremate and incinerate.

This litany was designed to drive snakes from his mind. The litany also explained the frequent silences during our conversations. . . .

Sam and I worked together for three years. We started by looking at a picture of a snake bracelet, and very gradually we worked our way up to pictures of real snakes. We made forays into unfamiliar neighborhoods and looked in pet-shop windows (never seeing a snake, mostly kittens and puppies and birds). We walked through Central Park; we even sat on the grass. All the while we were cause-and-effecting ("What is the medium by which a snake will appear when we think about it?") and reality testing ("How many snakes did we encounter on our last walk down Broadway?").

On many occasions during those three years Sam angrily announced that he was quitting therapy because it didn't work. Always, when we analyzed his diary (he was a scrupulous diary keeper) we found that the incident that set off the checking, the scrubbing, and the litanies had nothing to do with snakes. Very early in our work together when he was still looking at the picture of the snake bracelet (and doing exceedingly well at limiting his litanies), Sam's boss called him to say that if he wasn't able to come back to work full-time by a specific date, he would have to fire him.

Sam did resume his old job. For the first two weeks I met him at the elevator and together we went into his office and opened his desk drawer. I was identified by his coworkers as "Sam's snake woman." During this period I was on the company payroll because Sam unabashedly announced to the organization, "You guys made me crazy. You guys can pay for making me uncrazy." They did.

Response and Analysis

1. What is the difference between a fear of something and a phobia? In your own life, have you ever been unable to talk yourself out of dread or anxiety over something, even though you knew the dread was not entirely rational? What did the dread or anxiety feel like?

2. Raeann Dumont describes Sam's hierarchy of feared objects and situations. What is the purpose of creating this hierarchy? Describe how it might be used in treatment.

3. Dumont suggests that Sam showed signs of psychological problems in childhood. What were the signs? With which disorder(s) are Sam's early signs most consistent?

4. People who suffer from various illnesses not only need medical care but may need time off from work. Do you believe that companies should provide benefits or insurance to cover treatments such as the type Sam received? Why or why not? Would your answer be different under different conditions—for example, if the company were operated by a small family with only a handful of employees versus a large company with hundreds of employees?

Research

Therapists who treat persons with phobias might use several techniques. One technique involves exposing the individual to the feared stimulus either gradually or suddenly. Sudden exposure to the stimulus is called *flooding*.

Suppose you want to design a study to examine the effectiveness of gradual exposure versus flooding in treating various phobias. What types of phobias might you compare? Which phobias do you think would be most responsive to gradual exposure? To flooding? How would you determine whether the technique was effective?

THE ACCIDENT THAT DIDN'T HAPPEN

Judith L. Rapoport

Psychological Concept
obsessive-compulsive disorder

Dr. S., a clinical psychologist, recalls driving down the highway and thinking, "What if I hit someone on the road?" Once that thought entered his mind, he felt compelled to drive back to the place of the mythical mishap and check the area for a body. Dr. S. says that it is impossible to describe the anguish an obsessive-compulsive attack can bring. The sufferer becomes a slave to the disorder. For example, between the ages of twenty-two and thirty-three, Dr. S. experienced repeated incidents like the one described here. Dr. S.'s family relations were made even more difficult because his young son suffered from the disorder as well. What behavior does his son, Jeffrey, engage in, and what conclusions does Dr. S. draw about obsessive-compulsive disorder?

I'm driving down the highway doing 55 MPH. I'm on my way to take a final exam. My seat belt is buckled and I'm vigilantly following all the rules of the road. No one is on the highway—not a living soul.

Out of nowhere an obsessive-compulsive disorder (OCD) attack strikes. It's almost magical the way it distorts my perception of reality. While in reality no one is on the road, I'm intruded with the heinous thought that I *might* have hit someone . . . a human being! God knows where such a fantasy comes from.

I think about this for a second, and then say to myself, "That's ridiculous. I didn't hit anybody." Nonetheless, a gnawing anxiety is born. An anxiety I will ultimately not be able to put away until an enormous emotional price has been paid.

I try to make reality chase away this fantasy. I reason, "Well, if I hit someone while driving, I would have *felt* it." This brief trip into reality helps the pain dissipate . . . but only for a second. Why? Because the gnawing anxiety that I really did commit the illusionary accident is growing larger—so is the pain.

The pain is a terrible guilt that I have committed an unthinkable, negligent act. At one level, I know this is ridiculous, but there's a terrible pain in my stomach telling me something quite different.

Again, I try putting to rest this insane thought and that ugly feeling of guilt. "Come on," I think to myself, "this is *really* insane!"

But the awful feeling persists. The anxious pain says to me, "*You Really Did Hit*

Someone." The attack is now in full control. Reality no longer has meaning. My sensory system is distorted. I have to get rid of the pain. Checking out this fantasy is the only way I know how.

I start ruminating, "Maybe I did hit someone and didn't realize it . . . Oh my God! I might have killed somebody! I have to go back and check." Checking is the only way to calm the anxiety. It brings me closer to truth somehow. I can't live with the thought that I actually may have killed someone—I have to check it out.

Now I'm sweating . . . literally. I pray this outrageous act of negligence never happened. My fantasies run wild. I desperately hope the jury will be merciful. I'm particularly concerned about whether my parents will be understanding. After all, I'm now a criminal. I must control the anxiety by checking it out. Did it really happen? There's always an infinitesimally small kernel of truth (or potential truth) in all my OC fantasies.

I think to myself, "Rush to check it out. Get rid of the hurt by checking it out. Hurry back to check it out. God, I'll be late for my final exam if I check it out. But I have no choice. Someone could be lying on the road, bloody, close to death." Fantasy is now my only reality. So is my pain.

I've driven five miles farther down the road since the attack's onset. I turn the car around and head back to the scene of the mythical mishap. I return to the spot on the road where I "think" it "might" have occurred. Naturally, nothing is there. No police car and no bloodied body. Relieved, I turn around again to get to my exam on time.

Feeling better, I drive for about twenty seconds and then the lingering thoughts and pain start gnawing away again. Only this time they're even more intense. I think, "Maybe I should have pulled *off* the road and checked the side brush where the injured body was thrown and now lies? Maybe I didn't go *far enough* back on the road and the accident occurred a mile farther back."

The pain of my possibly having hurt someone is now so intense that I have no choice—I really see it this way.

I turn the car around a second time and head an extra mile farther down the road to find the corpse. I drive by quickly. Assured that this time I've gone far enough I head back to school to take my exam. But I'm not through yet.

"My God," my attack relentlessly continues, "I didn't get *out* of the car to actually *look* on the side of the road!"

So I turn back a third time. I drive to the part of the highway where I think the accident happened. I park the car on the highway's shoulder. I get out and begin rummaging around in the brush. A police car comes up. I feel like I'm going out of my mind.

The policeman, seeing me thrash through the brush, asks, "What are you doing? Maybe I can help you?"

Well, I'm in a dilemma. I can't say, "Officer, please don't worry. You see, I've got obsessive-compulsive disorder, along with four million other Americans. I'm simply acting out a compulsion with obsessive qualities." I can't even say, "I'm really sick. Please help me." The disease is so insidious and embarrassing that it cannot be admitted to anyone. Anyway, so few really understand it, including myself.

So I tell the officer I was nervous about my exam and pulled off to the roadside to throw up. The policeman gives me a sincere and knowing smile and wishes me well.

But I start thinking again: "Maybe an accident did happen and the body has been cleared off the road. The policeman's here to see if I came back to the scene of the crime. God, maybe I really did hit someone . . . why else would a police car be in the area?" Then I realize he would have asked me about it. But would he, if he was trying to catch me?

I'm so caught up in the anxiety and these awful thoughts that I momentarily forget why I am standing on the side of the road. I'm back on the road again. The anxiety is peaking. Maybe the policeman didn't know about the accident? I should go back and conduct my search more *thoroughly*.

I want to go back and check more . . . but I can't. You see, the police car is tailing me on the highway. I'm now close to hysteria because I honestly believe someone is lying in the brush bleeding to death. Yes . . . the pain makes me believe this. "After all," I reason, "why would the pain be there in the first place?"

I arrive at school late for the exam. I have trouble taking the exam because I can't stop obsessing on the fantasy. The thoughts of the mythical accident keep intruding. Somehow I get through it.

The moment I get out of the exam I'm back on the road checking again. But now I'm checking two things. First that I didn't kill or maim someone and second, that the policeman doesn't catch me checking. After all, if I should be spotted on the roadside rummaging around the brush a second time, how in the world can I possibly explain such an incriminating and aimless action? I'm totally exhausted, but that awful anxiety keeps me checking, though a part of my psyche keeps telling me that this checking behavior is ridiculous, that it serves absolutely no purpose. But, with OCD, there is no other way.

Finally, after repeated checks, I'm able to break the ritual. I head home, dead tired. I know that if I can sleep it off, I'll feel better. Sometimes the pain dissipates through an escape into sleep.

I manage to lie down on my bed—hoping for sleep. But the incident has not totally left me—nor has the anxiety. I think, "If I really did hit someone, there would be a dent in the car's fender."

What I now do is no mystery to anyone. I haul myself up from bed and run out to the garage to check the fenders on the car. First I check the front two fenders, see no damage, and head back to bed. But . . . *did I check it well enough?*

I get up from bed again and now find myself checking the *whole body* of the car. I know this is absurd, but I can't help myself. Finally . . . finally, I disengage and head off to my room to sleep. Before I nod off, my last thought is, "I wonder what I'll check next?"

Let me tell you about myself. I'm thirty-six years old and have had obsessions, at least in mild form, since I was six years old. My son Jeffrey, age five, has had the illness since at least age two. My two brothers most probably have the disease, though less severely. There is a good chance my nephew, age eight, has OCD as well as my father and his father also. I can write this here, but families with OCD almost never tell each other about it if they can help it. I am the one who broke the silence. My brother has had a remarkable response to imipramine [which occasionally helps OCD]. He said, "I never thought I would live my life without the pain and anxiety of all my 'dread' thoughts." Perhaps my other brother and nephew will consider treatment also.

I cannot really describe the torturous pain of the anxiety brought on by an obsessive-compulsive disorder attack. The checking incident I just relayed to you used to happen to me often. Between the ages of twenty-two and thirty-three (save for one or two brief remissions) this kind of an attack occurred every day. Many times it stayed with me all day long and, if it disappeared, a new attack, spawned from the old one, would quickly replace it. Later, other forms of checking began. I have stayed till midnight at my laboratory compelled to check my computer's simplest calculations by hand. The work is unpublished because I can never be certain that the numbers were averaged correctly.

I do not intend to sound dramatic, nor am I soliciting sympathy or pity. It's simply a fact of life that it's the pain—the deep, searing, never-ending pain—that makes this illness so unbearable. I know the pain. So do all the other OCs out there who share this illness with me and my family members. . . .

While there were indications from early childhood that I had the disease, it didn't clearly manifest itself until I was twenty-two years old. My symptoms were typical of obsessive-compulsives. I would check the gas oven and door locks, sometimes 20 times before I could go to bed at night. I would worry about poisoning myself and others with insecticides or cleaning fluids I may have touched. I would drive home from work, thinking that I left the light on in my office and drive all the way back to see if it was off: "It could start a fire." Sometimes I did this more than once in a day.

Many of the obsessions and compulsions were based in an extraordinary fear that my aggressive impulses, my anger, would, without me knowing it, leak out. I always thought I would start a fire by being negligent with cigarettes or kill someone by being a reckless driver. My vigilance was ongoing . . . and exhausting.

Each obsessive incident was accompanied by the fantasy that if I *didn't* act on it, something terrible would happen to me or someone else. Losing my job, being sent to prison, or hurting someone else were average catastrophic fantasies. Making *sure* these outcomes would not occur drove my compulsive behaviors.

The energy and time I would exert toward a hundred aimless acts has me shaking my head in disgust right now. I look back and wonder how I lived this way for over ten years. It was unbearable.

I hid my disease. I was like an alcoholic hiding his drink. My greatest fear was to be discovered. At times, my wife hated me for the illness. I hated myself. But I couldn't help it. The disease controls you, not the reverse.

In 1973, one year after the first onset, I went into therapy. The psychiatrist was very good. Over the next three years I made some excellent progress. I learned ways to cope and adapt. If there was an emotional source to the illness, the psychiatrist did as much as could be done to eliminate it.

Shortly thereafter, I went into remission and was okay for about a year or so. Not perfect, but substantially improved. After five years in therapy, it became clear that normal life-stress events seemed to trigger obsessive-compulsive episodes. After the birth of my first child, the disease struck again. This time it was worse than ever before.

My Son's Story

I went to father's night at my Jeffrey's pre-school. He was playing with a Fisher-Price toy, a schoolhouse, but his play was strange. He stood before the toy, jumped up and down, and flapped his arms as if excited by it. (We later labeled this behavior "flapping"). His muscles from head to toe contracted and relaxed over and over again. He would grunt and contort his face as if he was exerting great effort. When the jumping stopped, he would put his arms together and wiggle his fingers just above eye level (we later labeled this behavior, "wormies"). The finger movement was a form of self-stimulation; the grunting and muscle contraction, relaxation sequence would continue during "wormies" as well. He did this nonstop for 35 minutes. I could not disengage him. No matter what I tried, he simply wouldn't stop.

Occasionally he would bring a person, toy, chair, or desk into the play, but these self-stimulating behaviors and the self-induced muscle contractions continued. When I tried to disengage him I was met with repeated and rigid resistance. He *had to do* this bizarre behavior. He also had to play with the toy "his" way. Any change I introduced was vehemently rejected.

That night I spoke with my wife. We had a strong hunch that something wasn't right.

We carefully reviewed his behavior over the past year. We noted his excitability and extremely low attention span. He could not sit still, nor could he focus on a task. It would literally take him 15 minutes to put his socks on because he was so distracted by other things. We discussed how he would wiggle his fingers or dangle strings in front of his eyes for long periods of time (labeled "stringing") while doing muscle contractions and grunting. His resistance to change and new experiences were all too easy to identify. His obsessions with counting, serializing, and the repetition of questions to which he already had heard the answers a hundred times before were also recalled. At age two he would throw a fit if an object was not in its "proper" location on his night table and when he would get upset, he would cry, "Mommy, calm me down!"

We couldn't engage him in activity that was right for his age. When we did get him involved in some normal play—say, block building—he would bring "stringing," "wormies," and "flapping," along with the muscle contractions, into the play.

As we began to identify all the puzzle's pieces, we knew we could no longer chalk all this up to developmental lag or immaturity. We desperately wanted to, but we couldn't. Something was fundamentally wrong. And he was getting worse.

Often we look back and ask ourselves, how could we have waited so long to get help? The question is really a variation of another one: "How could we have been so negligent?" The answers can be found in several places.

Denial is one. What parent wants to face the fact that his or her child is handicapped? Jeffrey was so young—just four years old—that it was easy to rationalize away much of his aberrant behavior: "He'll grow out of it." "It's only temporary." "He's a boy and boys mature slower than girls."

Moreover, he had so many healthy positive attributes. His intelligence was apparent. His language skills were consistently improving. His attitude was generally good and he expressed a wide range of feelings—sadness, joy, silliness, boredom, and he loved to laugh. A strong need to please his parents, especially Mommy, was developing. He was insatiably curious about spatial locations: "Kroger's is next to Wendy's? Right, Mommy?" He was gentle and kind, perhaps to a fault, and affectionate—he would hug and kiss and snuggle with us.

Yet when a child dangles strings in front of his eyes four hours a day and tells you he can't help himself, or asks, "Mommy, why do I play with strings?", rationalizations soon wear painfully thin. Our child was very sick. We could no longer pretend, and we also knew that we had to do something about it.

A parent of an obsessive-compulsive child must understand the pain of the anxiety and also its control over one's behavior. Your child has absolutely *no control* over what he or she is doing . . . NONE. Your child's rituals may be totally aimless. They will make no sense to you. You cannot intellectually understand why your child does what he or she does. Don't try to understand in this way because all it will do is frustrate you; normal human reasoning and logic does not exist with this disease. The only logic is your child's relentless pain, his enormous need to stop this pain, and his involuntary behavior geared to this end.

Response and Analysis

1. Most of us have likely rechecked a door lock even though we knew that we had done so just a few moments earlier. We may even have driven back home to make certain that we had unplugged an iron. But imagine if thoughts to check if the door were locked or if the iron were turned off played repeatedly in our heads dozens or hundreds of times a day. What might you do to try to control your urge to recheck every previous action you had taken? How might your repetitive behavior affect your daily routines? Your relationships with others?

2. What is the difference between an obsession and a compulsion? Describe the obsession(s) and compulsion(s) experienced by Dr. S. and his son. How does OCD affect Dr. S.'s daily activities?

3. Persons with OCD often recognize the irrationality of their obsessions and compulsions and try to resist them. What happens to their symptoms, especially anxiety, if they resist performing their rituals? What happens if they perform the rituals?

4. What did Dr. S. learn in therapy about the events that trigger his episodes? How might cognitive or behavioral therapists treat persons with OCD?

Research

Suppose you want to investigate the therapeutic effects of support groups for sufferers of OCD. Your first task is to contact support groups and obtain their cooperation. What ethical issues might be involved in conducting research with participants who suffer from OCD? How might you solve these ethical problems?

POSTTRAUMATIC STRESS DISORDER IN VIETNAM VETERANS

Jonathan Shay

Psychological Concept
posttraumatic stress disorder

The Vietnam War left in its wake many men who were unable to return to the life they had known, and many veterans suffered from posttraumatic stress disorder (PTSD). Some became abusive, alcoholic, and unable to find satisfying work. Many of their marriages ended in divorce.

Psychiatrist Jonathan Shay works with veterans who fought in the Vietnam War and who have been diagnosed with PTSD. These veterans speak of suffering from depression, emotional paralysis, headaches, isolation, and nightmares about Vietnam. When young men become "screaming military fanatics," who are taught to kill, then we can't, says one veteran, "bring them home unbriefed, untrained, and expect them to be normal."[1] Here is the story of a Vietnam veteran—one of Dr. Shay's patients—who reveals his anger and suffering as he speaks about his experiences. Why is it important that he tell his story?

I haven't really slept for twenty years. I lie down, but I don't sleep. I'm always watching the door, the window, then back to the door. I get up at least five times to walk my perimeter, sometimes it's ten or fifteen times. There's always something within reach, maybe a baseball bat or a knife, at every door. I used to sleep with a gun under my pillow, another under my mattress, and another in the drawer next to the bed. You made me get rid of them when I came into the program here. They're over at my mother's, so I know I can get them any time, but I don't. Sometimes I think about them—I want to have a gun in my hands so bad at night it makes my arms ache.

So it's like that until the sun begins to come up, then I can sleep for an hour or two.

It wasn't any different when I was working for ____ before I lost it and they put me in the psych hospital. I remember the company doctor putting Valiums in

---

[1] Shirley Dicks (1990). *From Vietnam to Hell: Interviews with Victims of Post-Traumatic Stress Disorder*, p. 57. Jefferson, NC: McFarland & Company.

my mouth, and they strapped me to a stretcher. I was screaming, and I thought the Gooks had overrun us and were pouring through the place. Everyone I looked at looked like a Gook.

I worked a lot of overtime and also went to school and had a second job. I didn't sleep any more then than now. Maybe two hours a night. But I sure made a lot of money. Workaholic. That's me—no, that *was* me. I was real lucky they kept me so long. They understood that sometimes I just had to leave work. And they never laughed at me when I hit the floor if there was a loud bang or something. I know guys here [in the treatment program] who work other places who had fire-crackers lit off just to see them dive over a conveyer belt or something like that. Or their supervisors pushing them, mind-fucking them, pushing them till they lost it, so they could get rid of them. That never happened to me. Once a lamp in the ceiling exploded with a loud bang, and I dove into a tank of lubricant for the cutting machines. Oof! It was awful. But nobody laughed at me. They were real good to me, and they respected what I could do. They made me the head of the Emergency Response Team, like for explosions and injuries.

Once a guy was burned real bad when some hydraulic fluid caught fire. I was the only one who didn't freeze. I got in there with the fire blanket—see, I still got the scars here on my leg where I got hit too with the burning hydraulics. I got through Vietnam without a scratch and get a Purple Heart for the ____ Company. [Laughs, then silence.] The smell of burning flesh fucked me up real bad afterward, though. I didn't notice it at the time the guy caught fire, but for the next few weeks I kept having flashbacks of the time the fast-mover [jet] laid a canister of napalm on my company. I couldn't get the smell out of my nose, out of my mouth.

I don't deserve my wife. What kind of life is it for her married to me? She says, "Let's take the kids out for dinner." And I say, "Sure, let's go." So we get to the restaurant and we walk in the door and I say, "Whoa!" when I look around and see all those people. So the hostess shows us to a table right in the middle, and I say, "How about there in the corner?" and she says, "There's people there," and I say, "We'll wait." Meantime my wife is looking at me and there's sweat running down my face. I can't sit with my back uncovered. If I know you're back there covering me, it's okay, but a bunch of strangers, and some of them Gooks—no way. I sit in the corner where I can see everyone who comes in and everyone who leaves. So after we wait thirty minutes for the table in the corner we start walking through the restaurant to it and my heart's pounding, pounding and the sweat's rolling off me and I say, "I gotta go." So they sit down and eat and I stand up in the parking garage, the second floor overlooking the entrance to the restaurant where I have a real good line on everything going on.

Or another thing, y'know my wife's real social, and of course I'm not. She understands now because of the couples therapy ____ did with her and me together. So we don't fight anymore about a lot of those things, and she even helps me now with the embarrassment. Like at my in-laws' she'll even make up something she forgot in the car when she sees that there's getting [to be] too many people in the room, so I can get out of there. But one thing she still don't understand is the mail. She gets so mad at me because I'll drive into town to buy cigarettes but

I don't pick the mail up—it's right next to the 7-Eleven. What she doesn't understand is that every time I think it's ____'s kid sister writing me to find out how he died. She wrote to him every day—and I mean *every day*. Sometimes we wouldn't get our mail for six weeks, and when we'd get it there'd be more letters for him than for the rest of the platoon put together. It's better she don't know. If it was my big brother I wouldn't want to know the truth about the way *he* died.

Of course in another way I'm real good to her [laughs], compared to what I was like to other women before. [Pauses.] Whew! I was one mean motherfucker. She didn't want to know me. You didn't want to know me. You don't want to *know* the number of people I fucked up [pauses], or how I fucked them up.

I don't have very long to live. No, Doc, no, no, I'm not suicidal, it's just that sometimes I don't give a fuck. I don't care if I live or die. I've been waiting to die ever since I got back from Vietnam. When I get that way, my wife, my kids—and I really love them—it's "Get the fuck away from me!" Once when my daughter was younger and I was that way, she came up behind me and before I knew it I had her by the throat up against the wall. I can still see her eyes. I put her down and just walked out of the house without saying anything to anybody and didn't come back for a week. I felt lower than dogshit. I hate it that my kids behave so *careful* around me. I made them that way, and I hate it. Every time I see them being so careful I think of that look in her eyes and I get this feeling here [puts his palm on his belly] like a big stone sitting there.

I think I don't have long to live because I have these dreams of guys in my unit standing at the end of the sofa and blood coming down off them and up the sofa. I wake up screaming and the sofa soaked with sweat. It seems like if the blood reaches me I'm going to die when it does. Other nights I dream of the guys calling to me from the graveyard. They're calling to me, "Come on, come on. Time to rest. You paid your dues. Time to rest."

I never tried to kill myself, but a lot of the time I just don't care. For years I used to go down to the Combat Zone [the Boston red-light district] after midnight and just walk the alleys. If I saw someone down an alley in the dark, I wouldn't go the other way, I'd go down there thinking, "Maybe I'll get lucky." I'm amazed I wasn't killed. I guess I wanted to be killed. Once I came on a guy raping a hooker. She was screaming and screaming, and it was easy to tell he was hurting her bad. I yelled at him, and he turned around and started reaching behind his back. He was carrying. I ran on him so fast and had his elbow before he could pull out the piece [gun], and I pounded the shit out of him. That felt so-o go-o-od. I don't know what happened to the woman. I guess she screwed [ran away] while I was doing him. After that I started bringing a meat fork to the Combat Zone. You know like from a carving set with two—what do they call them—tines. I sharpened them real good. I didn't want to kill anybody, and I figured you could only stick that into somebody just so far before it stopped. When I went to the Combat Zone I never went with a gun. And there was a time I was really crazy and driving around town with a shotgun on the seat next to me.

I haven't spent a complete night in bed with my wife for at least ten years. I always end up on the sofa. It's safer for her, and I don't have to worry about waking her when I get up to walk the perimeter. When I was working sixteen hours a day I'd come home; she'd already be in bed. I'd do a couple hours of things around the house and meanwhile put away a case of beer and a fifth so I'd be able to sleep. Then I'd get in bed with her for two, three hours until it was time for work again. But after I couldn't work anymore, and really bad after I stopped drinking, I'd do this crazy shit at night. I once threw her out of bed so hard it broke her shoulder. I thought there was an NVA potato-masher [a grenade] come in on us. Another time I thought *she* was a Gook, and I had my hands around her throat before I woke up. So since I stopped drinking I never let myself fall asleep in bed with her. I lie there quiet until she's asleep and then get up, check the perimeter, and lie down on the sofa where I can see the door.

It's not much of a life for her, I guess. We haven't had sex in four years. She deserves better.

She says I always mess up a good thing—like I don't deserve it. At Christmas I try to make it perfect for the kids with a big, fresh tree trimmed just right and lots of presents, but it's like I'm watching them through a dirty window. I'm not really there and they're not really there, I don't know which is which. Maybe none of us is real. It's like I'm wrapped up in some kind of transparent cocoon and everything gets to me kind of muffled—oh fuck, I don't know how to explain it.

My son asks me if I'll come to his Little League game and I can't ever promise. He wants me to promise, but I can't. It's not that I don't want to go. I was in Little League myself, and I go sometime just at the last minute and watch from the tree line in the outfield. He has a great arm, and once he hit a home run into the trees where I was standing. I had to pull back real quick. You can't have somebody knowing where you'll be.

I'm so envious of all the normal people who can just go to the mall and hold hands with their wife and walk around. You see, I could never do that, because I'd be looking everywhere. Fuck! I even envy you. I see you walking up the street to the clinic and you're not checking the rooftops for snipers or looking between cars as you pass to make sure there's nobody going to jump you, and I'll bet you have *no idea* who's on the street with you. I can tell you every person two blocks ahead of me and two blocks behind me every second. I see you coming down the street, but you don't see me, because you're in your own world not looking for ambush. How come you're like that? I envy you.

You know, when I go into the men's room here at the clinic I have to pop open the door of each stall with my fist to make sure there's nobody waiting there for me. Sometimes there's guys in there taking a shit and they look at me like I'm a queer or something, but I got to do it or I'm too nervous to pee. Once I was in there and I was washing my hands and you walked in and just said, "Hi," and walked over to the urinal and peed without checking the stalls. How can you do that?

You know, people ask me if I work out. I look very healthy, athletic and stuff. I don't work out. I don't do anything. Maybe it's muscle tension that keeps me this way. But you know, I'm not really healthy. I went to the ___ Fair a bunch of years ago and they had a Take Your Blood Pressure for Free table, and they made me lie down and wanted to call an ambulance it was so high. They were afraid I was going to die on them right there. They worked me up at the hospital for a feo-something, a tumor that makes your blood pressure go through the roof, but they never found anything. Then when I told them that I had stomach pains a lot and vomit every morning, they told me I had ulcers and worked me up for something else, I can't remember the name, but again they thought it was another kind of tumor that makes your stomach pump out acid all the time by the bucketfull. They didn't find anything, but they gave me those pills to stop the acid, and now I don't vomit every day, only around my anniversaries. My skin is still all black in my groin from the jungle rot and Agent Orange, but my hands are better—see? It's only cracked a little here between the fingers and only kicks up during the summer. For years it was all around my waist cracked and oozing blood. My undershirt'd get caked to my skin and I'd have to change it three times a day or the smell would get to you. I was sprayed with Agent Orange during my second tour when we were working the Cambodian border. I thought they were spraying for mosquitoes, but it was Agent Orange, I found out afterward. This big plane came over putting out this big cloud behind it, and it came down on us like a mist, and I thought, "Ain't this amazing, they're spraying the mosquitoes all the way out here." But maybe it's all nerves and not Agent Orange. That's what Dr. ____ told me. I don't know what to believe.

I know it all kicks up around the time of year we went into ____. I can't tell you what we were doing there, it's still secret and I've never been too comfortable with these dropped ceilings here in the clinic. It's just too easy to hide a microphone here. Maybe someday I'll be able to talk about it, but for now you never know who might be listening, and I'm not allowed to say anything about it. I shouldn't even have said we were in ____. I guess they need to keep tabs, because you know we still have our people over there who'd be dead in a minute if the wrong thing was said. There've been times I took every stick of furniture out of my house, took all the plates off the plugs in the walls and replaced every light fixture, and I had a guy sweep my house for bugs—cost me $600, but I still had the feeling I was being watched. I don't know if it was the NVA [North Vietnamese Army] or a CIT [U.S. Marine counterintelligence], or maybe both. You *know* the NVA has people over here disguised as refugees. Maybe that sounds paranoid, but I can't help thinking it. Here I did three fucking combat tours serving my country and I feel like a fucking fugitive.

It still makes me mad the way nobody understands what we did over there. When I first came back it was like I was living under a toilet and every five minutes somebody had diarrhea on me. There's nothing I can do. I feel like a complete freak, maybe like the Elephant Man—that's me. Nobody can understand, 'cept maybe another 'Nam vet. If only I could cry like I cried the day ____ had his face shot off. I haven't cried since then. Never.

Well, I guess it's something that I can even talk to you like this, and you not even a 'Nam vet and all. Remember how long it took me to say *anything*? I just had to watch until I could trust ____ and ____ and you. It was almost three years till I started to open up.

The people who read this book ain't going to believe any of this shit. And *you* better look out. Nobody's going to believe you when you tell them, and you'll end up an outcast like us.

Response and Analysis

1. What happened to this Vietnam veteran that caused him to be so massively shaken? What belief systems and perceptions were altered by his experience?

2. Is there any potential for him to recover from this trauma, and, if not, what do we do with this man? If you believe he could recover, how would you go about achieving recovery, and whom would you bring in to be of help to him? What could we do to help him feel safe and be a member of the community?

3. What recurring painful memories, emotional withdrawal, avoidance, and heightened arousal does this veteran experience?

Research

Many Vietnam veterans participated in open interviews in which they were asked questions and were allowed to respond in whatever way they wished. What are two advantages and two disadvantages of an open interview? Do you believe that the advantages outweigh the disadvantages, or vice versa? Why or why not? Briefly describe another way to study how the Vietnam War affected veterans.

chapter 2

DISSOCIATIVE
DISORDERS

Which I is I?

Theodore Roethke, *In a Dark Time*

From time to time, certain psychological disorders capture the public's imagination, arousing curiosity, sympathy, and heated controversy. Recently, dissociative disorders have done that. Multiple personalities (dissociative identity disorder) and repressed memories (dissociative amnesia) have taken center stage as areas of scientific and public debate.

Dissociative phenomena are certainly not new. Several dissociative states—trance, amnesia, hypnotic states—have been recognized for centuries and may take various forms in different cultures. One of the earliest forms of psychological treatment, hypnosis, relies explicitly on suspending normal experiences of time and self.

The cases of dissociation that we often hear about in the media might lead us to believe that dissociative experiences are always strange and bizarre, but they are not. Dissociative experiences occur regularly in everyday life. We all experience forgetting; we all have discontinuities in the flow of our experiences; many of us have had the feeling that something seems, for a brief time, unreal. But these are not psychological disorders because we typically fill in the gaps—we knit together our experiences into reasonably integrated wholes. Our life and our experiences seem to have unity. But people with dissociative disorders have disruptions in consciousness, memory, identity, or perception that they cannot repair or integrate.

In recent years, there has been an increase in the frequency of dissociative-disorder diagnoses. Some argue that the increase is due to recent recognition that the prevalence of physical and sexual abuse—a contributing factor in many cases—is greater than previously believed. Others fear that the increase is the result of a diagnostic fad among some mental health professionals. A few skeptics even doubt the validity of these diagnoses.

One type of memory disorder that may result from severe trauma or stress is dissociative amnesia. This form of amnesia is different from amnesia brought on by other causes, such as head injury, dementia, or physical illness. The story of Jane Loring (written by Sidney Katz with the assistance of Jane Loring and Dr. Lionel

Solursh, who treated her) presents a case of dissociative amnesia. Her case was brought to the attention of the medical community because Loring could not remember who she was, where she had been, who her parents were, or what she had been doing for several days. There was no physical explanation for her amnesia, so she began a long course of therapy. In the course of treatment, Loring recovered her memories, some of which centered on recent stresses and childhood traumas.

Much of the controversy surrounding dissociative amnesia relates to the controversy over repressed memory—memories that are lost to consciousness because of the psychological trauma surrounding them. Memory researchers, such as Elizabeth Loftus, have argued that memory is not at all like a videotape recording. We remember events imperfectly, with many gaps. Her research has shown that people often fill in the gaps in memory, sometimes with information from other sources. From this perspective, some repressed memories of abuse, though honestly believed by the persons who hold them, may be untrue—they are fabrications that combine bits of reality with information from other sources. In the next selection, Elizabeth Loftus and Katherine Ketcham present many sides of the repressed memory controversy.

The final selection is by Quiet Storm (a pseudonym). It is one of several works published recently by persons diagnosed with dissociative identity disorder and who, through treatment, have begun to recognize and address the painful dissociations of identity.

There is still much we do not understand about memory, dissociation, and how personality is integrated. We do know, however, that the pain and confusion experienced by persons with dissociative identity disorder, amnesia, or depersonalization disorder is real. Mental health professionals will continue to seek better ways to diagnose and treat persons with these disorders while sorting through the cultural, scientific, and legal controversies.

THE DIVIDED WOMAN

Sidney Katz

Psychological Concept
dissociative amnesia

Amnesia can be caused by illness, traumatic injury, dementia, or severe psychological stress. According to the neurologist who examined her and the psychiatrist who treated her, psychological stress was the primary cause of Jane Loring's generalized dissociative amnesia (called *hysteria* at the time this was written). Loring was a second-year pharmacy student who, upon returning home from a trip, suddenly forgot her entire life. She was unable to remember her parents, her friends, or what she had learned in pharmacy school. She had no idea who she was. Loring began a course of treatment that involved psychotherapy, hypnosis, and medication. Through treatment, she was ultimately able to recover her past, including the incident that seemed to precipitate her amnesia. This selection presents the onset of Loring's amnesia and the beginning of her treatment.

The crisis that sent Jane Loring in frantic search of help began on the evening of November 6, 1966. She found herself lying on a sofa in an unfamiliar living room, looking up into the anxious faces of a middle-aged man and woman who were unknown to her. Her confusion quickly turned to astonishment and fear as they told her that they were her parents, and that she was in the Toronto home where she had lived all her life. As she stared at them blankly, they said her name was Jane Loring.

A painful silence followed, as they realized that she still didn't recognize them. Then the older woman—her mother—held out a folded piece of paper which she said she'd found in Jane's coat pocket. It was a cancelled airline ticket for a Toronto-Chicago flight, and the return-date stamped across it was six P.M., November 6, 1966.

As Jane gazed at the ticket, she could vaguely recall buckling her seat-belt before take-off from O'Hare Airport in Chicago. But she could remember nothing else. Abruptly, and for no apparent reason, her entire past life had been completely erased from her memory, leaving her mind like a blank piece of paper.

On the advice of their family doctor, the Lorings immediately summoned Dr. P. Weyman, a neurologist, to examine their daughter. Since Jane had previously been treated for epilepsy, they thought perhaps she had had another seizure.

But Dr. Weyman at once ruled out this possibility. "Your daughter's memory loss," he told the Lorings, "is due to amnesia, not epilepsy. It has a psychological basis. I'd suggest she see a psychiatrist, someone like Lionel Solursh. I'll refer Jane to him if you like."

A few days later, Dr. Weyman's letter of referral was delivered to a small psychiatric office on the sixth floor of Toronto Western Hospital. It read as follows.

Dr. P. T. Weyman, Neurologist
Medical Towers
Toronto, Ontario
November 9, 1966

Dr. Lionel Solursh
Dept. of Psychiatry
Toronto Western Hospital

Dear Dr. Solursh:

Re: LORING, Margaret Jane, age 22, single

Would it be possible for you to see the above patient as quickly as possible— tomorrow, if it's convenient? She is suffering acute anxiety and distress because of a state of amnesia which suddenly began four days ago, after she had returned from a brief visit to Chicago. I can find no neurological basis for her memory loss and conclude that it has a psychological basis. Indeed, this type of memory loss is more typical of an hysterical reaction.

Miss Loring was referred to me by her family physician and I have little personal information about her.

The events immediately preceding the onset of her amnesia are somewhat vague and puzzling. She flew to Chicago to visit a Miss Mary Manchester, a friend who is about ten years her senior and with whom she worked last summer in a girls' camp in upper New York State. Miss Manchester was the program director and Miss Loring was a counsellor.

For some reason, Miss Loring concealed the visit from her parents by telling them that she was spending the weekend with a local girl friend. The deception was detected when her flight was delayed by bad weather and her parents phoned the girl friend inquiring as to the whereabouts of their daughter.

Although I have no details, since Miss Loring can remember nothing, I would speculate that there was considerable emotional upheaval surrounding her visit to Chicago.

Miss Loring states that the last thing she can remember is boarding the plane in Chicago for the flight back to Toronto. According to her parents she entered her home and collapsed in the living room. When she regained consciousness, she could remember nothing of her past.

Yours truly,
P. T. Weyman, M.D., F.R.C.P. (C)

Weyman had a particular reason for referring his patient to Dr. Solursh.

Solursh's professional achievements were impressive. He was a senior psychiatrist on the staff of one of Toronto's leading teaching hospitals and a teacher of psychiatry at the University of Toronto medical school. He had written scores of professional papers and was an acknowledged authority on the symptoms and treatment of drug abuse. And lastly, Solursh had a special interest in cases of hysteria.

On November 11, 1966, the day after he received Weyman's letter, Dr. Solursh saw Jane Loring for the first time.

Dr. Solursh, notebook in hand, asked her name, address, and age.

Jane hesitated, then carefully consulted several cards which she had taken from her purse. "They tell me," she said somewhat tentatively, "that my name is Jane Loring and my age is twenty-two." She examined one of the cards again and added, "My whole name appears to be Margaret Jane Loring, but everyone seems to call me Jane." She lapsed into silence and fidgeted in her chair, obviously uncertain and frightened.

Her emotional state was not uncharacteristic of a patient's first visit to a psychiatrist. Dr. Solursh was aware that the prospect of revealing private feelings and information to a stranger was unnerving. And heaven knew what was in store for Jane. Endless courses of treatment, perhaps including such frightening methods as electric shock and powerful drugs. Where would it all end? Was there any real hope for recovery?

"Tell me what you *do* know about yourself," the doctor urged.

Jane shrugged helplessly. "All I'm really sure of is what's happened in the past five days since I woke up on the couch in my home. My parents tell me I had just returned from visiting a friend in Chicago, Mary Manchester, and that I had kept my trip a secret from them.

"My Chicago friend phoned me yesterday and told me that I'd had several epileptic seizures while I was at camp last summer. Apparently I never told my parents about them. Now they feel my loss of memory is related to the fact that I've been secretive about my seizures and my visit to Mary.

"Maybe I didn't really want to tell them about it but I have no idea why. And I can't believe I've completely lost my memory over something as simple as that." She twisted her hair nervously round her fingers as she talked.

"I just don't remember anything about myself. My parents tell me I've been feeling tired this fall and worrying about school—I'm in second-year pharmacy— even though I apparently stood in the top fifth of my class last year. But now it's so strange when I look at my books. They don't make sense, although some of the terms sound awfully familiar."

Dr. Solursh asked, "Can you tell me who your best friends are at school?"

Silence. Jane shook her head and bit her lip, frowning.

"What about places? Are there rooms or buildings or streets that mean anything special to you?"

More tense silence.

After a succession of unanswered questions the psychiatrist realized that, in her present state, Jane Loring was unable to supply any further information about herself.

Her desire to cooperate was obviously sincere. "I'm trying to remember but I can't," she said, almost to herself. "It's like a thick black wall is separating me from my past. I want to beat this thing, and by myself, without help from my parents.

My mother keeps prodding me, and I don't want her interference. But I'm frightened—please help me. It's terrible."

Already the skimpy interview had posed a number of central questions to Dr. Solursh. What had transpired in Chicago to precipitate such a severe reaction—total loss of memory? Why was Jane so secretive in her dealings with her parents? Her comments indicated that a considerable strain existed between her and her parents; but if she could not remember anything, including her parents, then why should she act so strongly independent? What problems had been weighing her down before the Chicago trip? Who was Mary and what part did she play in Jane's life?

"I'd like to see you tomorrow," said Dr. Solursh. "We'll use hypnosis to try and get your memory back. I'd like to help you return to school as quickly as possible."

On a Saturday morning the psychiatric ward of a large city hospital is less busy than usual. Many patients are home on weekend passes and only a skeleton medical and nursing staff is on duty.

On Saturday, November 12, Jane Loring was back in Dr. Solursh's office.

"How are you today?"

There was a lengthy silence, during which she appeared to be forcing herself to speak. Finally the words came rushing out. "I think you can help me but I'm so frightened. I can't stand the memory loss any longer. It's ridiculous and I have to get over it. Please try hypnosis—anything to get my memory back. I've got to find out who I am."

She described living without memory as a weird and embarrassing ordeal. She was unable to recognize a single object in her own room at home, including a cherished teddy bear she'd been given on her sixth birthday. She had to depend on a street map to find her way around Toronto, the city where she had spent her entire lifetime. "There are no familiar landmarks," she complained. "It's like waking up in Timbuktu." Some of her oldest friends were offended because she only responded to their greetings with a puzzled look. And her mother even had to introduce her to Peter, the boy she'd been going steady with for years and had become engaged to last fall.

Peter, she explained, had given her a crash course in reconstructing her university career and her personal relationships. Mary, her Chicago friend, had flown to Toronto to try to help Jane remember incidents that had occurred at the summer camp where they had worked together.

"The things Peter and Mary have told me about my past have been of practical value," Jane told her doctor, "but I'm left just as confused as ever."

Strangely, the first inklings of Jane's past to return were about her life as a counsellor at camp. She could recall, now, that she had been nicknamed "Mighty Mouse" and that another girl was called "Super-Rat." She also had a photographic impression of approaching a boat dock in a canoe, and seeing the name of the camp emblazoned in red paint on a piece of rough lumber.

Yet despite this slight progress, Mary's presence in Toronto was not welcomed by Mrs. Loring. Her mother, explained Jane, had taken an instant dislike to the thirty-four-year-old petite blonde who now worked on the staff of a Chicago social agency. Her mother had said to her, "I have a funny feeling Mary's a bad influence on you. She's somehow involved in your breakdown. I think you should keep away from her."

Jane Loring's dissatisfaction with her present condition was a hopeful sign to Dr. Solursh, since patients who feel comfortable with their symptoms are reluctant to cooperate with a therapist. Jane would make every attempt, he felt, to learn how to enter a hypnotic trance, and this technique should enable her to break through the memory barrier that had blocked out her past less than a week ago.

"Hypnosis," he explained, "is just a matter of learning how to get into a relaxed, sleep-like state. I want you to sit in as comfortable a position as you can. Fix your eyes on the buckle of my briefcase. When your eyelids become heavy, let them close."

Jane shifted in the big leather chair until she was comfortable and focussed on the briefcase that leaned against the wall eight feet away.

Solursh continued. "Notice the weight of your arms as they rest on the sides of the chair . . . they're getting heavy. The weight of your legs against the floor . . . they're growing heavy. The weight of your head on your neck . . . growing heavy. Your eyelids are heavy and you want to close your eyes. . . ."

Her eyes closing, Jane mumbled, "I'm sleepy . . . I'm growing heavier all over." Her body was visibly relaxed.

The psychiatrist continued, almost in a whisper. "Your body continues to feel heavier. I'm going to count from one to twenty, and with each number you're going to enter a heavier and sleepier state . . . one . . . two . . . three . . ."

Jane's reactions were almost ideal. In less than five minutes she had reached a profound hypnotic state. "Now," said Dr. Solursh, "I'm going to count to five. At five, you will recall boarding the plane in Chicago to fly home to Toronto."

Vanished memories now began coming back. Jane recalled boarding the plane at O'Hare Airport. "I'm unhappy about something but I don't know why. It's just a feeling. The flying weather is hell—all rain and fog. We have to cut the trip short and land in Buffalo." She remembered getting on a bus to complete the journey to Toronto. "Seated next to me is this old lecher. He won't stop talking. He keeps making passes at me and tries to date me in Toronto. It's a relief when the trip is over and I take a cab home."

She went on to vividly describe her arrival home. "I can see the house now. It's small, made of red brick, and has two stories. There's a large maple tree in the front lawn. And I can see a cat sitting in the window. It's my cat. Oh . . . there's a door. It's green. I'm walking towards it . . ."

She hesitated and then her voice became tense. "But I can't do it! I just can't go through the door."

For the next few minutes Solursh gently urged Jane to enter her home. "You are turning your key . . . you step into the house. What happens next? What are you thinking? What are you feeling?"

She remained silent, her face strained. Obviously, she was not yet able to face whatever awaited her within.

By persistent suggestion, I can ram her through the door, thought Solursh, but it might be risky. Re-entering the home probably symbolizes reuniting with a family situation that is painful to her. If I force her in, it might precipitate a psychotic breakdown.

He decided to bring the trance to an end. "Jane . . . I'm going to count backwards from five to one. With each number, you will feel lighter and more awake. At one, you will be wide awake but still very relaxed . . . five . . . four . . . three . . . two . . . one."

Jane opened her eyes quite readily. In spite of the frustrating experience of the door, she appeared less emotionally flat than when she had arrived. But she was still somewhat depressed by her sense of loss and confusion. She realized now that there would probably be no dramatic, one-shot cure for her condition.

Response and Analysis

1. Most people occasionally forget the names of people they have recently met or what they did the day before. How do these experiences differ from dissociative amnesia?

2. The neurologist who first examined Jane Loring determined that her memory loss had no physical cause; it was psychological. How do you think the doctor came to this conclusion? Why would it be important to know what caused the memory loss?

3. Dr. Solursh used hypnosis to help Loring recover her lost memories. Would you expect people who experience dissociative disorders to be more or less easily hypnotized? Why? What risks accompany recovering memory under hypnosis? What other methods might Dr. Solursh use to help Loring recover her memories?

4. When Loring was under hypnosis, Dr. Solursh chose not to pressure her to enter the door to her home. Why? What assumptions about her memory loss and its recovery does he seem to be making?

Research

Suppose you want to investigate the frequency with which therapists identify and treat clients with repressed memories of abuse. You discover that therapists vary greatly in the number of clients who they believe have repressed memories of abuse. For example, suppose in a three-year period, some therapists diagnosed no cases of repressed memories or dissociative disorders, whereas other therapists diagnosed over 60% of their clients with dissociative disorders and in need of treatment for repressed memories. How could you explain this discrepancy? How might you be able to tell if the therapists actually had different types of clients or if diagnosis was in the eye of the beholder?

THE MYTH OF REPRESSED
MEMORY

Elizabeth Loftus and Katherine Ketcham

Psychological Concept
repressed memory

Elizabeth Loftus is a research psychologist and a renowned expert in the field of memory. She became interested in the phenomenon of repressed memory because of the important questions it raises about how memory works. She is in the midst of an important debate between those who adamantly and without question support all stories of repressed memory, including childhood sexual abuse, and those who are skeptical and demand substantial evidence for such claims. With coauthor Katherine Ketcham, Loftus presents the views and painful stories from each side, the social and political influences on the debate, and her struggle to remain dedicated to the principles of science.

Something has gone wrong with therapy, and because that something has to do with memory, I find myself at the center of an increasingly bitter and fractious controversy. On one side are the "True Believers," who insist that the mind is capable of repressing memories and who accept without reservation or question the authenticity of recovered memories. On the other side are the "Skeptics," who argue that the notion of repression is purely hypothetical and essentially untestable, based as it is on unsubstantiated speculation and anecdotes that are impossible to confirm or deny. Some Skeptics are less circumspect, referring to repression as "psychomagic," "smoke and mirrors," or just plain "balderdash."

The True Believers claim the moral high ground. They are, they insist, on the front line, fighting to protect children from sexual predators and assisting survivors as they struggle through the arduous healing process. The implication, unspoken but not unheard, is that anyone who refuses to join the True Believers in their quest to uncover the hidden past and to gain legitimacy for the concept of repression is either antiwoman, antichild, antiprogress, or, at the worst extreme, "dirty," i.e., a practicing pedophile or satanist.

The Skeptics attempt to evade these accusations with talk of proof, corroboration, and scientific truth-seeking, but they are not afraid to hurl some deadly grenades of their own. According to the most outspoken and vituperative Skeptics, therapists specializing in recovered memory therapy operate in a neverland of fairy dust and mythic monsters. Woefully out of touch with modern research, engaging in "crude psychiatric analysis," guilty of oversimplification, overextension, and "incestuous opinion citing," these misguided, undertrained, and overzealous clinicians are implanting false memories in the minds of suggestible clients, making "therapeutic lifers" out of their patients and ripping families apart.

This is obviously more than an academic discussion about the mind's ability to bury a memory and then bring it back into consciousness years later. The issues evoked by the simple notion of repression are among the most controversial concerns of cognitive and clinical psychology: the role of hypnosis in therapy and courts of law; the power of suggestion; social influence theory; the currently popular diagnoses of posttraumatic stress disorder (PTSD) and multiple personality disorder (MPD, labeled in the fourth edition of the American Psychiatric Association's *Diagnostic and Statistical Manual* as dissociative identity disorder, DID); the inner child and the dysfunctional family; pornography; satanic cults; rumor mills; moral crusades; alien abduction; media-inspired hysteria; and, of course, the question of political correctness.

I watch the bullets fly, and I duck for cover. My research into the malleability of memory aligns me with the Skeptics, but I am also sympathetic to the True Believers' concerns. I do not want to see a return of those days, not so very long ago, when a victim's cries for help went unheard and accusations of sexual abuse were automatically dismissed as fantasy or wish-fulfillment and shunted away into the backwaters of the public conscience. Nor can I automatically accept the idea that significant numbers of fanatical therapists are carelessly implanting memories in their clients' vulnerable minds.

I don't believe the world is so purely black and white. And so I insist on entering the gray areas of ambiguity and paradox, asking questions, listening carefully, struggling to sort out the conflicting and contentious points of view. I answer ten-page, single-spaced letters from the True Believers; I talk to them for hours on the phone; I meet them in airport coffee shops and hotel restaurants where they tell me their stories and plead with me to come over to their side.

"Can't you see the damage you are doing?" they ask.

"All the gains the feminist movement has made in the last twenty years will be destroyed if you and others like you continue to question these memories," they insist.

"If you could only see the pain that I see, if you could only witness the intensity of my clients' anguish," a therapist pleads, "you would know that these memories arise from real, not imagined, events."

I listen and try to balance their passion with the pain I have witnessed in the stories of "the accused." A balding man in his seventies hands me a letter he recently received from his daughter's lawyer. He and his wife hold hands and wait patiently as I read through the official-looking document with "Attorney at Law" embossed in scrolled script at the top.

"Dear *Mr. Smith*," the letter begins:

I have been retained by your daughter, who is prepared to file a lawsuit against you for severe emotional damage inflicted during her childhood. She has recently recovered memories of perverse physical and sexual abuse perpetrated upon her by you, her father, when she was a minor. We are prepared to settle this case for $250,000. If we do not hear from you within four weeks from the date of this letter, we will file a law-suit requesting a substantially larger sum of money.

An accused mother shows me the fading color photograph of her "baby," the youngest of five children, whom she hasn't seen in more than three years. "She went to a therapist for help after she was severely beaten by her alcoholic husband," the gray-haired woman explains, cradling the thirty-year-old photograph in her arms. "While she was in therapy, she left her two young children with us. But after a few months she began to have flashbacks of her father sexually abusing her, beginning when she was just five months old. She wrote us a letter and said she never wanted to see us again. She has forbidden us to see or talk to our grandchildren."

"I'm not a baby-raper," an accused father tells me, tears running down his cheeks. "How could my daughter say these things about me? Where did these memories come from?"

I pick up the phone and call the accusing children, hoping for—what? Reconciliation?

"I can't take back the truth," the voices tell me.

"He did what he did, and he needs to admit it and ask for my forgiveness."

"I'm not responsible for my parents' pain."

"People need to believe in the children."

"The world is an unsafe place."

"I only want to protect other children."

"The truth has set me free."

"Parents lie," a child-abuse advocate tells me, her face red with anger. She quotes me the oft-repeated but always shocking statistic: One in three women have been sexually abused by the time they reach the age of eighteen.

"But those statistics," I interrupt gently, "are based on a very broad definition of sexual abuse that would include grabbing at breasts or buttocks covered with clothes, stroking a leg, or snatching a sloppy, unasked-for kiss at a drunken wedding reception."

"If you doubt the statistics"—the woman's voice rises—"why don't you visit the county rape center or the battered women's shelter? These women and children are not statistics; they are real people in real pain."

I have stopped arguing statistics.

"I can't describe the pain," an accused mother tells me. "If a child dies, you learn how to deal with the grief, but every morning I wake up to this nightmare, and every night I go to bed with it, and in between nothing changes."

"I think, My God, could this have happened? Did *I* repress the memories of abusing my children?" her husband says, waiting patiently for his turn to put words to his anguish. "And then I think: How could you forget something like that, how could I have touched my child and repressed all knowledge of it? No, no, no. I didn't forget this because it never happened. It simply never happened."

They look pleadingly at me. *Do you understand? Do you believe me?*

One of the most heartbreaking stories I've heard was told by a thirty-year-old woman who happens to be trained as a therapist. Her story is, perhaps, more complicated than most because she was a victim of childhood sexual abuse.

I know a lot about victimization, because I have been a victim. When I was in grade school, I was sexually molested. For the record, it was not my parents. And also for the record, I have never forgotten it, not for one day. But out of a deep sense of shame, just as many other victims experience, I remained silent for more than twenty years.

Then, one day, I shared my story of my abuse experience with my sister. Eventually she began to suspect that she, too, had been abused. She had no memories, no clues, no reason, no faces, no names, not one shred of evidence. She and my other sister began discussing their ideas and suspicions. As they bounced their thoughts and feelings off each other, they began having dreams about being molested.

They accused my grandfather, my uncle, and then my father. Their allegations became more bizarre and included my mother and older brother, aunts, uncles, cousins, friends, and neighbors. My parents stood by and watched as their family went down like dominoes, and they could do nothing.

My six-year-old nephew, who had been in therapy for more than a year and was now seeing his second counselor because his first counselor couldn't find any evidence of sexual abuse, began to make some disclosures. He said that my mother, my father, and my older brother, whom he had not seen in four years, had sexually molested him. Two weeks after my parents were named, I began my career as a therapist. I worked for three days, and on the fourth day, my supervisor called me into the office to inform me that my nephew had named more people who allegedly molested him. I was among the people he named. I was fired on the spot and was investigated by the Children's Services Board and the police. The investigation took almost four months before my name was cleared.

Having been a victim of sexual abuse, I would rather be found standing with a bloody knife next to a corpse than be accused of sexually molesting a child. Not a day goes by when I don't feel the emptiness of all the things and all the people that I have lost. But in the deepest part of my soul, I know the truth—the fact of my innocence, known only for certain to me and to God. No one can take that from me.

"These people are in denial," therapists counter.

"You are being used by them," a friend tells me. "They need your expertise to give their denials some kind of legitimacy. You're just a pawn in their hands."

"Get out of this whole field before your reputation is destroyed," another friend warns.

The Skeptics tell me to stop being so wishy-washy. "This is not a fence-sitting issue," they say.

"Naive patients are being led like lambs to slaughter by incompetent therapists."

"These therapists are worse than misinformed, poorly trained fools," a sociology professor fumes. "They are dangerous zealots, and they must be stopped."

Both sides tell me to watch my step. "Take very good care of yourself," a therapist writes.

"Watch yourself," a colleague warns.

"Be careful," a journalist cautions.

An anonymous letter postmarked from a mid-sized city in the Midwest accuses me of collaborating with satanists. "Please consider your work to be on the same level as those who deny the existence of the extermination camps during World War II," the letterwriter concludes.

"Is this the memory doctor who hates children?" a soft female voice inquires when I pick up the phone.

"I have an opinion about Dr. Loftus," a caller to a local radio program announces. "I think she's connected with the right-wing Christian groups who are trying to advance the cause of male patriarchy . . ."

I open the newspaper to read that a man I testified for in a child molestation case was brutally murdered. Two years earlier Kaare Sortland and his wife Judy had been charged with sexually molesting three young children at their day-care center. They were acquitted of one charge, and the judge dismissed the other two charges, noting that the children had originally denied that they were abused and only changed their minds after numerous therapy sessions and intensive interviews with interrogators.

On the night Kaare was murdered he heard noises outside his home and went outside to investigate. His wife heard him shout, "I didn't do it!" Seconds later he lay dying in the gravel driveway, shot three times in the chest with a large-caliber handgun.

I remember—was it just a few years ago?—sitting in a hotel coffee shop in Washington, D.C., with Herb Spiegel, a giant in the field of psychiatry and hypnosis, and Ed Frischholz, a young cognitive psychologist with a clinical practice in Chicago. Over coffee and Danish, we were having a lively discussion about memory, the media, and the amazing rebirth of the phenomenon known as repression. I related some of the odd stories and bewildering legal cases I'd become involved in, and we talked about the media frenzy that began with *People* magazine's cover stories featuring the repressed memories of Roseanne Barr Arnold and of 1958's Miss America, Marilyn Van Derbur.

During a lull in the conversation, Ed leaned back in his chair and said, "What do you suppose is going on out there?" By "out there" he meant, of course, the real world.

We were genuinely confused and caught a bit off guard. I couldn't know then where the question would take me, how far I would wander from the ivory tower of safe, scholarly pursuits. I remember laughing a bit nervously, hugging my friends good-bye, and, as I rushed out to catch my plane, promising to mail reprints of my recent papers. It was a familiar routine. But my world and my life were already in the process of a radical and irrevocable shift.

I want to understand "what is going on out there." I live, breathe, eat, and sleep repression. I have surrendered to this obsession because I believe that what is going on in the real world is vitally important to an understanding of how memory works and how it fails. I have been willing to step out of my role as a laboratory scientist and into this messy field experiment because I believe that this is where science begins: with puzzled questions about the causes of a phenomenon and the meticulous untangling of coincidence and design.

What is repression? Where do repressed memories come from? Are they authentic relics dredged from a forgotten past, or are they "smoke and mirrors" images that develop when a suggestion is implanted in a vulnerable person's mind? Whatever the answers turn out to be, these are critically important questions. I believe that the phenomenon of repression holds up a mirror in which we can catch glimpses of our own psyche. If we are willing to look without prejudice and preconception, we may be able to discover profound truths about our need to belong, to be loved, to be accepted, to be understood, to recover.

To recover—from what? That, of course, is the question.

Response and Analysis

1. How would you characterize the two sides of the debate over repressed memory? What do you think about the issue?

2. Many important decisions—including those about whether someone repressed memories of abuse—risk two different kinds of errors: false-positive errors affirm something that is not true, and false-negative errors deny something that is true. What are the personal and social costs of making each kind of error in cases of repressed memory?

3. Imagine that you are a therapist or counselor and a client tells you she recently read something about abuse and repression. She wonders if she might be a victim of child sexual abuse and has repressed the memory. How would you respond? What factors would you consider in deciding how to work with the client? Would you consult with colleagues? Why or why not?

4. Repression involves the separation of certain memories from consciousness. Many cases of repressed memory involve childhood memories. What therapeutic approaches would attempt to recover these memories as part of treatment? Would a cognitive thera-

pist be likely to work with these memories? A behavioral therapist? A psychodynamic therapist? What assumptions about the past's influence on the present are probably made when therapists encourage clients to recover repressed memories?

Research

Suppose a researcher is interested in the relationship between people's reports of poor relationships with adult caregivers and the frequency of dreams that contain themes of abuse. The researcher has participants answer an extensive questionnaire that includes information about their childhood and relationships with significant adults. Then she has participants record their dreams for one month. She codes the dreams as having or not having themes of abuse. The researcher finds that people who reported poor relationships had more dreams with themes of abuse than those with more positive adult relationships. She concludes that dreams containing themes of abuse are good indicators of having been abused as a child. What flaws can you find in this study? What are the problems with its design or procedures? Are there problems with the researcher's conclusions? If so, what are they? What alternative explanations can be made?

I HAVE MULTIPLE
PERSONALITY DISORDER

Quiet Storm

Psychological Concept
>   dissociative identity disorder
>   (formerly called multiple personality disorder)

Quiet Storm, a pseudonym the writer gave herself to symbolize the quiet surface that covers an inner storm, writes of the several people who she believes live within her. Each has a separate identity, career, and "memories, talents, dreams, and fears." She describes several of the women who are a part of her, and tells how they evolved as defenders against child abuse. Storm's interior world is vast, filled with children, adolescents, and adults. People often notice great changes in her and remark that she sometimes seems like a completely different person. All of her selves are gradually healing, but integration is not an issue she is ready to confront. Some readers may find portions of Storm's article disturbing because of the abusive ordeals she presents as causes of her illness.

Elaina is a licensed clinical therapist. Connie is a nurse. Sydney is a delightful little girl who likes to collect bugs in an old mayonnaise jar. Lynn is shy and has trouble saying her *l*'s, and Heather—Heather is a teenager trying hard to be grown-up. We are many different people, but we have one very important thing in common: We share a single body.

We have Multiple Personality Disorder (MPD). We have dozens of different people living inside us, each with our own memories, talents, dreams, and fears. Some of us "come out" to work or play or cook or sleep. Some of us only watch from inside. Some of us are still lost in the past, a tortured past full of incest and abuse. And there are many who were so damaged by this past and who have fled so deep inside, we fear we may never reach them.

Imagine a little girl walking with her parents through a bookstore. She's only four, but she already knows how to read. She sees a book she really wants, and asks her parents if she can have it. They tell her no, and a single tear of disappointment rolls down her cheek. A single tear, but it is one tear too many.

The little girl's parents don't say anything in the store, but when they get home they take off her panties and beat her until her bottom is raw and bleeding. The panties are replaced with a diaper that is fastened to her skin with silver duct tape. She is locked in a closet for three days. She is fed laxative mixed with milk in a baby bottle; her diaper is never changed. Her parents tell her again and again that she is a dirty little baby and will never grow up. They are right.

There is more, worse, but the little girl does not remember it. It's too painful to remember more. If she stays in that closet and refuses to acknowledge the passing of time, then maybe those awful things didn't really happen. Maybe there can be some other ending to her story.

In a way, that little girl never left that closet. Another little girl did, one who shared the same body but whose existence began the moment the closet door opened. Where there was one, now there were two—one who understood that she must never ever cry to her parents for any reason and another who huddled forever in a dark inner closet, because to remember what happened next, when her parents finally came to get her, would be too much for a single young mind to bear.

Many of our Alter personalities were born of abuse. Some came because they were needed, others came to protect.

Leah came whenever she heard our father say "Come lay awhile with me." If she came, none of our other Alters would have to do those things he wanted. She could do them for us, and protect us from that part of our childhood.

Halfcup came when we were left at home for days on end with nothing to eat. She cooked meals for us. She cleaned up afterward so our parents wouldn't know we'd found a way to unlock our bedroom door. Halfcup still loves to cook. Last Christmas we bought her a new set of pots and pans.

Connie came when the body was beaten so badly that somebody had to come who didn't feel the pain, who could comfort the Alters who hurt, who could tell the doctor we'd fallen off our bike. We couldn't let anyone tell him what really happened. That would have made our parents even madder.

Unlike many of our Alters, Connie grew up into an adult as our body did. She was created to be a healer, so it was only natural that when she was old enough, she would enroll in nursing school.

Connie didn't know that at the same time she was in nursing school, Elaina was in grad school working on her social work degree. Nor did Elaina know about Connie. All they knew was that, even with only three hours of sleep each night, there never was enough time to get things done.

MPD is not a disease. It is not a sickness. It is a highly developed coping mechanism that allows the young mind to compartmentalize, or dissociate, repeated and traumatic abuse. The six-year-old who smiles at her teacher at school cannot hold back the tears when her father enters her room in the middle of the night. Somebody else has to come, somebody who can do those things without crying because crying isn't ever allowed. And the little girl whose mother tucks her in at night and calls her Peaches will never understand why that same mother ties her to the bed when she has a fever and beats her and tells her only bad little girls get sick. Somebody else has to come—somebody whose nose isn't stuffy and who doesn't have a fever.

Being able to create Alter personalities to cope with the abuse is the only thing that allowed us to survive our childhood alive. MPD was never a disease—it was a gift, the gift of life we gave to ourselves.

Once we were grown up and had escaped from our abusive parents, the system that protected us for so many years became unnecessary. But still our internal system of multiple personalities survived, and the longer we went untreated the worse things became for us. We lost time, as Alters unknown to us took control of the body. Sometimes they went shopping. Sometimes they haunted libraries. Sometimes they cowered on the floor in the closet because one of our Alters saw a little girl walking hand in hand with her father and the very sight of it terrified her. Often an innocent remark from a friend would trigger old memories of abuse, and for the Alter who held those memories it was as if the abuse were still going on. We couldn't stand to be touched, or to have anyone tell us they cared for us. We felt worthless and alone.

It took five years and as many therapists before we found someone who recognized our MPD. It was another year before we fully accepted the diagnosis. Only then did we truly begin to know ourselves.

The more we learn about ourselves and the abuse that created us, the stronger our system becomes. We've become one another's friends. We form alliances, accept responsibilities. We take care of each other.

Elaina and Connie work for our living. Elaina is a respected therapist who is building an extensive private practice. Connie works weekends at one of the local emergency rooms. Heather drives the car, and watches out for all the children we still have inside of us. Sydney sits with the tiniest ones when they are crying, and Lynn holds the stuffed polar bear while we sleep and pesters Heather to make sure we have plenty of crayons on hand for when she and her inside friends want to color.

Like many Multiples, we have constructed a large internal house where we go to live when we are not occupying the body. It's several stories high, with crystal chandeliers and big picture windows, and there's an inner yard filled with rainbows where the little ones go to play while Elaina and Connie are busy at work. The little ones are never allowed out when the adults are at their jobs. We have enough trouble hiding our MPD from people as it is. We have to wear tinted contacts because our eye color changes every time a different Alter comes out, and if we had a dollar for every time somebody has said to us, "Jeez, it's like you're a completely different person," we wouldn't have to worry so much about paying the $7,000 a year we have to spend on therapy because our medical insurance doesn't cover MPD.

We each have our own rooms in our internal house. We can decorate them the way we want, and lock the door and be absolutely safe from harm. But it's sad to know there are many doors in this house of ours that have never been opened. Late at night we hear the sobs and screams of those who live behind these doors, Alters who are still imprisoned by their abusive pasts and for whom there is yet no peace.

One of our Alters named Molly recently told our therapist that the very first thing she can remember was being locked in a closet. There was someone in there with her, a little girl dressed only in a diaper that was taped to her skin. Molly remembered leaving the closet, but didn't know what became of that other little girl.

Our therapist tried hard to reach Molly's companion, but she wouldn't talk to him. She was too afraid to come out, terrified of the devastating memories that loomed just beyond her closet door.

That was the day of the tremendous thunderstorm. There were high winds, pelting sheets of rain, lightning, hail, and thunder. We seem to gather a lot of internal energy from storms. We feel electric inside and sometimes seem to feel a part of the storm itself. We think of ourselves as a storm, a quiet storm where outside everything may appear calm and peaceful but inside violent tornadoes rage.

Anyway, as soon as the storm began, we went driving in Heather's car. All around us the storm was swirling and howling. We could see, we could practically feel, the rain pelting down on us through the glass T-top roof.

While Heather drove, Molly led many of us to the place deep inside where that little girl still cowered in her closet. She opened the door and went inside. She held the little girl in her arms, and told her about all of us and how we were waiting outside to love her and take care of her. All she had to do was remember the past and by remembering, free herself from it.

Bravely, the little girl took Molly's hand and walked with her out of that closet. Everything appeared misty to her at first, but then the memories coalesced and we all looked on as she remembered what happened more than a quarter of a century ago so vividly that it all seemed to be happening to her again, right then and there. She remembered the baths, the boiling hot water, the acrid lye soap, the wire brush with the rounded wooden handle. She remembered the pain, the blood, the searing violation of her private parts.

You won't be a bad little girl anymore, will you?

No, Mama! No, Daddy!

We remembered too. We wept, we screamed, we shared the pain while Heather drove us through streets full of water that sloshed against the wheel rims, through bolts of lightning that lit up the sky and through thunder that shook the car.

We named the little girl Misty, and when she was through remembering, Molly took her to her room where she removed her soiled diaper and bathed her ever so gently, and then helped her into a pink night dress and a pair of big-girl panties. The two curled up on fluffy pillows.

Outside, the storm was still raging, but inside, for a time, all was quiet in the eye of our storm.

Little by little we were healing ourselves and freeing ourselves from the tyranny of our past. Our therapist tells us that when we have remembered everything and worked through the pain associated with these memories, we will no longer need Alter personalities to protect us, and then and only then we can begin the process of integration into a single, cohesive personality. But that will be our decision—whether or not we will even want to turn from many back into one.

Integration isn't something we even think about right now. Right now we're far too busy working to heal all the wounded children inside us, the frightened adolescents and angry adults. Together we will continue to reclaim what was stolen from us by the perpetrators of our abuse. We cannot recapture the lost years, the shattered innocence, but we will not let our past destroy our future. We are survivors of our abuse, not its victims. We know that the loudest cries are often very, very quiet. We will listen to these cries, and we will honor each part of us that endured the pain in silence.

For us, the silence is broken.

Response and Analysis

1. How do you react to the description provided by Quiet Storm? What most affected you about the reading?

2. What tragic events does Quiet Storm suggest led to her developing dissociative identity disorder (formerly called multiple personality disorder or MPD)? Why does she believe the personalities were needed? How strong is the link between dissociative identity disorder and abuse?

3. Quiet Storm says that dissociative identity disorder is not a disease; it is a gift. What does she mean by this? Why might it have taken "five years and as many therapists before we found someone who recognized our MPD"?

4. With which theoretical orientation do the causes of this disorder fit? How would MPD be explained by insight-oriented approaches? By behavioral approaches? By biological approaches?

Research

Suppose you conducted a research project examining the prevalence of dissociative identity disorder worldwide. Imagine that your results show that the prevalence of dissociative identity disorder varies considerably across cultures. In what ways could you explain this finding?

chapter 3

SOMATOFORM
DISORDERS
AND FACTITIOUS
DISORDERS

_It is easy to see how the condition is part of
the psyche's apparatus of defense; unwilling
to accept its own gathering deterioration,
the mind announces to its indwelling
consciousness that it is the body with its
perhaps correctable defects—not the precious
and irreplaceable mind—that is going
haywire._

WILLIAM STYRON, _Darkness Visible_

Somatoform disorders and factitious disorders are psychological problems that manifest as physical problems. The symptoms resemble those of medical conditions, but neither medical examinations nor other disorders (e.g., panic disorder) can adequately explain them. In somatoform disorders, the symptoms are real and genuinely distressing to the sufferer; in factitious disorders, the symptoms are feigned for psychological gains.

These disorders have fascinated psychologists since the discipline began. Some of the earliest records of psychotherapeutic treatment concern patients exhibiting somatoform disorder, particularly conversion disorder (an unexplained loss of motor or sensory functioning in one part of the body). These disorders raise important questions about the relationship between mind and body, psyche and soma.

This chapter includes two readings on somatoform disorder and one on factitious disorder. In the first selection, Carla Cantor struggled to understand the phantom illness that plagued her. Suffering from a persistent pain in her wrist and unable to get relief from any treatment, she began to read medical journals; her research convinced her that she had lupus, a disabling autoimmune disease. But facts did not support her self-diagnosis. Gradually, she came to recognize her symptoms as hypochondriasis. Persons with hypochondriasis experience constant or recurring dread of physical illness. Physical symptoms are often misinterpreted as indicators or signs of serious illness.

In the second reading, Katharine A. Phillips presents the story of Jennifer, a young woman suffering from body dysmorphic disorder. Persons with body dysmorphic disorder appear physically normal but either are preoccupied with an imagined physical defect or exaggerate a slight physical defect. They often severely constrict their lives to avoid exposing their imagined defect to others. Jennifer's troubles first began when she was eleven. At that time, she believed that her nose was misshapen; then she became convinced that her facial skin was covered with blotches and that these were physical deformities that made her ugly. She avoided social contact, was depressed, and sought surgery for the imagined defect.

It is sometimes difficult to distinguish between somatoform disorders and factitious disorders. In somatoform disorders, the symptoms are not under the person's voluntary control—they are not deliberately contrived or consciously made up. People experience them as real, distressing, and unwanted. Sufferers often have trouble believing that their symptoms are not strictly physical in origin. In factitious disorders, physical symptoms are intentionally created for psychological gain such as attention, concern, or sympathy. Though they might not be aware of their motivations for doing so, persons with factitious disorder consciously adopt a sick role. In a severe form of this disorder, Munchausen's syndrome, persons might inject themselves with chemicals or ingest feces to produce fevers or gain admission to a hospital; they might submit to unnecessary exploratory surgery. Marc D. Feldman and Charles V. Ford present the story of Jenny, who suffers from a factitious disorder. Though she continues to work productively at her job and attend school, she feigns having cancer because life seems more fulfilling that way. Her status as a cancer patient becomes part of her self-definition.

PHANTOM ILLNESS

Carla Cantor

Psychological Concept
hypochondriasis

Carla Cantor believed that she was seriously ill. Convinced that she had lupus, a "disabling autoimmune disease with an array of horrifying symptoms . . . and nearly as deadly as cancer," Cantor sought a firm diagnosis and treatment. However, her physicians could not find anything wrong with her. She eventually recognized that, although she did not have the illness she imagined herself to have, she was suffering from hypochondriasis.

Cantor writes of the feelings of shame wrought by this illness and believes it important to bring hypochondriasis to the public's attention. The antidepressant Prozac, psychotherapy, and a more tolerant attitude toward her psychological disorder helped alleviate her condition.

One warm June evening I found myself imprisoned, a patient on a psychiatric ward of a hospital a few miles from my New Jersey home. It was not at all what I had intended. I had come to the emergency room earlier that day in desperation: I *had* to talk to someone about the undiagnosed pain in my wrist, my thinning hair, and the unrelenting fear that I was morbidly ill. Physical symptoms had plagued me for nearly a year, the problems starting a few months after the birth of my son, Michael, in April 1990.

That spring had begun so beautifully; my husband and I were thrilled when our second child turned out to be a boy, a complement for his three-year-old sister, Danielle. One of each, we thought, the ideal family. But while I was nursing Michael, I developed an excruciating pain whenever I moved my left wrist. My internist said it might be carpal tunnel syndrome brought on by hormonal changes. He suggested that I stop nursing and give the wrist a rest. I consulted an orthopedist, who advised me to try a splint. When that didn't work, another specialist injected my wrist with cortisone. Nothing alleviated the pain, which had spread to my shoulder, and, confusing the situation, tests that initially showed a borderline case of carpal tunnel syndrome—a benign though painful ailment—were now negative.

I felt betrayed by the medical profession. The doctors couldn't figure out what was wrong with me, nor did they seem to care. So I began to search for my own diagnosis, requesting sophisticated tests to rule out obscure disorders I had read about, like thoracic outlet syndrome and de Quervain's disease, tenosynovitis. All that showed up was a mild inflammation of the left wrist on a bone scan, a sensitive, expensive procedure used to screen for arthritis and cancer. The physicians didn't seem to find the laboratory results at all disturbing. Just a stiff wrist! One doctor prescribed physical therapy, which only made the pain worse.

Without any suggestion from a doctor, I settled on a diagnosis of lupus, a frightening, disabling autoimmune disease with an array of horrifying symptoms—arthritis, hair loss, skin rashes, mouth sores—and nearly as deadly as cancer. It was a disease with which I had some familiarity. Ten years earlier, after a traumatic breakup with a man I'd been living with, I had fallen sick with something doctors couldn't explain. As they prodded and prescribed, I pored over medical texts in the library—where I discovered this hideous, heartwrenching illness.

Each day during the winter of 1983 I'd catalog my lupus-like symptoms—joint aches, rashes, itching attacks, black and blue marks, exhaustion. I'd bring the list to doctors, begging them to confirm my diagnosis. I shook up one rheumatologist enough that he admitted me to a hospital for a five-day physical workup. It turned out to be just the right prescription. Tests, treatments, attention from visitors, time off from my demanding job as a newspaper reporter, a rest for mind and body. My discharge diagnosis: psychophysiological reaction/muscular-skeletal system.

Finally, I allowed the doctors to convince me that whatever was going on in my body was not symptomatic of a deadly disease, but the psychological dimension of the diagnosis had little impact. By the time I left the hospital, I was ready to put lupus and everything it signified behind me. Without realizing it, I'd spent months grieving for the loss of my relationship. I had recovered my sense of self and could function. Although, on my doctor's advice, I consulted a psychiatrist—I had seen a social worker for a number of years but was not in therapy at the time—I resisted insight and went on my way, chalking up the experience to a "weird episode." I returned to my job, offering a vague explanation of my illness to colleagues, and began a new relationship.

Now, a decade later, lupus was back and *this* time it seemed my fears were justified. I was unable to bend my wrist without pain; my hair, which had turned brittle, was falling out; and I had sun allergies—on several occasions I had developed a rash in tropical sunlight—all markers for the disease. Tests were negative, but no matter how many doctors tried to reassure me that I didn't have lupus, I wasn't convinced. I knew about the bizarre and fluctuating symptoms that make lupus so tough to diagnose and that no test was entirely accurate in ruling it out. No one could offer a 100 percent guarantee that the disease wasn't in the early stages of the illness—and nothing less would do. Perhaps, I thought irrationally, the earlier episode had been its initial onset.

As months went by I became increasingly distracted and depressed as my husband grew resentful and impatient. My work as a freelance writer suffered and, worst of all, my children weren't getting the love and attention they deserved. Yet despite my conviction, no doctor would pronounce the diagnosis I dreaded but in some perverse way wanted. One young rheumatologist, in retrospect among the wisest doctors I consulted, hinted that this obsession with my wrist and well-being might be related to the birth of my son, a latent postpartum depression of sorts. He suggested psychological help, which I resisted.

My trip to the hospital was a last desperate plea for help. I was on the verge of a breakdown, though it wasn't clear to me why. Was it because of my intolerable symptoms? That doctors couldn't find what was wrong? Or was I possibly going crazy because I *was* crazy? . . . something I briefly and reluctantly considered. I picked a sweltering Friday afternoon when I had just completed a writing assignment and expected my in-laws from out of town for a visit. I knew that they would be supportive of my family and help my husband with our children should I be gone for some time. At the hospital I waited hours in the emergency room to see the physician on call, who after examining me sent in a third-year medical resident in psychiatry. This brash young doctor listened to my woes of the past year: the pain, the tests, the physicians, my exhaustive search for an answer. After a few questions, he looked at me squarely and said, "I believe you are suffering from clinical depression. I want to admit you to the psychiatric ward."

After the initial shock of hearing his words, I felt relief. My shoulders relaxed and my stomach stopped churning as I sat calmly at the edge of the examining table, waiting for a nurse to take me to my room. A pleasant male orderly asked if I was hungry and brought me a cup of tea and a sandwich, the first food I had eaten all day. Finally, my illness would be diagnosed! Doctors would examine my inflamed wrist, psychiatrists would listen to me talk about the psychic pain of the past year, and they would all figure out whether I was really sick or just plain crazy. Being in a hospital also seemed like a reasonable excuse for leaving behind the responsibilities and stresses that go with being a freelance writer and mother of two young children.

But when the nurse arrived with a wheelchair—hospital policy—things got a little strange. Riding up in the elevator with her, I hung my head to avoid eye contact. *What if I didn't have a disease? Maybe I really was a fraud!* Then I was wheeled down a dingy hall into a sterile, forbidding-looking place: the psychiatric ward. I sucked in all that was disagreeable at once: the drugged-out patients sprawled on vinyl couches, watching a communal television set mounted on the ceiling, the group and occupational therapy schedules posted on the wall, the No Visitors sign. This, I knew, was no Club Med.

"Let me see your bag, miss," said a stern-looking woman with a sergeant's voice. I watched in horror as she rifled through my pocketbook and pulled out a pair of eyebrow tweezers. "I need those!" I cried, an edge of hysteria in my voice. (Now they'll really think I'm nuts, I thought.) She replied, "You'll get these back, miss. Hospital policy. The patients can't keep any sharp objects." . . .

Early the next morning I departed. I told the director it had all been a terrible mistake. What could he say? My husband came to get me and I walked back into my life with the joy and relief of waking from a nightmare. My kind, accepting in-laws asked no questions, and the children were overjoyed to have Mommy home.

It was time to take stock of my life. Perhaps the best thing to do was to leave the pain alone. Accept the symptoms, ignore them. After the hospital fiasco, I was able to do that for a while and there was a slight reprieve, but unwelcome and frightening thoughts intruded and the wrist was still stiff. I made the occasional visit to a doctor, getting a blood test for reassurance that never lasted long. Then one summer day I spotted a *New York Times* article headlined, "Patients Refusing to Be Well, A Disease of Many Symptoms." The subject was hypochondria, a pre-occupation with the fear of having or getting a serious disease. I had never before read anything about the topic. The article talked about people who suffer from symptoms for which no cause can be found or whose complaints are inappropriate in relation to their symptoms. In the past such patients had been dismissed by doctors and left to shuttle from medical laboratories to specialists to emergency rooms. But an effort was under way in the medical community to identify these patients, whose problems ranged from cancer phobias to chronic pain, to help them find relief. Physicians were even giving them a less pejorative name—somatizers ("soma" from the Greek word for body), a term psychiatrists use to describe people who unconsciously convert emotions into bodily ills. . . .

I spent an hour telling Dr. Fallon about my inflamed wrist, the hair loss, the photosensitivity, and the now wavering conviction that all these symptoms were signs of early lupus. He administered a psychological questionnaire to evaluate my problem and asked me to participate in the Prozac experiments. I never did take part in them. My husband and my parents, whom I had told of my troubles, were supportive and encouraged me to begin treatment with Prozac, but not as a partic-ipant in a double-blind study, in which I might be administered only placebos. So I established a relationship with another psychiatrist and began a trial of Prozac, my initial course on the drug lasting five months, less than the usual duration. Within weeks I felt better. The obsessive thoughts lifted; the pain and stiffness receded; the lost hair began growing back. After a year of misery I was happy and produc-tive again.

I telephoned Dr. Fallon, who was delighted to hear of my progress and curi-ous about my treatment. I couldn't explain why things were going so well. Had Prozac been a catalyst for change? Was it the working out of issues with my new therapist? Or had my growing recognition that for years I had been expressing emotions through physical symptoms finally reached a new stage? A former thera-pist had tried to convince me that my maladies and fears were symptomatic of other problems, but it hadn't sunk in. Or perhaps I wasn't ready to face my prob-lems until now, even to consider that my intrusive thoughts could be related to deeper psychological troubles or biochemical imbalances. . . .

The truth is that most who suffer from hypochondria do not need an "offi-cial" diagnosis to know that they have a problem. Like people with obsessive-compulsive disorder, who think the same senseless thoughts over and over, hypochondriacs tend to be painfully aware of the irrational nature of their fears. They are besieged by irrational beliefs pertaining to their bodies and ill health but feel powerless to dismiss them. Though preoccupations may range from mild to disabling, be episodic or unremitting, the fears are rarely delusional in intensity. And in the unusual case when health obsessions reach psychotic proportions, as I believe my lupus phobia came close to doing, the psychosis tends to be limited to this single aspect of experience. . . .

During the decade between the two lupus scares, I lived a high-strung but productive life: I attended graduate school, held jobs, was married, had children.

But my existence was peppered with episodes of illness. When the going got tough, I'd get sick. Or just the opposite: when things seemed to be going well, I'd come down with a symptom, or at least what I interpreted as one. It might be stomach pain, dizziness, black and blue marks, swollen glands, an achy heel, anything. Whatever the symptom, I always interpreted it as a precursor of some crippling illness: leukemia, Lou Gehrig's disease, scleroderma. I knew just enough about most diseases to cause trouble. Eventually I'd get past each episode, but it always took time—the cure a mysterious concoction of enough negative tests, a lessening of symptoms, some positive change in my life. And when the event was over, the realization that I was healthy and wasn't going to die, at least not immediately, was like a high, a reprieve, a new lease on life. That is, until the next time. The two hospital stays—interestingly, one for the physical workup, the other a mental one—were like bookends; they represented the two times in my life when symptoms, regardless of whether they were labeled organic or psychiatric, did not abate, when the way I usually coped with life just didn't work. . . .

Yes, Prozac has helped me quiet my intrusive thoughts, so much so that when I first began taking the drug I felt more like myself and freer than I had in years. It was as if all the wisdom accumulated in all that time in talk therapy suddenly came alive. The drug let loose the best in me, or perhaps the best me, the one without the internal battlefield. It restored my capacity for pleasure. I had symptoms, but they no longer terrified me. So natural did this new emotional balance seem, the side effects of Prozac so minimal, that I thought I was making it happen. Twice I went off the drug to try to do just that and was disappointed. Both times the preoccupations came back. Not always as fears about illness, but the same catastrophic thinking would manifest itself in other ways: in obsessions about my work, my ability to be a good mother, my relationship with my husband, my friends. Working with my psychiatrist, I came to realize that my style is an obsessional one. I worry, I fixate, and unwelcome negative thoughts intrude into many areas of my life. Hypochondria just tends to focus the worries in a particular direction.

When I first recognized this fragility in myself, I thought I was the unusual one, feeling my vulnerability so acutely, fixating on what I fixated on, suffering the way I suffered. I thought I might even know why. When I was seventeen, I was involved in a fatal car accident. I was a new driver behind the wheel of my parents' Chevy, my friend Toby beside me in the passenger seat. We were on our way to the ski slopes. Then I missed a curve on a winding mountain road obscured by a snowbank and in a flash had a fiery collision with a tractor-trailer. Fate let Toby die while I survived with barely an injury.

The accident was the worst thing that ever happened to me. Even twenty-four years later it is difficult for me to say that without guilt and without hearing a condemning voice over my shoulder: "Bad for you, huh? But so much worse for her."

The sense of culpability in the accident's aftermath which filled me with shame, despair, and self-hate was so intense that it endures to this day. Directly afterward, I was numb, and then for many years punitive: I wouldn't allow myself to feel healthy, happy, and strong. I carried the guilt in my body, exorcising it during my early twenties in the rebuking self-starvation of anorexia, and later in a constant certainty of being struck down by illness or death. I couldn't connect the symptoms on any emotional level with the earlier event, but years afterward in psychotherapy, my therapist drew the links and tried to make me see. I worked diligently at insight and even achieved the connection intellectually, but knowledge wasn't powerful enough to allow me to let go of the punitory system I had created, or of the hypochondriacal fears.

Then two things happened: a drug changed some essential biological substrate within me, and I met other people who had suffered and are suffering in a way I completely understood. These were not necessarily people who had survived an accident, but nonetheless they had lived their own version of survivor syndrome that had caused them to be emotionally frail, unable to withstand the irony of our peculiar existence. There had been an alcoholic father, a depressed mother, physical or emotional abuse, some trauma, or a series of smaller blows, which had burst upon already weakened ground. I was not the only one who experienced the phenomenon of getting symptoms when things were going well, who couldn't juggle too many stressful events, who didn't let joy in too easily.

Meeting these people made me realize that we humans are boundlessly complex, and that my "accident equals hypochondria" insight was only one clue to an ever more intricate puzzle. No one walks away from trauma unscathed, but not everyone who is traumatized starves herself or develops hypochondria. Why I became more afraid of living and of dying than others will forever remain an enigma. I can point to the car accident. I can point to my father's tendency to brood and be hard on himself, which I have internalized. I can point to a very early preoccupation with my body, not liking my nose, my wispy curls, my bushy eyebrows, which I perceived as too dark. I can also point to a certain naive recklessness I have displayed in my life; a tendency to flirt with disaster—hitchhiking alone through Europe and Central America, putting trust in unworthy relationships, experimenting with more drugs than I should have—a side of myself for which hypochondria may have provided a balance. Other events have had their impact: a distant cousin, beautiful, sweet, and courageous, dies of lymphoma at twenty-five; a childhood classmate gets married and is dead of a brain tumor within a year; my great uncle Charlie, who shortly after his acceptance to medical school diagnoses his own leukemia and dies before his graduation. . . .

With Prozac's help, I've learned to control my anxiety and phobic tendencies and keep hypochondria at bay. I've been back on the drug for nearly two years, and although it helps greatly in managing everyday life, I know that it's not a panacea. Many people, including myself, are leery about medication, especially of a relatively new drug whose clinical trials evaluating the effects of long-term use are still in the early stages. . . .

In my personal odyssey, what has probably helped as much as anything is the realization that I'm not the only one fighting this battle. The knowledge that one is not alone—which dawned for me in reading the *New York Times* article—can be the first step toward self-acceptance and recovery. . . .

Response and Analysis

1. Most people have heard the term *hypochon-driac* applied to a person. Prior to reading this article, what did you think the term meant? In what ways was your understanding of hypochondriasis accurate? Inaccurate?

2 What is Carla Cantor's understanding of the causes of her disorder? To what extent would you say she understands what brought on her disorder? Why? What functions might her symptoms serve?

3. How are the symptoms of hypochondriasis similar to those of anxiety disorders such as panic disorder, phobia, or obsessive-compulsive disorder? Why should hypochondriasis be included among somatoform disorders rather than anxiety disorders?

4. Cantor maintains that the antidepressant Prozac helped control her anxiety and her phobic tendencies. In addition to biomedical approaches such as this, what other treatment approaches are often prescribed for persons suffering from hypochondriasis? In general, how effective are these treatments?

Research

One theory holds that persons with hypochondriasis are acutely aware of physical (somatic) changes within their own bodies. These somatic changes are misinterpreted as indicating physical problems or serious illness. Suppose you want to examine whether persons with hypochondriasis are in fact more sensitive to minor somatic changes than are persons in a control group. One way to test your idea is to expose the participants to stimuli (e.g., various noises, images, mild exercise), record their physiological arousal (e.g., heart rate, galvanic skin response, electroencephalogram recordings), and then ask them if they experienced any physical (somatic) changes. This procedure would allow you to correlate the physiological arousal measures with the participants' self-reports about their perceptions of physical changes. What would you hypothesize the results of the study would be? Why? What ethical issues should you consider before telling participants about how accurately they estimated changes in their physiology?

THE BROKEN MIRROR

Katharine A. Phillips

Psychological Concept
body dysmorphic disorder

Jennifer suffers from body dysmorphic disorder, a diagnosis that is given when persons whose bodies appear normal are consumed with the idea that part of their body is physically defective. Although she has normal, attractive skin, Jennifer is obsessed with the thought that her skin is not normal. She has twice undergone dermabrasion, a painful face peel given to those suffering from severe acne. Both times, her dermatologist advised against the procedure. Jennifer is frustrated because her family, friends, coworkers, and physicians are unable to confirm her perceptions of herself. In the following story, note how Jennifer's condition escalates to the point where she is barely able to leave her home.

"This is incredibly embarrassing," Jennifer began. "It's really hard for me to talk about this. I don't want to be here." She fidgeted anxiously in her chair and looked at the floor. Her hands shook, and she seemed close to tears. Jennifer had in fact canceled her first two appointments with me, and she'd finally agreed to come in only at her mother's insistence. I had spoken briefly with her mother on the phone, who said she was feeling desperate—her daughter had a serious problem that neither of them could cope with any longer.

I asked Jennifer if she could explain what was so embarrassing. "I don't like talking about my problem," she said. "You'll probably think I'm silly or vain. But I'm not," she said with tears in her eyes. "This is a very serious problem. I can't even tell you how bad it is." She sat silently for a minute, looking down anxiously, as if trying to decide what to say and how to express it. "Well, I guess I should tell you what it is. I think I'm really ugly. In fact, I think I'm one of the ugliest people in the whole world."

Jennifer was by anyone's standards attractive. She was a 22-year-old woman with long strawberry-blond hair, large green eyes, and a beautiful complexion. She reminded me of the captain of my high school cheerleading squad, a pretty and vivacious young woman. How could Jennifer think she was ugly? What could she possibly believe was wrong with how she looked? I wondered what it could be. I couldn't see any flaws anywhere.

At first, Jennifer was reluctant to discuss the details. "Well, I just think I'm not pretty," she said. "I've felt this way for a long time, and I can't seem to convince myself that I'm wrong. I know what you're going to say. You're probably going to tell me I look fine—everyone does—but I know it's not true. I look terrible!"

"What is it about your appearance that upsets you so much?" I asked. "My skin," she replied, after some hesitation. "See all these pimples and scars and marks?" I really couldn't see what she was describing. From where I was sitting, her skin looked clear. Jennifer stood up and walked over toward me. "See these marks?" she asked again, pointing at her cheek and nose. In some of the places she pointed to I could discern some small whiteheads, but I had to be within a foot of her to see them. Even then I had to look closely.

Jennifer sat down again and went on to describe how since her early teenage years she'd been preoccupied with the "acne" and "marks" she'd just pointed out. She also thought her skin was too pale. "I look like a ghost. Everyone else looks really good; I stick out like a sore thumb. I'm the one who looks ugly," she said.

"When did the problem start?" I asked her. "When I was around 11," she replied. "It started with my nose. One of my nostrils stuck out more than the other. I remember catching a view of myself in the mirror one day and panicking. I thought, 'Is that what you look like? You look terrible, like a freak!'

"My nostrils don't really bother me anymore. My skin took over for them. Now all I think about is how bad my skin looks. I think about it for most of the day. People can see it from 50 feet away!" Jennifer cried as she said this—she truly believed that she was ugly and that her ugliness was visible to the entire world.

At this point Jennifer wasn't sure she wanted to continue. It was too upsetting to talk about her problem. But, with encouragement, she managed to go on. "I try not to think about it, but I have to," she said. "I think about it for most of the day. It's the first thing I think of when I wake up in the morning. I rush to the mirror, wondering 'How does it look?' How my skin looks in the morning totally determines how my day goes. Unfortunately, 80% of the time it looks horrible."

In high school Jennifer thought so much about her supposed ugliness that she couldn't concentrate in class. Her preoccupations crowded her mind and sapped her energy. "I dressed up a lot, I got really tan, wore blue eye shadow, and did a lot of things with my hair to distract people from my skin. But it didn't work. I couldn't concentrate on my school work, and I didn't want to be seen. It was too hard for me to stay in school," she said. "I started calling my mother in the middle of the day to pick me up. She didn't want to get me because I was supposed to be in class, but I was so upset and cried so much she'd come and take me home."

While doing her homework, Jennifer spent so much time examining her face in a mirror she kept on her desk that she couldn't complete her assignments. When she started reading, she felt compelled to check the mirror. "I had to see how my skin looked," she explained. "I had to see if it was any worse. Sometimes I'd get stuck there for hours, examining it for imperfections.

"I'd pick at it, too," she added, "which just made it worse. Sometimes I'd pick and pick with pins dipped in alcohol trying to get rid of the pimples and get the pus out. I'd pick at all kinds of things—little bumps, blackheads, any mark or imperfection. Sometimes I'd be up doing this at 1:00 or 2:00 in the morning, and then I'd fall asleep in class the next day, if I even went. Sometimes it would even bleed. I always felt terrible afterward. I'd make such a mess of my skin that I'd get totally hysterical."

As a result of her skin concerns, Jennifer's grades slipped from As and Bs to Ds, and she was put in a class for students with academic difficulties, even though she was bright. After missing many days of school, she dropped out of the ninth grade, even though she'd wanted to go to college. "I really tried to stay in school," she said. "But I couldn't do it. It was too much."

Jennifer also missed parties because, as she explained it, "No one would want to hang out with me because I'm so ugly." When her friends encouraged her to go, telling her how pretty she was, Jennifer didn't believe them. "They were just feeling sorry for me and trying to be nice. How could I go when I looked so horrendous?"

She did date one boy after she'd dropped out of school but saw him largely in her own house. "I hardly ever went out with him because I didn't want anyone to see my skin. I'd have him come over to my house. When he came over, I pulled all the shades down and turned down the lights so he couldn't see how bad my skin looked. But I stopped seeing him because I figured he'd just leave me anyway when he found out how bad I looked."

After dropping out of high school Jennifer tried waitressing three different times, but each time she quit or was fired because she missed so much work. "I wouldn't go if I had even one pimple. Sometimes I left in the middle of the day because I thought the customers were making fun of my skin behind my back." A job as a filing clerk was more tolerable, since she didn't have to be around other people as much, but she had trouble with that job, too. She thought about her skin for most of the day and secretly checked it in a pocket mirror over and over. "I tried not to," she explained, "because it took me away from my work. But I couldn't resist. *I couldn't stop thinking about my face, and I had to check it.* I *had* to make sure I looked okay, but I usually thought it looked bad. When I looked in the mirror I felt totally panicked seeing all those pimples and marks. Sometimes I even had to leave work and go to bed for the rest of the day. It was just like when I was in school."

When Jennifer had to work in a room with several other people and sit under fluorescent lights, she quit her job. "Sitting that close to other people was really hard because they could see how bad my skin was," she explained. "And the fluorescent lights were the last straw. I remember the day I quit. I was doing some filing, and all I could think of was that those awful lights showed up all the marks and pimples and holes in my face. I looked like a monster. I couldn't stop thinking that everyone in the room was looking at me! I tried to calm myself down and focus on what I was doing, but I couldn't. I had a panic attack. I ran out of that room and never went back."

Jennifer went on disability because she was unable to work, and continued to live with her parents even though she wanted to live on her own. Her parents bought her most of what she needed, and she rarely went out. "I do go out sometimes, but mostly at night when no one can see me," she said. "Sometimes I go to a 24-hour grocery store at midnight, when I know no one else will be there. For a long time I've bought most of my clothes through catalogs. I'm too scared to go out—everyone will see how ugly I am," she explained. When she did venture out she first spent at least two hours putting on makeup. "I look as though I'm wearing a mask, but at least I sort of cover up the pimples and scars," she said. She also painstakingly covered herself from head to toe with a bronzer to make her skin less white and to look "less like a ghost." She couldn't go out if there was any chance of rain because her bronzer would streak and run.

"It's getting worse," she said. "Last week, I got up my courage and decided to go out in the daylight, which I hardly ever do. I started driving to the store, and, just my luck, I got stuck in a major traffic jam. I was sitting there, in four lanes of traffic, waiting for the traffic to move, but it wasn't moving, and these people in the other cars were looking at me. All I could think was that they were looking at my face, thinking 'That poor girl; look how ugly she is. How can she go out in public when her skin looks so bad?' I tried to convince myself that it wasn't true, but my heart started racing, and I was sweating and shaking. I couldn't stop thinking that they were laughing at me. I got so panicked I had to leave. So I left my car in the middle of the traffic jam, and I ran until I found a phone booth. I called my mother and I stayed there hiding until she got me. That's how bad it got—I left my car sitting in the middle of the highway!"

Jennifer thought her problem was physical, not psychiatric, so she'd seen at least 15 different dermatologists. Some gave her antibiotics and other medications, but most said she didn't need treatment. "I'm every dermatologist's nightmare," Jennifer said. "I keep going back to see them, asking them over and over if my skin looks okay. I didn't believe them when they said my skin was fine. I wouldn't go away. I asked and asked them about my skin, and I begged them for treatment. A lot of them refused to see me anymore. They're probably all seeing therapists because of me!"

One of the dermatologists had in fact called to refer Jennifer to me for treatment. He told me that Jennifer had beautiful skin but was so obsessed with it that she might benefit from seeing a psychiatrist. But, at that time, Jennifer preferred to continue seeing dermatologists.

She finally did see a dermatologist whom she convinced to do a dermabrasion, a painful face peel usually reserved for treating severe acne. "The dermatologist really didn't want to do it," Jennifer said, "but I was so desperate that she gave in." After the dermabrasion Jennifer felt better about her skin for several months, even though her friends asked her what had happened to it. "They all thought it looked worse because it was red for a while," she said. "But I was thrilled. I didn't care if it was red because at least the pimples and marks went away." But within several months Jennifer's preoccupation returned and was even worse. She then had another dermabrasion, even though her parents implored her not to and the dermatologist was reluctant to repeat it. But Jennifer felt so desperate that it was done. That procedure didn't help her feel any better either. She was so depressed over this, over the fact that her "last hope" didn't help, that she thought about suicide.

When she first saw me, Jennifer still believed her problem was physical, not psychiatric, and she really wanted to see another dermatologist, not a psychiatrist. But her mother had insisted. "All my daughter does is ask me if she looks okay, over and over again, all day long," she told me. "She looks through magazines, asking me if her skin looks as good as the models'. No matter what I say, she can't be reassured. She's a pretty girl—I don't know what to do!" She had even told Jennifer that she'd have to move out of the house if she didn't stop her questioning, but Jennifer couldn't stop. "I have to ask her," Jennifer said. "I ask her at least a hundred times a day. I try not to, but I can't stop."

Jennifer also insisted that her mother hold magnifying glasses and shine light on her face from different angles when she inspected herself in the mirror so she could get a better look at her skin. Her mother reluctantly did it because Jennifer was so upset if she refused, but this took more than an hour a day and never really helped. "If it helped I might be willing to keep doing it," her mother said, "but she just keeps asking me if her skin looks okay and if she has scars, and she just keeps looking in the mirror. It might be hard for you to believe this, Doctor, but this problem is ruining our family—the constant questioning, the constant tears. She won't go out. We've tried to be patient, but nothing we do seems to help. We love our daughter and want to help her, but we can't take it anymore!"

Jennifer's story is not unusual. Although her body dysmorphic disorder was severe, her long struggle is typical of what many people experience. Body dysmorphic disorder, or BDD, is a painful yet virtually unknown psychiatric disorder—one in which normal-looking or even attractive people are preoccupied with a defect or flaw in their appearance. What's unusual about the defect is that it isn't visible—or is hardly visible—to others. People with this disorder may, for example, think that their hair is too curly, too straight, or too thin. Or that they have "veins" on their cheeks, scars on their nose, or skin that's too red or too pale. Or that their nose is too big, their lips too thin, their hips too big, or their breasts too small. Any body part can be the focus of concern. In reality they look fine. Often they have no defect at all. If they do have a flaw, it's generally minimal—something other people don't particularly notice. When I meet someone with BDD, I can almost never figure out what the supposed defect is by looking at them. Other people usually can't either. The "defects" are more in their minds than their bodies.

People with BDD not only focus on a defect that others don't notice—they think about it excessively. They worry. They obsess. It causes them pain. And it often interferes with their life.

BDD is a fascinating disorder. How can a person with no perceptible flaw, or only a minimal flaw, in his or her appearance focus so excessively on something others don't notice? How can an attractive young woman like Jennifer think she looks monstrously ugly—that she's "one of the ugliest people in the whole world"?

I've found BDD particularly intriguing because it's largely undiscovered and unknown. Many people with this disorder have gone from doctor to doctor—dermatologists, plastic surgeons, ophthalmologists, psychiatrists—without finding out what their problem is. Until very recently, many professionals and laypersons alike had never heard of BDD. Even though this is beginning to change, BDD is still an underrecognized disorder. And even though there's much that we know about BDD, much about it remains mysterious.

Response and Analysis

1. Imagine you know someone who is suffering from body dysmorphic disorder. How do you think you might feel about his or her excessive concerns about appearance? Would you try to reason with the person? Reassure him or her? Avoid the person? Why or why not?

2. Cosmetic surgery is relatively common in the United States, and many Americans are concerned or dissatisfied about some aspect of their appearance. To what extent might cultural influences be a cause of body dysmorphic disorder? Would you expect body dysmorphic disorder to be less or more prevalent in other societies? Why or why not?

3. What is the etiology of body dysmorphic disorder according to the following psychological approaches: psychoanalytic, biological, and behavioral? Which of these approaches do you think best explains the etiology? Why? Which approach do you think has the highest treatment success rates?

Research

Body dysmorphic disorder represents both a delusion—a firmly held belief not grounded in reality—and an obsession—the appearance of persistent, intrusive thoughts. Suppose a researcher discovers that persons with body dysmorphic disorder are more likely to have family members who have disorders characterized by delusions (e.g., schizophrenia) and obsessions (e.g., obsessive-compulsive disorder). Would this finding make a strong argument for a genetic or biological cause of the disorder? Why or why not? How might a psychologist who follows the psychoanalytic approach or the social learning theory approach interpret the finding?

PATIENT OR PRETENDER

Marc D. Feldman and Charles V. Ford

Psychological Concept
factitious disorder

Jenny is a young and responsible woman, working effectively on her job, engaged to be married, and planning for her future. When her fiancé broke off the engagement, Jenny was bereft and began taking extreme measures to get much-needed attention from others. Although she was not physically ill, she announced to family and friends that she had cancer. She began losing weight and attending a support group for cancer patients. Jenny had a factitious disorder. Persons with a factitious disorder deliberately simulate or induce a physical or psychological condition in order to assume the role of a person who is sick. Factitious disorder is different from malingering, which is when someone deliberately fakes illness to obtain a material gain such as avoidance of work or military service or to obtain worker's compensation. Unlike factitious disorder, malingering is not a psychological disorder. What stages does Jenny move through from the onset of her disorder to the time she begins to face up to her fiction?

Jenny, one of those "invisible" people we all know and overlook each day, was a secretary for a manufacturing firm. She had earned a reputation for being dependable and efficient even if she wasn't ambitious, and these characteristics contributed to her unassuming presence. She hadn't developed strong personal relationships at work, but 35-year-old Jenny didn't seem to miss that kind of camaraderie, looking instead to her after-five existence for comfort, companionship, and security. She lived with the man to whom she had been engaged for more than a year, had a small circle of casual friends, and periodically saw her mother, who lived in the same western city. Week in and week out, Jenny's world seemed never to change, until one day it suddenly, quietly, fell apart.

Without any warnings that had been evident to Jenny, her fiancé announced that he was breaking their engagement. She needn't grope for solutions, he told her. The relationship was over and Jenny would have to move out of his apartment.

Jenny had existed to please her man, happily performing all the tasks of a homemaker, even though it meant working for hours each evening after returning from her outside job. Fancying herself an old-fashioned girl at heart, she had filled her leisure time with activities such as baking, preparing lavish dinners, and meticulously ironing everything from sheets to shirts. She yearned to be married and even had a hope chest full of items for her wedding day, but she never pressured her fiancé to set a date. And although she was hardly a creative lover, Jenny was faithful and devoted and always put her fiancé's needs before her own.

Jenny reeled with the prospect of having to leave this man. She blamed herself for the breakup even though she didn't know what she had done to cause it. Bewildered, Jenny surrendered the relationship amidst tears and pleas for answers, but without a fight. With nowhere else to turn, she went to live with her mother, a workaholic elementary school teacher whose prescription for coping was "keep busy."

In an effort to fill the empty hours after work, the lonely, depressed Jenny began sewing for the drama club at her mother's school. The children loved her kind, mild manner, and Jenny spent many hours fitting them for costumes for the semiannual productions at the school. Sadly, this wasn't enough to meet her emotional needs or rescue her from becoming increasingly introverted at work and in her personal life. Whereas she used to feel worthy of sharing in conversations, Jenny now felt she had nothing of interest to discuss. She also felt so overwhelmed by her feelings of abandonment and betrayal that she couldn't begin to express herself to anyone, let alone resolve her troubles by herself. Silence and overwork became her coping mechanisms.

After months of functioning under intense emotional strain, Jenny went to work one day and confessed to everyone there: "I have terminal breast cancer."

Jenny became an instant "somebody," the object of sympathy and attention from people who never noticed her before. Suddenly coworkers became best friends. Everyone rallied to her support. People were willing to change their own life-styles to accommodate Jenny. They offered to include her in carpools to cut down on the amount of traveling she had to do, and to share her work load, even though that meant they might have to work overtime without compensation. But Jenny declined their offers, saying that she wanted to carry on as she had before in spite of her illness. Her coworkers were moved by her spirit.

Jenny was rewarded with the kind of nurturance and support she had been craving. She had watched a neighbor suffer from breast cancer and knew how a woman would look as the disease progressed. Gradually, Jenny, too, lost her hair. She seemed to lose any incentive to wear makeup that would help hide her haggard appearance, and her already slight figure reflected drastic weight loss.

As her hair disappeared (later to be replaced by a wig), as her weight dropped 20 pounds, making her look more gaunt and pale each day, Jenny's life was, ironically, transformed into that of someone "special." Emotionally she was finally fulfilled.

Jenny cut back her already limited social activities. At home, her mother sometimes questioned her about her appointments with doctors, but also became even busier than usual to keep her mind off her daughter. Jenny's hair could regularly be found in the bathroom sink, but her mother's concern seemed muted until Jenny became entirely bald. "Oh my God, Jenny! Your hair! It's *all* gone!" cried her mother, her face contorted with horror and tears welling into her eyes. Jenny touched her smooth scalp wistfully and replied, "It's all part of the therapy, Mother. I just have to be strong and bear it. The doctors are doing everything possible. It's going to be okay, really." Jenny's calm response alleviated her mother's worries somewhat and Jenny maintained her "brave victim" persona.

Several months after breaking the news about her illness, Jenny enrolled in a weekly hospital support group for women with breast cancer. She became a diligent member, never missing an opportunity to be with the caring group of cancer patients and the social support team from the local cancer center. Jenny mirrored the appearance and tribulations of the other women in the group.

Because Jenny had emphasized the deadly nature of her illness, coworkers naturally talked among themselves about what would happen to her as she got closer to the time when the cancer would claim her life. But when months passed and Jenny's condition didn't seem to get worse, support from coworkers leveled off and even began to wane. At that point, Jenny shared another personal tragedy— her beloved grandfather had been seriously injured in a fire. A few people rolled their eyes as if to ask, "What next?" but most of her coworkers were upset by the thought of the increased emotional burden Jenny would have to bear and they pitied her. One woman spent her lunch hour reassuring Jenny and sharing intimacies about how she had dealt with the death of her grandmother. She even offered to accompany Jenny to a death and dying counseling group which was sponsored by a local church. But Jenny boldly squared her shoulders and pronounced, "I'll be all right. I'm learning to deal with these things in my cancer group."

The student body of her mother's elementary school supported Jenny as well.

The children raised money to help Jenny pay for chemotherapy treatments. Jenny didn't want to take the money, but her mother insisted, saying she shouldn't disappoint the students. Feeling guilty about accepting money from the children, Jenny squirreled it away with the intention of somehow paying them back. At school, Jenny became a role model for students and teachers alike because, despite her illness, she continued sewing costumes for the upcoming school production. Students promised to dedicate the musical to Jenny. A local newspaper wrote about her courage and strength.

Although some people wondered about Jenny's ability to report to work every day, there were surprisingly few questions from her coworkers and supervisors, despite Jenny's failure to file insurance claims. It wasn't until her support group leaders tried to gain more information about her medical status that suspicions arose. "Jenny, we haven't been able to reach one of the doctors whom you said has been treating you, and the other doctor you referred us to doesn't know you," a counselor told her one night. "Can you help us?" Jenny hesitated momentarily, then quickly explained: "One of them retired and moved to Florida, but the other is my specialist. Of course he knows me. Call him again." She gently touched the hand of the counselor and thanked her for being so concerned. Jenny continued to provide the group's leaders with the names of doctors who had treated her, but it seemed that she was sending them on one wild goose chase after another. After following Jenny's dead-end maps, the leaders became convinced that she was lying. . . .

"How could you accuse me of such a thing?" Jenny cried indignantly. "I shouldn't have to go through this awful grilling after all I've been through. Do I have to die to prove how sick I am? Will you believe me *when* I die?" Jenny angrily paced back and forth, her arms folded across her chest in a gesture of defiance. "It won't do you any good to refute this, Jenny," the group's leaders calmly told her. "We know that you never had cancer, but something else really *is* troubling you and we want to help." Eventually, as Jenny began to accept that the counselors did want to help her and not exact retribution, she collapsed into a chair, admitting her ruse in a flood of emotion. "You're right," she sobbed. "I faked everything right from the beginning. I just needed someone to care about me. I'm so sorry, so very, very sorry. I beg you to forgive me. Are you going to report me to someone? How will I ever be able to face everyone?" The counselors assured her that now that the truth was known, help for her emotional problems was available, and they recommended that she accept psychiatric counseling. Before the episode was over, Jenny agreed. She also promised to tell others that she had concocted the entire story and, when she lived up to her word, she felt the repercussions of her actions. Jenny sheepishly returned to work and confided in her supervisor, a no-nonsense woman who had lightened Jenny's work load because of her "illness." The supervisor was enraged by Jenny's tearful confession. She chastised her for "all the pain and anguish" she had caused her coworkers. "You took advantage of everyone and for what! You should be ashamed of yourself," the woman shouted, and with that she fired Jenny. By then, Jenny had carried out her simulation of cancer for two years.

Losing her job compounded Jenny's embarrassment, but her mother's reactions made her wish for death. "I can't believe that you put me through all these months of worry," her stunned mother said. "I prayed and prayed for you. How could you do this to someone who loves you and who you supposedly love? What's wrong with you?" she asked, shaking her head in disbelief. "Do you know how many times I imagined myself at your funeral? I've mourned for you over these months as if you were already gone. How could you do this to me? Say something to make me understand!" But Jenny couldn't explain; she hardly understood what was happening herself. . . .

Although physically well, Jenny was one of the countless people who suffer from the strange psychological illnesses called *factitious disorders*. While well known to psychiatrists and psychologists, factitious disorders are often misinterpreted by the uninformed to be merely lying; a vicious way to use others for personal gain. Factitious disorders are far more complex than that, however, and surprisingly far-reaching in their effects upon the general public and medical community. . . .

Some of Jenny's actions were typical of virtually all factitial patients, but it is also true that certain aspects of her care are atypical. First, Jenny was able to carry out a deception involving a serious illness for a long time in one place; most disease portrayals last a relatively short time before the patient is discovered and takes the portrayal elsewhere, abandons it, or switches to a different illness. Second, Jenny did not flee when confronted; rather she accepted the advice to admit the deception to her coworkers and employer. And third, Jenny then accepted and profited from treatment, which is contrary to most psychiatrists' experiences with factitial patients. . . .

It isn't as hard to fool doctors as one might expect. Time and time again we see in the factitious disorders literature that patients expose themselves to multiple tests, exploratory operations, and diagnostic procedures. These tests may be repeated several times, even by the same doctors, because the doctors want so much to believe their patients. They just assume they missed something the first time.

And as in any business, physicians want to satisfy their patients. If a patient says, "You're missing something; I'm still in pain," doctors make every effort to please the patient and so they perform more tests. In other situations, a doctor may say, "Everything looks normal, but since you're so sure of the ailment let's just go ahead and treat it." As a result, people end up with unnecessary medications and surgeries. Doctors often find it very difficult to believe that somebody would actually feign a serious illness or self-induce dangerous symptoms.

It's the same with counselors and other health care professionals. Their first thoughts are not about whether or not someone is faking an illness. Although Jenny never actually presented herself to physicians, she did something that may well have been more exotic—she enrolled in group therapy. Surrounded by people with breast cancer, she said that she too had breast cancer. This lie actually represented a very primitive way of reaching out for help. It was so literal that it was pathetic.

The leaders of the group with whom Jenny aligned herself had been working with cancer patients for a long time. When Jenny showed up, she appeared emaciated and readily talked about her chemotherapy and the vomiting it caused as an explanation for her appearance. With such a convincing presentation, why would the group leaders have initially cross-examined Jenny or turned her away? But Jenny backed herself into a corner. She dared to put herself into an environment with genuinely sick women and stay around them for more than a year. Over time there were some deaths in the group, and some women improved while others deteriorated. Yet Jenny was there every week looking the same. Women in the group became suspicious, but none of them wanted to appear insensitive and question Jenny outright, so they voiced their suspicions behind her back. . . .

We don't know all the factors that contribute to the development of these disorders, making certain people react so differently than others in the same traumatic situation. Many women, for example, have broken up with fiancés. Why did Jenny choose her particular course? Is it biological? Is it situational? Is it due to early life experiences? Or is it a combination? All of these factors have contributed to specific cases of factitious disorders.

Response and Analysis

1. What are your reactions to Jenny's behavior? Empathy? Condemnation? To what extent do you believe Jenny was aware of (a) her motivations; (b) her behavior; and (c) the effects her behavior had on others? Do you think she had voluntary control over her behavior? Why or why not?

2. Jenny's feigned illness was a symptom of underlying problems with which she was not coping. What were these problems?

3. What benefits did Jenny receive by pretending she was dying of breast cancer? What skills does Jenny need to gain so that she will not resort to this behavior again?

4. What are the differences among factitious disorder, hypochondriasis, conversion disorder, Munchausen's syndrome, and malingering? What criteria do treatment professionals use to distinguish them?

Research

Suppose you have used a correlational design to examine the relationship between age and the diagnosis of factitious disorder. Assume that you have conducted the study with participants between the ages of eighteen and sixty years and have analyzed the data. Your analysis shows a correlation coefficient of −.39 between age and the diagnosis of factitious disorder. Does this indicate that the relationship is (a) positive or negative, and (b) strong, moderate, or weak? Based on your findings, what conclusions might you be able to make?

chapter 4

MOOD DISORDERS

In the middle of the journey of our life
I found myself in a dark wood.
For I had lost the right path.

DANTE, cited in William Styron,
Darkness Visible

Who has not felt the world bright with color, filled with laughter and joy? And who has not been downcast or melancholy? To be human is to have felt both. For those suffering from a mood disorder, however, these opposites have a very different meaning. In depressive disorders, people experience feelings of futility, fatigue, insomnia, irritability, loss of interest and pleasure in most activities, and recurrent thoughts of death or suicide. In bipolar disorder (formerly called *manic depression*), people experience periods of depression alternating with periods of mania. Mania involves feelings of intense energy, elevated mood, expansiveness, and hyperactivity. These moods are qualitatively and quantitatively different from ordinary happiness and sadness—they are long lasting, engulfing, and often incapacitating.

Mood disorders are among the most common and most devastating of psychological disorders. They can leave people unable to meet the simplest demands of daily life. Lifetime prevalence of depression in women may be as high as 25%, for men as high as 12%. The prevalence of bipolar disorders is lower, around 1% for adults. However, when one considers all mood disorders combined (including, for instance, dysthymic disorder and cyclothymic disorder), as many as 15% to 20% of Americans can expect to be affected at some time in their lives. The personal and social costs of these disorders are staggering.

Elizabeth Wurtzel has written about depression from the viewpoint of a young woman at the center of youth culture. A popular music critic for the *New Yorker* and *New York Magazine*, Wurtzel describes what it is like to be depressed and young in America. For her, as for many depressed persons, enjoyment of life seems entirely beyond reach. Note how difficult she finds it to make others understand the oppressive ache of her depression and how, despite her obvious intelligence and insight, she seems unable to pin down how she became clinically depressed. Finally, note how she was ultimately able to manage and overcome her depression.

Kay Redfield Jamison, who suffers from bipolar disorder and has become an expert in the field, describes the emotional extremes she experienced—from euphoric highs to devastating lows. She also discusses her resistance to recognizing that she was ill and how she recovered once she acknowledged her illness. In Jamison's view—a view shared by many others—bipolar disorder can be explained largely by genetic and biological factors. Though few people would doubt some role for genetics, other competing explanations for causes of the disorder exist.

SUFFERING FROM DEPRESSION

Elizabeth Wurtzel

Psychological Concept
depression

Elizabeth Wurtzel, a graduate of Harvard College and a writer-journalist living in New York City, was twenty-seven years old when she wrote *Prozac Nation*, a book that received wide acclaim. Wurtzel suffered from depression's steady progression and eventually recognized that she was truly ill. Here she describes her intense loneliness and anguish, cites the effects of parental discord and financial burden, and acknowledges that the antidepressant Prozac did help. What benefits of this medication does she describe? What questions does she raise about the origins of her illness?

Some catastrophic situations invite clarity, explode in split moments: You smash your hand through a windowpane and then there is blood and shattered glass stained with red all over the place; you fall out a window and break some bones and scrape some skin. Stitches and casts and bandages and antiseptic solve and salve the wounds. But depression is not a sudden disaster. It is more like a cancer: At first its tumorous mass is not even noticeable to the careful eye, and then one day—wham!—there is a huge, deadly seven-pound lump lodged in your brain or your stomach or your shoulder blade, and this thing that your own body has produced is actually trying to kill you. Depression is a lot like that: Slowly, over the years, the data will accumulate in your heart and mind, a computer program for total negativity will build into your system, making life feel more and more unbearable. But you won't even notice it coming on, thinking that it is somehow normal, something about getting older, about turning eight or turning twelve or turning fifteen, and then one day you realize that your entire life is just awful, not worth living, a horror and a black blot on the white terrain of human existence. One morning you wake up afraid you are going to live.

In my case, I was not frightened in the least bit at the thought that I might live because I was certain, quite certain, that I was already dead. The actual dying part, the withering away of my physical body, was a mere formality. My spirit, my emotional being, whatever you want to call all that inner turmoil that has nothing to do with physical existence, were long gone, dead and gone, and only a mass of the most fucking god-awful excruciating pain like a pair of boiling hot tongs clamped tight around my spine and pressing on all my nerves was left in its wake.

That's the thing I want to make clear about depression: It's got nothing at all to do with life. In the course of life, there is sadness and pain and sorrow, all of which, in their right time and season, are normal—unpleasant, but normal. Depression is in an altogether different zone because it involves a complete absence: absence of affect, absence of feeling, absence of response, absence of interest. The pain you feel in the course of a major clinical depression is an attempt on nature's part (nature, after all, abhors a vacuum) to fill up the empty space. But for all intents and purposes, the deeply depressed are just the walking, waking dead.

And the scariest part is that if you ask anyone in the throes of depression how he got there, to pin down the turning point, he'll never know. There is a classic moment in *The Sun Also Rises* when someone asks Mike Campbell how he went bankrupt, and all he can say in response is, "Gradually and then suddenly." When someone asks how I lost my mind, that is all I can say too.

Note: Elizabeth Wurtzel had flown to Minneapolis to visit her boyfriend. Suffering for many years from depression, she phoned Dr. Sterling, her psychiatrist in Cambridge, Massachusetts, who suggested that Wurtzel fly to Boston and receive more aggressive treatment at Stillman Hospital. In these next paragraphs Wurtzel describes her emotional states in Minneapolis and soon thereafter in the hospital.

I am depressed to the point of being incapable of much else besides lying in this white room with these white sheets and white blankets, watching a television set suspended from the ceiling which changes channels with a remote control that you squeeze like a lemon that might be souring your tea. I know I can do so much more than this, I know that I could be a life force, could love with a heart full of soul, could feel with the power that flies men to the moon. I know that if I could just get out from under this depression, there is so much I could do besides cry in front of the TV on a Saturday night.

Dr. Sterling agrees, when I first check into the infirmary, that I can lie there for as long as I like, but I need to get my work done. Always, always, no matter how bad life seems to be, I must hand in my papers on time or take my finals when I am supposed to or meet deadlines for stories. So my word processor and all my books make the trek to Stillman with me, where I entertain fantasies of finding solace in my studies as I was once able to do.

But I'm too far gone for that now. It seems that I have spent so much time trying to convince people that I really am depressed, that I really can't cope—but now that it's finally true, I don't want to admit it. I am petrified by what is happening to me, so frightened of what the bottom of the well will look like once I sink down there, so frightened that in fact this is it. How did this happen to me? It seems not so long ago, maybe only a decade ago, I was a little girl trying out a new persona, trying on morbid depression as some kind of punk rock statement, and now here I am, the real thing.

I find myself calling Dr. Sterling every five minutes to get her to assure and reassure me that I will come out of this one day. And she always does, always says the right things. But a few seconds after I hang up, I'm frightened all over again. So I call all over again.

"Elizabeth, we just went through this," she says. "What can I do to make you believe me?"

"You can't," I say through tears. "Don't you get it? Nothing sticks. That's my whole problem. Rafe leaves the room for five minutes, and I'm sure he's never coming back. And that's how it is for me with everything. Nothing is real to me unless it's right in front of me."

"What a terrible way to live."

"That's what I'm trying to tell you!"

I wonder if she understands that I can't go on like this.

And still, I keep telling myself that recovery is an act of will, that if I decide one day that I simply must get up and get out of this bed, that I must be happy, I will be able to force it to happen. Why do I believe this is possible?

I suppose because the alternative is too frightening. The alternative will lead to my inevitable suicide. Up until now, I always thought of self-destructive behavior as a red flag to wave at the world, a way of getting the help I needed. But the truth is, lying here in Stillman, for the first time ever I am contemplating suicide completely seriously, because this pain is too much. I wonder if all the nurses who traipse through here to bring me meals, to change the sheets, to remind me to shower—I wonder if any of them can tell from just looking at me that all I am is the sum total of my pain, a raw woundedness so extreme that it might be terminal. It might be terminal velocity, the speed of the sound of a girl falling down to a place from where she can't be retrieved. What if I am stuck down here for good?

I call Dr. Sterling again, ask her the same questions again, and she decides, finally, that I must be given some kind of drug. After all, I am not her only patient, I am not her only problem, and every time she says something to me about feeling like she really needs to spend time with her children, I start to cry and tell her that if I die, there will be blood on her hands. If for no reason other than that she wants her private life back, Dr. Sterling is willing to try a chemical cure. She thinks that with the right medication, I might even be able to get my work done. Both my academic adviser and Dr. Sterling, along with several friends, have suggested that I just take incompletes in my courses and make up the work some other time, but, for some reason, I just can't. It would be too demoralizing. If I can write my papers, I keep telling myself, then I'll know that I don't yet have to abandon all hope. I know that if I don't do my schoolwork, I really will be compelled to kill myself because the last bit of what I have to hold on to will be gone. Other kids with emotional troubles take time off from school, but they have families, they have some sense of a place in this world that can absorb them in all their pain; all I have is the semblance of a life that I have made for myself here at Harvard, and I can't let go of it. I *must* do my work.

My main symptoms, Dr. Sterling believes, are anxiety and agitation. In her opinion, even worse than the depression itself is the fear I seem to have about never escaping from it. As usual, my problem seems to be that I am one step removed from my problems, more a nervous audience member at a horror movie than the movie itself. "So you think I'm suffering from meta-depression?" I ask Dr. Sterling in a moment of humor.

"That's one way to see it," she replies.

Dr. Sterling believes that the best drug for me, at least until I go for a thorough evaluation with a psychopharmacologist at McLean, is Xanax, mainly because it will have an immediate effect. An antidepressant might ultimately be a more appropriate antidote for my ills, but Dr. Sterling doesn't think I'll live to see the results of that kind of drug, which will take a few weeks to kick in, if we don't find a solution to my immediate depression.

In a strange way, I had fallen in love with my depression. Dr. Sterling was right about that. I loved it because I thought it was all I had. I thought depression was the part of my character that made me worthwhile. I thought so little of myself, felt that I had such scant offerings to give to the world, that the one thing that justified my existence at all was my agony. Taking a hypersensitive approach to life had come to seem so much more pure and honest than joining the ranks of the numb masses who could let it all slide by. What I'd stopped realizing was that if you feel everything intensely, ultimately you feeling nothing at all. Everything registers at the same decibel so that the death of a roach crawling across a Formica counter can seem as tragic as the death of your own father. The people on the outside—and that's the right word, because to a depressive everyone else is outside—who are selectively expending their emotional energy are actually a lot more honest than anyone who is depressed and has replaced all nuance with a constant, persistent, droning despair.

But depression gave me more than just a brooding introspection. It gave me humor, it gave me a certain what-a-fuck-up-I-am schtick to play with when the worst was over. I couldn't kid myself and think that anyone enjoyed my tears and hysteria—plainly, they didn't—but the side effects, the byproducts of depression, seemed to keep me going. I had developed a persona that could be extremely melodramatic and entertaining. It had, at times, all the selling points of madness, all the aspects of performance art. I was always able to reduce whatever craziness I'd experienced into the perfect anecdote, the ideal cocktail party monologue, and until that final year of real lows, I think most people would have said that when I wasn't being carted off to the emergency room I was fun . . .

Anyway, I thought this ability, to tell away my personal life as if it didn't belong to me, to be queerly chatty and energetic at moments that most people found inappropriate, was what my friends liked about me. In fact, over time, in the years of my recovery from depression, most of them let me know, one by one, that while they didn't mind that I said things that were thoughtless and out of line, they excused this behavior as a sad flaw. It wasn't what they liked about me at all. It was what they put up with, because when I wasn't busy flying around the room and ranting about nothing, I was actually just good to talk to, even a good friend. That's all their feelings for me were about. They'd be just as happy to see all the affectation go.

But before I knew this, I was so scared to give up depression, fearing that somehow the worst part of me was actually all of me. The idea of throwing away my depression, of having to create a whole personality, a whole way of living and being that did not contain misery as its leitmotif, was daunting. Depression had for so long been a convenient—and honest—explanation for everything that was wrong with me, and it had been a handicap that helped accentuate everything that was right. Now, with the help of a biochemical cure, it was going to go away. I mean, wild animals raised in captivity will perish if placed back into their natural habitats because they don't know the laws of prey and predator and they don't know the ways of the jungle, even if that's where they belong. How would I ever survive as my normal self? And after all these years, who was that person anyway?

Note: Eventually Elizabeth Wurtzel does try to commit suicide.

The day after the suicide attempt, Dr. Sterling lets me leave Stillman, and I get up and go to work at the Harvest as if nothing is wrong. It is my first day, and it is pretty clear as the manager tries to show me how to tilt a decanter of milk in different ways to produce different consistencies of steam, that this is one in a series of menial jobs I will miserably fail at. Nonetheless, I am almost happy to be behind the cash register and in front of the coffee maker today. I'm happy to be doing anything routine and normal.

At some point, when things slow down during lunch, I call Dr. Sterling to tell her I feel strange and lonely because my friends were mostly angry at me about what had happened. Eben insisted that he felt just as bad as me sometimes and didn't do things like that. Alec lectured me about how I had let myself fall into this funk and he wasn't surprised that I felt so awful considering I'd wrecked my life by spending most of first semester in Rhode Island and most of second semester in California and England. Everybody I'd spoken to about the overdose in its immediate aftermath was almost mean about it. I had expected some version of sympathy, and instead people kept telling me I'd brought this on myself. From the way they were talking, you'd think I'd committed murder—not attempted suicide. Even Samantha, my bedrock, my sob sister, seemed annoyed. I think she said, What a stupid thing to do!

Dr. Sterling explains that this is normal. She says people can be understanding about almost anything but suicide. "Remember," she says, "these are people who feel like they're doing the best they can to be helpful, and you do something that indicates your utter rejection and dissatisfaction with their efforts. It's infuriating."

After I hang up the receiver, I return to one waiter demanding a double espresso, a decaf cappuccino, and a café au lait, while another wants two espressos, a decaf double espresso, and a tea, and everyone needs to deliver the orders at once, everyone is shouting at me at once, I can't remember what anyone says, and I think: What if they knew? Just as I walked around the day after I lost my virginity, wondering if my aspect had changed, if my cheeks revealed this new experience in a rosier glow, today I wonder if people know I'm a failed suicide.

And then something just kind of changed in me. Over the next few days, I became all right, safe in my own skin. It happened just like that. One morning I woke up, and I really did want to live, really looked forward to greeting the day, imagined errands to run, phone calls to return, and it was not with a feeling of great dread, not with the sense that the first person who stepped on my toe as I walked through the square may well have driven me to suicide. It was as if the miasma of depression had lifted off me, gone smoothly about its business, in the same way that the fog in San Francisco rises as the day wears on. Was it the Prozac? No doubt. . . . Just as I always said that I went down gradually and then suddenly, I also got up that way. All the therapy, all the traveling, all the sleeping, all the drugs, all the crying, all the missed classes, all the lost time—all of that was part of some slow recovery process that came to the end of its tether at the same time that I reached mine.

It took a long time for me to get used to my contentedness. It was so hard for me to formulate a way of being and thinking in which the starting point was not depression. Dr. Sterling agrees that it's hard, because depression is an addiction the way many substances and most modes of behavior are, and like most addictions it is miserable but still hard to break. On Prozac, I often walk around so conscious of how not-terrible I feel that I am petrified that I'm going to lose this new equilibrium. I spend so much time worrying about staying happy that I threaten to become unhappy all over again. Any time I am bothered about anything, whether it's a line that's too long at the bank or a man who doesn't return my love, I have to remind myself that these emotional experiences (petty annoyance in the former instance, heartbreak in the latter) are reasonable and discrete unto themselves. They don't have to precipitate a depressive episode. It takes me a long time to realize that when I get upset about something it doesn't mean that the tears will never stop. It is so hard to learn to put sadness in perspective, so hard to understand that it is a feeling that comes in degrees, it can be a candle burning gently and harmlessly in your home, or it can be a full-fledged forest fire that destroys almost everything and is controlled by almost nothing. It can also be so much in-between.

In-between. There's a phrase that is far too underappreciated. What a great day it was, what a moment of pure triumph, to have discovered that there are in-betweens. What freedom it is to live in a spectral world that most people take for granted. Being somewhere in the middle is anathema in our culture, it connotes mediocrity, middlingness, an item that is so-so, okay, not bad, not good, not much of anything. So many people feel a need to go bungee jumping or to take vacations in Third World countries full of scorpions and armed dictators. So many people spend so much time in adventures meant only to take them out of that boring middle range, that placid emotional state where it feels, no doubt, like nothing ever happens. But me, all I want is that nice even keel. All I want is a life where the extremes are in check, where I am in check.

All I want is to live in between.

I will never not be on guard for depression, but the constancy, the obsessive and totalizing effect of that disease, the sense that life is something happening to other people I am watching through an opaque cloud, is gone.

The black wave, for the most part, is gone.

On a good day, I don't even think about it anymore.

In the case of my own depression, I have gone from a thorough certainty that its origins are in bad biology to a more flexible belief that after an accumulation of life events made my head such an ugly thing to be stuck in, my brain's chemicals started to agree. There's no way to know any of this for sure right now. There isn't some blood test, akin to those for mononucleosis or HIV, that you can take to find a mental imbalance. And the anecdotal evidence leads only to a lot of chicken-and-egg types of questions: After all, depression does run in my family, but that might just be because we're all subject to being raised by other depressives. Where my depression is concerned, the fact that Prozac in combination with other drugs has been, for the most part, a successful antidote, leads me to believe that regardless of how I got started on my path of misery, by the time I got treatment the problem was certainly chemical. What many people don't realize is that the cause-and-effect relationship in mental disorders is a two-way shuttle: It's not just that an a priori imbalance can make you depressed. It's that years and years of exogenous depression (a malaise caused by external events) can actually fuck up your internal chemistry so much that you need a drug to get it working properly again. Had I been treated by a competent therapist at the onset of my depression, perhaps its mere kindling would not have turned into a nightmarish psychic bonfire, and I might not have arrived at the point, a decade later, where I needed medication just to be able to get out of bed in the morning.

As it stands, for a few years after I first began taking medication, after leaving Cambridge and coming back to New York, I stayed away from psychotherapy. I saw a psychopharmacologist who was basically a drug pusher with a medical degree, I filled my prescriptions, and believed that that was enough. After Dr. Sterling, I could not imagine ever being able to find a therapist who was good enough. And besides, it seemed that with occasional lapses, drugs really were the answer. But then, as I found myself ruining relationships, alienating employers and other people I worked with, and falling all too frequently into depressive blackouts that would go on for days and would feel as desolate and unyielding as the black wave scares I'd spent much of my pre-Prozac life running from, I realized I needed therapy. Years and years of bad habits, of being attracted to the wrong kinds of men, of responding to every bad mood with impulsive behavior (cheating on my boyfriend or being lax about my work assignments), had turned me into a person who had no idea how to function within the boundaries of the normal, nondepressive world. I needed a good therapist to help me learn to be a grown-up, to show me how to live in a world where the phone company doesn't care that you're too depressed to pay the phone bill, that it turns off your line with complete indifference to such nuances. I needed a psychologist to teach me how to live in a world where, no matter how many people seem to be on Prozac, the vast majority are not, and they've got problems and concerns and interests that are often going to be at odds with my own.

It has taken me so long to learn to live a life where depression is not a constant resort, is not the state I huddle into as surely as a drunk returns to his gin, a junkie goes back to her needle—but I'm starting to get to that place. At age twenty-six, I feel like I am finally going through adolescence.

Response and Analysis

1. How did Elizabeth Wurtzel get "in the throes of depression"?

2. What help did Wurtzel finally get? What were the results of treatment?

3. What does Wurtzel mean by living in an "in-between" period?

4. What prompted Wurtzel to consider suicide? How did she react after her attempt?

5. How is depression different from the blues, sadness, or grief? Is there any evidence that depression differs from these other states physiologically?

Research

Suppose you wanted to examine Kay Redfield Jamison's assertion (see her story *An Unquiet Mind* in this chapter) that our perception of psychological disorders is influenced by gender-related expectations. Jamison says that depression is more in line with society's expectations for women while mania is more in line with expectations for men. You decide to design a research project to determine whether people interpret the symptoms of depression differently for men and women. You will give therapists the same portion from Elizabeth Wurtzel's account of her experiences with depression, but you will tell half the therapists that the author is a man and the other half that the author is a woman. In this design, what is the independent variable? What outcomes would you measure (i.e., what are the dependent variables)? How would you measure them? What do you expect to happen? State your expectation in the form of a hypothesis.

AN UNQUIET MIND

Kay Redfield Jamison

Psychological Concept
bipolar disorder

Clinical psychologist Kay Redfield Jamison suffers from bipolar disorder. Throughout college and graduate school, Jamison had great periods of energy. When her manic periods took hold, she would stay up all night for several nights in a row, reading any book she could find and writing plays and poems. She was all motion, spending too much money, socializing too often, talking too fast. Her mind never stopped, never seemed clearer. Invariably, however, her periods of elation gave way to their polar opposite. She would become tired, depressed, unable to concentrate. It was a struggle to make it through each day. Yet not until she joined the faculty at the University of California, Los Angeles, did she recognize that she needed medical help, and then only after a colleague gently confronted her with his suspicion of her illness. How did Jamison respond to her colleague? Did she show any ambivalent feelings about either having the disorder or gaining control over it?

I was a senior in high school when I had my first attack of manic-depressive illness; once the siege began, I lost my mind rather rapidly. At first, everything seemed so easy. I raced about like a crazed weasel, bubbling with plans and enthusiasms, immersed in sports, and staying up all night, night after night, out with friends, reading everything that wasn't nailed down, filling manuscript books with poems and fragments of plays, and making expansive, completely unrealistic, plans for my future. The world was filled with pleasure and promise; I felt great. Not just great, I felt *really* great. I felt I could do anything, that no task was too difficult. My mind seemed clear, fabulously focused, and able to make intuitive mathematical leaps that had up to that point entirely eluded me. Indeed, they elude me still. At the time, however, not only did everything make perfect sense, but it all began to fit into a marvelous kind of cosmic relatedness. My sense of enchantment with the laws of the natural world caused me to fizz over, and I found myself buttonholing my friends to tell them how beautiful it all was. They were less than transfixed by my insights into the webbings and beauties of the universe, although considerably impressed by how exhausting it was to be around my enthusiastic ramblings: You're talking too fast, Kay. Slow down, Kay. You're wearing me out, Kay. Slow down, Kay. And those times when they didn't actually come out and say it, I still could see it in their eyes: For God's sake, Kay, slow down.

I did, finally, slow down. In fact, I came to a grinding halt. Unlike the very severe manic episodes that came a few years later and escalated wildly and psychotically out of control, this first sustained wave of mild mania was a light, lovely tincture of true mania; like hundreds of subsequent periods of high enthusiasms it was short-lived and quickly burned itself out: tiresome to my friends, perhaps; exhausting and exhilarating to me, definitely; but not disturbingly over the top. Then the bottom began to fall out of my life and mind. My thinking, far from being clearer than a crystal, was tortuous. I would read the same passage over and over again only to realize that I had no memory at all for what I just had read. Each book or poem I picked up was the same way. Incomprehensible. Nothing made sense. I could not begin to follow the material presented in my classes, and I would find myself staring out the window with no idea of what was going on around me. It was very frightening.

I was used to my mind being my best friend; of carrying on endless conversations within my head; of having a built-in source of laughter or analytic thought to rescue me from boring or painful surroundings. I counted upon my mind's acuity, interest, and loyalty as a matter of course. Now, all of a sudden, my mind had turned on me: it mocked me for my vapid enthusiasms; it laughed at all of my foolish plans; it no longer found anything interesting or enjoyable or worthwhile. It was incapable of concentrated thought and turned time and again to the subject of death: I was going to die, what difference did anything make? Life's run was only a short and meaningless one, why live? I was totally exhausted and could scarcely pull myself out of bed in the mornings. It took me twice as long to walk anywhere as it ordinarily did, and I wore the same clothes over and over again, as it was otherwise too much of an effort to make a decision about what to put on. I dreaded having to talk with people, avoided my friends whenever possible, and sat in the school library in the early mornings and late afternoons, virtually inert, with a dead heart and a brain as cold as clay. . . .

College, for many people I know, was the best time of their lives. This is inconceivable to me. College was, for the most part, a terrible struggle, a recurring nightmare of violent and dreadful moods spelled only now and again by weeks, sometimes months, of great fun, passion, high enthusiasms, and long runs of very hard but enjoyable work. This pattern of shifting moods and energies had a very seductive side to it, in large part because of fitful reinfusions of the intoxicating moods that I had enjoyed in high school. These were quite extraordinary, filling my brain with a cataract of ideas and more than enough energy to give me at least the illusion of carrying them out. My normal Brooks Brothers conservatism would go by the board; my hemlines would go up, my neckline down, and I would enjoy the sensuality of my youth. Almost everything was done to excess: instead of buying one Beethoven symphony, I would buy nine; instead of enrolling for five classes, I would enroll in seven; instead of buying two tickets for a concert I would buy eight or ten. . . .

Much as it had during my senior year in high school, my classwork during these galvanized periods seemed very straightforward, and I found examinations, laboratory work, and papers almost absurdly easy during the weeks that the high-flying times would last. I also would become immersed in a variety of political and social causes that included everything from campus antiwar activities to slightly more idiosyncratic zealotries, such as protesting cosmetic firms that killed turtles in order to manufacture and sell beauty products. . . .

But then as night inevitably goes after the day, my mood would crash, and my mind again would grind to a halt. I lost all interest in my schoolwork, friends, reading, wandering, or daydreaming. I had no idea of what was happening to me, and I would wake up in the morning with a profound sense of dread that I was going to have to somehow make it through another entire day. I would sit for hour after hour in the undergraduate library, unable to muster up enough energy to go to class. I would stare out the window, stare at my books, rearrange them, shuffle them around, leave them unopened, and think about dropping out of college. When I did go to class it was pointless. Pointless and painful. I understood very little of what was going on, and I felt as though only dying would release me from the overwhelming sense of inadequacy and blackness that surrounded me. I felt utterly alone, and watching the animated conversations between my fellow students only made me feel more so. I stopped answering the telephone and took endless hot baths in the vain hope that I might somehow escape from the deadness and dreariness. . . .

I reaped a bitter harvest from my own refusal to take Lithium on a consistent basis. A floridly psychotic mania was followed, inevitably, by a long and lacerating, black, suicidal depression; it lasted more than a year and a half. From the time I woke up in the morning until the time I went to bed at night, I was unbearably miserable and seemingly incapable of any kind of joy or enthusiasm. Everything—every thought, word, movement—was an effort. Everything that once was sparkling now was flat. I seemed to myself to be dull, boring, inadequate, thick brained, unlit, unresponsive, chill skinned, bloodless, and sparrow drab. I doubted, completely, my ability to do anything well. It seemed as though my mind had slowed down and burned out to the point of being virtually useless. The wretched, convoluted, and pathetically confused mass of gray worked only well enough to torment me with a dreary litany of my inadequacies and shortcomings in character, and to taunt me with the total, the desperate, hopelessness of it all. What is the point in going on like this? I would ask myself. Others would say to me, "It is only temporary, it will pass, you will get over it," but of course they had no idea how I felt, although they were certain that they did. Over and over and over I would say to myself, If I can't feel, if I can't move, if I can't think, and I can't care, then what conceivable point is there in living?

The morbidity of my mind was astonishing: Death and its kin were constant companions. I saw Death everywhere, and I saw winding sheets and toe tags and body bags in my mind's eye. Everything was a reminder that everything ended at the charnel house. My memory always took the black line of the mind's underground system; thoughts would go from one tormented moment of my past to the next. Each stop along the way was worse than the preceding one. And, always, everything was an effort. Washing my hair took hours to do, and it drained me for hours afterward; filling the ice-cube tray was beyond my capacity, and I occasionally slept in the same clothes I had worn during the day because I was too exhausted to undress.

During this time I was seeing my psychiatrist two or three times a week and, finally, again taking Lithium on a regular basis. His notes, in addition to keeping track of the medications I was taking—I had briefly taken antidepressants, for example, but they had only made me more dangerously agitated—also recorded the unrelenting, day-in and day-out, week-in and week-out, despair, hopelessness, and shame that the depression was causing: *"Patient intermittently suicidal. Wishes to jump from the top of hospital stairwell"*; *"Patient continues to be a significant suicide risk. Hospitalization is totally unacceptable to her and in my view she cannot be held under LPS [the California commitment law]"*; *"Despairs for the future; fears recurrence and fears having to deal with the fact that she has felt what she has felt"*; *"Patient feels very embarrassed about feelings she has and takes attitude that regardless of the course of her depression she 'won't put up with it'"*; *"Patient reluctant to be with people when depressed because she feels her depression is such an intolerable burden on others"*; *"Afraid to leave my office. Hasn't slept in days. Desperate."* At this point there was a brief lull in my depression, only to be followed by its seemingly inevitable, dreadful return: *"Patient feels as if she has cracked. Hopeless that depressed feelings have returned."*

My psychiatrist repeatedly tried to persuade me to go into a psychiatric hospital, but I refused. I was horrified at the thought of being locked up; being away from familiar surroundings; having to attend group therapy meetings; and having to put up with all of the indignities and invasions of privacy that go into being on a psychiatric ward. I was working on a locked ward at the time, and I didn't relish the idea of not having the key. Mostly, however, I was concerned that if it became public knowledge that I had been hospitalized, my clinical work and privileges at best would be suspended; at worst, they would be revoked on a permanent basis. I continued to resist voluntary hospitalization; and, because the California commitment code is designed more for the well-being of lawyers than of patients, it would have been relatively easy for me to talk my way out of an involuntary commitment. Even had I been committed, there was no guarantee at all that I would not have attempted or committed suicide while on the ward; psychiatric hospitals are not uncommon places for suicide. (After this experience, I drew up a clear arrangement with my psychiatrist and family that if I again become severely depressed they have the authority to approve, against my will if necessary, both electroconvulsive therapy, or ECT, an excellent treatment for certain types of severe depression, and hospitalization.)

At the time, nothing seemed to be working, despite excellent medical care, and I simply wanted to die and be done with it. I resolved to kill myself. I was cold-bloodedly determined not to give any indication of my plans or the state of my mind; I was successful. The only note made by my psychiatrist on the day before I attempted suicide was: *Severely depressed. Very quiet. . . .*

Both my manias and depressions had violent sides to them. Violence, especially if you are a woman, is not something spoken about with ease. Being wildly out of control—physically assaultive, screaming insanely at the top of one's lungs, running frenetically with no purpose or limit, or impulsively trying to leap from cars—is frightening to others and unspeakably terrifying to oneself. In blind manic rages I have done all of these things, at one time or another, and some of them repeatedly; I remain acutely and painfully aware of how difficult it is to control or understand such behaviors, much less explain them to others. I have, in my psychotic, seizurelike attacks—my black, agitated manias—destroyed things I cherish, pushed to the utter edge people I love, and survived to think I could never recover from the shame. I have been physically restrained by terrible, brute force; kicked and pushed to the floor; thrown on my stomach with my hands pinned behind my back; and heavily medicated against my will.

I do not know how I have recovered from having done the things that necessitated such actions, any more than I know how and why my relationships with friends and lovers have survived the grinding wear and tear of such dark, fierce, and damaging energy. The aftermath of such violence, like the aftermath of a suicide attempt, is deeply bruising to all concerned. And, as with a suicide attempt, living with the knowledge that one has been violent forces a difficult reconciliation of totally divergent notions of oneself. After my suicide attempt, I had to reconcile my image of myself as a young girl who had been filled with enthusiasm, high hopes, great expectations, enormous energy, and dreams and love of life, with that of a dreary, crabbed, pained woman who desperately wished only for death and took a lethal dose of Lithium in order to accomplish it. After each of my violent psychotic episodes, I had to try and reconcile my notion of myself as a reasonably quiet-spoken and highly disciplined person, one at least generally sensitive to the moods and feelings of others, with an enraged, utterly insane, and abusive woman who lost access to all control or reason. . . .

Depression, somehow, is much more in line with society's notions of what women are all about: passive, sensitive, hopeless, helpless, stricken, dependent, confused, rather tiresome, and with limited aspirations. Manic states, on the other hand, seem to be more the provenance of men: restless, fiery, aggressive, volatile, energetic, risk taking, grandiose and visionary, and impatient with the status quo. Anger or irritability in men, under such circumstances, is more tolerated and understandable; leaders or takers of voyages are permitted a wider latitude for being temperamental. Journalists and other writers, quite understandably, have tended to focus on women and depression, rather than women and mania. This is not surprising: depression is twice as common in women as men. But manic-depressive illness occurs equally often in women and men, and, being a relatively common condition, mania ends up affecting a large number of women. They, in turn, often are misdiagnosed, receive poor, if any, psychiatric treatment, and are at high risk for suicide, alcoholism, drug abuse, and violence. But they, like men who have manic-depressive illness, also often contribute a great deal of energy, fire, enthusiasm, and imagination to the people and world around them.

Manic-depression is a disease that both kills and gives life. Fire, by its nature, both creates and destroys. "The force that through the green fuse drives the flower," wrote Dylan Thomas, "Drives my green age; that blasts the roots of trees / Is my destroyer." Mania is a strange and driving force, a destroyer, a fire in the blood. Fortunately, having fire in one's blood is not without its benefits in the world of academic medicine, especially in the pursuit of tenure. . . .

The debt I owe my psychiatrist is beyond description. I remember sitting in his office a hundred times during those grim months and each time thinking, What on earth can he say that will make me feel better or keep me alive? Well, there never was anything he could say, that's the funny thing. It was all the stupid, desperately optimistic, condescending things he *didn't* say that kept me alive; all the compassion and warmth I felt from him that could not have been said; all the intelligence, competence, and time he put into it; and his granite belief that mine was a life worth living. He was terribly direct, which was terribly important, and he was willing to admit the limits of his understanding and treatments and when he was wrong. Most difficult to put into words, but in many ways the essence of everything: he taught me that the road from suicide to life is cold and colder and colder still, but—with steely effort, the grace of God, and an inevitable break in the weather—that I could make it.

Response and Analysis

1. Describe Kay Redfield Jamison's manic behavior. What symptoms of depression did she experience? Why was she concerned about being admitted to a hospital?

2. Jamison describes Lithium as an important part of her treatment. What are the most common means of treating bipolar disorder?

3. How might differences in prevalence for depression and bipolar disorder be the result of social expectations, clinicians' interpretations, or women's greater willingness than men to report distress?

4. How do you feel about someone who has been diagnosed with a psychological disorder treating others? Would you go (or recommend a close friend go) to a therapist who had once been in treatment? Why or why not?

Research

Suppose you suspect that a client's income level affects the quality of treatment she or he receives. You hypothesize that persons with higher incomes have better treatment outcomes because they may have access to higher-quality treatment than those with lower incomes. You conduct a study examining how treatment outcomes are affected by the following variables: client's income, client's education level, therapist's training, therapist's years of experience, and therapist's fees. Which among these variables do you suspect would correlate most strongly with successful treatment rates? Why? How else might the results be explained?

chapter 5

SUICIDE

*There is but one truly serious philosophical
problem, and that is suicide. . . . I see many
people die because they judge that life is not
worth living. I see others paradoxically getting killed for the ideas or illusions that
give them a reason for living. I therefore
conclude that the meaning of life is the
most urgent of questions.*

ALBERT CAMUS, *The Myth of Sisyphus*

Suicide is always tragic, always a puzzle. It is not considered a psychological disorder in its own right, yet it is often associated with psychological disorders such
as depression and schizophrenia. But suicide has many causes beyond these. In
the United States, someone takes her or his life every twenty to thirty minutes. It is
one of the leading causes of death in the industrialized world, and it raises many
moral and legal questions.

As a way of seeking help, many people give clues to others about their intent
to kill themselves. Such clues show how ambivalent most sufferers feel about taking
their own life. A common myth is that one should never mention the word "suicide"
around people who seem despondent because that might make them more likely to
take their own life. In fact, people contemplating suicide often benefit from talking
about their thoughts and feelings with an empathetic listener. But there are no guar-
antees; while some people do benefit from help or find ways to pull through on their
own, others seem intent on dying.

In this chapter, we look at the stories of three people whose lives have been
touched by suicide. Patricia Hermes has directed her energies toward suicide prevention. In this selection, Hermes interviews Kelly O'Connor, a teenager who no
longer wanted to live. Even though Kelly was bright, friendly, and attractive, she
often felt lonely and discouraged. She was ambivalent about committing suicide and
indirectly sought help by sharing her plans with a friend. The selection also includes
Hermes's interview with Dr. Skowronski, a counselor who runs one of the youth
groups to which Kelly belonged.

The tragedy of suicide can deeply affect survivors. What happens to family and
friends who are left behind in pain and sorrow? Here Karen Kenyon tells of her

stages of grieving as she tried to recover from the suicide of her young husband. In her journal, she records the process she and her son went through to rebuild their lives. Today, Kenyon is a freelance writer and lecturer.

Pulitzer prize–winning author William Styron discloses his addiction to alcohol and his life-long struggle with depression. He had planned to commit suicide, but one evening he had an epiphany, an epiphany that came through music that he loved. He perceived life in a new way, no longer wanted to die, and found the courage to seek treatment.

A TIME TO LISTEN:
PREVENTING YOUTH SUICIDE

Patricia Hermes

Psychological Concept
preventing youth suicide

Concerned about the frequency of suicides among young people, Patricia Hermes believes that troubled youth need someone to listen to their fears and despairs, and that listening and caring may help prevent suicide. Hermes interviewed Kelly O'Connor, an outgoing and bright teenager who, during a period of depression, seriously considered suicide. O'Connor shares her pain and discusses how she indirectly sought help. We include further analysis and reflection in a conversation between Hermes and Dr. Cheryl Skowronski, a minister and counselor at the Silver Point Presbyterian Church in Greenville, North Carolina, where Kelly O'Connor was a member of a group of teenagers who were dealing with their suicidal feelings.

Q: Could you talk now about why you felt so bad, or what led up to the crisis?

K: A lot of things built up to it, some of which, two years later, I'm just beginning to work on. I grew up holding in all my feelings—anger, for instance. Tears. I didn't cry. After I was about five years old, I cried very little if at all. Never with my family. I would cry with my cat—he was my best friend. He was the only one I talked to about my problems.

Q: That sounds so lonely. A cat doesn't talk back.

K: Yes, but I liked that, given the alternative of talking to my family and having them respond in a way that just made me angrier or more upset. If he didn't respond, at least he didn't increase the bad feelings. So I could kind of believe that he understood.

In grade school, I had very few friends. I was very much a loner. I got very good grades. I used to spend about seven hours a night on homework. When I wasn't doing homework, I was watching television. There was even a period of time when I didn't eat with the family. I'd sit downstairs and watch TV while I was eating my dinner. When I hit high school, I started making friends and having fun. I didn't need to work as hard, because I'd gone to a good grade school and I'd learned a lot of things they were teaching in the freshman year. My second year, I had some problems getting along with my best friend, and my grades slipped a little bit—down to C's in a few of my classes. And then junior year, they took a nose dive. I failed chemistry first quarter, and was able to get a doctor's note to get out of classes. I didn't like chemistry and I wasn't interested in it, but failing really upset me. I had so much on my mind—problems with school, anger at my family—but more than that, just this sad, sad feeling that felt so awful. I got out of that class, but then about mid-year everything went—D's, F's.

Q: You couldn't concentrate? Or didn't care?

K: No, I just didn't even *know* it was happening. I wasn't in the habit of keeping track of my grades and figuring out what my grades would be at the end of the quarter. I'd get a bad paper, and figure, well, it was behind me now, there wasn't anything I could do about it. So I wasn't even expecting the bad grades. And my parents just freaked out. For the first time in my life, they grounded me. I could only go to school or to work. And only fifteen minutes on the phone, which really limited the contact I could have with my friends. And, at that point, my friends were the only thing that was keeping me alive.

Q: Was it a specific thing that was wrong then? Something that you knew and could identify?

K: More than anything, it was just this huge sadness. This huge, huge sad feeling inside. I began feeling more and more depressed. Later, my parents told me that they had grounded me not so much to punish me, but to keep an eye on me, because they knew that something was wrong for my grades to go like that. But they were angry at me, and yelling, and giving me a hard time, and it was so hard to deal with. It was just a few weeks later—maybe not even a few weeks—that I started talking about suicide to my friends.

Q: But not to your parents?

K: No. I was always very good at putting on an act around them. Inside, I could be so upset that I was about to fall apart, but I'd walk in that front door and the smile would go on—nothing's wrong, no problems, not upset, not angry! That kind of acting was something I'd been doing for seventeen years. So they didn't really know anything was going on. But finally I was getting to the point where I wanted help. I knew I was getting too close to doing something.

Q: Like what?

K: I would have OD'd. I had it all planned out. Painkillers, aspirin. I was always the last one to bed, so I'd take them right before I went to bed, and no one would be missing me till six o'clock in the morning. I figured by then it would be too late. I started talking to my friends about it, and they were getting worried.

Q: Why were you telling your friends? Did you want them to stop you?

K: Yes. I didn't know who to ask for help. I didn't know who could help me, who could make the pain go away. But I was hoping that maybe by telling my friends, the word would get out to someone who could get in there and help me. Finally my best friend, Andrea, talked to one of my teachers about it, and the teacher had Andrea talk to the school nurse. That day at lunch, I was called up to the administration office. This woman from the office came down and walked with me to the administration office, and she didn't say a word to me the whole time. I walked in, and there were my parents and Andrea and the nurse. I sat down between my mother and Andrea—I would really rather just have been sitting next to Andrea—and they started talking about it. It was after that that I began seeing my first psychiatrist.

Q: So you were allowed to continue in school after that—home and school, life as usual? As long as you were seeing a psychiatrist?

K: Yes, because at that point, I was able to say to the psychiatrist that I wasn't about to do anything to hurt myself.

Q: And mean it?

K: Yes.

Q: But it was only three weeks later that you felt desperate enough to make plans again?

K: Yes. I wish I could remember what we discussed in that last session. I remember driving home from that session with my arms straight out, pushing my back into the back of the driver's seat, and having to fight to keep my foot up on the accelerator—having to fight to keep it from jamming down.

But when I got home, the smile went on: "No problems! The appointment was fine!" I went to my room. At that point, I was getting home-bound assignments—the school was letting me get my work done at my own pace. And that's when my own pace was not at all, so the assignments just weren't getting done. I had been given two weeks to do them, and now it was the end of the two weeks. I was in my room, staring at my books, and I felt like throwing them out the window, or running away from them, or just getting away.

And that's when I decided that the only way out was to get out. It's going to be over! I thought. All my problems are going to be over! And I believe in heaven. And even though it's probably a sin to kill yourself, well, I believed that if you killed yourself, it was because you had gotten to the point where you couldn't handle it. There was something emotionally wrong, you weren't thinking straight. And I figured God wouldn't blame you for that. I figured that the people who loved me would have to understand that I was hurting too bad to go on and that now I wasn't hurting anymore. So I rationalized: Great, my problems will be over and I'll get to go to heaven. Had written a poem about it. So I was ecstatic. Really happy. Went to bed happy.

But it was the next day that I went into school—hoping that someone would pick up on what was happening to me. And ended up telling the nurse who would stop me. . . .

I wish I could say more to kids. You just never seem to find the right words. Maybe just this: If you choose to live now, you can choose to die later. But if you choose to die now, you can't choose to live later. It just doesn't work that way.

Dr. Skowronski: As Kelly's been talking about contemplating suicide and yet *wanting* to be stopped, I've been thinking of what other kids in the group and my other teenage groups say—that they fight against what they want. It's sort of "Please hear what I'm not saying."

Q: What do you mean?

Dr. S: Most people do want to be heard—do want help—but they don't know how to ask for it. At least, I know that almost everybody I've met wants help.

So, since they don't want to go to an adult for help—it's very rare that anyone in that age group will go to an adult—they go to their peers. And usually they'll ask their friends, "Please don't tell anyone."

Many teenagers say to me, "Oh, I don't want to break that confidence, because I'll break my friendship." Confidence and confidentiality is a very important issue with kids. But every peer can break that confidentiality. Because, as Kelly so succinctly said, better to break that friendship than to lose a friend forever.

Q: And as Kelly has also said, maybe it's not a confidence at all, but a cry for help?

Dr. S: Yes. They want you to *drag* them to a hospital. Or *drag* them to some kind of help.

Q: Because they don't have the energy to do it themselves?

Dr. S: The energy, the concentration level, is zip, nothing. That's why you can't do anything, can't do homework, can't concentrate. What's happening is that you're unable to concentrate on anything because you're wasting your energy— you can't help it, the energy is being wasted for you. If you've ever been depressed, you know that's what happens. The energy is gone. Then you get more angry at yourself because you can't do anything. And then anger gets turned inward.

So teens go to someone their age because they know it'll be someone who will understand them. Understanding is the key word. And an adult sometimes has a great deal of trouble understanding a teenager. We want to forget how we felt when we were going through that period. We don't want to recall the pain. As Kelly said, there are bills to be paid, other things to do, and so adults' lives get complicated with other things. We tend to forget those very awkward, *difficult* years that we all went through. And we all had feelings of suicide, by the way. Maybe we didn't do anything about them, but we've all had feelings that "maybe the world would be better off without me." And that's particularly true if you're a sensitive person. So, once the teen years are over, we adults want to forget.

Q: Could the parents' denial also be because it hurts so much for parents to see their kids hurting?

Dr. S: Exactly. So parents sometimes say, "Oh, well, they'll work through it. *I* worked through it. Pull up the old bootstraps and just get on with it." Which is *not* what a teenager needs to hear.

That's also why statements such as—"Oh, you're wonderful, oh, you're great. Hey, all you have to do is just get through this little period and everything's going to be fine"—that kind of thing just makes a person who's depressed go up the wall. Because it doesn't help a bit.

And saying things like "Look at your wonderful family—you have four brothers, mother, father—"

K: Words like that tell you that the person didn't understand!

Dr. S: Yes. And it also makes you feel guiltier. Because you already *know* that you have these people who love you and care for you.

K: For me, once I decided definitely to do it, I was ecstatic about it. My problems were going to be over. But immediately something else was going "Uh-oh. Wait a minute. There's something big-time wrong to be this happy about killing yourself." It was like two opposing forces. Then people say, "Think of your family, think of what it would do to them." And you're thinking: Think of what it's doing to *me*! Now! You really feel misunderstood.

Dr. S: That's one of the things I had to more or less demythologize myself about. Because I always thought a person who was suicidal, *really* making plans, *really* going to do something about it, was someone who was *not* surrounded by loving family or friends. When in truth many are. As we find in the group.

Q: Could you tell me a little about the group? How it works—and how it might work for others?

Dr. S: The group is run by a number of different counselors besides me—three of us who are trained. Last night, for instance, we had seventy kids in the group. We were talking about feelings, feelings that we have all gone through about being lonely. The theme was "Alone in the Crowd." All the kids were really involved in communicating with each other. It was so exciting to hear them able to speak about their deepest emotion. Because it's hard—how *do* you tell your deepest emotion if you're really hurting?

Kelly is able to speak it now because in a way she's rehearsed it by talking to doctors, peers, and others. Most people do it in silence. And that silence is detrimental.

Kelly has just recently come back, and she's such a welcome addition to the group—almost as a role model. She can eloquently express how she feels about what she's gone through. She can point out that it's not as though once you've been through depression, you'll *never have it again*. But it also doesn't mean that you're *suicidal* again. It just means: I made it once, I can make it now again. It's very important for a person who is suicidal to hear that. Kelly knows how they feel.

We were trying to decide on names for this group. I was caught up in all that "initial" stuff—making up initials to stand for a name. But at our first meeting the kids said, call it what it is—Suicide Prevention. But it does take time for parents to agree to this.

Sometimes we have trouble getting kids to this group. We have to rely on parents to drop their kids off (if the kids aren't driving yet). And a great number of parents don't agree that they have any problems in the family.

Kelly used to pick kids up and bring them here. Frankly, we need that. Kids will call here, leave their number. When I call back, parents answer and say, "What do you want?" I say, "I'd like to speak to Chris"—or whoever left the message. And the parent says, "Well, she's fine."

It's very difficult to get parents to agree that there's any problem. Sometimes they agree only when their child does what Kelly did.

Q: Do you think parents today are just not hearing?

Dr. S: Well, our parents didn't hear us, either. I mean, I love my mother, but there were some things we didn't talk about, either. No, it's not just parents today. It was true of our parents, too. It's very hard to communicate with parents. It's just not something you normally do at certain ages. In the first place, you wouldn't *want* your mother and father to know everything about you. Even to this day, there are certain things I wouldn't tell my mother.

But the defense mechanisms are up with families if they have to take their kids to a support group.

Q: So it's not just today? There have been similar problems all along?

Dr. S: No, there are some things different. It's coping mechanisms that it seems to me are missing today. What we're trying to do with our suicide prevention council, all the agencies that are trying to help with teens—the Y, the child abuse agencies, the councils on crime—is get a curriculum written and get it in the schools. We've just persuaded the superintendent of schools that it is needed—some kind of program that will help a person learn how to cope.

You know, all the time that Kelly sat in front of the TV alone, eating her dinner, spending seven hours a night on homework, is not healthy. What could have changed that? She had some problems at home. Well, we've had problems at home with parents forever, and always will. So why did it affect Kelly? Why has it affected others her age more than it did ten years ago? We don't know. But maybe if there had been a program in schools that dealt with feelings, that said, "How do you feel when a parent does or says what your parent said or did?"—it might have helped Kelly find different ways of coping.

That's what we're seeing—that if we deal with the problems as they come up, it is helpful. That's why the suicide support group is so helpful. Why talking to a psychiatrist is helpful. Talking to someone who understands.

It comes out often in the support group: that it is all right to talk about suicidal feelings. It is okay to say it. It is okay to share it. That doesn't mean you're going to do it. It doesn't mean you're crazy or sick. It just means you're hurting.

Therapy is a process, just as it was a *process* getting to the point of being suicidal. Suicide is not just one impulsive act. By seventeen years old, a person has usually given it some thought—some great thought. Usually most of us don't speak about what's deep inside us. But when we use silence, we close down. What we try to do with the group is help them talk about—and hear about—some of the feelings *all* of us have been through. That's what this group is all about—suicide *prevention*.

Response and Analysis

1. What reasons do teenagers sometimes give for wanting to commit suicide?

2. Why is it sometimes difficult for a potential suicide victim to find help before it is too late? Why might it be difficult for others to respond in ways that would be most helpful?

3. If someone reveals plans to commit suicide and asks for confidentiality, should the confidante honor that request? Why or why not?

4. Why might even close, caring parents be unaware that their child is considering suicide?

5. What might support groups offer in the way of help to those who have contemplated or attempted suicide?

Research

Most large communities have telephone crisis centers that are staffed by trained volunteers. People contemplating suicide sometimes call these centers. Suppose you want to assess the effectiveness of various training programs for volunteers in preventing suicide. To measure effectiveness, you have trained observers sit with the volunteers and record their comments. The observers rate the volunteers' skills according to criteria provided by experts in suicide prevention. There are several independent variables that might be related to effectiveness. Consider the following independent variables: number of hours of training, number of hours discussing suicide in training, number of hours trainees spent in simulated phone conversations with mock suicide callers, years of experience of the training staff, quality of the relationship between the crisis center and other community health-care facilities, and the reputation of the center in the community. Which variables would you expect to relate most strongly with ratings of effectiveness? Why? What variables other than those listed might predict effectiveness of volunteers in preventing suicide? How might the procedures of the study bias the findings?

SUNSHOWER

Karen Kenyon

Psychological Concept
recovering from the suicide of a loved one

When Karen Kenyon and her husband, Dick, were in their late thirties, life was full of exciting beginnings. Dick Kenyon had accepted a position in administration at the University of California, San Diego; they had purchased a home, and they and their young son enjoyed exploring the treasures of Southern California. One night, Dick was so late coming home from work that Karen called the campus police. The police found his car with a note inside that indicated that Dick felt his job had become unbearable. Dick had jumped from the eleventh floor of a building on campus. As part of healing, Karen kept a journal that recorded her anguish and that of her son, and the process of recovery that they went through. The following account is a selection from her journal.

Dick's suicide brings forth the full range of emotion. Some feel they understand it, some hate it, some accept it, some condemn it, some don't even want to see it, but its presence stays and won't be denied. . . .

The views of Dick's suicide were many and varied:

"He was a martyr, maybe like Jesus. He was definitely trying to make a statement."

"He did it on campus, not at home, and so he hated the campus."

"He wouldn't have wanted you to find him. He was protecting you."

"He was an angry man."

"He was not an angry man. It was an act of despair."

"He was too good."

"He was totally out of touch with reality."

"He was not mentally ill. It was a logical choice he made."

"How do you know it wasn't best for him? Not best for you, but best for Dick?"

"He should have had medication."

"He wouldn't have done that. I just can't believe he would have done that."

"Some say childhood causes these things, but I think it has to do with chemical imbalance."

"It was definitely a chemical imbalance. He was losing weight."

"It didn't fit his psychological make-up."

"It was his job—all the pressure."

"It wasn't his job. It was that he was ill."

"It was just a choice he made."

"I feel so angry at Dick's act—it is why I haven't written you."

"He turned against you. Can't you see that? Can't you feel his rejection of you?"

"He did it for you."

Or as one friend said, "Perhaps it was a part of Dick that was like one of the moons of Saturn—always there—but no one knew about it—and it was unknown even to Dick."

The question "Why?" plays on our deepest fear, our deepest guilt, self-doubt, and sense of failure, our fear of loss of control, of others, of ourselves. I couldn't keep him from doing it, and he couldn't keep himself from doing it. But the line is thin. Perhaps for Dick it was total control. They look the same. The result was the same.

Was it for no reason, or was it for all the reasons, or was it for no apparent reason? Why that choice? The truth is we don't really know, though we can conjecture. The existence of the fact and the acceptance of the unknowingness, is perhaps all. That is the "faith," the "faith" written on the side of the boat as it passed us on his last trip out to sea.

All the words are only attempts to make clear, and still the true clearness exists only in the acknowledgement.

In my heart only one reality exists. He is no longer here, and I am still alive. There don't have to be "reasons" for anything anymore. It's that simple. It's that complex. . . .

I am pained and saddened to think of the mental suffering he must have gone through. And yet, in his state of mind, in his reality, it must have seemed the perfect thing to do. He didn't do what I wanted him to do, what Richard wanted him to do. This was not his parents' choice, his coworkers' or his friends' choice. This final choice was made totally alone. It was Dick's choice. He labored through the night, and he gave birth to his death.

He must have wanted release, and I guess he has that now, though I wish he hadn't had to do it. The ultimate question, after all, isn't "Did he have the right to do it?" but is perhaps "Why should he have had to do it?"

On the other hand, when someone is left as I was, there is the opposite question, "Do I have the right to live?" I have struggled not with taking my life, in the sense of losing it, but with taking my life, using it, and feeling I have a right to live, in the fullest sense.

Maybe that is the hardest hurdle for survivors. There is grief. There is loss. But are we ever absolved? My thoughts for a long time questioned if I deserved to live.

Journal excerpt, December 4, 1979:

The hardest thing, and it's getting better, is to believe that I deserve this new life. It's here for the taking—the sun, the sea, my friends, my son, art, music, touching someone's hand.

I know my old self died. I know my new self is infinitely wiser, though far from wise. . . . Do I deserve to be loved is not the essential question. The essential question is, do I deserve to love?

And even if I don't deserve to—shouldn't I anyway? The question of to be or not—is really to love or die. If we live, then we must love. If we love, we live. They are inseparable.

Now piece by piece I am trying to take back my right to life, trying to learn to live for myself, for Richard,[1] and with friends, and new people in my life.

Now for the first time in my life I'm beginning to truly know myself alone, and to be able, then, to share that self here and there with others, and to have a beginning sense of purpose.

Deserving to live is much more than survival. . . .

How does a gentle man survive? In Dick's case, he doesn't, except in our hearts, and on these pages. His tragedy, I think, is the tragedy of that gentle side of all men—larger in some, barely noticeable in others. His tragedy was perhaps that of being too sensitive, feeling too much of the pain of the world while not acknowledging enough of his own pain, his own needs, and the tragedy of being locked into a job which gave him no real creative outlet. When he tried to bring his human values into it, those values were dismissed. Unseeing eyes denied them over and over again. And his was perhaps also the tragedy of not being seen by me, or others, as he truly was, and of not being able to show himself as he was, and of letting feelings of failure gnaw away at his sense of worth.

But the need to persevere was perhaps the tragic flaw, the tragedy of insisting upon enduring, never crying for help. Dick could stick with something and concentrate intensely on it. He was utterly lacking in self-indulgence. He didn't feel, as most people do, that his desires were of utmost importance. He had a strong nurturing side, but this nurturing did not extend to himself.

As James Kavanaugh has said in one of his poems, "There are men too gentle to live among wolves.". . .

He could muster strength from nowhere to live—only persevere to die—only try to take the darkness that surrounded him and finally become it—in order to find light. . . .

Was it easier for him to kill himself than to come home and say he just couldn't make it anymore?. . .

The beginning stages of grief seemed to me to be as heavy and gray as battleships, heavy as dark curtains, and yet those curtains did very gradually lift.

> Journal excerpt, August 16, 1979:
> There seem to be two phases, major phases, so far, for me. The first was the almost prenatal stage, the curling up in bed with Dick's ring on a chain around my neck, as I clutched it like a rosary—the seeking of comfort—those were the first few weeks. Now nine months later the world is opening more for me. It is in many ways more difficult. The shock is still there, the unreality, and mixed in now is an increase in questioning. I haven't accepted it—the fact—or not knowing the reason—or that I must go on. Layered on this is now the reality of life decisions. . . .

Every place I went for a long time reminded me of Dick, whether I had been with him in that place or not. The old places were haunted by him, but the new places too were expectant with "What would he think of this?" or "Would he like that?"

Stores cried out with shirts he would like, records he might want, books he would have read, even presents he would have given me.

---

[1] Dick and Karen Kenyon's son

A friend of mine, Stefanie Ramsdell, wrote simply one day, capturing a facet of grief:

> You went suddenly
> Left my hands brimming with gifts —
> Nowhere to bring them.

All the "unfinished business" as Elizabeth Kübler-Ross has said, must be finished. The words unsaid, the gifts never given, are like threads in a tapestry that must be rewoven.

I thought constantly of all I hadn't said. I wanted to say, "I just didn't know . . ." but of course the words I wanted most to say—the essential message in life—is "I love you."

Grief is the price we pay for that love—said or unsaid, and it is the ship that eventually carries us through the passage of separation.

Shock

In the beginning, grief took the form of shock. It covered me with an ability to go on. It looked like courage—maybe—but it is something that protects against the unacceptable and anesthetizes.

I did many things while in that initial state of shock. Besides planning the memorial service, in a week I made a little pamphlet with a picture of Dick to give to friends. In it I told them what happened, and what he was like. It was a tribute to him, so that people would remember and know him, and it helped my feelings have a place to go. I could express love for Dick in those words—love I had no other way to express.

Every night I sat at the kitchen table with bills I'd never paid before, trying to figure out finances—something I'd never wanted to know—and finding an unusual pleasure in their dependability and lack of emotion. I made lists of tasks. Rote thinking worked best. It held back the fear and terror.

I tried to create an order to life. I was working then from nine in the morning until one. Never mind that I often cried in the car, driving to and fro, or that I at least once screamed at the top of my lungs in that car. I would come home, pick up Richard at 2:15 after school, and we'd run errands, or do anything to be out of the house. In the state of shock, life is shot apart and makes no sense, until gradually a new sense comes. . . .

I think guilt must be the most difficult emotion for the survivors of suicide. It is so easy to blame ourselves, and it is so hard to let go of that last remnant of connection with the person we have lost, and so to finally say goodbye.

But it is guilt that will keep us from living, and if we give in to that, then we too have committed a kind of psychological suicide. And in a sense guilt puts a stain on the whole world.

When I was first told of Dick's note, indicating he would do harm to himself, my first words were words of guilt, "Oh, no—oh, God—I don't deserve to live. . . ." All I could think was that I had done it. Somehow I must have driven him to it, or not seen where he was headed.

For months I tried to feel his pain, tried to know how he must have felt. I tormented myself as much as I could and still remain functional. I felt my hair would turn gray and I would get cancer—and that it was what I deserved, though I never said that to anyone. It frightens me still to remember those thoughts, but helps me realize too how we do wish ourselves illness. . . .

I knew too, though, that his final act was one thing he couldn't have shared with me, because I would have fought to keep him alive, and he knew that. I would have clung to him, and not let him go. And he wanted to go. He wanted to die. . . .

Anger is a feeling I didn't and haven't felt consistently. It is hard to know who or what to be angry with, and yet it has woven its way through me. Anger can be very good at times. It can give some strength to get us through until a bit of real inner strength builds up. We can use it to protect ourselves, but it is important to be aware if we are doing that. Both guilt and anger are excesses of emotion our minds build cases around. . . .

Some of the anger does come from the fear and the loss, and some of it is justifiable. The paradox is that death gives us anger, but that especially in the face of death, we should be able to go beyond it, and to reach some kind of peace in this our limited time. . . .

One day I decided I should put out some of Dick's clothes for Goodwill. I didn't at that point want to give much of anything away—only T-shirts, underwear, and socks; and I had put in the bags house shoes he had worn much of the time. I drove off to work that day, after setting the bags on the front step. Then about a mile from home terrible guilt feelings overtook me. How could I give them away? I didn't want those shoes, but somehow they symbolized Dick, I guess. I drove back and took them out of the sack. I just couldn't do that yet.

This early time was a time of hanging on, in more ways than one—to Dick, to pain, to others, and to myself, but little by little I also found what could help start to make a pathway.

The most important thing to me was the contact with people. It was necessary and vital. Warm human voices and personalities, just being near, or present, touching my hand, hugging me—desperately were needed, but not always available. . . .

The phone rang in the house several times a day for the first few weeks. I would talk until my voice ached. I needed that talking, that telling and retelling of the events. When I told the story to others, I was telling the story to myself. Though the story was no longer the event, though there were no answers to my questions, at least it was something. I could hang on to the story, say his name— and so in a sense I still had Dick, and I was making the event real. After a few weeks, calls stopped, but needs to be in touch remained.

The most appreciated gift friends could give me was just to be there. Some disappointed me. Others that I wouldn't have expected to came forward. People who *could* be with me *were* with me. There is a rightness in that. At times there were phone conversations where ten-minute spaces elapsed. Words can only say so much. We were together, connected in silence by a telephone, by caring.

It seems such a simple thing, such a mundane thing, but I cherish friends who took Richard and me to dinner, or invited us to their homes for dinner. Food and friendship are full of life. A special emptiness, particularly at the ritual of dinnertime, reigns in a house emptied by someone's dying. Life felt cold, little nourished. It helped to be out of the house and in warm, caring, life-supporting surroundings, because we lived on the edge of darkness. . . .

My job was a blessing. It was essential to have to get out of bed every day and have someplace I needed to be. The importance or unimportance of tasks I dressed for didn't matter. My friends at work filled in my life every day. They provided the nest, without which I don't know how I could have gone on.

Somehow during this time I managed to write an article on widowhood for a local newspaper. I recall that beginning this article was so important to me. My real work, writing, has always given me strength. Someone said to me—you won't finish that—widows start a lot of things and don't finish them. But I knew I would. It was essential to me.

Response and Analysis

1. How does Karen Kenyon explain her husband's suicide?

2. How does Kenyon respond to the various reactions of others toward her husband's suicide?

3. Describe the process Kenyon goes through in order to survive the tragic loss of her husband.

4. How does telling her story help Kenyon? In what way can writing and speaking out be a psychologically sound way to deal with tragic events?

Research

Suppose you wish to conduct a study to examine whether writing about a traumatic event can reduce stress. Before conducting the study, you must secure approval from the human subjects Institutional Review Board at your college or university. Two of the purposes of the Review Board are to ensure that your procedures are ethical and to protect the rights and dignity of the participants.

Most Review Boards require the researcher to submit a form describing, among other things, the activities in which the students will participate. Suppose the procedures for your experiment are as follows. When the participants arrive at your lab, you will escort them to individual cubicles where they cannot see the other participants or the experimenter. You then ask the participants to read and sign a consent form, and allow students who do not wish to participate to leave. Next, you will ask half of the participants to write for thirty minutes about a distressing or traumatic event that they have experienced. You will ask the other half to write for thirty minutes about their favorite summer vacation. You tell all participants that their essays are anonymous and that they should not put their names on their essay. At the end of the thirty-minute period, you ask the participants to place their essays in an unmarked envelope. Finally, you ask each participant to complete a brief survey indicating whether they gained new insights about themselves by participating in the study.

In addition to a description of the procedures, most Institutional Review Boards ask the researcher to list the potential benefits and risks of the study to the participants. Based on the above description, list the potential benefits and risks (e.g., writing about the event may induce a negative mood) to students who will participate in the study. Do you believe the risks outweigh the benefits, or vice versa? Why? Why is it important to allow those students to leave who do not want to participate? Why is it important to debrief participants about the experiment at the end of the session?

DARKNESS VISIBLE

William Styron

Psychological Concept
deciding not to commit suicide

Author William Styron suffered from depression, an illness he didn't recognize for years but which he self-treated with alcohol until it affected his health. At the age of sixty-three, Styron fell into a great apathy, and the wondrous sight of a flock of Canadian geese left him not with a sense of their beauty but with a terrible dread that made him believe that the words of Baudelaire, "I have felt the wind of the wing of madness," applied to him. Only after the name *depression* had been given to his illness did his wife recognize that Styron had been under a cloud of despondency for years. Many of his novels (*Sophie's Choice, Lie Down in Darkness*) deal with suicide and despair. Styron made plans to commit suicide, but a moment of epiphany stopped him. In the following account, Styron describes what prevented him from taking his life and prompted him to check into a hospital. Since his treatment, Styron has felt once again both serenity and joy.

I was on Martha's Vineyard, where I've spent a good part of each year since the 1960s, during that exceptionally beautiful summer. But I had begun to respond indifferently to the island's pleasures. I felt a kind of numbness, an enervation, but more particularly an odd fragility—as if my body had actually become frail, hypersensitive, and somehow disjointed and clumsy, lacking normal coordination. And soon I was in the throes of a pervasive hypochondria. Nothing felt quite right with my corporeal self; there were twitches and pains, sometimes intermittent, often seemingly constant, that seemed to presage all sorts of dire infirmities. . . .

I had moved back to my house in Connecticut. It was October, and one of the unforgettable features of this stage of my disorder was the way in which my own farmhouse, my beloved home for thirty years, took on for me at that point when my spirits regularly sank to their nadir an almost palpable quality of ominousness. The fading evening light—akin to that famous "slant of light" of Emily Dickinson's, which spoke to her of death, of chill extinction—had none of its familiar autumnal loveliness, but ensnared me in a suffocating gloom. I wondered how this friendly place, teeming with such memories of (again in her words) "Lads and Girls," of "laughter and ability and Sighing, / And Frocks and Curls," could almost perceptibly seem so hostile and forbidding. Physically, I was not alone. As always Rose[1] was pre-

---

[1] Styron's wife

sent and listened with unflagging patience to my complaints. But I felt an immense and aching solitude. I could no longer concentrate during those afternoon hours, which for years had been my working time, and the act of writing itself, becoming more and more difficult and exhausting, stalled, then finally ceased.

There were also dreadful, pouncing seizures of anxiety. One bright day on a walk through the woods with my dog I heard a flock of Canada geese honking high above trees ablaze with foliage; ordinarily a sight and sound that would have exhilarated me, the flight of birds caused me to stop, riveted with fear, and I stood stranded there, helpless, shivering, aware for the first time that I had been stricken by no mere pangs of withdrawal but by a serious illness whose name and actuality I was able finally to acknowledge. Going home, I couldn't rid my mind of the line of Baudelaire's, dredged up from the distant past, that for several days had been skittering around at the edge of my consciousness: "I have felt the wind of the wing of madness." . . .

My few hours of sleep were usually terminated at three or four in the morning, when I stared up into yawning darkness, wondering and writhing at the devastation taking place in my mind, and awaiting the dawn, which usually permitted me a feverish, dreamless nap. I'm fairly certain that it was during one of these insomniac trances that there came over me the knowledge—a weird and shocking revelation, like that of some long-beshrouded metaphysical truth—that this condition would cost me my life if it continued on such a course. This must have been just before my trip to Paris. Death, as I have said, was now a daily presence, blowing over me in cold gusts. I had not conceived precisely how my end would come. In short, I was still keeping the idea of suicide at bay. But plainly the possibility was around the corner, and I would soon meet it face to face. . . .

A phenomenon that a number of people have noted while in deep depression is the sense of being accompanied by a second self—a wraithlike observer who, not sharing the dementia of his double, is able to watch with dispassionate curiosity as his companion struggles against the oncoming disaster, or decides to embrace it. There is a theatrical quality about all this, and during the next several days, as I went about stolidly preparing for extinction, I couldn't shake off a sense of melodrama—a melodrama in which I, the victim-to-be of self-murder, was both the solitary actor and lone member of the audience. I had not as yet chosen the mode of my departure, but I knew that that step would come next, and soon, as inescapable as nightfall.

I watched myself in mingled terror and fascination as I began to make the necessary preparation: going to see my lawyer in the nearby town—there rewriting my will—and spending part of a couple of afternoons in a muddled attempt to bestow upon posterity a letter of farewell. It turned out that putting together a suicide note, which I felt obsessed with a necessity to compose, was the most difficult task of writing that I had ever tackled. There were too many people to acknowledge, to thank, to bequeath final bouquets. . . .

But even a few words came to seem to me too long-winded, and I tore up all my efforts, resolving to go out in silence. Late one bitterly cold night, when I knew that I could not possibly get myself through the following day, I sat in the living room of the house bundled up against the chill; something had happened to the furnace. My wife had gone to bed, and I had forced myself to watch the tape of a movie in which a young actress, who had been in a play of mine, was cast in a small part. At one point in the film, which was set in late-nineteenth-century Boston, the characters moved down the hallway of a music conservatory, beyond the walls of which, from unseen musicians, came a contralto voice, a sudden soaring passage from the Brahms *Alto Rhapsody*.

This sound, which like all music—indeed, like all pleasure—I had been numbly unresponsive to for months, pierced my heart like a dagger, and in a flood of swift recollection I thought of all the joys the house had known: the children who had rushed through its rooms, the festivals, the love and work, the honestly earned slumber, the voices and the nimble commotion, the perennial tribe of cats and dogs and birds, "laughter and ability and Sighing, / And Frocks and Curls." All this I realized was more than I could ever abandon, even as what I had set out so deliberately to do was more than I could inflict on those memories, and upon those, so close to me, with whom the memories were bound. And just as powerfully I realized I could not commit this desecration on myself. I drew upon some last gleam of sanity to perceive the terrifying dimensions of the mortal predicament I had fallen into. I woke up my wife and soon telephone calls were made. The next day I was admitted to the hospital.

Response and Analysis

1. How did William Styron's depression affect his perceptions of life? What are possible sources of his decision to commit suicide?

2. What happened that made Styron decide against committing suicide?

3. What risk factors and psychological disorders are associated with suicide?

Research

Suppose you want to know the extent to which people suffering from depression abuse alcohol. One of the problems in conducting research to answer this question is that people may not be willing to accurately report how much alcohol they consume. For example, they may be concerned about social sanctions—their employers or other people might find out. How might you structure your study to make participants more willing to accurately report their experiences with alcohol? What ethical issues might be involved in ensuring anonymity or confidentiality?

chapter 6

PSYCHOLOGICAL FACTORS AND MEDICAL CONDITIONS

*Ask not what disease the person has,
but rather what person the disease has.*

(Attributed to) SIR WILLIAM OSLER

Physical and psychological health affect each other in numerous ways. Physical conditions can directly affect psychological well-being, such as when injury or aging produce dementia or amnesia. They also have indirect effects and may influence the development of psychological problems, such as depression or anxiety disorders. The relationship also works in the other direction—one's attitudes, emotions, and cognitions affect numerous ailments, including hypertension, asthma, headaches, stomachaches, and ulcers. A DSM-IV diagnosis of psychological factors affecting a medical condition is made when a medical condition (Axis III) is complicated by psychological problems that constitute an additional health risk. Treatment usually involves a combination of medication and psychotherapy.

One of the most researched factors affecting psychological and physical health is stress. Stress is an internal response to a perceived demand, which may be biological (e.g., illness, injury), psychological (e.g., guilt, high aspirations), or social (e.g., large crowds, poverty). Stress calls the body to action, but if the call continues for long periods or is too overwhelming, it can cause exhaustion and vulnerability to illness. In the first selection, Robert Eliot says that he was three years behind his self-imposed career timetable and pushing hard to catch up. The demands he placed on himself eventually took their toll on his physical health, until he learned to recognize and control stress.

Anyone who has ever had a headache knows that it can be brought on by stress and can affect mood. People who suffer from migraine headaches know that they can affect more than that. While migraines vary in intensity and duration, they are often severe, may be accompanied by nausea, and can last from a few hours to several days. Fortunately, new drugs show promise for bringing relief to migraine sufferers. In the second selection, Joan Didion describes how she learned to live with migraines and how they affect her physical and mental health.

Tennis professional Arthur Ashe was at the peak of his life when he learned that he had acquired immune deficiency syndrome (AIDS). In the final years before his death, Ashe began writing about his life and how he coped with AIDS. Ashe writes that he never asked why it was he who had to suffer this tragic illness because then he would have to ask why it was he who had also been so fortunate. In the third selection, Ashe tells how he drew on personal discipline and training to help sustain him.

In the final selection, Floyd Skloot tells of coping with chronic fatigue syndrome. This illness is controversial because its causes are not fully understood; some even question whether it should be regarded as a medical illness. Nevertheless, Skloot experiences impairment and must adapt. He shows that people who have certain medical conditions often must make psychological and lifestyle adjustments. The right adjustments, though not always easily made, can enhance the quality of life.

IS IT WORTH DYING FOR?

Robert S. Eliot and Dennis L. Breo

Psychological Concepts
heart attack, stress, type A behavior

Robert Eliot kept telling himself that he was late: he was three years behind his self-imposed schedule to become chief of cardiology at a major university hospital. Eliot was an active and in-demand physician, researcher, and lecturer, and he displayed many of the characteristics associated with the type A behavior pattern. The type A behavior pattern includes impatience, competitiveness, hostility; it means being hardworking and more concerned about personal achievements than social relationships. Rushing on his way to a dynamic career, Eliot was felled by a heart attack.

Eliot's reaction to and recovery from the heart attack led him to explore how stress affects health. Through insight and subsequent changes in the way he lived and thought, he restored his health and developed more rewarding professional goals and personal relationships. In this selection, Eliot looks at the impact of stress on health and offers suggestions for being less vulnerable to pressure.

My body cried out for rest, but my brain wasn't listening. I was behind schedule. My timetable read that by the age of forty I should be the chief of cardiology at a major university. I was forty-three when I left the University of Florida at Gainesville and accepted the position of chief of cardiology at the University of Nebraska in 1972. All I had to do was run a little faster and I'd be back on track.

Years of preparation had led to this opportunity, starting with medical school and cardiology residency at the University of Colorado. Then came five years of practicing academic and private cardiology at the University of Minnesota, where I trained and worked with giants like cardiovascular pathologist Jesse Edwards and open-heart surgeons C. Walton Lillehei, Richard Lillehei, Aldo Castenada, Norman Shumway, and Christiaan Barnard. Then it was on to the University of Florida for five years as a professor and as chief of cardiology at the Gainesville Veterans Administration Hospital.

It was time to find out if I could build something myself, a cardiovascular center that would do innovative research. Nebraska needed such a center. I saw the university as a place of opportunity and promise.

What I didn't see was how hard it is to start an expensive new project in an established institution. I thought we'd worked out the essential issues in advance, but when I arrived the frustrations started to pile up. I would argue for autonomy, facilities, and funds, and would run into ever-growing problems of bureaucracy, budget, manpower, and timing. I came to feel that the walls were closing in on me and I would never break free to make my dream a reality.

Desperately, I did what I had been doing all my life. I picked up the pace. I tried to force things through. I criss-crossed the state to provide on-the-spot cardiology education to rural Nebraska physicians and build support among them for the university's cardiovascular program. I scheduled academic lectures across the country, continually flying in and out at a moment's notice. I remember that on one trip on which my wife Phyllis helped with the business arrangements, a seminar went superbly, and on the plane ride home Phyllis wanted to savor the memory. Not me. I was rushing through the evaluation forms, worrying about how to make the next seminar better.

I had no time for family and friends, relaxation and diversion. When Phyllis bought me an exercise bike for Christmas, I was offended. How could I possibly find time to sit down and pedal a bicycle?

I was often overtired, but I put that out of my mind. I wasn't concerned about my health. What did I have to worry about? I was an expert in diseases of the heart, and I knew I didn't have any of the risk factors. My father had lived to be seventy-eight and my mother, at eighty-five, showed no sign of heart disease. I didn't smoke. I wasn't overweight. I didn't have high blood pressure. I didn't have high cholesterol. I didn't have diabetes. I thought I was immune to heart disease.

But I was running a big risk for other reasons. I had been pushing too hard for too long. Now all my efforts seemed futile, and I carried an extra burden, knowing I had brought promising associates to what looked like a losing situation. A feeling of disillusionment descended on me, a sense of *invisible entrapment*.

I didn't know it then, but my body was continuously reacting to this inner turmoil. For nine months I was softened for the blow. It came two weeks after my forty-fourth birthday.

It was a Friday afternoon, the first day of spring, and my adrenaline was pumping. I had been lecturing in New Orleans and had had little sleep before flying back to Omaha and heading straight into a confrontation with administrators over support for the planned cardiovascular center. I ran into a brick wall: again, problems with bureaucracy, budget, manpower, timing. Suddenly I snapped, exploding with anger. I thought my life's work and that of my colleagues was being torpedoed. Leaving the office, I was still enraged, and could not calm down as I started a two-hundred-mile drive west for a weekend cardiology conference at a community hospital—a trip on which my family was coming along so the kids could finally have a weekend with Daddy.

I was too angry to drive, so Phyllis did. I was bone-tired, past the point of exhaustion, and as we pushed on through miserable weather—a rainstorm that beat down on the car for hours—I realized that my resources were all but gone. Yet that night I could not sleep; the events of the day left my mind no rest.

The next morning I lectured on heart attacks and sudden death. After a heavy lunch, I began to discuss some heart attack cases. One of the faculty members from my department showed some slides. I tried to provide the commentary.

I couldn't think straight.

Normally I could have diagnosed the cases being shown on the slides in a second. Today, the faculty member had to gently lead me into making the correct diagnoses. I could not concentrate, could not assemble any thoughts. I felt exhausted. My voice was hoarse. My eyes were blurry. Vaguely aware of my fuzziness, I continued to talk and somehow made it through the hour.

The next speaker was our youngest faculty member. I had known him since he was a medical student, had watched him develop over the years, and was very proud of him. But, sitting in the back of the room, I was still having trouble concentrating. He was young and energetic, and I felt old and weary. I sat watching him, anxious for him to do well.

Suddenly it hit: an elephant sat on my chest.

The pressure was intense and went from my breastbone up into my shoulders and neck and jaws, and down both arms. I had trouble breathing. Two minutes of pain seemed to last an eternity. I changed my breathing; I changed my seating position. The pain persisted.

Indigestion? Incredibly, I thought it must be the fatty, spicy cold cuts I had eaten for lunch.

I started to sweat. The room must be too warm, I thought. I walked outside, but the discomfort continued. Could I have a hiatal hernia—was my stomach pushing up into my chest? I got on the elevator and made it to the coronary care unit, where only that morning I had conducted grand rounds.

I asked the head nurse for nitroglycerin. She gave me a funny look but brought two tablets. I went outside and put one under my tongue. I had never taken nitroglycerin before.

The pain didn't go away. I took a second tablet. No relief. I began getting bowel cramps. Nausea. It must be gallbladder trouble, I told myself. I went to the bathroom. The pain got worse. The game was over.

I diagnosed myself: myocardial infarction of the inferior wall.

I went back to the head nurse and asked to be taken to a vacant bed. As I stretched out, I said, "I've just had a heart attack."

I was lucky. I had the kind of heart attack everyone should have—mild and in a hospital. From the time the elephant sat on my chest until the time I was strapped up to an electrocardiograph to have my heartbeat checked, only twenty minutes passed. Had the trouble started before we reached the hospital, I probably would have died.

As I looked up from the wrong side of the sheets in the coronary care unit, I realized that this insult to my heart was providing me with a new insight into my life:

I had brought on my own heart attack. I knew this because, when I asked myself if I could have avoided it, the answer was, "Yes, I really believe I could have." The way I reacted emotionally to work stress had made me vulnerable. For years, I had pushed myself. Jobs during high school and college. Completing a four-year premed course in three. And after that, my constant drive for achievement as a resident, teacher, public speaker, and consultant. I had won recognition, but at what price? Worse, I was a prime candidate for a second heart attack if I didn't change my ways.

It took several hours for tests to confirm the diagnosis. Finally there came a burst of rapid heartbeats, proof of the heart attack. The doctor injected Xylocaine, a local anaesthetic, into a vein, and the danger was over. I could go to sleep now. As I drifted off, I came to a second conclusion:

Life was not a matter of victory or defeat. Ever since childhood I had been told, and had believed, that success was worth any demand, any sacrifice. But now I had to ask myself: Is it worth dying for?

During my recovery, I began to piece together my past and to construct a new future. My life had been a blur of overachievement to gain rewards, but I had never asked what I really wanted for myself. The only child of a Lebanese immigrant and a British blueblood, I had been told from birth that if you worked hard you would be treated as an equal in America, but it was best to be your own boss. My mother, Ruth Buffington, was a delightful, optimistic Victorian lady. My father, Salim Elia, was a wise, complex, brilliant, and scholarly research chemist who worked for thirty-five years for a pharmaceutical firm, and felt that his best ideas had been pirated by others who were higher up in the company and politically more shrewd. He was bitter to the day of his death.

We lived on what some considered the wrong side of the tracks in Wilmette, Illinois, an affluent suburb north of Chicago that borders some of the wealthiest communities in the nation. I grew up knowing that the only way for the son of an immigrant to belong on the North Shore was to become a lawyer or an executive—maybe a professor, definitely a doctor. My father had always admired doctors because they were compassionate scientists who had independence. When I won a scholarship and was accepted to medical school in Colorado, it was the happiest day of his life. The next month, he died.

After my father's death, I changed my name to Eliot, though retaining his first name, Salim, as my middle name. It was my father's wish: "Son, there's no sense handicapping yourself by going through life with a name that people don't understand."

Other changes came with those years. As a junior in medical school, when I finally got to put on the white coat and look at people instead of cadavers and frogs, I began to feel for the first time that I might amount to something. That year was also when Phyllis Allman, a dietitian from Wisconsin, came into my life. After a stormy three-and-a-half-year courtship, we settled down to a long, stable marriage. But I was always busy taking care of business. We never had enough time to be with each other—until my heart attack.

It sounds strange, but the heart attack was the best thing in the world for me. With a week in the hospital, an additional week of bedrest at a vacation cabin, and three months at home, I had a lot of time to think, with a loving wife to help me sort it all out. I realized how much Phyllis really loved me. She protected me like a mother grizzly bear. I realized that my children, Bill and Susan, were surprisingly sensitive and loving. I also realized that my blind pursuit of academic medicine would have left my family in a terrible financial predicament if I had died. Money had never been a motivating force for me, but it was frightening to realize that the ones I loved were financially so vulnerable.

I took time to rediscover my wife. We spent many hours renewing memories and making plans for our future life together. I rediscovered an old romance with model railroading and turned a room of our basement into an elaborate railroad complete with whistles, steam, and brakemen. I took time to rediscover my body. After years of treating it like a sack of potatoes, I began to listen to it. I took walks. I made time to sleep. I learned how to say "no" to things when I was tired. I watched my diet. I was again becoming a human being instead of a robot.

During three months of recuperation, I rethought my life and clarified my values. As Nietzsche has observed, "If you stare long enough into the abyss, it begins to stare back." I had stared into the abyss of death and it made me a believer in life. I would face up to stress and make it friend, not foe.

Years later my wife testified to the difference it made after I decided to confront stress and do something about it. "You know, Bob," she said, "if you had died from your heart attack, I don't think the kids and I would have missed you. We never really knew you. If you were to die now, we would miss you very much."

Response and Analysis

1. What new insights about life did Robert Eliot have after his heart attack? How did these insights influence Eliot to change his lifestyle?

2. Eliot says that he brought on his own heart attack. What psychological, social, and cultural factors does Eliot suggest contributed to his heart attack?

3. How might stress contribute to coronary heart disease? What does the most recent research say about the relationship between stress and heart disease?

4. How can social support reduce the effects of stress, emotional distress, and vulnerability to illness?

Research

Before his heart attack, Robert Eliot displayed many of the characteristics associated with the type A behavior pattern. Suppose you are interested in whether the type A behavior pattern is a risk factor for coronary heart disease, independent of other known risk factors, such as heredity, smoking, diet, and substance abuse. You conduct a correlational study to examine the relationship between the type A and type B behavior patterns and the incidence of coronary heart disease. Your study, which takes place over a ten-year period, asks participants to complete surveys designed to determine whether their behaviors were consistent with the type A or type B pattern, and whether they developed coronary heart disease. Your results suggest that the type A behavior pattern is positively associated with coronary heart disease. Based on the results, could you conclude that the type A behavior pattern caused coronary heart disease? What alternative explanations might be relevant?

IN BED

Joan Didion

Psychological Concept
migraine headaches

Joan Didion is a novelist, essayist, journalist, and screenwriter. Her writings are diverse, from coauthoring the screenplay for *A Star Is Born* to her most recent fictional work, *The Last Thing He Wanted*, which deals with women journalists. Earlier works such as *Miami* and *El Salvador* reflect her concern for political refugees and civil rights.

Didion suffers from migraine headaches, a condition caused by changes in the size of cranial blood vessels. In the following essay, she tells of her battles and subsequent truces with them. When are migraines most likely to attack? Not when catastrophe strikes. Rather, they occur during small moments of frustration: when she has misplaced some item or when she has too many interruptions. Didion describes the physical manifestations of migraines and speaks of the misunderstandings that can occur with those who make false assumptions about migraine sufferers. Of special interest is Didion's solution to living with severe pain.

Three, four, sometimes five times a month, I spend the day in bed with a migraine headache, insensible to the world around me. Almost every day of every month, between these attacks, I feel the sudden irrational irritation and the flush of blood into the cerebral arteries which tell me that migraine is on its way, and I take certain drugs to avert its arrival. If I did not take the drugs, I would be able to function perhaps one day in four. The physiological error called migraine is, in brief, central to the given of my life. When I was 15, 16, even 25, I used to think that I could rid myself of this error by simply denying it, character over chemistry. "Do you have headaches *sometimes? frequently? never?*" the application forms would demand. "Check one." Wary of the trap, wanting whatever it was that the successful circumnavigation of that particular form could bring (a job, a scholarship, the respect of mankind, and the grace of God), I would check one. "*Sometimes,*" I would lie. That in fact I spent one or two days a week almost unconscious with pain seemed a shameful secret, evidence not merely of some chemical inferiority but of all my bad attitudes, unpleasant tempers, wrongthink.

For I had no brain tumor, no eyestrain, no high blood pressure, nothing wrong with me at all: I simply had migraine headaches, and migraine headaches were, as everyone who did not have them knew, imaginary. I fought migraine then, ignored the warnings it sent, went to school and later to work in spite of it, sat through lectures in Middle English and presentations to advertisers with involuntary tears running down the right side of my face, threw up in washrooms, stumbled home by instinct, emptied ice trays onto my bed and tried to freeze the pain in my right temple, wished only for a neurosurgeon who would do a lobotomy on house call, and cursed my imagination.

It was a long time before I began thinking mechanistically enough to accept migraine for what it was: something with which I would be living, the way some people live with diabetes. Migraine is something more than the fancy of a neurotic imagination. It is an essentially hereditary complex of symptoms, the most frequently noted but by no means the most unpleasant of which is a vascular headache of blinding severity, suffered by a surprising number of women, a fair number of men (Thomas Jefferson had migraine, and so did Ulysses S. Grant, the day he accepted Lee's surrender), and by some unfortunate children as young as two years old. (I had my first when I was eight. It came on during a fire drill at the Columbia School in Colorado Springs, Colorado. I was taken first home and then to the infirmary at Peterson Field, where my father was stationed. The Air Corps doctor prescribed an enema.) Almost anything can trigger a specific attack of migraine: stress, allergy, fatigue, an abrupt change in barometric pressure, a contretemps over a parking ticket. A flashing light. A fire drill. One inherits, of course, only the predisposition. In other words I spent yesterday in bed with a headache not merely because of my bad attitudes, unpleasant tempers, and wrongthink, but because both my grandmothers had migraine, my father has migraine, and my mother has migraine.

No one knows precisely what it is that is inherited. The chemistry of migraine, however, seems to have some connection with the nerve hormone named serotonin, which is naturally present in the brain. The amount of serotonin in the blood falls sharply at the onset of migraine, and one migraine drug, methysergide, or Sansert, seems to have some effect on serotonin. Methysergide is a derivative of lysergic acid (in fact Sandoz Pharmaceuticals first synthesized LSD-25 while looking for a migraine cure), and its use is hemmed about with so many contraindications and side effects that most doctors prescribe it only in the most incapacitating cases. Methysergide, when it is prescribed, is taken daily, as a preventive; another preventive which works for some people is old-fashioned ergotamine tartrate, which helps to constrict the swelling blood vessels during the "aura," the period which in most cases precedes the actual headache.

Once an attack is under way, however, no drug touches it. Migraine gives some people mild hallucinations, temporarily blinds others, shows up not only as a headache but as a gastrointestinal disturbance, a painful sensitivity to all sensory stimuli, an abrupt overpowering fatigue, a strokelike aphasia, and a crippling inability to make even the most routine connections. When I am in a migraine aura (for some people the aura lasts fifteen minutes, for others several hours), I will drive through red lights, lose the house keys, spill whatever I am holding, lose the ability to focus my eyes or frame coherent sentences, and generally give the appearance of being on drugs, or drunk. The actual headache, when it comes, brings with it chills, sweating, nausea, a debility that seems to stretch the very limits of endurance. That no one dies of migraine seems, to someone deep into an attack, an ambiguous blessing.

My husband also has migraine, which is unfortunate for him but fortunate for me: perhaps nothing so tends to prolong an attack as the accusing eye of someone who has never had a headache. "Why not take a couple of aspirin," the unafflicted will say from the doorway, or "I'd have a headache, too, spending a beautiful day like this inside with all the shades drawn." All of us who have migraine suffer not only from the attacks themselves but from this common conviction that we are perversely refusing to cure ourselves by taking a couple of aspirin, that we are making ourselves sick, that we "bring it on ourselves." And in the most immediate sense, the sense of why we have a headache this Tuesday and not last Thursday, of course we often do. There certainly is what doctors call a "migraine personality," and that personality tends to be ambitious, inward, intolerant of error, rather rigidly organized, perfectionist. "You don't look like a migraine personality," a doctor once said to me. "Your hair's messy. But I suppose you're a compulsive housekeeper." Actually my house is kept even more negligently than my hair, but the doctor was right nonetheless: perfectionism can also take the form of spending most of a week writing and rewriting and not writing a single paragraph.

But not all perfectionists have migraine, and not all migrainous people have migraine personalities. We do not escape heredity. I have tried in most of the available ways to escape my own migrainous heredity (at one point I learned to give myself two daily injections of histamine with a hypodermic needle, even though the needle so frightened me that I had to close my eyes when I did it), but I still have migraine. And I have learned now to live with it, learned when to expect it, how to outwit it, even how to regard it, when it does come, as more friend than lodger. We have reached a certain understanding, my migraine and I. It never comes when I am in real trouble. Tell me that my house is burned down, my husband has left me, that there is gunfighting in the streets and panic in the banks, and I will not respond by getting a headache. It comes instead when I am fighting not an open but a guerrilla war with my own life, during weeks of small household confusions, lost laundry, unhappy help, canceled appointments, on days when the telephone rings too much and I get no work done and the wind is coming up. On days like that my friend comes uninvited.

And once it comes, now that I am wise in its ways, I no longer fight it. I lie down and let it happen. At first every small apprehension is magnified, every anxiety a pounding terror. Then the pain comes, and I concentrate only on that. Right there is the usefulness of migraine, there in that imposed yoga, the concentration on the pain. For when the pain recedes, ten or twelve hours later, everything goes with it, all the hidden resentments, all the vain anxieties. The migraine has acted as a circuit breaker, and the fuses have emerged intact. There is a pleasant convalescent euphoria. I open the windows and feel the air, eat gratefully, sleep well. I notice the particular nature of a flower in a glass on the stair landing. I count my blessings.

Response and Analysis

1. How do migraine headaches affect Joan Didion's daily life? How does she manage the headaches?

2. What factors or conditions are likely to bring on a migraine headache? Why?

3. How might a person who is predisposed to migraine headaches control the onset of the headache? Discuss how relaxation training, biofeedback, and cognitive therapy might be used in the treatment of migraine headaches.

Research

Suppose you want to conduct a study to determine which biofeedback technique most effectively controls migraine headaches. Your study has one independent variable, biofeedback technique, which has three levels or conditions: (a) present a tone and a light when blood pressure lowers; (b) present a constant digital display of blood pressure; and (c) do not present any feedback about blood pressure. The dependent variable is a blood pressure reading that you can monitor in all three conditions.

You must now choose whether the participants should participate in all three conditions or in only one condition. If they participate in all three conditions, in what order should you present the conditions? For example, should the participants first hear the tone and see the light when their blood pressure lowers, then see a constant digital display, and then receive no feedback? Or should you vary the order in which you present the stimuli? Why?

List one advantage and one disadvantage to having the participants participate in (a) all three conditions; and (b) only one condition. Which approach will you choose? Why?

DAYS OF GRACE

Arthur Ashe and Arnold Rampersad

Psychological Concepts
AIDS, coping, social support

Tennis champion Arthur Ashe was only thirty-eight years old when he suffered a heart attack. Four years later, he had double-bypass heart surgery and received a blood transfusion to help him heal faster. That transfusion cost him his life: the blood was tainted with the human immunodeficiency virus (HIV). In February 1993, at the age of forty-nine, Ashe died of AIDS.

In his autobiography, Ashe says that the qualities that helped him cope with his illnesses were those that had shaped his character: respect for reputation, honor, discipline, and dignity. These he learned from his parents. Later, his tennis coach taught him sportsmanship: to behave with grace, to keep anger in control, and to not let despair take over. He knew that to give in to anxiety or fear—even for a second—could lose a game.

Ashe had lived with hardship from birth. When he was asked by a reporter if having AIDS was the heaviest burden of his life, he hesitated but a second and then replied, "No, it isn't. It's a burden all right . . . but being black is the greatest burden I've had to bear."

No one in my hospital room that day had to ask the question I knew would be on many people's minds, perhaps on most people's minds. But the rest of the world would ask: How had Arthur Ashe become infected?

To almost all Americans, AIDS meant one of two conditions: intravenous drug use or homosexuality. They had good reason to think so. Of the 210,000 reported cases of Americans, male and female, afflicted with AIDS by February 1992, 60 percent were men who had been sexually active with another man; about 23 percent had been intravenous illicit drug users; at least 6 percent more had been both homosexual and drug abusers; another 6 percent or so had been heterosexual; 2 percent had contracted the disease from blood transfusions; and 1 percent were persons with hemophilia or other blood-coagulant disorders.

The link between individual behavior and infection is crucial to AIDS. Indeed, AIDS was "discovered" in North America in 1980, when doctors in New York and Los Angeles noticed that an unusually high number of young male homosexuals had contracted *Pneumocystis carinii* pneumonia without the usual precondition, an immune system depressed by prescribed medicine. At about the same time, a normally quite rare disease, Kaposi's sarcoma, also began to spread; and once more the victims were young male homosexuals. Later that year, Dr. Michael Gottlieb at UCLA, a federally funded clinical investigator, was the first to notify the Centers for Disease Control about the puzzling outbreak of infections.

By the middle of the following year, the evidence was conclusive and alarming that a new disease was with us, and that it was becoming a nationwide epidemic. The search then began for its cause. After much hard work, HIV was isolated and identified in 1983. An individual tested positive for HIV when a blood test determined the presence in the blood of antibodies fighting the attack by the human immunodeficiency virus, or HIV. Then AIDS was finally defined as a combination in any person of HIV and one or more of over two dozen opportunistic diseases. The search for a cure continued—and continues. . . .

So how, the public would want to know, did Arthur Ashe contract AIDS? Had I been quietly shooting up heroin over the years? Or was I a closet homosexual or bisexual, hiding behind a marriage but pursuing and bedding men on the sly? . . .

The facts of the case are simple. Recovering from double-bypass heart surgery in 1983, I felt miserable even though I had experienced post-operative pain before. I can remember a conversation I had with a doctor in which I complained about feeling unbelievably low, and he laid out my options for me.

"You can wait it out, Arthur, and you'll feel better after a while," he said. "Or we can give you a couple of units of blood. That would be no problem at all."

"I would like the blood," I replied. I don't think I hesitated for a moment. Why feel miserable when a palliative is at hand? Surely there was nothing to be feared from the blood bank of a major American hospital, one of the most respected medical facilities in New York City. In fact, less than a month later, in July 1983, Margaret Heckler, President Reagan's Secretary of Health and Human Services, confidently made an announcement to the people of the United States: "The nation's blood supply is safe." Her words are etched in my memory. . . .

The news that I had AIDS hit me hard but did not knock me down. I had read of people committing suicide because of despair caused by infection with HIV. Indeed, in the preceding year, 1987, men suffering from AIDS were 10.5 times more likely to commit suicide than non-HIV-infected people who were otherwise similar to them.

In 1988, the AIDS suicide rate fell, but only to 7.4 times the expected rate. In 1990, it was 6 times the expected rate. The drop continued, but the far greater likelihood of suicide among AIDS patients persists, according to a 1992 issue of the *Journal of the American Medical Association*. (Incidentally, most of the HIV-infected men who kill themselves use prescription drugs to do so, instead of the guns that most male suicides use.) The main reason for the decline in this suicide rate, according to the report, was the general improvement in treatment, including the development of drugs that gave AIDS patients more hope. By 1992, however, the suicide rate was starting to rise again, as many of the therapies for AIDS, including those I was dependent on, began to show their limitations.

For me, suicide is out of the question. Despair is a state of mind to which I refuse to surrender. I resist moods of despondency because I know how they feed upon themselves and upon the despondent. I fight vigorously at the first sign of depression. I know that some depression can be physically induced, generated by the body rather than the mind. Such depression is obviously hard to contain. But depression caused by brooding on circumstances, especially circumstances one cannot avoid or over which one has no control, is another matter. I refuse to surrender myself to such a depression and have never suffered from it in my life.

Here is an area in which there are very close parallels between ordinary life and world-class athletic competition. The most important factor determining success in athletic competition is often the ability to control mood swings that result from unfavorable changes in the score. A close look at any athletic competition, and especially at facial expressions and body language, reveals that many individuals or even entire teams go into momentary lapses of confidence that often prove disastrous within a game or match. The ever-threatening danger, which I know well from experience, is that a momentary lapse will begin to deepen almost of its own accord. Once it is set in motion, it seems to gather enough momentum on its own to run its course. A few falling pebbles build into an avalanche. The initiative goes to one's opponent, who seems to be impossibly "hot" or "on a roll"; soon, victory is utterly out of one's reach. I've seen it happen to others on the tennis court; it has sometimes happened to me. In life-threatening situations, such as the one in which I now found myself, I knew that I had to do everything possible to keep this avalanche of deadly emotion from starting. One simply must not despair, even for a moment.

I cannot say that even the news that I have AIDS devastated me, or drove me into bitter reflection and depression even for a short time. I do not remember any night, from that first moment until now, when the thought of my AIDS condition and its fatality kept me from sleeping soundly. The physical discomfort may keep me up now and then, but not the psychological or philosophical discomfort.

I have been able to stay calm in part because my heart condition is a sufficient source of danger, were I to be terrified by illness. My first heart attack, in 1979, could have ended my life in a few chest-ravaging seconds. Both of my heart operations were major surgeries, with the risks attendant on all major surgery. And surely no brain operation is routine. Mainly because I have been through these battles with death, I have lost much of my fear of it.

I was not always that way. I had been a sickly child, but for most of the first thirty-six years of my life, until 1979, I nurtured a sense of myself as indestructible, if not actually immortal. This feeling persisted even after my heel surgery in 1977. For nine years since my first heart attack, however, I had been living with a powerful sense of my own mortality. And I have had many other signs, in the deaths of others, that have led me to think of my own end as something that could be imminent. So AIDS did not devastate me. AIDS was little more than something new to deal with, something new to understand and respond to, something to accept as a challenge, as if I might defeat it.

One can ready oneself for death. I see death as more of a dynamic than a static event. The actual physical manifestation of the absence of life is simply the ultimate step of a process that leads inevitably to that stage. In the interim, before the absolute end, one can do much to make life as meaningful as possible.

What would have devastated me was to discover that I had infected my wife, Jeanne, and my daughter, Camera. I do not think it would make any difference, on this score, whether I had contracted AIDS "innocently" from a blood transfusion or in one of the ways that most of society disapproves of, such as homosexual contacts or drug addiction. The overwhelming sense of guilt and shame would be the same in either case, if I had infected another human being.

A friend of mine has ventured the opinion that much as I love Jeanne, I am truly crazy about Camera. Well, Jeanne loves me, but I think she, too, is truly crazy about Camera. The thought that this beautiful child, not yet two years old, who has brought more pure joy into our lives than we had ever known before we laid eyes on her, could be infected with this horrible disease, because of me, was almost too much even to think about.

Both Jeanne and Camera were quickly tested. Both, thank God, were found to be free of any trace of HIV. Their testing has continued, and they remain free of infection. . . .

With AIDS, I have good days and bad days. The good days, thank goodness, greatly outnumber the bad. And the bad days are not unendurable. Mainly my stomach lets me down and I suffer from diarrhea. I take my pills, and I am disciplined enough to stick to my schedule. Sometimes I become a little tired, but I have learned anew to pace myself, to take short rests that invigorate me. In this matter of AIDS, as in so many aspects of my life, I am a lucky man.

I believe that there are five essential pillars to support the health and well-being of every individual. The first is unhindered access to physicians who will render primary care, listen to and advise the patient, and follow up with treatments in a professional manner. The second is the availability of medicines, treatments, and other therapies. The third is the support of family and friends. The fourth is the determination of the patient to make himself or herself better, to take charge of his or her well-being in cooperation with others. The fifth essential pillar is health insurance, because few people can bear the cost of a serious illness without falling irretrievably into debt. Take away any of these five pillars, I believe, and the structure of individual health and welfare starts to collapse.

I have been fortunate to have all five pillars solidly in place: excellent physicians, perhaps the best that can be had; the most efficacious medicines, no matter what the cost; the loving support of a skilled, intelligent spouse and the most loyal and resourceful group of friends anyone could have; self-reliance taught from my boyhood by my father but reinforced by decades of rigorous training in a sport based on individualism; and no fewer than three generous health-insurance policies.

AIDS does not make me despair, but unquestionably it often makes me somber. For some time I have wrestled with certain of Susan Sontag's ideas or insights in her remarkable books *Illness as Metaphor* and *AIDS and Its Metaphors*. In the former, inspired by her battle against cancer, Sontag writes about "the punitive or sentimental fantasies concocted about" illness, especially illnesses such as leprosy, tuberculosis, and cancer. "My point is that illness is *not* a metaphor, and that the most truthful way of regarding illness—and the healthiest way of being ill—is one purified of, most resistant to, metaphoric thinking." AIDS is not a metaphor for me, but a fact; and yet I find it hard to avoid its metaphoric energy, which is almost irresistible. I reject the notion that it is God's retribution for the sins of homosexuals and drug abusers, as some people argue, but on occasion I find its elements and properties peculiarly appropriate to our age.

I live in undeniable comfort—some would say luxury—in a spacious, lovely apartment high above Manhattan. When I venture out to walk the streets below, I see how others live who have not been dealt as generous a hand. I see poverty, usually with a face as dark as mine or darker, sitting on a box in front of my bank with a cup in her hand; or trudging wearily along the sidewalks; or fallen down into foul gutters. Around the corner, huddled on chilly stoops near the Greek Orthodox church, I see loneliness gnawing at human beings who surely deserve a far better fate. I hear madness crying out in the indifferent streets.

Sometimes, gloomily, I wonder about a connection between AIDS and where we in the United States are headed as a people and a nation as this century moves to a close. Too many people seem determined to forget that although we are of different colors and beliefs, we are all members of the same human race, united by much more than the factors and forces that separate us. Sometimes I wonder what is becoming of our vaunted American society, or even Western civilization, as an unmistakable darkness seems to settle over our lives and our history, blocking out the sun. Our national destiny, which at times seems as bright as in the past, sometimes also appears tragically foreshortened, even doomed, as the fabric of our society is threatened by endless waves of crime, by the weakening of our family structures, by the deterioration of our schools, and by the decline of religion and spiritual values. AIDS then takes on a specially ominous cast, as if in its savagery and mystery it mirrors our fate.

Surely we need to resist surrendering to such a fatalistic analogy. Some people profess to see little purpose to the struggle for life. And yet that is precisely the task to which, in my fight against the ravages of AIDS, I devote myself every day: the struggle for life, aided by science in my fight with this disease. I know that we are all, as human beings, going to our death, and that I may be called, because of AIDS, to go faster than most others. Still, I resolutely do battle with this opponent, as I boldly did battle with my opponents on the tennis court. True, this fight is different. The biggest difference is that I now fight not so much to win as not to lose. This enemy is different, too—dark and mysterious, springing on civilization just when civilization was sure that it had almost rid itself of mysterious beasts forever. But it must be fought with science, and with calm, clear thinking.

I know that I must govern that part of my imagination that endows AIDS with properties it does not intrinsically possess. I must be as resolute and poised as I can be in the face of its threat. I tell myself that I must never surrender to its power to terrify, even under its constant threat of death.

Response and Analysis

1. Arthur Ashe applied lessons that he learned through his professional tennis career and through other illnesses to help him cope with AIDS. Briefly describe an emotion-focused and problem-focused coping strategy he used.

2. Why was social support important to Ashe? How might social support reduce the effects of stress, emotional distress, and vulnerability to illness?

3. Ashe presented "five essential pillars to support the health and well-being of every indi-

vidual." What are the five pillars? Does psychological research suggest that any of these "pillars" positively promote health and well-being?

Research

Arthur Ashe believed that the support of family and friends is important to health and well-being. Suppose you want to design a study to test this idea. Write Ashe's idea in the form of a hypothesis. How might you measure social support? How might you assess health and well-being?

THORNS INTO FEATHERS:
COPING WITH CHRONIC ILLNESS

Floyd Skloot

Psychological Concepts
chronic fatigue syndrome, stress, coping

Floyd Skloot has chronic fatigue syndrome, a condition that affected his immune system, and his "balance, memory, abstract reasoning, concentration, coordination, and stamina." Skloot realized that only after he became sick did he really listen to his body. He recognized the need for significant changes in his lifestyle and moved with his family from Portland to the small town of Amity, Oregon, where the pace was slower. Skloot outlines the ways in which his adaptation to his body has enhanced his life. Skloot is an author and poet whose writings have appeared in *The American Scholar, The Harvard Review*, and *The Best American Essays of 1993*.

If you knew me five years ago, before I got sick, you would not know me now. Some of it is style, of course, or style reflecting substance. Cannot run anymore, so I have hand-carved hazelwood and cocobolo canes in place of running gear. Cannot work, so there is a wardrobe of baggy sweats or wildly patterned, floppy pants instead of the trim three-piece suits and shirts with snug collars. Look down and there are clogs instead of wing-tips, since for years it was a challenge just to tie my shoelaces. I wear a small hermatite ball in my left earlobe now and use fingers instead of a brush to manage my hair, which—like my beard—is shot with gray. Though it is no heavier, the lean and hard body that I worked so diligently to sculpt is much softer now. As my wife Beverly says, it seems like my armor is gone.

But it is more than style. A lifelong city boy, I now live in the country and love it, despite the spiders and carpenter ants, despite skunks and the occasional porcupine, despite poison oak or a well that threatens to go dry and its iron-rich water that stains me amber. And I am slow now. I used to move through my world like a halfback, zigging and zagging, always trying for that extra yard, very difficult to bring down. Now I conserve, I loiter, I move as in a dream; because if I don't, I will either fall or smack into something. But of this necessity has come a whole new way of being in my life. This goes for talking too, which I do at a more leisurely pace, interspersed now with actual listening. Something different and vital has emerged. My secret is that I have found the places within me that illness could not touch. I have learned to honor them. . . .

I averaged four-hours-a-day supine and surrounded by classical music during the first two years of my illness. It was not all sweetness and light: sometimes music took me to the very center of my experience, to the conflicts I was feeling about all that had changed in my life, to the vortex of emotions. But sometimes it took me outside myself altogether, into a realm of pure sound where there could be peace. . . .

Without music, I would still have survived. But music helped me understand that my body's score had been completely revised. The symphony now included an extended movement of deep discord, a dark and confusing interlude that would, however, end up in a place worth knowing, provided that I listened well.

This was a deep, intuitive way to understand what my illness—Chronic Fatigue Syndrome—does to the body, throwing its intricately balanced, complex systems into disarray so that nothing works as expected any more, a cacophony of symptoms. Calling it Chronic Fatigue Syndrome is like calling Beethoven's Ninth Symphony a little music recital. It is like calling polio Chronic Stiffness Syndrome. A viral infection I had in December 1988 started it all. The infection, which probably targeted my brain, triggered an immune system cascade that my brain has never been able to turn off. Blood flow to the brain stem is reduced. Balance, memory, abstract reasoning, concentration, coordination, and stamina are damaged. I look away from people when I talk to them because their physical responses make me forget what I am saying. I often cannot find words that are in my vocabulary, so there are either long pauses while I search for them or I become a chorus of malapropisms, given to such pronouncements as "the charms are burning" instead of "the leaves are turning," or to saying over the dinner table, for reasons I still cannot figure out, "cross the bristle."

This is not the way I used to be. But music has taught me my being could still contain harmony, if I could only hear the whole thing through.

Or take time. I have come to see that it is entirely possible to do just that, to *take* time, to seize control of it rather than be controlled by it. Paradoxically, the way to take control of time is to let it go altogether.

Time changes when a person is chronically ill. Often alone, I experienced the timelessness of solitude, the way everything slows down long enough to speed up while a person is immersed in illness. Though John Donne says, in his fifth devotion, that "as sickness is the greatest misery, so the greatest misery of sickness is solitude," I did not find this to be true for me. Solitude became a kind of chamber in which my separation from time and the world of measured change made sense. Because I was removed from the world of work—meetings, lunches, schedules, deadlines—and outside the rhythm of a traditional day—I found that a week's very shape was lost. Days dragged by. Unless people were coming over to visit or I had a doctor's appointment, it hardly mattered what time it was.

Soon I learned to eat when I was hungry and sleep when I was tired. I found that I did not have to eat three meals a day, or eat at fixed times; I could graze all day long if I wanted to. I found myself approaching sleep the same way. I napped a couple of hours in the morning and again in the afternoon because that was when I was too tired to be awake.

Finally, I weaned myself from the constant measuring of slow change that accompanies chronic illness. I gave up the thrice-daily graphing of body temperature (mine was sub-normal) and the compilation of sleep totals. I stopped weighing myself every morning. Oddly enough, all these changes did was provide a sense of greater control. "What poor elements are our happinesses made of," Donne writes in his fourteenth devotion, "if time, time which we can scarce consider to be any thing, be an essential part of our happiness!" The man certainly had a point.

None of this should have been surprising to me. Before getting sick, I would have said that as a competitive runner I knew my body and its needs. That was why I was running, to help body and soul deal with working full-time, being a parent to my children and the family's chief cook, and writing for a couple of hours every night. Time was a matter of being where I had to be when I had to be there; it was a matter of pace and records to beat. Good runners, the books and magazines said, listened to their bodies; I was one of those listeners.

Baloney. After getting sick, I saw that I might have listened to my body before, but did not really hear it.

So time, and the way my body functioned in time, turned out to be something I did not understand until getting sick. Time turns out to be a truly inner phenomenon. Despite clocks, agendas, and appointments, regardless of records, goals, and setting aside calendars, time measured how I experienced my self moving through my life. My illness had not stolen time from me after all; it had instead placed time in my own hands.

Then there is love. I am talking about passionate, intense love, the kind of connection that seems impossible when someone is seriously and chronically ill. The kind that comes from so deep inside, the place seems to have been closed off by illness. Or worse, poisoned by it.

People who are sick frequently despair of loving like this. It seems so difficult to sustain if they are married and ill; finding it is beyond imagining if they are single and ill. If fortunate, they might have something else in their lives, a supportive, nurturing love, familiar and comfortable, that becomes romance's version of the sick-bed: a place to rest, to convalesce, to take care.

Ill and weakened, I was no longer the person who knew himself capable of passion's true eloquence. I felt as removed from it as from the rest of my old life's defining activities. It was astounding to feel passion touch the arid places within me and saturate them, reaching me where I had given up hope of ever being reached again. Then astonishment was replaced by the understanding that I must act on what I felt, that I could and must respond to the erotic feelings I was capable of having. Not that I could suddenly run a marathon again, or spell and do math reliably; not that I could remember birthdates, or walk without a cane, or get through a day without at least one long nap. Of course I could not miraculously function as though my central nervous system and immune system were normal again. But I found that Eros can be a healing power, assertive of life's wonder and surviving force.

So is touch. For years before we married, Beverly was my massage therapist, bringing me the healing power of touch. We were never intimate in the sense of being lovers then; Beverly would never compromise her professional ethics. But we became close friends through those years—me lying there with my eyes closed, the sheets smelling of sweet almond oil, Beverly moving around me for an hour with her powerful hands, her resonant voice becoming familiar as a recurring dream while we spoke softly to one another about our lives. In my illness there have been times when my joints and bones were so tender that her touch nearly jolted me from the table, but we found a way to manage that pain and bring ease to my body. I think we built a connection based on shared openness, on the sonorousness of intimate conversation.

"The disease hath established a kingdom," Donne writes in his tenth devotion, "an empire in me." It often seems to those who live there that passion has been banished from the land. Curiously, I found it locked in the Emperor's own dungeon and together with Beverly set it free.

For all they take away, chronic pain and illness also bring opportunity. The great challenge is to cope, but coping may not mean what people initially think it means.

The word "cope" comes from the Latin for "strike" or "blow." It implies activity, not passivity, engagement rather than withdrawal. I think it is among our signal responsibilities to accept the opportunities illness brings us and do something with them. That is how we cope, fighting back at the diseases which challenge us.

In his seventeenth devotion, Donne says "affliction is a treasure, and scarce any man hath enough of it." I cannot say that I agree with him there, but I am with him when he goes on to say, "No man hath affliction enough that is not matured and ripened by it."

Now I live in a round house Beverly built in the middle of twenty hilly acres above a small town called Amity in the Willamette Valley. How appropriate that the word *amity* means "peaceful relations," since this is the place where I have found the peace that is part of converting the thorns of illness into feathers. From the room where I write for the one or two hours a day that I *can* write, I see the pond that Beverly dug amid Douglas fir, maple, wild cherry, and scrub oak. One of the cats is plump, queenly Zola, who looks far too equable to be the fierce hunter—has just sashayed past the window, a mouse dangling from her mouth. Two Adirondack chairs scream "Spring will come! Spring will come!" while rakishly tilting back toward a winter sun that has not yet burned through the fog. Beverly bought and painted them magenta over two years ago, on that first weekend she brought me out here from Portland.

I am not saying that listening to music, modifying eating and sleeping habits, loving, and moving to the country will give control of a life taken over by illness and pain. For each person, surely, the details will vary, the untouched places will be different. But finding the places within that illness cannot reach, and learning to honor them, can help transform the bed of thorns that is illness.

Response and Analysis

1. How has living with chronic fatigue syndrome changed Floyd Skloot's daily life? His social relationships? Life with his wife?

2. People may use one or more coping strategies to deal with stressful situations. How does Skloot use emotion-focused and problem-focused coping strategies to deal with chronic fatigue syndrome?

3. How has chronic fatigue syndrome affected Skloot's memory, abstract reasoning, and concentration? What challenges do they create for Skloot and his family?

Research

Suppose you want to conduct a cross-cultural study to examine how persons suffering from chronic illness cope with their conditions. You will recruit persons in the United States, France, Malaysia, South Africa, and Russia to participate in the study. The participants will complete a standardized questionnaire that measures coping behaviors.

How might differences in socioeconomic status, education, size of the community in which the participants live, and number of family members living in the home influence the results? What other possible confounding variables might influence the findings? How could you minimize the influence of these variables?

chapter 7

SCHIZOPHRENIA

*When I first had the breakdown, it was
like dropping an egg on the kitchen floor.
Part of the shell is still intact, but part of
it's shattered, and my personality is the
yolk, leaking away. And I cannot get it
back together.*

ANNE DEVESON, *Tell Me I'm Here*

Schizophrenia is a brutal illness. Imagine suddenly hearing a voice come to you at unexpected moments, giving you orders, making cruel or bizarre comments. You are sure the voices are real: You hear them clearly. What do you do as these voices continue to speak to you daily? Your once orderly world becomes chaotic, setting you adrift.

Those who suffer from schizophrenia may hear such imaginary voices coming from strangers on the street, from pictures hanging on a wall, from talk show hosts on television. They often have great difficulty maintaining a train of thought. Their once orderly, coherent world becomes more than chaotic; it has the sensation, said one young man, of rats eating away at the brain. In addition to difficulty organizing thoughts, persons with schizophrenia often experience delusions, persistently held illogical beliefs (such as the belief that aliens are transmitting personal messages through one's dental work). They might also have hallucinations—sensations and perceptions not attributable to environmental stimuli (such as having the sensation of bugs crawling on the skin or hearing voices). The disorder strikes most often in the late teens, but symptoms of the disorder can begin in childhood, or later in life.

Schizophrenia can be characterized by the presence of positive symptoms, such as delusions, hallucinations, disorganized speech, or bizarre behavior. It can also be characterized by negative symptoms, deficits such as flattened affect or social withdrawal. Diagnosis can be difficult because other disorders can produce symptoms similar to schizophrenia. For instance, severe mania in bipolar disorder or extreme anxiety in obsessive-compulsive disorder can produce psychotic symptoms, as can drug-induced psychosis.

This chapter presents the stories of three people suffering from schizophrenia.

The first is written by Carol S. North, who had been hospitalized frequently and diagnosed with schizophrenia before she finished medical school. North had been plagued by voices giving her directions, by suspicions that the air dust she breathed may have been particles from King Tut's body "floating aimlessly on the wind for centuries." With the help of Dr. Hemingway and some experimental therapy, North recovered and is now a practicing psychiatrist.

The second story is written by the mother of a young man who had shown some early signs of schizophrenia. Jonathan's boyhood was relatively uneventful; he was a bit high strung, but he did well in school, loved art, and was advanced in general knowledge. When he entered high school, the disorder began to develop in full. He threw food on the floor, spoke incoherently, became violent, and threatened his family. Anne Deveson's powerful account conveys not only the pain the family suffered but the anguish that eventually led Jonathan to take his life.

The third story is that of Allan Davis. When Davis was a junior at Princeton University, he began to believe that people on television were talking to and about him. Over time, he developed a delusional belief system focused on sexuality, secret codes, and organized crime. Davis, now in his forties, lived several chaotic years before he found a treatment program that helped him. Here he details his experiences with schizophrenia and the treatment program.

WELCOME SILENCE: MY TRIUMPH OVER SCHIZOPHRENIA

Carol S. North

Psychological Concept
schizophrenia

When Carol S. North was in medical school and studying the physiology of heart sounds, she put the stethoscope to her own heart and heard the barking of dogs, a barking that had come to her at odd moments since the time she had attended dog surgery labs. When she took an exam, voices told her which answers to give (she failed the test). On another occasion, when she was studying at home and let her bird out of its cage, the bird landed on her head and North felt messages coming to her brain from the bird. Other times, she believed that plants in her home were engulfing her or that the spirit world was controlling her body. Faculty and friends suggested that she seek help, and in the segment that follows, North tells of her first visit to Dr. Hemingway, a psychiatrist. North desperately wanted to stay in medical school, and she didn't want him to learn that she had previously been hospitalized for psychiatric problems. Here we see North's description of her behavior, thoughts, and feelings during her interview, and some of Dr. Hemingway's perceptions.

The psychiatrist was sitting behind his desk waiting for me to arrive. It was eight-thirty to the exact second. I thought that would make a good impression; my punctuality would demonstrate that I was sane and had things well under control.

He didn't seem to notice that I was on time.

"Carol?" he asked. "Are you Carol North?"

I nodded.

"Hi, I'm Dr. Hemingway."

"Hemingway, ocean spray. Love is blind, wined, and dined."

The voices were apparently still with me. I couldn't locate the speakers they were blaring from.

I took a closer look at Dr. Hemingway and wilted. This guy looked like a true Freud. He appeared to be in his fifties, and his beard and hair were pure white. He wore little round wire-rim spectacles which somehow seemed to complete the professorial effect of his tidy three-piece plaid wool suit. This guy did not look as if he would understand anything. I doubted he had ever had any metaphysical experiences like mine.

"What brought you here today?" he asked.

At first I thought he meant my car, but then he politely rephrased his query to ask what kind of problems I was having. I told him I had been treated for psychiatric problems in the past, but I didn't say that I had been in this hospital, or that I had been having psychiatric symptoms continuously ever since. I didn't want him to think I was a crazy, hopeless case.

He sat quietly while I described the disruptions in my concentration caused by the barking dogs in the lectures and in the stethoscopes. I told him I was having problems understanding exam questions and that they got me all mixed up, although I wasn't sure exactly how. Feeling guilty, I added that I'd been skipping too many classes. But, I explained, this was only because I couldn't make much sense out of the lectures and my time would be better spent at home studying or sleeping.

After a moment's pause to reflect over what I'd said and to think if there was anything I might have left out, I added, "I can't concentrate when I'm hearing the voices." (That was enough; I didn't want to have to tell him all about the Other Worlds' phenomena because it would have taken all day.)

Suddenly the voices turned on their Echo Machine, to get me to shut up about them, I supposed. My words didn't sound at all normal. They echoed. Next I heard Frank Zappa and the Mothers of Invention singing "Who Are the Brain Police?" behind the wall, with more echoes. It all sounded increasingly sinister. So many things had seemed sinister lately. Yes, there was something going on today.

"Where do these voices come from?" The doctor's voice was echoing just as everything else was.

"I don't know, exactly. I think they're from somewhere else."

He looked puzzled. Twitching his eyebrows, he repeated, "From somewhere else?"

I nodded. "Yeah. Sometimes they come through speakers that are disguised in the walls. I can't ever find them."

"What do the voices say?"

His echo was starting to bother me.

"I can't always understand them," I tried to explain. "Sometimes they repeat snatches of conversation or make rhymes to it. How they sometimes sound is like they're having a cocktail party in the next room and I can make out only some of the words or phrases. It doesn't make a lot of sense."

I wished that frigging Echo Machine would quit. It made it hard to concentrate on the discussion.

I had to work hard to stay on the same subject. It took me a while to reconnect my thoughts. Finally, I resumed speaking, hoping I hadn't drifted too far. "Sometimes the voices talk about what I'm doing, like they're sports commentators, saying things like 'She is walking out of the Medical Sciences Building' or 'She doesn't know it but she's about to flunk this exam'—only they say things very calmly. Or they might tell me to do something ridiculous like walk across town and back in the middle of the night. A few times they've wakened me in the night by yelling in my ear, and I've been too scared to get back to sleep."

"You appear to be having some trouble concentrating on what you're saying today," said Dr. Hemingway. "Is there any particular problem?"

"Well, yes. They have sound-effect machines. Like now they are using an Echo Machine that makes both of our voices reverberate, and that bothers me so I can't think very well. There are other machines like the Barking Dogs Machine and the Helicopter Machine that they can use to produce sounds out of nowhere. Sometimes I can't tell whether noises are my neighbors or the sound-effects machines."

I felt creepy talking about the voices. It was like talking about them behind their backs, except even worse because I knew they knew what I was saying about them. I hoped I hadn't gotten them irritated. The consequences could be severe. They could transform my next exam score from passing to failing at a whim.

"Do you ever hear your thoughts as if they had been spoken aloud?" Dr. Hemingway asked.

Wow, how does he know about that? Has he been reading my mind? I glared at him.

Finally I responded to his question: "Yes, I hear my thoughts out loud. In lecture. It bothers me." I wanted to cooperate yet not reveal too much now. I needed his help for my exams.

"Do you think other people can read your mind?" he probed.

Amazing how he knew about that too! Maybe he'd been listening to the same voices. "Yes," I said. "That's been a big problem for me."

He did seem to have good empathy. He was listening intently to everything I said. Nodding slowly, he muttered, "Mm-hmm," as if he was thinking hard. He didn't look totally convinced. "How do you know people are reading your thoughts?"

"My head's transparent. I can't protect my thoughts. Some one sucks all the thoughts out of my head and then I can't say anything because I don't have any thoughts left to say."

"Can you give me an example? When was the last time that happened?"

I felt my skin turning gray and starting to slide off my forearms right there in the psychiatrist's office. The sensation was so alarming that I couldn't possibly think to answer his question. It took all my concentration just to hold on to my skin. I was too embarrassed to tell him about my skin problem because I was sure it was a result of mental weakness.

"Is there some reason why you aren't saying anything?" he asked, firing off multiple twitches from his eyebrows. "Has someone stolen your thoughts? Do you think I have stolen your thoughts?"

His twitches had to be an anxiety gauge or a puzzlement gauge. I didn't know which. I thought it would probably be better for me to tell him about my skin problem than for him to hear it from the voices or pick it up from my own thought waves. I explained to him that I had been quiet for a minute because I had been using all my concentration to keep my forearm skin from sliding off.

He offered up another "Mm-hmm."

"The shrink is pink," said Hal.

I started to smile, but stopped myself. Hal was right. That was funny.

Dr. Hemingway asked me various other questions about my life, including my medical and family history, educational background, and current living arrangements. Then he announced, "I'd like to prescribe you some medicine. If things get bad enough for you, you might have to quit school or go into the hospital."

Just as I'd suspected. If this guy was going to talk about my quitting school and hospitalization or other ruinous alternatives, he wasn't going to be any help at all. What I needed was someone to help me stay *in* school, not help me *out*. What I needed was a way to be strong against the Forces of Chaos. Couldn't he see my problem was essentially spiritual, even cosmic—and not really psychiatric at all? I refused even to think of hospitalization or quitting school.

To appease Dr. Hemingway I agreed to take small amounts of Navane, a major antipsychotic tranquilizer that he prescribed for me. That would make me seem cooperative and might help buy time until he could understand my problem in its broader sense and give me some real help. But I warned him that if the medicine made me groggy or sluggish or otherwise interfered with my schoolwork, I would have to discontinue it immediately. I needed my energy and my resources for medical school.

Dr. Hemingway wanted to see me again on Monday.

After I left he dictated a note which included the following statements about me:

> The patient looks rather quiet, answers questions with some degree of thought disorder, and has trouble such as reaching her goal. She appears somewhat confused about her thought processes and what is going on and about the meaning which she sees in many things. There is no push of speech, no flight of ideas. She seems to be on the concerned and sober side. Occasionally, answers are somewhat retarded. She appears to have some insight into her illness, but this is definitely impaired. Judgment also seems to be impaired. Impression: probable schizophreniform illness. The history of an acute episode a number of years ago with rather relatively good health in between would seem to support this, although the possibility of a manic-depressive illness cannot be ruled out.

The following Monday I returned to Dr. Hemingway's office for the follow-up appointment he had scheduled. I didn't know that in the interim he had found my old hospital record.

The first thing Dr. Hemingway wanted to know was whether I was having any problem with the Navane. As he studied my face, his bushy white eyebrows arched upward and then subtly furrowed into his wire-rim glasses. Simultaneously his nose twitched.

That is undoubtedly a signal. This is some kind of a test. He has somehow observed me all weekend and is now fully equipped to detect the inconsistency or lie that he is expecting me to blurt out.

The voices might have filled him in on the details. He couldn't be trusted.

I couldn't decide what to say. I wanted to accuse him outright. But I didn't know exactly what to accuse him of. I would have to pretend I didn't know anything until I had more evidence. The conflicting thoughts about what to say collided with each other in my brain and vaporized, leaving a vacuum where the thoughts were just a second before.

I felt pressured. He was sitting there twitching his eyebrows and nose and mustache, waiting for me to answer his question. I didn't have any thoughts, so how could I answer his question? I had to think of something to say quickly, something consistent. He was still twitching and waiting.

I was falling through space and time again, only he couldn't tell that. I was the only one who could tell.

He broke my fall by speaking. Instantly I had thoughts again.

"Did you take the Navane?" he asked.

"Yes," I answered him in the most normal voice I could summon. It didn't sound like my voice. The voices must have put in a substitute.

The doctor was grinning. He was frowning, too. His face was one huge grin-frown.

"Did you have any problem with the medicine?" he asked again.

With my substitute voice I projected the words "I'm a bit dizzy when I first wake up in the morning." I wondered what they'd done with my usual voice.

"That dizziness is just a side effect which should wear off in a few days," he told me. "Until then, don't stand up too fast first thing in the morning."

His facial expression began to alternate between grinning and frowning at a speed of about four times a second. That made it nearly impossible for me to be able to read his true facial expression. He didn't appear to be so intent on catching me in an inconsistency or a lie now. He looked more trustworthy. Maybe I had misjudged him.

"What did you do this weekend?" he asked.

That sounded like a reasonably innocent question. I relaxed a little.

"Well, you remember on Friday I told you I had to move to a different apartment last month?"

"Oh yes, after the spring rains when your roof leaked so bad?" His eyebrows and nose twitched noticeably as he spoke.

"Right. Yesterday just before dawn I sneaked back to see the old apartment," I continued, still trying to sound as normal as I could. "I got in because I kept a duplicate key." I was doing fine, I thought.

"Well, what did you see?" His twitches were becoming almost rhythmic.

Maybe his twitches meant he knew the answer to his question. I didn't even need to tell him, since he knew. I studied his grinfrown for a minute. The sentence "What did you see?" echoed around in my head several times until I didn't know whether I'd said it or he'd said it or maybe even the voices had said it. He looked as if he expected me to say something. I didn't know what we were talking about anymore.

It was up to me to fill the silence.

Dr. Hemingway's office was dusty. I was inhaling dust particles into my lungs. No telling where all those dust particles had come from. Some of the molecules in the air might have diffused from someone passing gas earlier and now I was breathing them in. Maybe one of the dust particles I was breathing had come from breaking off of King Tut's body and floating aimlessly on the wind for centuries, to finally wander into this room. This was a conceptual equivalent of the Interference

Patterns. Maybe some plants had once incorporated a few atoms originally from Joan of Arc's body into their structure and then a cow had eaten the plants and defecated on the ground and some oats growing out of that soil had taken nourishment from the cow manure and had eventually been harvested and processed, and I had consumed the famous atoms in my Cheerios that morning! The idea became fixed in my head. This had happened, without a doubt.

"I am breathing King Tut and I have swallowed Joan of Arc," I told Dr. Hemingway. This was a very profound thought. It seemed intrinsically relevant to the discussion because of its profundity, although I was not quite sure how it related. The depth of its profundity seemed to far outweigh any qualms I had about saying it. It had been a good statement and would at least get the conversation moving again. The responsibility of making the next contribution to the discussion would be off my shoulders for the moment.

"Mm-hmmmm." Dr. Hemingway was momentarily taken aback by the absurdity of my statement.

I was still marveling at the brilliance of my observation when Dr. Hemingway said, "But what do swallowing Joan of Arc and breathing King Tut have to do with how your apartment looked?"

I felt my cheeks burning hot from the inside out. He must have been simultaneously seeing my cheeks turn cherry-red from the outside in. I was embarrassed that I had gotten mixed up and forgotten that we were talking about my old apartment, and then said something completely off the wall. Was Dr. Hemingway trying to trick me?

Dr. Hemingway pretended I hadn't said anything crazy. "Tell me about your old apartment," he said.

I was relieved he chose not to embarrass me further by making a big deal out of my confusion. "Well," I said, "when I got up to Megan's[1] old room I saw the ceiling bulging downward. The bulging was a Sign that the Other Worlds are impinging on this world, right? Pretty soon it will all come crashing in. Isn't that what it means?"

Dr. Hemingway didn't answer my question. He was twitching a lot. I couldn't tell for sure, but I thought he looked worried.

"I know it's true," I said soberly, "because I felt a touch of the SuperReal when I saw it." The SuperReal was such a profoundly significant concept that I couldn't convey its meaning to him in ordinary words. Instead I translated the concept into wordless thought waves which I transmitted to him through the air medium linking our minds. He didn't look at all receptive. I was finding communication with him difficult.

"Something else I saw over there upset me," I heard my substitute voice say.

That elicited a double-twitch response of his eyebrows.

"There were little green plants growing out of the carpet in Megan's old room. I didn't know what to make of them."

"Mm-hmm," he said along with his next facial twitch. It sounded like an mm-hmm of disbelief to me.

---

[1] North's former neighbor

"But I *saw* them," I insisted. "They were really there. There were about five or six of them. They were about six inches tall, all single stalks. A couple of them even had little buds on their tips."

"Mm-hmm," he responded again. This doctor sure wasn't too quick with original responses. "Has Megan seen the little green plants?"

This was hopeless. Dr. Hemingway would never believe me, much less be able to offer an acceptable interpretation of these Signs. "No, I haven't shown them to her yet," I said, making a mental note to do just that.

He twitched again to signal a change of subject. He hadn't seemed satisfied with the last one. I hoped the next would be easier to discuss.

"Were you able to study over the weekend?" he asked.

I wished he'd quit twitching. It made me nervous. I still suspected it was some kind of signal. I answered his question: "I studied the whole weekend, but it was hard to concentrate because of the interference."

I anticipated another twitch from him at this point, but he just sat back in his chair grinfrowning.

I must have judged him right in the first place. I interpreted his ambiguous grinfrown to mean that he already knew about the interference, most likely from the voices. He was carefully poised in readiness for a swift pounce on me with a shocking verbal assault as soon as I said the wrong thing. He had all the evidence he needed to incriminate me. I shouldn't have let him in on such a personal concept as the interference.

"Can you tell me a little bit about the interference?" he asked, looking sincerely interested now. He was starting to back off.

Now I felt a little safer. I answered, "The interference is like static on the radio. It—well, it interferes."

"Interferes?" he asked. "How?" His face appeared immensely friendlier than it had a minute before. I had never been able to judge faces.

"It impinges," I explained further. "Like the voices. Like the barking dogs."

"Can you be more specific—to help me understand a little better?" He looked as if he sincerely wanted to understand. Nobody had ever responded to me like this before. In the past, people had just dismissed me as some kind of nut, instead of showing interest in my ideas like the OtherWorldly phenomena. I knew the Other Worlds weren't a delusion I had cooked up out of a state of mental derangement. They couldn't be. Delusions were simpler than that, like when people thought the FBI was after them. The Other Worlds were far too sophisticated and intricate to be a delusion. And they stood up under too many kinds of logic. They had too much consistency and reliability over time to be false. I wanted Dr. Hemingway to understand that.

I explained, "The interference is other things besides voices, helicopters, and barking dogs. It's also patterns. The patterns jump around and flow in and out of each other and change colors. They march over walls, spaces, and people's faces— like radio static, but only in the visual sense. The interference spills into our perceptual grounds from leaks from other systems. *You* can see and hear it, I think. You have the capability within you now, but you have to learn how to perceive—

just as the medical student must learn how to appreciate subtle clinical nuances that seem obvious to the seasoned physician."

I paused, but Dr. Hemingway was listening intently, expecting me to finish.

I continued, "I think everybody sees the interference—but they haven't learned to recognize what they're observing." That was what I meant to say, but I actually conveyed only about half of it, leaving Dr. Hemingway wondering what exactly I was trying to tell him.

He nodded thoughtfully. If I could get him to see that I had stumbled onto other dimensions, he might be my key to enlightening the world. People would be more likely to listen to a psychiatrist than to a former mental patient labeled schizophrenic.

"Have you ever discovered your phosphenes?" I asked him.

I could see I'd lost him there.

"Phosphenes," I explained, "are the brilliant colored patterns you see when you close your eyes and press on your eyeballs with your fingers. Try it."

"I know what those are," he said. "I've seen them."

"Good. The interference looks something like them."

I felt I was starting to fall again. It was going to be difficult trying to explain things with this happening.

Dr. Hemingway persisted with his own questions: "Can you tell me about this SuperReal feeling you mentioned?"

"SuperReal, reel-to-reel banana peel," I heard one of the voices say playfully from a far-off world.

That was funny. I tried to subdue an uncontrollable smile.

Dr. Hemingway responded with the slightest hint of an involuntary grin and asked, "What about this SuperReal feeling? What's that like?" He was trying not to acknowledge my smile.

I managed to get my mouth straight again and explain, "The SuperReal is a feeling of reality that is stronger and harsher than the usual reality I know—it's like biting down on something cold when you have a cavity. It impinges, like the inter-ference. It's a feeling that overwhelms me when we collide with the Parallel Worlds and part of their systems leak into this one."

Dr. Hemingway looked puzzled. He couldn't understand why I believed such absurd ideas. (What he didn't understand was that schizophrenic logic transcended ordinary logic.) I couldn't explain the SuperReal to him. He was in the wrong logic set. There weren't earth words to describe it. "SuperReal" was the closest I could come to describing it.

"What are these Other Worlds you keep telling me about?" he asked. "What's it like over there?"

I thought back to my last visit to the Other Side. Right then I was sitting on the wrong side of the SuperReal Barrier to be able to tell him about it. My mind over here couldn't grasp it. His probably couldn't either. I could only suggest vaguely that it was totally different from here. It was something you just had to experience for yourself.

Dr. Hemingway was still wearing his grinfrown. He hadn't stopped grin-frowning for more than a few seconds while I'd been talking to him. I wanted to ask him about it, but I thought maybe I was already supposed to know somehow, so I didn't ask. I didn't want to look stupid.

The unmistakable putter of a helicopter vibrated through the windowpane right behind Dr. Hemingway. He pretended not to notice it.

Why? Was he somehow involved in it? Had he informed them of my whereabouts? I tried to block my thoughts out completely in hopes that the helicopters couldn't locate me by homing in on my thought waves.

After an insufferably long minute the helicopter faded into the nondescript drone of the background interference, and I no longer heard it. I was aware that neither Dr. Hemingway nor I had said anything for quite a while. His twitch had quit. He was looking directly into my eyes. I thought he was trying to read my naked thoughts right through my pupils. He had me under some kind of a spell. It felt creepy. He was doing it with the power of his eyes. He was hypnotizing me. He could make me do weird things. He could make me do things I didn't want to do.

Well, stop staring at him, then!

But I couldn't.

"I'm going to increase your Navane from ten to fifteen milligrams a day," he said. "And I'd like you to come back and see me again in a week. Can you do that?" he said with another twitch.

I was under his spell. He could make me do that. I couldn't possibly fail.

He set me up another appointment for the following Monday. As Dr. Hemingway opened the door to his office, Hal announced, "You're leaving Dr. Hemingway's office now. You're about to step off the edge of the earth."

I gazed out the door in the direction of the voice. I looked back at Dr. Hemingway. He hadn't heard the voice. Well, then, I hadn't either.

"See you next Monday," he said as I stepped into the hallway with my book pack over my shoulder. I didn't glance back.

Dr. Hemingway dictated the following note:

> It turns out that Miss North has a very large record compiled here at the psychiatric hospital with at least one admission here, numerous outpatient visits. On the occasion of her admission to the hospital . . . she was diagnosed as catatonic schizophrenic. Apparently, when admitted to the hospital, she showed many of the present symptoms which she is complaining of. It is evident that this girl has had a serious and possibly chronic condition going back . . . at least [four years] but has been able to function reasonably effectively in the school situation despite the chronicity of her complaints.

As I changed into my sweat clothes to prepare for my morning jog my breasts felt lumpy and tender. This had to be a side effect of the Navane. I'd also gained several pounds, thanks to the medicine. But the worst side effect was when I started finding wet spots on the front of my blouses, also from the Navane. I phoned Dr. Hemingway to complain that the medicine was making my breasts leak milk. Having previously experienced psychiatrists who were intolerant of "patient noncompliance," I thought Dr. Hemingway might get all huffy and demand that I either cooperate or terminate treatment. But at this point I didn't care; I couldn't tolerate these side effects.

To my surprise, he was sympathetic. He told me I was apparently very sensitive to side effects of drugs, and he elected to switch my medicine to small doses of a different antipsychotic tranquilizer, Haldol. I had had trouble with Haldol when I was being treated by Dr. Falmouth, but the doses had been large. Dr. Hemingway began my dose at a minimal half milligram at bedtime, and over the next week he gradually increased it to four milligrams. After a few days I began to notice that the voices were not bothering me quite as continuously, and that the interference was growing fainter and less disruptive.

I continued regular appointments with Dr. Hemingway. I began thinking it was time to be honest with him. He seemed trustworthy. I decided he knew me well enough by now that his opinions of me were already formed and he might not be so likely to be swayed by my old records if he read them now. . . .

"Keep taking the Haldol," he advised me. "It should help stop those confusing thoughts and the voices too. It will probably make it easier for you to study."

That's exactly what I wanted, to be able to study better. Maybe this guy really was trying to help me. . . .

I wasn't too crazy to be able to sense genuineness. Even through the heavy interference storm, I could detect Dr. Hemingway's caring attitude. He was unlike any other psychiatrist I'd seen. He seemed sincerely interested in my welfare and in the quality of my existence. I sense this was how he could understand my inability to tolerate certain drug side effects, when former psychiatrists had not taken the same complaints seriously. What I really feared was being forced to take drugs that would prevent me from studying effectively. I would do everything possible to prevent another interruption of my education.

Response and Analysis

1. What symptoms of schizophrenia did Carol North exhibit during her meetings with Dr. Hemingway? For instance, do you find examples of clang associations, ideas of reference, or certain types of hallucinations?

2. What differences do you see in the way North perceives herself during the sessions and the way Dr. Hemingway perceives North? What might cause these differences in perception?

3. What does Dr. Hemingway do to earn North's trust? What strengths does North show that may have aided in her recovery?

Research

Suppose you want to conduct a study to investigate the degree to which individuals are correctly diagnosed with schizophrenia. You will videotape an interview with an individual who demonstrates symptoms associated with schizophrenia. Then you will send the videotape and a detailed history of the individual to a random sample of one hundred clinical psychologists. How might you select the psychologists? Why might it be important to give all of the participants the same instructions? What instructions might you give?

TELL ME I'M HERE

Anne Deveson

Psychological Concept
schizophrenia and the family

When Jonathan Deveson turned seventeen, he became ill with schizophrenia. Jonathan's childhood had not been unusual: he loved music from Pink Floyd to Mozart and loved to read the works of J. R. R. Tolkien. In the early stages of his disorder, he began to believe that people were against him; he sometimes behaved erratically, alternating periods of quiet with shouting. As the disease progressed, Jonathan was often violent and threatening. His suffering was intense, and he inflicted some of his pain on others. This young man, who cried out "What's wrong with me? All I want is a simple life," felt that his brain was being destroyed. This selection, written by his mother, is her testimony about this disorder and what it can do to its victims and their families.

*A*pril 1979. We had just moved to South Australia, and I was in the kitchen one Sunday night in early autumn. The church bells had just rung, and I was making soup. . . .

The architect[1] was due for dinner and my two younger children, Georgia and Joshua, were in the garden.

The front door opened, banged shut, and Jonathan appeared with a friend called Paul, who led the way. They had been camping for the weekend. At this stage of the story, Jonathan was seventeen, Georgia fourteen, and Joshua ten.

Paul jerked his head toward Jonathan and said, 'I think he's sick.'

Jonathan wore a beige beanie on his long fair hair and had pulled it down so it almost covered his eyes and nose. His nose was long and straight but the bridge was a bit crooked from where a gang had jumped him at a swimming pool two years earlier. He had sensitive features, fair skin, and brown eyes. He was very tall and getting taller.

Sometimes he looked truly beautiful, like one of those angels in Italian Renaissance paintings. I nearly do not write this, because I think it might sound mawkish. But at this time in his life, Jonathan was beautiful. He still held his head on one side, and had a dimple when he smiled. Tonight, he ignored everyone and wandered up and down the room talking to himself, and giggling. When I went up and hugged him, he looked over my head and his arms hung stiffly by his side.

---

[1] A friend of Anne Deveson

We sat at the table. It was one of those evenings that was going to be lumpy. The architect, who liked his meals to be candle-lit with Mozart, instead of with rowdy teenagers and wheezy dogs, tried valiantly to sustain an intelligent conversation. He asked us what we thought of Norman Mailer.

Georgia said Mailer was passé.

Jonathan turned his soup bowl upside-down on the table and made patterns on the polished wood. 'Yair, yair,' he said conspiratorially. He kept nodding his head. His eyes darted around the room. He looked frightened. I felt alarm, a lurch in my stomach.

Jonathan stood up suddenly, and the table shook. He strode purposefully into the garden like someone embarking on a marathon race. His head was thrust forward, his elbows were flapping, and his lips were moving as if he were having this intense conversation with himself. There was immense energy about this sudden action of his. It stopped just as suddenly. He came to rest beneath a plum tree. Under a darkening sky, he stood there for a moment like a stork, one leg tucked under the other. The plum tree was brazenly beautiful, its fruit dark red and ripe. Lots of plums had fallen on the ground, and he began systematically squashing them.

The architect echoed Paul's earlier remark. He said in a concerned voice (because he was, and is, a kindly man), 'I think he is sick.'

Jonathan wandered back in. He had been eating one of the plums and its red juice stained his mouth. The architect took his leave as soon as he could gracefully manage.

We all went to bed. I lay and worried. I don't usually worry, but tonight was different. My bed didn't help. It was pear-shaped and the sheets were black satin. This was an improbable feature of an improbable house which was built by a Russian in the 1950s and which the architect had rented for us so that we could have one year of settling in before we all lived together.

This house had a glass-brick façade and part of it was painted lime green. It was bow-fronted like a ship and belonged to a man who had spent his life in the South Seas and a mild-looking woman who was said to have been waiting for him. While she waited she had filled her cupboards full of hair rollers, and bird-seed for the pigeons.

Lying in my pear-shaped splendour, I dozed off, still uneasy. I was wakened to a sound that thrummed through my ears, my eyes, my head, my whole body. The house was shaking. At first I wasn't sure what was happening, then I realized it was music, loud music.

I fumbled my way downstairs and opened the door of the living-room. It was a big L-shaped room with a parquet floor, plastic armchairs, and several hideous metal sculptures on the wall which moved when you wound them up. The music was Pink Floyd, 'Dark Side of the Moon,' and it was thundering into such distortion that I had to put my hands over my ears. Although it was a warm night, Jonathan sat hunched up over the electric fire. All bars were blazing and his sneakers smelt of burning rubber. He was rocking back and forth, his arms tightly wrapped around himself as if he were holding himself together. His lips were moving. I turned off the music. He jumped up, turned it on again, and grabbed me by the wrists. Then he spat in my face.

'Fucking bitch,' he hissed. There was a ferocity about his anger that alarmed me. I wiped my face. I was angry. 'Don't!' I shouted.

'Fucking bitch!' he shouted again. He began banging his head with his hands, and then banging his head against the wall. He was screaming something about rats, only I couldn't hear him properly above the din. 'Rats, they're eating my brain,' I thought he said. I rushed to put my arms around him. 'There aren't any rats. No rats. No rats,' I crooned.

He pushed me away, so hard that I fell backwards on the floor. I looked up and saw the other two children standing in the doorway. Georgia had her hand to her mouth. I think she was screaming 'Don't Jonathan, don't Jonathan.' But then he was screaming too. And all the while the music was pounding through the room, through our heads, through the screaming. Joshua turned it off, and Jonathan went to grab him but changed his mind. He stood with his hands tucked in the top of his jeans, his feet apart.

'The PLO will get you,' he said, and spat on the floor. 'Now piss off,' he roared. 'Piss off!'

We retreated. Georgia and Joshua went back to bed and I returned to the living-room. Jonathan was back at the radiator, rocking to and fro. There was no music, only his keening, a strange high lament. When he saw me he became agitated, and I withdrew. I thought about calling a doctor, but the whole incident had been so bizarre, so unexpected that I felt shocked and bemused. My head ached, but I guess I must have dropped off to sleep because I woke, startled. It was the silence that disturbed me, made me stumble down the stairs, to find Jonathan sprawled out in an armchair. His face was flushed, but otherwise he looked like a boy who had fallen asleep on an ordinary night in an ordinary house in an ordinary town. I turned off the fire and closed the door.

Next day, we were exhausted. Jonathan was no longer in the living-room. He had gone up to his bedroom and crashed, fully clothed, on his bed. He came downstairs at about two in the afternoon, and went straight to the bread crock. He made himself large hunks of bread and jam and sat cross-legged on the floor, shoving the bread into his mouth as if he hadn't eaten in days.

'What happened last night?' I asked him.

He giggled.

'You said rats were eating your brain.'

He giggled again, and walked out of the house.

I followed him, but he was too fast for me and I had to let him go. I watched him as he padded barefoot down the road, hands in his pockets. He was wearing an old, grey, Tibetan wool jacket I had bought him, striped with many different colored braids.

I had tried to ring the architect earlier in the day, but he was out on a job. Georgia and Joshua were at school. I barely knew anyone else in Adelaide. I comforted myself by eating almost as many hunks of bread and jam as Jonathan had.

Then I remembered I had seen a Youth Refuge at the end of our street. I went straight there.

The staff were young and confident. They said that I did not have to put up with such aggressive behavior and I agreed. They also said that it could be a drug reaction, and they gave me the name of a general practitioner and a drug-and-alcohol counselling service. The general practitioner said to bring the boy in. The counselling service said the boy had to want to come in. But Jonathan had disappeared.

The architect arrived for dinner, and I told him what had happened. He said, not unreasonably, 'Oh, Lord, I hope it doesn't happen tonight.' That night would be one of the nights the architect stayed. He was a man given to regularity in his life.

During dinner in the garden, Jonathan joined us and sat with his eyes downcast. His lips were tightly held together and he spoke in monosyllables. The other two children were also quiet. We all felt tense. I went to bed in apprehension but all was well. The house was quiet. Everyone slept or appeared to sleep. A pale moon hovered low in the sky.

For the next week or so, Jonathan flitted through the house like a grey moth. He was supposed to be looking for a job, but he rarely appeared before early afternoon, when he would dart into the kitchen, make himself some food, and return to his room. At night, he paced up and down, talking and laughing, or he went downstairs and played Pink Floyd, over and over again. I bought him headphones which he sometimes remembered to use. Often, as he listened to the music, he rocked and repeated his lament. Several times, he went out in the early hours of the morning, leaving the front door swinging wide open. His hair was matted and he refused to change his clothes. Most worrying of all was his withdrawal from everyone around him. If we tried to break through to him, he would either walk right past us, or erupt in a rage. I sensed a build-up of energy inside him, as if there were an engine racing inside his head that was about to explode.

When I suggested that he visit a doctor because I was worried about him, he looked at me as if I had offered him a visit to a torture chamber. Then he became obsequious, wringing his hands like Uriah Heap. 'No thank you,' he said. 'No thank you, I do not think that would be a good idea. But thank you.'

I tackled him about drugs. When Jonathan first went to high school we were at the end of the flower-power era, and drugs—mainly marijuana—were readily available. He hung his head, mumbling, 'No, nothing like that.' Then he scuttled off giggling.

This endless giggling was driving us all up the wall. We did not know whether to join in or to tell him to shut up. And what would we have said: 'Laughing is forbidden around here'?

I contacted his friend Paul, who was defensive. He said they had smoked some dope while they were camping, but not much, and after all he, Paul, was okay. No, he didn't know what had happened except that when they woke up on Sunday morning Jonathan had begun trembling and behaving strangely.

When I rang Jonathan's father in Sydney, Ellis said he was sorry, and that it must be very worrying for me. Ellis and Jenny (his new wife) had spent Easter with us, just a few days earlier. 'Get him to a doctor,' Ellis advised. I said that I was trying to get Jonathan to a doctor but he kept refusing. 'My heart bleeds for you,' said Ellis, who was given to hyperbole, but had also just learned he had cancer. In the same circumstances, I doubt if I would have done any better. I put the telephone down and felt very alone. This was a time I needed family, but both my parents had died when the children were very young, and my brothers lived overseas.

I climbed the stairs to Jonathan's room which looked out at tree tops and sky. Since he was a child, Jonathan had drawn and painted. His images were usually bold. But today, he had a piece of charcoal clenched in his hand and was making small cramped marks on the paper. His face was bent so low over his desk that I wondered how he could see. He was drawing snakes and spiders and strange tormented faces, swastikas and machine guns, mushroom clouds and knives. When the charcoal disintegrated because he was pressing so hard, he picked up another piece as if he hadn't noticed what had occurred. He was giggling.

I said, 'Tell me . . .' My voice sounded desperate.

'Yes?'

'Tell me what's happening for you.'

'Nothing.'

'But I feel . . .' Oh God, what did I feel? Frightened, confused, needing to convince him that he was behaving strangely, when either he did not want to know about it, or did not comprehend it.

He thrust his face and body so close to mine that I could feel his breath on my forehead. Then he spun me round several times and peered at me. 'Mars Bar,' he said. 'You're a fucking Mars Bar.'

He rocked me backwards and forwards. I began crying. He stopped and put his arms around me. 'I'm sorry.'

'Jonathan, are you all right?'

'I'm all right. And now get out before I kill you.' He said it casually, and then continued his drawing.

He looked up when I didn't leave. '*Get out!*' he yelled.

A friend gave me the name of two psychiatrists but they were booked up for many weeks. One of them said Jonathan should be making his own appointments. The other, a psychiatrist at a public hospital, said he would see Jonathan but that I would have to bring him in. He said it was probably youthful rebellion. Later that day, Jonathan threw two plates across the kitchen, emptied a cordial bottle over the floor, said that Jane Fonda was his mother, and pushed past me into the street. That night we heard him running up and down the living-room, howling. These were not howls of rebellion; these were howls of pain.

I made an appointment for Jonathan to see one of the psychiatrists but Jonathan was nowhere to be found when I went to take him. So I went myself. The psychiatrist was young and earnest. He made copious notes as I proffered up every detail of my life. Afterwards, I felt disembowelled. The psychiatrists and the general practitioner all declined to make home visits.

I found a social worker and then wished I hadn't. She wore sandals and a denim skirt, touched my arm several times, and spoke with a rising inflection at the end of every sentence. I decided she had taken a counselling course by correspondence.

'Try not to be down-hearted.'

'What am I going to do?'

'Show him you love him.'

'But what-am-I-going-to-do?'. . .

22 January. Jonathan . . . left at midday saying he was going to visit some friends. At the end of the afternoon I was driving through North Adelaide when I spotted him walking along the middle of the road. He waved at me to stop. He asked me for a milkshake so we went into a café, and talked for a few minutes before he began glowering at me, and muttering. The tension of the past few weeks . . . was bound to erupt sometime. It erupted over me.

One minute Jonathan was blowing into his chocolate-malted. The next, he had thrown the milkshake at my face, followed by the pepper and salt, upturned the table, and chucked a chair at me. People gasped, the waiter came running and Jonathan shot off, out the door and up the street.

I shook the milk off me and tried to rub the pepper out of my eyes, which made it worse. The waiter hovered, hoping for an explanation. I couldn't think of one that wouldn't take half an hour, so I paid the bill and left.

Brenda and Margaret[2] thought I should charge Jonathan with assault. They said I had to set limits. The idea appalled me. But I did feel angry: angry with Jonathan for hurting me, angry with the system for not helping him, angry with the illness. The hardest anger to deal with was the anger with Jonathan, because of its paradox. Can you be angry with someone if it is their illness that makes them so destructive? But I was angry, so angry that I felt like thumping anyone and everyone, so angry that I had to belt my rage out on some cushions, and even then could not assuage it because I felt so powerless.

23 January. As Jonathan hadn't called to see Brenda, she went looking for him. She called round to the commune, and wrote in her report:

> Jonathan was lying half on and half off his mattress. He did not respond when I spoke to him and the radio was blaring away. He looked very pale and at first I thought he was dead but was very relieved to find he was breathing. There was no evidence that he had taken anything and I understand that he does become almost unconscious when he is having psychotic episodes. So I left. The room was in its usual grotty state with a shower of bus tickets around the place.

24 January. Jonathan arrived home in the middle of the night by forcing one of the windows. He was psychotic, laughing and talking to himself, going into high-pitched giggles, and racing up and down the stairs. At one stage he pulled down all the medical books, followed by the Bible. I sat on the floor with him and tried to get him to talk about what was happening, but he ignored me and raced through the pages like a fast-track film sequence, reading aloud made-up words, and scrumpling the pages as he turned them. I phoned the crisis centre but they told me to phone the police. I phoned the police but, by the time they arrived, two hours later, Jonathan had left.

Early next morning I went out to my car and found Jonathan slumped over the driving wheel. He looked as if he were unconscious or dead. He was neither.

---

[2] Friends of Anne Deveson

When I got in the car, he took my finger and bit it so hard that I yelled in pain. He forced my head back against the seat, so that I began to choke, while his teeth kept gripping my finger. He giggled. Then he let go of my finger and my throat, suddenly, and leapt out of the car and ran down the road. I sat in the car for about five minutes, hugging my finger and crying, and then dragged myself into the house. I felt sick and desolate.

It seemed as if I were the one who mainly precipitated the violent outbursts. When Jonathan was psychotic, he incorporated me into his delusions and he would hear voices commanding him to hurt me. His internal conflicts must have been terrible. He had written on the blotched and mouldy walls of his squat a large message in black texta: *Don't harm Anne*. Over the years I would find scraps of paper on which he had scrawled similar injunctions. The more psychotic Jonathan became, the greater his terror, and the stronger his need to protect himself. Once, he said that God had told him I was the Devil and should be destroyed. Perhaps, as he looked at me my face was distorting so greatly that, to him, I looked like the Devil.

Response and Analysis

1. What symptoms of schizophrenia does Anne Deveson say her son experienced? Give examples of disorganized thinking, auditory hallucinations, emotional disturbances, and difficulties interacting with other people.

2. How might having a schizophrenic person in one's family affect family dynamics?

3. What are the involuntary commitment procedures in Australia as described by Deveson? How might these procedures differ from those in your state?

Research

Suppose you conduct a twenty-year longitudinal study to investigate the degree to which symptoms associated with schizophrenia improve over time. The participants are fifty people who are twenty years old and meet the DSM-IV criteria for schizophrenia. Your objective is to assess the participants at the same time each year for twenty years. Unfortunately, you have increasing difficulty locating the participants over the years. By the twentieth year, you are able to contact only 40% of the original fifty participants. How might the loss of the participants affect your conclusions?

I FEEL CHEATED BY
HAVING THIS ILLNESS

Allan Davis

Psychological Concept
schizophrenia

Allan Davis had to cope with being homeless and schizophrenic. After he had completed a degree in English Language and Literature at Princeton University, Davis's life deteriorated as his schizophrenia progressed. His symptoms improved when he received antipsychotic medication during his first hospitalization, but they returned when he discontinued the medication. He was constantly beset with anxiety and fear, so he began using illegal drugs to blunt his feelings. Eventually, his behavior brought him into contact with the courts, and from there he was transferred to a hospital where he received treatment.

My schizophrenia sneaked up on me and filled my life with danger. When my schizophrenia became obvious in 1977, I was 23, an African-American junior at Princeton University, and a drug abuser.

The first abnormal thing I remember was my perception that people on television were talking to me and about me. Later, I became convinced that everybody at Princeton was gay, and I became frightened by the prospect of flunking out if I didn't match that standard, which I did not. I also believed I learned a color code known only to members of organized crime or the intelligence community.

Then, Memorial Day weekend of 1977, my girlfriend's brother was killed in a car accident. That was the beginning of a major delusion in my life: that people don't really die. I convinced myself that the body in the casket was a dummy. My girlfriend didn't understand that I was becoming ill with schizophrenia, but she had her own problem. She was devastated by her brother's death and spent her time crying in my arms or angrily physically attacking me for not doing anything to make her feel better. We finally separated.

By 1982, at 28, I had constructed a fantasy world where I was the only male capable of having sex and where people didn't really die, they just became other people, always female. Occasionally I would doubt my fantasy and become depressed, but eventually I would simply take more illegal drugs until I was high enough to convince myself again.

I came home to Topeka in late 1982. A psychiatrist diagnosed my problem as schizophrenia, but no medication was prescribed. I didn't know what schizophrenia was and neither did my parents. Even now I don't think they fully understand. My parents thought my problem behavior was a result of my drug use, but, in truth, my schizophrenic delusion was the cause of my problems. Even when I didn't use drugs, my delusions remained.

Within a few months, Mr. Davis began treatment at the Menninger Community Service Office, a Topeka outpatient clinic.[1] He first saw a psychiatrist and later was in psychotherapy with a social worker. He recalls that he was not invested in treatment at that time and eventually dropped out. Because he was too ill to hold a job, he received a monthly disability check that made it possible for him to move from his parents' home to a place of his own. It also supported his drug habit.

Today I know for sure that I have schizophrenia, because I had visual and auditory disturbances. But for a long time I refused to believe the diagnosis of schizophrenia meant anything was seriously wrong with me. I still believed in my fantasy world, and I thought the diagnosis of schizophrenia was just a convenient way to get a disability check.

In 1986 I began to experience severe, unexplained physical problems which I now attribute to anxiety. I would be asleep but aware and unable to breathe or move for what seemed like a minute. I had this problem occasionally as a child, but now it occurred with regularity. I also had heart palpitations, which scared me so much that my fantasy world collapsed. I was afraid I was dying, and I was afraid to die. I stopped using drugs because they made me more anxious.

These palpitations led Mr. Davis to see his general physician, who suggested that his symptoms might be related to a mental illness.

I followed my physician's advice and checked into the psychiatric ward at a local general hospital. I came out with a prescription for an antipsychotic medication.

With the medication, Mr. Davis's thought disturbances abated, but he was extremely depressed and withdrawn. He stayed in bed until late in the morning, then went to his parents' home to eat, watch television, and nap. Returning to his home by 8 P.M., he would take his medication and be in bed by 8:30 P.M. With no friends, his only social contacts occurred when he attended the church where his father is pastor.

I gained 60 pounds, I stopped shaving, and my appearance basically became much worse. In truth, I was depressed because of the eventuality of death. Nobody noticed my depression; they just thought I was withdrawn.

I took the antipsychotic drug until 1988, when the prescribing psychiatrist discontinued it because he thought I was exhibiting symptoms of tardive dyskinesia.

Tardive dyskinesia is a serious side effect of some antipsychotic medications. It is marked by involuntary movements, frequently involving the mouth and tongue and sometimes the

---

[1] The italicized portions were added by the editors of *Menninger Perspective* and offer important information about Mr. Davis's illness and treatment.

limbs and trunk. Symptoms may remit in some patients who quit taking the offending drug, but they may be permanent for others.

From 1986 to 1989, Mr. Davis also returned to the Menninger Community Service Office, but he frequently was unable to talk to the therapist about his feelings and could not participate in the treatment process.

After the medication was discontinued, my delusion eventually returned. I also began using drugs again. My visual disturbances returned and were more numerous. I would see after-images of people where people no longer were, I would see lights in the night sky traveling between the stars, and more commonly I would see streaks of light or darkness in the daytime.

Escalating Problems

The years from 1989 to 1991 were especially turbulent for Mr. Davis and for members of his family. He lived with his parents, but disagreements with them led him to leave for extended periods. Once, he traveled to Texas, New York, Boston, and, finally, Seattle, where he lived in a shelter and briefly worked at a fast food restaurant. After six months, he returned to Topeka.

Later in 1991, I moved from Topeka to Los Angeles because marijuana was cheaper and more plentiful there. I obtained an apartment in a building for the homeless mentally ill, but then I started using daily a product sold to me as crack. I thought when I got high everybody and everything got high, so even though I was not impressed with the product, I would still use it and marijuana to—as I believed—bring peace and avoid earthquakes. I was deep into my delusion and terribly unaware that I lived in a dangerous world.

When my drug usage got me evicted from my apartment, I became officially homeless. I had been a Boy Scout as a kid, so I was neatly efficient at urban camping. I began spending much of my days in a park frequented by drug dealers and users. While there I found labels, still with legible lot numbers on them, from local anesthetics such as lidocaine, a novocaine substitute. I became convinced that the crack I was buying was nothing more than a drug from a dentist's office. I sought assistance from, in my opinion, the proper drug authority: the police who permitted the drug sales. Twice, when the police stopped while driving through the drug park I gave them the labels.

I never understood why one person who bought drugs in the park called me a snitch and threatened my life, but my deluded beliefs and lack of awareness of danger were getting me into trouble. I began to have more and more disagreements with the park residents who hung around and mooched off of the drug salesmen.

Because I believed I was a special drug user and deserved to be treated in a special way, I would say things that got me into altercations, but I almost always ran. One time I was being chased and a bystander blocked my path. I evaded him but stumbled and fell. When I got up, he hit me. I suffered a fractured jaw, because I was breathing through my open mouth when I was hit.

I was on the operating table having my jaw wired shut when I began to bleed from the nose and choke. The anesthesiologist didn't know that one sinus was smaller than the other, so I bled when the tubes were removed from my nose. The wires on my teeth shredded the insides of both lips as I struggled to breathe. I awoke in severe pain.

With my jaw wired shut, I returned to the drug park certain in my delusion that I was safe. My visual disturbances continued, and I began to experience mild auditory disturbances. The voices usually said "here" or "me."

One morning while I was in the park, I heard an auditory disturbance say, "Here's where he gets hurt." I guess I burned my finger on a marijuana cigarette. Then, as I was going somewhere, I looked behind me and saw a park resident who had never really threatened me following me. I tried to evade him, but I heard another voice in front of me—another auditory disturbance—say, "Here." By then I knew better than to do anything the voices said to do, so I stopped, because the voice was in front of me.

I felt a thud on my left shoulder and saw that my pursuer had kept running past me when I stopped. He was looking back at me, and he was holding a five-inch folding knife. I had been stabbed less than an inch from my spine. The wound was three or four inches deep, but no major blood vessels or organs were damaged.

Because of my delusional condition, because I referred to my visual disturbances as antipersonnel radar, and because one police officer considered me a troublemaker, I could not get the police to find and arrest my attacker when I returned to the park several days after being stabbed. It took a lot to get me to stay away from the drug park. In my fantasy world I was safe, but I had a knife wound that said I wasn't safe.

I finally left Los Angeles and came home after two years. One day I was arrested at the local mall.

One of the mall merchants accused Mr. Davis of creating a disturbance in her store. He left the store when asked, but the store manager called mall security anyway. The mall security chief told Mr. Davis he was banned from the entire mall and could not return. Mr. Davis went back inside to call the mall manager to verify that he could be banned from the entire mall and was arrested. Another shopper had observed his arrest, and she volunteered to testify at his trial.

When I got to court I was shocked to find that my court-appointed attorney had not prepared a defense for me or interviewed the witness, and the witness did not appear. I was convicted. When I complained to my attorney, he lost his temper, threatened to kick my "———— —," and chased me from the courtroom.

The judge didn't see what happened, and I guess he assumed that the mentally ill person was at fault, because he called me back into the courtroom and found me in contempt of court. My protestations that I hadn't done anything and my inability to follow the judge's order to be quiet landed me in jail.

The jail psychiatrist found me incompetent to be sentenced and recommended that I go to the Menninger hospital or stay in jail. I went to the Menninger hospital after almost a month in jail.

The Menninger Hospital

Menninger operates a spectrum of clinical programs for persons with chronic mental illnesses and has earned a reputation as a center of excellence for the treatment of persons like Mr. Davis. Central to these programs is the HOPE Unit of the C.F. Menninger Memorial Hospital. This unit, whose acronym stands for Health Opportunities and Psychological Enhancement, provides extended inpatient treatment for persons with severe mental illnesses.

The HOPE Unit was particularly appropriate for Mr. Davis because of the comprehensive treatment it provides. Primary symptoms of schizophrenia, such as delusions, disturbances of association, and excessive ambivalence, seem to be of biological origin and can often be treated with psychotropic drugs. However, the negative symptoms, such as apathy and deterioration of healthy daily living habits, are, at least in part, actually psychological reactions to the biological disorder. They must be treated using approaches such as individual psychotherapy, group psychotherapy, and psychosocial treatment. The HOPE unit provides all of these.

Nevertheless, Mr. Davis remained reluctant to participate in treatment. In his state of delusion, he continued to believe that the street drugs that he had been taking would be most beneficial for him. Fearing that medications would cause serious side effects, he refused to take the antipsychotic medications prescribed by his psychiatrist.

Thus, the first task for staff was to develop a trusting relationship with Mr. Davis. Through daily contact, psychiatrist Katherine Weyrens and members of the nursing team addressed his fears. Without pressuring or pushing too hard, they encouraged him to relax and talk, as he was able. Knowing his fears about medications, they provided sound, accurate information about psychotropic drugs and what he might expect from them.

In addition, Mr. Davis participated in individual and group psychotherapy. His parents and brothers joined him in a meeting with his treatment team. Through this meeting, they came to better understand and accept his illness and were able to provide ongoing support for him.

Three months into his hospitalization, Mr. Davis agreed to take an antipsychotic medication.

After three months of refusing medication, which I regarded as virtually poison, I relented, really because I had no choice, and tried an antipsychotic drug. My understanding was that if I did not try the drug, the law would send me to a state facility where I would be forced to take it.

With no access to illegal drugs to reinforce the delusion and my back in a corner, it took me only two days to accept what is real: people do die, sex does occur, and so does violence. I was out of the fantasy for the final time, never more to return.

During his fourth and final month in the hospital, as his antipsychotic drug regimen was refined, Mr. Davis continued to improve. Working with staff and participating with other patients in therapy groups, he earned more privileges and was able to go unescorted to prescribed activities including the gym. He began working with an art therapist.

Leaving the Hospital

To sustain their gains, patients with serious, chronic mental illnesses like schizophrenia need a stable, supportive environment in which to continue treatment following hospital-

ization. Menninger Partial Hospitalization Services are designed to meet those needs by providing ongoing group therapy, opportunities for socialization, help in reentering society through volunteer work, school, or employment, and the monitoring of medications. As their condition allows, patients live in group homes, with family members, or on their own. It was to this program that Mr. Davis transferred, and he returned to his parents' home.

After moving home, I asked my prescribing psychiatrist for an antidepressant, and two weeks after beginning to take it I was pleasantly surprised that I was feeling better. Encouraged by that success, I then asked for an anti-anxiety agent, and a very small dosage was prescribed for me. That also helped.

The antipsychotic medication has eliminated the visual and auditory disturbances. I regret the years I spent in my nonmedicated condition. Now I need all three of my prescriptions.

Mr. Davis has been in the partial hospital program for 18 months. He spends a portion of each day five days a week at Menninger, participating in a variety of meetings and activities including yoga classes, a relapse prevention group, and a medications group in which patients learn about the medications they are taking and the effects—both good and bad—that they may produce. He writes for the patients' newsletter and attends classes at Washburn University in Topeka.

He meets weekly with his case coordinator, social worker Kay Kelly, to assess how his life is going and to get help with any problems, and he continues to see his psychiatrist.

Twice weekly he participates in a therapy group. "I know that social isolation is a symptom of both schizophrenia and depression," Mr. Davis said. "I'm not very talkative in groups, but I think I am benefiting from attending." Ms. Kelly said Mr. Davis also helps other group members through his understanding of their experiences and how they are feeling. Although it is difficult for him, with encouragement he has been able to reach out to others.

Mr. Davis also has made strides in developing a circle of friends through the Sunshine Connection, a drop-in center for consumers of mental health services. He is president of the center's board of directors. Funded by Kansas Social and Rehabilitation Services and located on the grounds of Topeka State Hospital, the Sunshine Connection provides activities for mental health patients on Friday nights and Saturday afternoons when most other outpatient programs are closed. Up to 50 people visit the center on Saturday to enjoy table tennis and other games, television, movie videos, live music, and snacks.

Looking to the Future

I keep myself neat and exercise regularly. I am studying journalism at Washburn University. My GPA (grade point average) is 3.5, and I optimistically expect it to go higher. I expect to have a real job someday. Maybe I'll write my autobiography, because there is a lot more to my story than can be told in this brief account and, besides, not many people come back from where I was.

Although his future is uncertain, Mr. Davis expects to complete his degree in mass media and likely will attend the University of Kansas to get a master's degree in a journalism-related field. He is interested in teaching at the college level.

Having come to grips with his own illness, he also has thought of working in the mental health field. One possibility, he said, would be to work as a case manager in a community mental health center, where he could apply what he has learned through his own struggle with schizophrenia to helping others with mental illnesses. "Based on my own experience, I know how difficult it is to convince consumers (patients) of things," he said.

Despite the progress he has made and his hard-earned understanding and acceptance of his illness and what life is like for a person with a chronic mental illness, Mr. Davis continues to face challenges. He feels cheated by having his illness and wonders why he couldn't have lived a "normal life like everybody else."

I am convinced that I have schizophrenia, and I am pretty sure I will be taking medications for the rest of my life. I'm 42 years old. I've never been married and I have no children. I have no love in my life. I have no relatives in the Midwest except my parents. I am very concerned about growing old alone. One of my major concerns is the inevitability of death, but there is nothing I can do about it.

I think about being stabbed, and it scares me. I am embarrassed by some of the things I did. I don't have any ill feelings about my arrest or the events in the courtroom, because that led to my recovery. I feel cheated by having this illness.

Response and Analysis

1. Notice how Allan Davis describes conflict with the courts, his attorney, and other persons who are homeless. Do you think he has felt cheated by society as well as by schizophrenia? Why or why not?

2. What symptoms of schizophrenia does Davis display? Give examples of visual, auditory, and emotional disturbances, and of his difficulties interacting with other people.

3. What reasons does Davis give for his using illegal drugs? How did his delusional beliefs concerning drug use get him into trouble?

4. What treatment did Davis finally receive? What helped him?

5. Three to four million Americans with schizophrenia are permanently unemployed, and many are unemployable. About half of all patients in mental hospitals are diagnosed with schizophrenia. Considering these statistics, how should society care for victims of schizophrenia? Where should people with schizophrenia live? Should society provide residences for those with schizophrenia? Who should assist victims of schizophrenia and other psychological disorders when they cannot work and cannot pay for living expenses or for mental health treatment?

Research

Suppose you want to conduct a study to determine the rates of schizophrenia among different ethnic groups in the United States. One of your primary concerns in designing the study is minimizing the effects of confounding variables (e.g., socioeconomic status, size of the community). How can you design the study to determine if differences between groups are caused by ethnicity or by the social and economic conditions faced by certain ethnic groups? How might you design the study to determine if homelessness is a cause of schizophrenia or if schizophrenia is a cause of homelessness?

chapter 8

PERSONALITY DISORDERS AND IMPULSE CONTROL DISORDERS

In the long journey out of the self,
There are many detours, washed-out
  interrupted raw places
Where the shale slides dangerously
and the back wheels hang almost over the edge
At the sudden veering, the moment of turning.

THEODORE ROETHKE, *Journey to the Interior*

The diagnosis of personality disorder is often difficult to make. Clinicians must discern long-standing patterns of inflexible and maladaptive behavior, cognitions, and emotions. They must determine that problem behaviors, which typically begin in adolescence or early adulthood, deviate markedly from society's expectations and are caused by enduring personality traits rather than by other disorders or situational factors. Persons with personality disorders do not always feel distress (e.g., persons with antisocial personality disorder often see others rather than themselves as the problem), so they may not present themselves for treatment. Even with correct diagnosis and treatment, however, change for persons with personality disorders can be difficult, as maladaptive behavior tends to be recurrent.

For convenience, personality disorders are sometimes grouped into three categories based on their dominant symptoms. Persons with paranoid or schizotypal personality disorder show eccentricity in thought and action. Persons with histrionic, borderline, or antisocial personality disorder behave in dramatic, emotional, or erratic ways. Those who have avoidant or dependent personality disorders are predominantly anxious or fearful. Personality disorders are diagnosed on Axis II in DSM-IV. Other Axis I disorders can occur along with these Axis II disorders, just as Axis I disorders can occur along with general medical conditions (Axis III).

In the first selection, Geoffrey Wolff painfully discovers that his father's behavior was frequently deceitful, impulsive, irresponsible, or criminal. Many of Duke's behaviors fit a diagnosis of antisocial personality disorder. Persons with this disorder often lack remorse over their chronic disregard for social and legal norms. They may have shallow or manipulative relationships with others, showing persistent patterns of dishonesty, impulsivity, or aggressiveness.

The second selection is by Susanna Kaysen, who was diagnosed with borderline personality disorder. Borderline personality disorder is one of the most commonly diagnosed personality disorders and is characterized by pronounced fluctuations in mood and self-image, and by unstable social relationships. Kaysen, who attempted suicide, writes with honesty and irony about her experience in a mental hospital. She critically examines how well her diagnosis fits with her behavior during this time, revealing that diagnoses are general characterizations that may not fit individuals perfectly.

Impulse control disorders include kleptomania, pathological gambling, pyromania, and intermittent explosive disorder. Each disorder in this Axis I category is characterized by repeated failure to control a particular type of impulse. Persons often feel strong urges to engage in behavior—similar to compulsions—with anxiety preceding completion of the act and released following it. They are usually aware of the destructive consequences of the behavior but feel unable to resist. Impulse control disorders raise important questions about voluntary control, or willpower, over impulses and appropriate social and legal responses to impulse-driven behaviors. In the last selection, Stuart and Dan, both pathological gamblers, describe their addiction to gambling. They tell of their reasons for gambling and the problems that have resulted from their addiction.

THE DUKE OF DECEPTION

Geoffrey Wolff

Psychological Concept
antisocial personality disorder

Persons diagnosed with antisocial personality disorder show a long-term pattern of disregard for and violations of the rights of others. Their behavior can be selfish, impulsive, irresponsible, even criminal. Deceit and manipulation are common features of the disorder, so con artists often fall into this category. Geoffrey Wolff tells of the two histories of his father: the real and the fabricated. Wolff's father, called Duke, said he was a Yale graduate; yet he wasn't. He said he wasn't Jewish; yet he was. He said he was a fighter pilot in World War II; yet he wasn't. What he was was a con artist. What prompts Duke to create an imaginary world and to lead a dishonest life? Note the way Duke treats other people and the impressions he wants to make. How many of the behaviors Wolff describes are consistent with antisocial personality disorder?

I listen for my father and I hear a stammer. This was explosive and unashamed, not a choking on words but a spray of words. His speech was headlong, edgy, breathless: there was neither room in his mouth nor time in the day to contain what he burned to utter. I have a remnant of that stammer, and I wish I did not; I stammer and blush, my father would stammer and grin. He depended on a listener's good will. My father depended excessively upon people's good will.

As he spoke straight at you, so did he look at you. He could stare down anyone, though this was a gift he rarely practiced. To me, everything about him seemed outsized. Doing a school report on the Easter Islanders I found in an encyclopedia pictures of their huge sculptures, and there he was, massive head and nose, nothing subtle or delicate. He was in fact (and how diminishing those words, *in fact*, look to me now) an inch or two above six feet, full bodied, a man who lumbered from here to there with deliberation. When I was a child I noticed that people were respectful of the cubic feet my father occupied; later I understood that I had confused respect with resentment.

I recollect things, a gentleman's accessories, deceptively simple fabrications of silver and burnished nickel, of brushed Swedish stainless, of silk and soft wool and brown leather. I remember his shoes, so meticulously selected and cared for and used, thin-soled, with cracked uppers, older than I was or could ever be, shining dully and from the depths. Just a pair of shoes? No: I knew before I knew any other complicated thing that for my father there was nothing he possessed that was "just" something. His pocket watch was not "just" a timepiece, it was a miraculous instrument with a hinged front and a representation on its back of porcelain ducks rising from a birch-girt porcelain pond. It struck the hour unassertively, musically, like a silver tine touched to a crystal glass, no hurry, you might like to know it's noon.

He despised black leather, said black shoes reminded him of black attaché cases, of bankers, lawyers, look-before-you-leapers anxious not to offend their clients. He owned nothing black except his dinner jacket and his umbrella. His umbrella doubled as a shooting-stick, and one afternoon at a polo match at Brandywine he was sitting on it when a man asked him what he would do if it rained, sit wet or stand dry? I laughed. My father laughed also, but tightly, and he did not reply; nor did he ever again use this quixotic contraption. He took things, *things*, seriously.

My father, called Duke, taught me skills and manners; he taught me to shoot and to drive fast and to read respectfully and to box and to handle a boat and to distinguish between good jazz music and bad jazz music. He was patient with me, led me to understand for myself why Billie Holiday's understatements were more interesting than Ella Fitzgerald's complications. His codes were not novel, but they were rigid, the rules of decorum that Hemingway prescribed. A gentleman kept his word, and favored simplicity of sentiment; a gentleman chose his words with care, as he chose his friends. A gentleman accepted responsibility for his acts, and welcomed the liberty to act unambiguously. A gentleman was a stickler for precision and punctilio; life was no more than an inventory of small choices that together formed a man's character, entire. A gentleman was this, and not that; a *man* did, did not, said, would not say.

My father could, however, be coaxed to reveal his bona fides. He had been schooled at Groton and passed along to Yale. He was just barely prepared to intimate that he had been tapped for "Bones," and I remember his pleasure when Levi Jackson, the black captain of Yale's 1948 football team, was similarly honored by that secret society. He was proud of Skull and Bones for its hospitality toward the exotic. He did sometimes wince, however, when he pronounced Jackson's Semitic Christian name, and I sensed that his tolerance for Jews was not inclusive; but I never heard him indulge express bigotry, and the first of half a dozen times he hit me was for having called a neighbor's kid a guinea.

There was much luxury in my father's affections, and he hated what was narrow, pinched, or mean. He understood exclusion, mind you, and lived his life believing the world to be divided between a few *us's* and many *thems*, but I was to understand that aristocracy was a function of taste, courage, and generosity. About two other virtues—candor and reticence—I was confused, for my father would sometimes proselytize the one, sometimes the other.

If Duke's preoccupation with bloodlines was finite, this did not cause him to be unmindful of his ancestors. He knew whence he had come, and whither he meant me to go. I saw visible evidence of this, a gold signet ring which I wear today, a heavy bit of business inscribed arsy-turvy with lions and flora and a motto, *nulla vestigium retrorsit*. "Don't look back" I was told it meant.

After Yale—class of late nineteen-twenty something, or early nineteen-thirty something—my father batted around the country, living a high life in New York among school and college chums, flying as a test pilot, marrying my mother, the daughter of a rear admiral. I was born a year after the marriage, in 1937, and three years after that my father went to England as a fighter pilot with Eagle Squadron, a group of American volunteers in the Royal Air Force. Later he transferred to the OSS, and was in Yugoslavia with the partisans; just before the Invasion he was parachuted into Normandy, where he served as a sapper with the Resistance, which my father pronounced *ray-zee-staunce*.

His career following the war was for me mysterious in its particulars; in the service of his nation, it was understood, candor was not always possible. This much was clear: my father mattered in the world, and was satisfied that he mattered, whether or not the world understood precisely why he mattered.

A pretty history for an American clubman. Its fault is that it was not true. My father was a bullshit artist. True, there were many boarding schools, each less pleased with the little Duke than the last, but none of them was Groton. There was no Yale, and by the time he walked from a room at a mention of Skull and Bones I knew this, and he knew that I knew it. No military service would have him; his teeth were bad. So he had his teeth pulled and replaced, but the Air Corps and Navy and Army and Coast Guard still thought he was a bad idea. The ring I wear was made according to his instructions by a jeweler two blocks from Schwab's drugstore in Hollywood, and was never paid for. The motto, engraved backwards so that it would come right on a red wax seal, is dog Latin and means in fact "leave no trace behind," but my father did not believe me when I told him this.

My father was a Jew. This did not seem to him a good idea, and so it was his notion to disassemble his history, begin at zero, and re-create himself. His sustaining line of work till shortly before he died was as a confidence man. If I now find his authentic history more surprising, more interesting, than his counterfeit history, he did not. He would not make peace with his actualities, and so he was the author of his own circumstances, and indifferent to the consequences of this nervy program.

There were some awful consequences, for other people as well as for him. He was lavish with money, with others' money. He preferred to stiff institutions: jewelers, car dealers, banks, fancy hotels. He was, that is, a thoughtful buccaneer, when thoughtfulness was convenient. But people were hurt by him. Much of his mischief was casual enough: I lost a tooth when I was six, and the Tooth Fairy, "financially inconvenienced" or "temporarily out of pocket," whichever was then his locution, left under my pillow an IOU, a sight draft for two bits, or two million.

I wish he hadn't selected from among the world's possible disguises the costume and credentials of a yacht club commodore. Beginning at scratch he might have reached further, tried something a bit more bold and odd, a bit less inexorably conventional, a bit less calculated to please. But it is true, of course, that a confidence man who cannot inspire confidence in his marks is nothing at all, so perhaps his tuneup of his bloodline, educational *vita*, and war record was merely the price of doing business in a culture preoccupied with appearances.

I'm not even now certain what I wish he had made of himself: I once believed that he was most naturally a fictioneer. But for all his preoccupation with make-believe, he never tried seriously to write it. A confidence man learns early in his career that to commit himself to paper is to court trouble. The successful bunco artist does his game, and disappears himself: Who *was* that masked man? No one, no one at all, *nulla vestigium [sic] retrorsit [sic]*, not a trace left behind.

Well, I'm left behind. One day, writing about my father with no want of astonishment and love, it came to me that I am his creature as well as his get. I cannot now shake this conviction, that I was trained as his instrument of perpetuation, put here to put him into the record. And that my father knew this, calculated it to a degree. How else explain his eruption of rage when I once gave up what he and I called "writing" for journalism? I had taken a job as the book critic of *The Washington Post*, was proud of myself; it seemed then like a wonderful job, honorable and enriching. My father saw it otherwise: "You have failed me," he wrote, "you have sold yourself at discount" he wrote to me, his prison number stamped below his name. . . .

[My father had purchased] a wrist watch from a jeweler, Donavan & Seamans, with a check for $248.70 from an account that had been closed more than four years. My father didn't need the watch—he had a dozen others—and he finally gave it to Toby [my brother] on Toby's way to Vietnam. The watch cost him two years in Chino [Correctional Facility].

He was wrong then, but he was usually right about me. He would listen to anything I wished to tell him, but would not tell me only what I wished to hear. He retained such solicitude for his clients. With me he was strict and straight, except about himself. And so I want to be strict and straight with him, and with myself. Writing to a friend . . . I said that I would not now for anything have had my father be other than what he was, except happier, and that most of the time he was happy enough, cheered on by imaginary successes. He gave me a great deal, and not merely life, and I didn't want to bellyache; I wanted, I told my friend, to thumb my nose on his behalf at everyone who had limited him. My friend was shrewd, though, and said that he didn't believe me, that I couldn't mean such a thing, that if I followed out its implications I would be led to a kind of ripe sentimentality, and to mere piety. Perhaps, he wrote me, you would not have wished him to lie to himself, to lie about being a Jew. Perhaps you would have him fool others but not so deeply trick himself. "In writing about a father," my friend wrote me about our fathers, "one clambers up a slippery mountain, carrying the balls of another in a bloody sack, and whether to eat them or worship them or bury them decently is never cleanly decided."

So I will try here to be exact. I wish my father had done more headlong, more elegant inventing. I believe he would respect my wish, be willing to speak with me seriously about it, find some nobility in it. But now he is dead, and he had been dead two weeks when they found him. And in his tiny fist at the edge of the Pacific they found no address book, no batch of letters held with a rubber band, no photograph. Not a thing to suggest that he had ever known another human being.

Response and Analysis

1. What aspects of Duke's behavior reflect antisocial personality disorder? What are the possible causes of antisocial personality disorder?

2. How did Duke's behavior affect Geoffrey Wolff? Did Wolff believe that Duke felt remorse or guilt about his actions? Why or why not?

3. In what ways did Duke's actions harm other people? Harm himself?

Research

Suppose you want to conduct a study to examine whether people who are diagnosed with antisocial personality disorder show less concern for punishment and pain than do other people. What is the null hypothesis? What is the research, or alternative, hypothesis?

GIRL, INTERRUPTED

Susanna Kaysen

Psychological Concept
borderline personality disorder

Susanna Kaysen was diagnosed with borderline personality disorder—a disorder characterized by mood swings, fluctuations in self-image, unstable interpersonal relationships, and feelings of emptiness. Her condition was so severe that she was hospitalized after a suicide attempt. During her nearly two years in the hospital, she experienced a variety of symptoms. On recovery, Kaysen enlisted the support of her physician to release her records so she could include them in *Girl, Interrupted*, a book about her experiences. Here, she describes her hospital admission and some of the symptoms and uncertainties that troubled her. She also critically examines how well her diagnosis fits her behaviors.

Perhaps it's still unclear how I ended up in there. It must have been something more than a pimple. I didn't mention that I'd never seen that doctor before, that he decided to put me away after only fifteen minutes. Twenty, maybe. What about me was so deranged that in less than half an hour a doctor would pack me off to the nuthouse? He tricked me, though: a couple of weeks. It was closer to two years. I was eighteen.

I signed myself in. I had to, because I was of age. It was that or a court order, though they could never have gotten a court order against me. I didn't know that, so I signed myself in.

I wasn't a danger to society. Was I a danger to myself? The fifty aspirin—but I've explained them. They were metaphorical. I wanted to get rid of a certain aspect of my character. I was performing a kind of self-abortion with those aspirin. It worked for a while. Then it stopped; but I had no heart to try again. . . .

I was having a problem with patterns. Oriental rugs, tile floors, printed curtains, things like that. Supermarkets were especially bad, because of the long, hypnotic checkerboard aisles. When I looked at these things, I saw other things within them. That sounds as though I was hallucinating, and I wasn't. I knew I was looking at a floor or a curtain. But all patterns seemed to contain potential representations, which in a dizzying array would flicker briefly to life. That could be . . . a forest, a flock of birds, my second-grade class picture. Well, it wasn't—it was a rug, or whatever it was, but my glimpses of the other things it might be were exhausting. Reality was getting too dense.

Something also was happening to my perceptions of people. When I looked at someone's face, I often did not maintain an unbroken connection to the concept of a face. Once you start parsing a face, it's a peculiar item: squishy, pointy, with lots of air vents and wet spots. This was the reverse of my problem with patterns. Instead of seeing too much meaning, I didn't see any meaning.

But I wasn't simply going nuts, tumbling down a shaft into Wonderland. It was my misfortune—or salvation—to be at all times perfectly conscious of my misperceptions of reality. I never "believed" anything I saw or thought I saw. Not only that, I correctly understood each new weird activity.

Now, I would say to myself, you are feeling alienated from people and unlike other people; therefore you are projecting your discomfort onto them. When you look at a face, you see a blob of rubber because you are worried that your face is a blob of rubber.

This clarity made me able to behave normally, which posed some interesting questions. Was everybody seeing this stuff and acting as though they weren't? Was insanity just a matter of dropping the act? If some people didn't see these things, what was the matter with them? Were they blind or something? These questions had me unsettled.

Something had been peeled back, a covering or shell that works to protect us. I couldn't decide whether the covering was something on me or something attached to every thing in the world. It didn't matter, really; wherever it had been, it wasn't there anymore.

And this was the main precondition, that anything might be something else. Once I'd accepted that, it followed that I might be mad, or that someone might think me mad. How could I say for certain that I wasn't, if I couldn't say for certain that a curtain wasn't a mountain range?

I have to admit, though, that I knew I wasn't mad.

It was a different precondition that tipped the balance: the state of contrariety. My ambition was to negate. The world, whether dense or hollow, provoked only my negations. When I was supposed to be awake, I was asleep; when I was supposed to speak, I was silent; when a pleasure offered itself to me, I avoided it. My hunger, my thirst, my loneliness and boredom and fear were all weapons aimed at my enemy, the world. They didn't matter a whit to the world, of course, and they tormented me, but I got a gruesome satisfaction from my sufferings. They proved my existence. All my integrity seemed to lie in saying No.

So the opportunity to be incarcerated was just too good to resist. It was a very big No—the biggest No this side of suicide. . . .

Two o'clock on a Saturday in August on a medium-security ward in Belmont. Old cigarette smoke, old magazines, green spotted rug, five yellow vinyl chairs, a broken-backed orange sofa: You couldn't mistake that room for anything but a loony-bin living room.

I sat in my yellow vinyl chair . . .

I looked at my hand. It occurred to me that my palm looked like a monkey's palm. The crinkle of the three lines running across it and the way my fingers curled in seemed simian to me. If I spread my fingers out, my hand looked more human, so I did that. But it was tiring holding my fingers apart. I let them relax, and then the monkey idea came back.

I turned my hand over quickly. The back of it wasn't much better. My veins bulged—maybe because it was such a hot day—and the skin around my knuckles was wrinkly and loose. If I moved my hand I could see the three long bones that stretched out from the wrist to the first joints of my fingers. Or perhaps those weren't bones but tendons? I poked one; it was resilient, so probably it was a tendon. Underneath, though, were bones. At least I hoped so.

I poked deeper, to feel the bones. They were hard to find. Knucklebones were easy, but I wanted to find the hand bones, the long ones going from my wrist to my fingers.

I started getting worried. Where were my bones? I put my hand in my mouth and bit it, to see if I crunched down on something hard. Everything slid away from me. There were nerves; there were blood vessels; there were tendons: All these things were slippery and elusive.

"Damn," I said.

Georgina and Polly[1] weren't paying attention.

I began scratching the back of my hand. My plan was to get hold of a flap of skin and peel it away, just to have a look. I wanted to see that my hand was a normal human hand, with bones. My hand got red and white—sort of like Polly's hands—but I couldn't get my skin to open up and let me in.

I put my hand in my mouth and chomped. Success! A bubble of blood came out near my last knuckle, where my incisor had pierced the skin.

"What the fuck are you doing?" Georgina asked.

"I'm trying to get to the bottom of this," I said.

"Bottom of what?" Georgina looked angry.

---

[1] Other patients in the hospital

"My hand," I said, waving it around. A dribble of blood went down my wrist.

"Well, stop it," she said.

"It's my hand," I said. I was angry too. And I was getting really nervous. Oh God, I thought, there aren't any bones in there, there's nothing in there.

"Do I have any bones?" I asked them. "Do I have any bones? Do you think I have any bones?" I couldn't stop asking.

"Everybody has bones," said Polly.

"But do *I* have any bones?"

"You've got them," said Georgina. Then she ran out of the room. She came back in half a minute with Valerie.[2]

"Look at her," Georgina said, pointing at me.

Valerie looked at me and went away.

"I just want to see them," I said. "I just have to be sure."

"They're in there—I promise you," said Georgina.

"I'm not safe," I said suddenly.

Valerie was back, with a full medication cup.

"Valerie, I'm not safe," I said.

"You take this." She gave me the cup.

I could tell it was Thorazine from the color. I'd never had it before. I tipped my head back and drank.

It was sticky and sour and it oozed into my stomach. The taste of it stayed in my throat. I swallowed a few times.

"Oh, Valerie," I said, "you promised —" Then the Thorazine hit me. It was like a wall of water, strong but soft.

"Wow," I said. I couldn't hear my own voice very well. I decided to stand up, but when I did, I found myself on the floor.

Valerie and Georgina picked me up under the arms and steered me down the hall to our room. My legs and feet felt like mattresses, they were so huge and dense. Valerie and Georgina felt like mattresses too, big soft mattresses pressing on either side of me. It was comforting.

"It'll be okay, won't it?" I asked. My voice was far away from me and I hadn't said what I meant. What I meant was that now I was safe, now I was really crazy, and nobody could take me out of there. . . .

So these were the charges against me. I didn't read them until twenty-five years later. "A character disorder" is what they'd told me then.

I had to find a lawyer to help me get my records from the hospital; I had to read line 32a of form A1 of the Case Record, and entry G on the Discharge on Visit Summary, and entry B of Part IV of the Case Report; then I had to locate a copy of the *Diagnostic and Statistical Manual of Mental Disorders* and look up Borderline Personality to see what they really thought about me.

It's a fairly accurate picture of me at eighteen, minus a few quirks like reckless driving and eating binges. It's accurate but isn't profound. Of course, it doesn't aim to be profound. It's not even a case study. It's a set of guidelines, a generalization.

---

[2] A nurse

I'm tempted to try refuting it, but then I would be open to the further charges of "defensiveness" and "resistance."

All I can do is give the particulars: an annotated diagnosis.

"[U]ncertainty about several life issues, such as self-image, sexual orientation, long-term goals or career choice, types of friends or lovers to have . . ." I relish that last phrase. Its awkwardness (the "to have" seems superfluous) gives it substance and heft. I still have that uncertainty. Is this the type of friend or lover I want to have? I ask myself every time I meet someone new. Charming but shallow; good-hearted but a bit conventional; too handsome for his own good; fascinating but probably unreliable; and so forth. I guess I've had my share of unreliables. More than my share? How many would constitute more than my share?

Fewer than for somebody else—somebody who'd never been called a borderline personality?

That's the nub of my problem here.

If my diagnosis had been bipolar illness, for instance, the reaction to me and to this story would be slightly different. That's a chemical problem, you'd say to yourself, manic-depression, Lithium, all that. I would be blameless, somehow. And what about schizophrenia—that would send a chill up your spine. After all, that's real insanity. People don't "recover" from schizophrenia. You'd have to wonder how much of what I'm telling you is true and how much imagined.

I'm simplifying, I know. But these words taint everything. The fact that I was locked up taints everything.

What does *borderline personality* mean, anyhow?

It appears to be a way station between neurosis and psychosis: a fractured but not disassembled psyche. Though to quote my post-Melvin psychiatrist: "It's what they call people whose lifestyles bother them."

He can say it because he's a doctor. If I said it, nobody would believe me.

An analyst I've known for years said, "Freud and his circle thought most people were hysterics, then in the fifties it was psychoneurotics, and lately, everyone's a borderline personality."

When I went to the corner bookstore to look up my diagnosis in the *Manual*, it occurred to me that I might not find it in there anymore. They do get rid of things—homosexuality, for instance. Until recently, quite a few of my friends would have found themselves documented in that book along with me. Well, they got out of the book and I didn't. Maybe in another twenty-five years I won't be in there either.

"[I]nstability of self-image, interpersonal relationships, and mood . . . uncertainty about . . . long-term goals or career choice . . ." Isn't this a good description of adolescence? Moody, fickle, faddish, insecure: in short, impossible.

"[S]elf-mutilating behavior (e.g., wrist-scratching) . . ." I've skipped forward a bit. This is the one that caught me by surprise as I sat on the floor of the bookstore reading my diagnosis. Wrist-scratching! I thought I'd invented it. Wrist-banging, to be precise.

This is where people stop being able to follow me. This is the sort of stuff you get locked up for. Nobody knew I was doing it, though. I never told anyone, until now.

I had a butterfly chair. In the sixties, everyone in Cambridge had a butterfly chair. The metal edge of its upturned seat was perfectly placed for wrist-banging. I had tried breaking ashtrays and walking on the shards, but I didn't have the nerve to tread firmly. Wrist-banging—slow, steady, mindless—was a better solution. It was cumulative injury, so each bang was tolerable.

A solution to what? I quote from the *Manual*: "This behavior may . . . counteract feelings of 'numbness' and depersonalization that arise during periods of extreme stress."

I spent hours in my butterfly chair banging my wrist. I did it in the evenings, like homework. I'd do some homework, then I'd spend half an hour wrist-banging, then finish my homework, then back in the chair for some more banging before brushing my teeth and going to bed. I banged the inside, where the veins converge. It swelled and turned a bit blue, but considering how hard and how much I banged it, the visible damage was slight. That was yet one more recommendation of it to me.

I'd had an earlier period of face-scratching. If my fingernails hadn't been quite short, I couldn't have gotten away with it. As it was, I definitely looked puffy and peculiar the next day. I used to scratch my cheeks and then rub soap on them. Maybe the soap prevented me from looking worse. But I looked bad enough that people asked, "Is something wrong with your face?" So I switched to wrist-banging.

I was like an anchorite with a hair shirt. Part of the point was that nobody knew about my suffering. If people knew and admired—or abominated—me, something important would be lost.

I was trying to explain my situation to myself. My situation was that I was in pain and nobody knew it; even I had trouble knowing it. So I told myself, over and over, You are in pain. It was the only way I could get through to myself ("counteract feelings of 'numbness'"). I was demonstrating, externally and irrefutably, an inward condition.

"Quite often social contrariness and a generally pessimistic outlook are observed." What do you suppose they mean by "social contrariness"? Putting my elbows on the table? Refusing to get a job as a dental technician? Disappointing my parents' hope that I would go to a first-rate university?

They don't define "social contrariness," and I can't define it, so I think it ought to be excluded from the list. I'll admit to the generally pessimistic outlook. Freud had one too.

I can honestly say that my misery has been transformed into common unhappiness, so by Freud's definition I have achieved mental health. And my discharge sheet, at line 41, Outcome with Regard to Mental Disorder, reads "Recovered."

Recovered. Had my personality crossed over that border, whatever and wherever it was, to resume life within the confines of the normal? Had I stopped arguing with my personality and learned to straddle the line between sane and insane? Perhaps I'd actually had an identity disorder. "In Identity Disorder there is a similar clinical picture, but Borderline Personality . . . preempts the diagnosis . . . if the disturbance is sufficiently pervasive and . . . it is unlikely that it will be limited to a developmental stage." Maybe I was a victim of improper preemption?

I'm not finished with this diagnosis.

"The person often experiences this instability of self-image as chronic feelings of emptiness or boredom." My chronic feelings of emptiness and boredom came from the fact that I was living a life based on my incapacities, which were numerous. A partial list follows. I could not and did not want to: ski, play tennis, or go to gym class; attend to any subject in school other than English and biology; write papers on any assigned topics (I wrote poems instead of papers for English topics; I got F's); plan to go or apply to college; give any reasonable explanation for these refusals.

My self-image was not unstable. I saw myself, quite correctly, as unfit for the educational and social systems.

But my parents and teachers did not share my self-image. Their image of me was unstable, since it was out of kilter with reality and based on their needs and wishes. They did not put much value on my capacities, which were admittedly few, but genuine. I read everything, I wrote constantly, and I had boyfriends by the barrelful.

"Why don't you do the assigned reading?" they'd ask. "Why don't you write your papers instead of whatever you're writing—what is that, a short story?" "Why don't you expend as much energy on your schoolwork as you do on your boyfriends?"

By my senior year I didn't even bother with excuses, let alone explanations.

"Where is your term paper?" asked my history teacher.

"I didn't write it. I have nothing to say on that topic."

"You could have picked another topic."

"I have nothing to say on any historical topic."

One of my teachers told me I was a nihilist. He meant it as an insult but I took it as a compliment.

Boyfriends and literature: How can you make a life out of those two things? As it turns out, I did; more literature than boyfriends lately, but I guess you can't have everything ("a generally pessimistic outlook [is] observed").

Back then I didn't know that I—or anyone—could make a life out of boyfriends and literature. As far as I could see, life demanded skills I didn't have. The result was chronic emptiness and boredom. There were more pernicious results as well: self-loathing, alternating with "inappropriately intense anger with frequent displays of temper . . ."

What would have been an appropriate level of intensity for my anger at feeling shut out of life? My classmates were spinning their fantasies for the future: lawyer, ethnobotanist, Buddhist monk (it was a very progressive high school). Even the dumb, uninteresting ones who were there to provide "balance" looked forward to their marriages and their children. I knew I wasn't going to have any of this because I knew I didn't want it. But did that mean I would have nothing?

I was the first person in the history of the school not to go to college. Of course, at least a third of my classmates never finished college. By 1968, people were dropping out daily.

Quite often now, people say to me, when I tell them I didn't go to college, "Oh, how marvelous!" They wouldn't have thought it was so marvelous back then. They didn't; my classmates were just the sorts of people who now tell me how marvelous I am. In 1966, I was a pariah.

What was I going to do? a few of my classmates asked.

"I'm going to join the WACs," I told one guy.

"Oh, yeah? That will be an interesting career."

"Just kidding," I said.

"Oh, uh, you mean you're not, really?"

I was stunned. Who did they think I was?

I'm sure they didn't think about me much. I was that one who wore black and—really, I've heard it from several people—slept with the English teacher. They were all seventeen and miserable, just like me. They didn't have time to wonder why I was a little more miserable than most.

Emptiness and boredom: what an understatement. What I felt was complete desolation. Desolation, despair, and depression.

Isn't there some other way to look at this? After all, angst of these dimensions is a luxury item. You need to be well fed, clothed, and housed to have time for this much self-pity. And the college business: My parents wanted me to go, I didn't want to go, and I didn't go. I got what I wanted. Those who don't go to college have to get jobs. I agreed with all this. I told myself all this over and over. I even got a job—my job breaking au gratin dishes.

But the fact that I couldn't hold my job was worrisome. I was probably crazy. I'd been skirting the idea of craziness for a year or two; now I was closing in on it.

Pull yourself together! I told myself. Stop indulging yourself. There's nothing wrong with you. You're just wayward.

One of the great pleasures of mental health (whatever that is) is how much less time I have to spend thinking about myself.

I have a few more annotations to my diagnosis.

"The disorder is more commonly diagnosed in women."

Note the construction of that sentence. They did not write, "The disorder is more common in women." It would still be suspect, but they didn't bother trying to cover their tracks.

Many disorders, judging by the hospital population, were more commonly diagnosed in women. . . .

In the list of six "potentially self-damaging" activities favored by the borderline personality, three are commonly associated with women (shopping sprees, shoplifting, and eating binges) and one with men (reckless driving). One is not "gender-specific," as they say these days (psychoactive substance abuse). And the definition of the other (casual sex) is in the eye of the beholder.

Then there is the question of "premature death" from suicide. Luckily, I avoided it, but I thought about suicide a lot. I'd think about it and make myself sad over my premature death, and then I'd feel better. The idea of suicide worked on me like a purgative or a cathartic. For some people it's different—Daisy, for instance. But was her death really "premature"? Ought she to have sat in her eat-in kitchen with her chicken and her anger for another fifty years? I'm assuming she wasn't going to change, and I may be wrong. She certainly made that assumption, and she may also have been wrong. And if she'd sat there for only thirty years, and killed herself at forty-nine instead of at nineteen, would her death still be "premature"?

I got better and Daisy didn't and I can't explain why. Maybe I was just flirting with madness the way I flirted with my teachers and my classmates. I wasn't convinced I was crazy, though I feared I was. Some people say that having any conscious opinion on the matter is a mark of sanity, but I'm not sure that's true. I still think about it. I'll always have to think about it.

I often ask myself if I'm crazy. I ask other people too.

"Is this a crazy thing to say?" I'll ask before saying something that probably isn't crazy.

I start a lot of sentences with "Maybe I'm totally nuts," or "Maybe I've gone 'round the bend."

If I do something out of the ordinary—take two baths in one day, for example—I say to myself: Are you crazy?

It's a common phrase, I know. But it means something particular to me: the tunnels, the security screens, the plastic forks, the shimmering, ever-shifting borderline that like all boundaries beckons and asks to be crossed. I do not want to cross it again.

Response and Analysis

1. How do you react to Susanna Kaysen's description of her experiences? What most affected you about the reading? Why?

2. Briefly describe Kaysen's mood changes, unstable interpersonal relationships, and identity problems.

3. Kaysen examines the extent to which her behaviors fit the criteria for her diagnosis, borderline personality disorder. Which of her behaviors does Kaysen believe fit and do not fit the diagnosis?

4. How do the psychodynamic, social learning, and cognitive perspectives conceptualize borderline personality disorder?

Research

Suppose you are interested in whether biases and expectations influence the judgment of diagnosticians in making their psychological diagnoses. Specifically, you want to know if members of one ethnic group are diagnosed with more severe disorders than are members of another group.

You recruit forty diagnosticians (twenty men, twenty women) to participate in your study. Their responses will be completely anonymous. Each diagnostician will receive the same case history. However, you tell half of the participants that the case history is for an African American male, and you tell the other half that the case is for a white male. After reviewing the case history, the participants will offer a diagnosis.

Do you believe that either the African American males or the white males will receive a more severe diagnosis? Why? Is this an adequate way to study how ethnicity might influence the judgments of diagnosticians? Why or why not? Do you think the ethnicity of the diagnosticians would influence their ratings? Why or why not?

LOSING YOUR SHIRT

Mary Heineman

Psychological Concept
compulsive gambling

Pathological gambling, kleptomania, and pyromania are common impulse control disorders. Persons suffering from these disorders often feel a growing tension that they release by behaving in ways that are harmful to themselves or to others. Unfortunately, these disorders can destroy lives and may result in large financial debts, poor health, emotional exhaustion, and even a prison sentence. The following are Stuart's and Dan's accounts of their addiction to gambling. Both came from families who gambled, but, other than that, their families were very different, as were their motives for gambling. Their stories help us understand how each succumbed to this destructive compulsion.

Stuart's Story—in the Beginning

I was born a gambler. My father was a compulsive gambler, and he taught me to gamble long before I started kindergarten. The only games we played were games of chance. I became my father's most devoted fan. I looked up to him the first ten years of my life. He was fun, exciting, active, and always doing something new and daring. I felt privileged when he would allow me to accompany him to the track or to off-track betting parlors. He taught me to read a scratch sheet. He used to have me call him at work after I got home from school to give him the results of the P.M. races. I knew Dad looked forward to my calls, and I would be especially excited if I was calling to tell him he had won. Often he gave me extra money when he had it, and boy, did I love that!

My first gambling experience with others was pitching pennies after school with two kids in fourth grade. I had already been pitching pennies for over three years, so I was pretty good at it. I couldn't wait for my father to get home from work so I could share my good luck with him. He always listened to me when the conversation was about gambling.

To me, gambling meant having a father who would talk to me, cared about me, and would be interested in what I had to say. I could always get his attention if I had a gambling experience to share.

By the time I was in junior high school, my father's gambling had gotten way out of hand. He and my mother were fighting all the time. We never had any money, she couldn't pay the bills, and we were getting endless phone calls from banks, department stores, and loan companies. It got so bad at times that we had to walk more than two miles to my grandparents' house to get food. Those visits were never pleasant. We would have to listen to Grandpa pressure Mom to leave Dad because of his gambling. That always scared me.

Shortly after my sixteenth birthday, I realized just how angry I was with my father. He had become so consumed by his gambling that we hardly ever talked. Our common interest and the fun we used to have sharing it had long since gone. It's ironic, because at that time, my gambling was going just great. I was winning much more than I was losing, I had a great reputation with my friends, and I felt great.

At that point in my life, the one thing I knew for sure was that I would never let my gambling control me like it controlled my father. I was too smart to let that happen.

Stuart's Story—in the End

What did gambling do for me? It brought me closer to my father, because it was a common interest. In addition, I got a great deal of excitement from gambling. I was always the kind of kid who could not stand boredom. I wanted to live "on the edge," and gambling let me do that. I could never feel bored while sitting on a bet that was made with money badly needed for living expenses or, better yet, with money that belonged to someone else.

When I gambled during my teens, I found out I could ignore things that others were concerned about—tests, getting a job, money to buy a car, or getting a date for high school dances. My main concern during that time was simply where to raise the money I needed to be in ACTION the following day. ACTION was my only interest. I could get a date anytime—that wasn't a problem. But I didn't want a date, because no girl ever made me feel the way I did when I won big.

Winning big made me feel important, strong, powerful, and potent. I was raised by a macho father and I guess I adopted his attitudes. My first twelve years of gambling kept my self-esteem high. Everyone knew I had a great deal of self-confidence. They could see it in my face and hear it in my voice. I feared no one. Gambling, with its occasional big wins, made me feel like a man.

That's what gambling did *for* me, and it would have been nice if that would have continued; however, I was much more affected by what gambling did *to* me.

Gambling prevented me from learning how to socialize. When my friends were beginning to interact with the opposite sex, I was at the track. While my friends were dating, I was out trying to raise the money I needed to be in ACTION. My nineteenth birthday came and went and I had never even had a single date. By the time I was twenty-one, I couldn't get up the nerve to ask a girl for a date. I just kept gambling and put the whole idea of dating out of my mind. The few friends I had started pairing off, marrying, and moving away. I pretended not to care. As long as I could be with the horses, I cared about little else.

Gambling prevented me from getting interested in any hobby or craft. I had no special talents. I couldn't play tennis or golf and I could barely swim. During my teen years, I devoted all my time and energy to my one love.

Eventually, as my gambling progressed, it took hold of me completely. No matter what was going on in my life, I had to gamble. I became the world's greatest liar. I had to lie to so many people to get the money I needed to pay debts or to gamble. I ignored my family and the people I cared about. No one could count on me ever showing up for an important occasion, because I would only go if it didn't interfere with my going to the track. Whenever I was invited anywhere, I would always answer yes, because I never cared about what I said. My only concern was that my answer make the other person happy. That prevented me from being pressured.

I was whatever anyone wanted me to be. I would promise anyone the world if it would get them off my back. My daily goal was to avoid conflict so I could be free to put my energy elsewhere.

I let everybody down. No one could trust me. No one would confide in me. In the end, no one needed me.

What did gambling do to me? It controlled me just like it had controlled my father, even though I had been so sure I was too smart to let that happen.

Dan's Story—in the Beginning

I was a spoiled brat. My dad was a very successful businessman and well-respected in the community. Despite his busy schedule, he always attended my school activities. He encouraged me to do the things that interested me. He tried to motivate me in anything he saw as a plus in my life, and he often praised me in front of others. I was an only child and I truly felt he was proud of me.

My mother wrote children's stories (one was made into a movie). Since she wrote at home, she was always there for me. Sometimes I felt she was too focused on me and overprotective, but even at an early age, I knew that she always had my best interests at heart.

If compulsive gamblers need parents to blame for their addiction, I am out in the cold. I loved and respected my parents more than any kid I knew. They did everything they could possibly do to show me their love.

Gambling was part of my family's lifestyle, and it was never a problem. Both my parents loved to visit the casinos a couple of times a year, and they'd have dinner at the racetrack every few months. It was one of their leisure activities, among many others: opera, theater, tennis, golf, traveling, and socializing at the country club.

My dad thought of gambling as a macho activity, so he didn't discourage me from an occasional wager on my favorite games, even at a young age. As a matter of fact, he often wagered with me. I enjoyed that because it gave us a common interest.

I started to gamble without my parents' knowledge when I was in the ninth grade. I was fifteen years old and the smallest kid in class. Although I loved sports, I never tried out because of my size. I did the only thing I could think of to get involved with sports: I became the high school bookie. I ran the pools for the weekend games. While I was managing the money and keeping book, I started to wager heavily myself. I didn't wager because I needed money (my parents were always generous with me). I wagered heavily to show off in front of my school friends. I wanted them to see me as a risk-taker, not a wimp. I felt that some of my classmates looked down on me because I was short and slight. They never really said anything derogatory, but they were somewhat sarcastic and I felt hurt. I needed their acceptance. I did not want to feel different.

At any rate, I found out very quickly that gambling was one way I could get what I needed. My reputation as a successful sports bettor spread fast and stuck with me throughout high school.

Gambling afforded me something my parents could not buy: the acceptance and respect of my schoolmates. I loved it.

Dan's Story—in the End

Gambling made me believe that all the things my parents said about me were true—that I was bright, creative, and intelligent. Before gambling, I never believed in myself because I never felt accepted by my classmates. I always felt like an outsider.

My first big win proved to me I could be popular. I fooled myself into thinking the kids liked me when I now know they liked my money and my generosity. Before I started winning, I was never invited to join the others at school activities. Because of my size, I couldn't get a date. I stopped asking girls to go out with me by the time I was a junior in high school. However, in my senior year, I had a number of girl-friends because I could afford to take them wherever they wanted to go.

Gambling and winning allowed me to grow approximately six inches in the eyes of others. It made me feel six feet tall.

Today I know it is more important for me to remember what gambling did *to* me and not for me.

By the time I graduated from college, I had few coping skills. I was irresponsible, very immature, and totally consumed by my gambling. The amounts I was betting and the frequency of my gambling caused many problems. The more problems I had, the more I gambled; and the more I gambled, the more problems I had.

My parents bailed me out over and over again to the tune of over thirty thousand dollars. Each time they came to my rescue, I promised them, often with my tears, that if they helped me I would never gamble again. I would have promised them anything, as long it got me whatever I needed to remain in ACTION.

Gambling made me so incredibly selfish. I felt resentful on the night our American prisoners of war were returning from Vietnam because I had to miss the football games that the news coverage preempted.

Gambling made me hate any family occasion when it was necessary to give a gift, because I wanted to spend my money on nothing but gambling.

Gambling made me make a new friend only if I thought he would be good for a touch when I was in need of money.

Gambling made it so that the only time I ever felt emotionally comfortable was when I was in ACTION.

Gambling convinced me that my problem was money and that one more big win would solve everything.

What did gambling do *to* me? It removed all the positive characteristics my parents worked so hard to foster within me, and it destroyed them emotionally. I knew that when they first realized my gambling was a serious problem, they blamed themselves. I used my knowledge of their guilt to manipulate them. They raised me in hopes I would adopt their most precious values, but I ignored every one of them. I didn't care about their values; I didn't care about their feelings; I didn't care about anything but being in ACTION. I cursed them, blamed them, stole from them, and, in the end, I attacked them physically—one day they refused to give me the money I needed to pay gambling debts in order to keep my credit with my loan shark and thus stay in ACTION.

What did gambling do *to* me? It resulted in losing the people most dear to me, my parents—the two people who would have died for me, the two people who gave me their hearts. I took those hearts and broke them.

Response and Analysis

1. Why did Stuart and Dan gamble before they began high school? During high school? During college? After college? What function did gambling serve in their lives?

2. How did Stuart's and Dan's preoccupation with gambling affect their social relationships? Academic success? Coping skills?

3. Why was it difficult for Stuart and Dan to overcome their compulsion to gamble?

Research

Suppose you want to examine the personality traits of persons diagnosed as pathological gamblers. You decide to administer the Minnesota Multiphasic Personality Inventory (MMPI) to serve one hundred college students in your state. However, because of scheduling difficulties, you are unable to administer the MMPI at the same time to the participants. Half of the participants (most of whom are freshmen) complete the MMPI in mid-December; the other half (most of whom are seniors) complete it in mid-July. How might the time of year and composition of the sample influence your findings?

chapter 9

SUBSTANCE-RELATED
DISORDERS

*In the story of Dracula the victim offers
himself, exposing his neck before Dracula
sucks the blood. Once bitten, he is Dracula's
slave. Here there are two aspects to the phenomenon of addiction—giving oneself over
and being taken and possessed. They are
inseparable.*

LINDA SCHIERSE LEONARD,
*Witness to the Fire: Creativity
and the Veil of Addiction*

Substance abuse remains an enormous social problem. Addiction, violence, crime, impairment of functioning, poor health, poverty, victimization of children—all of these may arise from misuse of drugs. Substance use is considered a psychological disorder when it impairs social or occupational functioning and causes dependence, or when contact with other toxic substances, such as heavy metals, paints, glues, pesticides, or carbon monoxide, produces psychological impairment.

Alcohol is the most frequently implicated substance among the substance-related disorders. It accounts for a staggering number of lost hours on the job and for well over 10% of the nation's total health costs. In the first selection, Caroline Knapp tells of her descent into alcoholism and of the difficulty in quitting. For a long time, Knapp, like many who are dependent on alcohol, did not recognize her problem as alcoholism because she thought alcoholics were unable to hold a job or maintain good professional and social relationships. She avoided acknowledging her condition and making others suspicious by hiding bottles or drinking in secret, but she was unable to mislead anyone for long.

In the next selection, Nan Robertson, a reporter for the *New York Times*, describes her battle to abstain from alcohol. Her recovery was sometimes rocky;

wherever she went, it seemed as though alcohol was served and people were drinking. Central to helping her recover was the support she received from members of Alcoholics Anonymous, as well as the medication Antabuse.

Young persons make up a disproportionately high percentage of substance abusers. In the third selection, D. H. tells about using steroids because he wanted to be a football star, whatever the cost. As he continued to use them, the initial effects (enhanced physique and performance) were overshadowed by the negative ones (emotional instability, aggressiveness, symptoms of sterility). But D. H. nonetheless found it difficult to quit because of his intense desire to increase his body's size and strength.

In the final selection, John C. Flynn tells the story of Helen, who abused cocaine, and Helen describes her initial interest in and progression with the drug. She was not knowledgeable or concerned about the long-term effects of the drug, and the force of the drug soon took hold. Helen became dependent on cocaine and suffered a seizure, was hospitalized, and had some irreparable loss of memory. For Helen, D. H., Robertson, Knapp, and for many other substance abusers, quitting is half the battle; avoiding relapse is the other half.

MY DESCENT INTO ALCOHOLISM

Caroline Knapp

Psychological Concept
alcohol dependence

Caroline Knapp, author, contributing editor, and columnist, writes of what she calls her "love affair" with alcohol. Knapp was addicted to alcohol but was convinced that she was not an alcoholic because she held a job and had friends, many of whom drank as much as she. Alcohol was everywhere. It was present at social gatherings and celebrations, at times of sadness, and at moments when she wanted to relax. It was the accompaniment to the action until it became the action itself. What reasons does Knapp suggest were responsible for her becoming an alcoholic?

Idrank.

I drank Fumé Blanc at the Ritz-Carlton Hotel, and I drank double shots of Johnnie Walker Black on the rocks at a dingy Chinese restaurant across the street from my office, and I drank at home. For a long time I drank expensive red wine, and I learned to appreciate the subtle differences between a silky Merlot and a tart Cabernet Sauvignon and a soft, earthy Beaucastel from the south of France, but I never really cared about those nuances because, honestly, they were beside the point. Toward the end I kept two bottles of Cognac in my house: the bottle for show, which I kept on the counter, and the real bottle, which I kept in the back of a cupboard beside an old toaster. The level of liquid in the show bottle was fairly consistent, decreasing by an inch or so, perhaps less, each week. The liquid in the real bottle disappeared quickly, sometimes within days. I was living alone at the time, when I did this, but I did it anyway and it didn't occur to me not to: it was always important to maintain appearances.

I drank when I was happy and I drank when I was anxious and I drank when I was bored and I drank when I was depressed, which was often. I started to raid my parents' liquor cabinet the year my father was dying. He'd be in the back of their house in Cambridge, lying in the hospital bed in their bedroom, and I'd steal into the front hall bathroom and pull out a bottle of Old Grand-dad that I'd hidden behind the toilet. It tasted vile—the bottle must have been fifteen years old—but my father was dying, dying very slowly and gradually from a brain tumor, so I drank it anyway and it helped.

My mother found that bottle, empty, that April, the day of my father's funeral. I'd thrown most of the others away but I must have forgotten that one, and she'd discovered it stashed behind the toilet as she was cleaning the front bathroom for guests.

I was sitting at the dining-room table and as she walked through the room, the bottle in her hand, she glared at me, a look of profound disappointment. So I lied.

"That was *before*," I said, referring to a promise I'd made her six months before my father died. "Two drinks a day," I'd said. "No more than that. I promise I'll cut down."

I'd made the promise on a Sunday the previous July, in the midst of a pounding hangover. I'd been visiting my parents at their summerhouse on Martha's Vineyard and I'd gotten so drunk the night before, I almost passed out on the sofa, sitting right there next to my mother. I'd done the drinking in secret, of course, stealing off to my bedroom every thirty minutes or so to take a slug off a bottle of Scotch I'd stashed in my bag, and I vaguely remember the end of the night, my words slurring when I tried to talk, my eyelids so droopy I had to strain to keep them open. I was usually more careful than that, careful to walk the line between being drunk enough and too drunk, careful to do most of the serious drinking at the very end of the night, after everyone else had gone to bed. But I slipped up that time and my mother caught me. The next day she asked me to take a walk with her on the beach, an unusual move for my mother, who requested a private audience only when she had something very serious to say. I remember it was a sunny morning, mid-July, with a stiff breeze and hot light, and I remember a feeling of dread and contrition; I was hoping she wouldn't be mad at me.

We made our way down the dirt path that led from our house to Menemsha Pond, a blue arc of water at the bottom of the hill, and then we walked for a while in silence. Finally she said, "I need to talk to you. I'm very worried about your drinking."

I said, "I know." I walked beside her, keeping my eyes on my feet in the sand, afraid that if I looked up I'd bump too abruptly into a truth I didn't really want to see. I added, softly, "I am too." I could tell from her tone that she wasn't angry, just worried, and I had to admit to her: I was too. Sort of.

We walked some more. She said, "This is very serious. It's more serious than smoking."

My mother was the sort of person who chose her words with the utmost care, and I understood that a wealth of meanings ran beneath that simple phrase: *more serious than smoking*. Smoking caused cancer, a disease that was killing my father, that had killed several women in her family, that would kill her just a few years later. She understood that drinking was more dangerous and she understood why: smoking could ruin my body; drinking could ruin my mind and my future. It could eat its way through my life in exactly the same way a physical cancer eats its way through bones and blood and tissue, destroying everything.

"It *really* is serious," she said.

I kept my head lowered. "I know."

And I meant it, at least just then. There are moments as an active alcoholic where you *do* know, where in a flash of clarity you grasp that alcohol is the central problem, a kind of liquid glue that gums up all the internal gears and keeps you stuck. The pond was beautiful that day, rippled and sparkling, turning the sand a deep sienna where it lapped against the shore, and for an instant, I did know, I could see it: I was thirty-three and I was drinking way too much and I was miserable, and there had to be a connection.

My mother was such a gentle woman. She said, "What can I do to help you? I'll do anything I can," and that's when I made the promise.

I looked out across the pond, not wanting to look her in the eyes. "I don't know," I said. "I know I have to deal with it." I told her I'd look into Alcoholics Anonymous. I said, "In the meantime I'll cut down. Two drinks a day. No more than that. I promise."

I'd meant it. That afternoon I took the ferry from Martha's Vineyard to Woods Hole, en route back to Boston where I lived, and I remember sitting there on the boat, vaguely nauseated, my head still aching from the night before. I wanted a beer, just one beer to help ease the headache, and I debated with myself about that for several long minutes: Shouldn't I prove to myself that I could go a day—just one simple day—without a drink? Shouldn't I? The ninety-minute ride to Boston loomed ahead. The sky was clear, with the sharp light of late afternoon, and people wearing windbreakers and sweatshirts and sunglasses lolled on the deck in canvas chairs, sipping Budweiser and Michelob Light from tall plastic cups.

I had the beer. And then, when I got back to my apartment, I had a little wine with dinner. Just a little: two glasses, but they were small ones, so I considered them half-glasses and counted them as one. From that point on, though, I was always very careful around my mother—careful not to drink more than two glasses of anything in front of her, careful never to call her when I was drunk—but I didn't keep my promise.

And that's how it works. Active alcoholics try and active alcoholics fail. We make the promises and we really do try to stick with them and we keep ignoring the fact that we can't do it, keep rationalizing the third drink, or the fourth or fifth. *Just today. Bad day. I deserve a reward. I'll deal with it tomorrow. . . .*

I get pangs of horror sometimes when I think about what was happening to my brain back then, how all that alcohol was wending its way into my bloodstream and vital organs, how liquor might have been throwing things out of whack from the very start.

Normal drinkers seem to have a kind of built-in alarm system that tells them at a certain point to stop drinking. They ingest alcohol, it passes through the stomach walls and small intestine and into the bloodstream, then moves through cell membranes and mixes in the entire water content of the body: brain, liver, heart, pancreas, lungs, kidneys, and every other organ and tissue system are affected. Alcohol basically depresses the central nervous system, although at low doses it gives the drinker a revved-up, pleasant feeling: at first alcohol increases blood flow, accelerates the heart rate, and stimulates brain cells, all of which makes the drinker feel giddy, talkative, energetic. At higher doses the depressive effects are felt: the drinker gets uncoordinated; vision may be impaired; reflexes are delayed; speech gets slurred. The normal drinker usually calls it quits well before that point: that elusive internal alarm goes off and says, *No more.* Some Asians, who typically have one of the lowest rates of alcoholism in the world, experience what's called the Asian Flush Syndrome: too much liquor makes them warm and queasy, causes the heart rate to rise and the blood pressure to drop. The feeling is unpleasant and the drinker's natural, self-protective tendency is to abstain.

Not mine. No one really knows precisely why some people become alcoholic while others don't, but scientists are closing in on some of the causes. Alcoholism is probably an inherited phenomenon—research over the last thirty years has begun to confirm that alcoholism runs in families, suggesting that although environmental factors may contribute to the development of the disease, most alcoholics probably have a genetic predisposition to it as well.

Addiction to alcohol is also a neurological phenomenon, the result of a complex set of molecular alterations that take place in the brain when it's excessively and repeatedly exposed to the drug. The science of addiction is complicated, but the basic idea is fairly straightforward: alcohol appears to wreak havoc on the brain's natural systems of craving and reward, compromising the functioning of the various neurotransmitters and proteins that create feelings of well-being.

Essentially, drinking artificially "activates" the brain's reward system: you have a martini or two and the alcohol acts on the part of the brain's circuitry that makes you feel good, increasing the release of the neurotransmitter dopamine, which is central to feelings of pleasure and reward. Over time (and given the right combination of vulnerability to alcoholism and actual alcohol abuse), the brain develops what are known as "compensatory adaptations" to all that artificial revving up: in an effort to bring its own chemistry back into its natural equilibrium, it works overtime to *decrease* dopamine release, ultimately leaving those same pleasure/reward circuits depleted.

A vicious cycle ensues: by drinking too much, you basically diminish your brain's ability to manufacture feelings of well-being and calm on its own and you come to depend increasingly on the artificial stimulus—alcohol—to produce those feelings. This is why an alcoholic may wake up after a night of heavy drinking struggling with two competing motivations. The logical, thinking part of the brain, taking note of the hangover and the feelings of remorse, kicks in with determination and resolve: *Drinking too much is bad; I'm going to cut down; I mean it.* But the far less rational part—this far more mysterious, primitive, and powerful circuitry of pleasure and need—speaks in a more urgent, compelling voice: *No,* it says. *I feel bad. And I need a very specific thing, alcohol, in order to feel good again.*

Seen in this light, alcoholism may be a disease in the purest sense: a physiological state producing a sense of overwhelming *disease.* . . .

So there I was at age twenty, then twenty-one, then twenty-five and older, literally pickling.

Response and Analysis

1. Describe Caroline Knapp's progression to becoming an alcoholic. Why might many alcoholics initially deny their addiction?

2. How was Knapp physiologically and psychologically addicted to alcohol? How did the addiction influence her self-concept, interpersonal relationships, and performance at work?

3. What are some of the challenges to overcoming alcohol addiction?

4. How would you know if a friend had a problem with alcohol?

Research

Caroline Knapp tells how alcohol abuse affected her relationships with others. Alcohol abuse is also associated with aggressive behavior. Suppose you want to replicate a study examining how expectations about alcohol influence aggressive behavior. You decide that all participants will be given the same amount of a beverage. Half will drink tonic water and half will drink alcohol that does not taste when it is mixed with tonic water. Participants drinking alcohol will receive enough alcohol to become legally intoxicated. Before you hand out the beverage, you tell half of the participants who receive tonic water and half who receive tonic water and alcohol that they are drinking tonic water; you tell the other half that they are drinking alcohol. That is, one quarter of the participants will

- expect alcohol and drink alcohol, or
- expect alcohol but drink tonic water only, or
- expect tonic water but drink alcohol, or
- expect tonic water and drink tonic water.

After the participants drink the beverage, your research assistant will pretend to be a participant and irritate and annoy the real participants. Then you will give the participants an opportunity to deliver electric shocks to your research assistant. The degree of electric shock delivered is your measure of aggression. In fact, no shocks will be delivered to the assistant; the participants do not know that the shock-generating machine is not operational.

Do you think that knowledge of having consumed (or not consumed) alcohol would affect participants' aggressiveness? Why or why not?

Is it ethical to have people drink alcohol without their knowledge? If not, how can a researcher inform potential participants without creating expectations about how they should behave? Is it ethical to tell participants that they have delivered electric shocks to someone when no shocks are going to be delivered? How might a researcher debrief his or her participants regarding these issues? Do you think that the human subjects Institutional Review Board at your college or university would approve this study? Why or why not?

GETTING BETTER: INSIDE ALCOHOLICS ANONYMOUS

Nan Robertson

Psychological Concept
recovery from alcohol dependence

Nan Robertson is a reporter for the *New York Times* and recipient of the Pulitzer Prize for an article on toxic shock syndrome. Robertson, who had always been a heavy drinker, found herself in a cycle that went from depression to loneliness to drinking. She received treatment in a hospital for her addiction to alcohol and vowed to refrain from alcohol and continue treatment upon her release. In this selection, Robertson tells of the ways the drug Antabuse and the support she received from members of Alcoholics Anonymous were essential parts of her recovery.

On the morning of December 8, 1975, I said good-bye to Smithers.[1] As usual, there were hugs and kisses from the other patients, the counselors, and the nurses. "I *know* you'll make it, Nan," said Donna, a patient. I thought, "It's a good thing she hasn't read the staff report on me." I pushed open the heavy glass and iron front door and went out into the noisy streets of Manhattan. I passed Nodeldini's, a restaurant-bar around the corner, where so many patients who had bolted Smithers had gone to tie one on. I hailed a taxi to take me home. I was nervous and disoriented but hopeful.

That night, armed with the meeting book that lists the days, times and places of hundreds of A.A. meetings every week in Manhattan, I went to the group that met each Monday in the parish house of an imposing Gothic church on Upper Fifth Avenue. Despite Smithers, I was not prepared for what I saw. I somehow expected a gathering of shabby depressives, yet there before me was a quintessentially Upper East Side Episcopalian congregation, some men in pinstripes, many women shod in low-heeled, perfect Ferragamo pumps, with bits of discreet family jewelry at the throat and wrists.

The hospitality committee of my fellow drunks welcomed me at the door with smiles and handshakes. Their warmth swept away my timidity. The meeting was as impeccably ordered as any Sunday service at my own church, St. James, a mile down Madison Avenue.

---

[1] A rehabilitation center that has an alcohol treatment program

During the weeks that followed, I went table-hopping every night to a different meeting, each featuring a slice of New York life. There were blocked writers expressing their angst on the Upper West Side and blue-collar workers in Brooklyn recalling bars they had loved. The beginners' meetings everywhere were charged with raw emotion, close to the edge. The people in them, only days or weeks away from their last drink, could be on pink clouds of jubilation or jittery, unstrung and sullen. In distinct contrast to the group I had gone to my first night out of Smithers, the dress code was universally casual.

Soon, I began to see why A.A. members kept going to meetings. They comforted and centered me. The people in them steadied and supported me in ways as small but crucial as an arm around my shoulder. Sometimes my attention wandered for stretches of time while I retreated into my own thoughts. Sometimes I was bored. But a speaker, or even a sentence uttered from the floor, would get through to me. At one meeting, a man said, "I began coming to these basements and I discovered that I was right about myself—I am a decent person." I thought with surprise, "So am I." I helped make coffee, unfolded chairs, cleaned ashtrays when the meetings were over. Veterans asked me to come with them to nearby coffee shops afterward, and in these little clusters I enjoyed their stories, told my own, made friends, swapped telephone numbers.

But I was afraid to speak up in meetings. A shyness foreign to me stopped me every time I wanted to open my mouth. Finally, after four months in A.A., I raised my hand in a group that gathered near my apartment, six floors up in the parish house of a Presbyterian church. The group was small, and after attending several meetings there I felt at home. Overwhelmed with nervousness, I said, "My name is Nan, and I am an alcoholic. I have been sober four months, and I am so grateful to be here." I could not go on. My voice trembled, and I knew that if I said anything more, I would burst into tears. Everybody in the little group turned to me, smiling and applauding. They knew that the beginners are the bravest ones, enduring the hardest times. They knew that as you go on, it gets easier.

Those first months, I simply put one foot ahead of another. I took everything the old-timers told me on faith. They told me not to take that first drink, and to go to meetings every night. Simpleminded as the advice seemed to me, I had nothing else to hold on to. I was often depressed. I disliked much of the A.A. official literature and its "onward and upward with Babbitt" tone. I was convinced I could never again enjoy life with my old gusto, never have fun at a party again. My work did not interest me. I was struggling in a fog of ennui and blunted feelings. I believed I would never again experience life with the intensity that had been natural to me in my best years.

In the winter of 1976, just two months out of Smithers, I experienced my first strong compulsion to have a drink. I had thrown out all the liquor in my apartment, and so, when three friends asked me to go to a theater matinee with them, I suggested that I fix them lunch at home and that they bring their own wine to accompany it. They arrived with two bottles of white wine but drank only one. I put the other in my refrigerator, and we went off to the theater. My mood darkened during the play. I could not concentrate. I went home and opened the refrigerator door. There was the bottle of wine, dewy and inviting. My mouth watered. I reached for it. Then I slammed the refrigerator door and rushed to telephone an A.A. friend. She told me: "Get that bottle of wine and pour it right now down the sink. *Now*. I'll hang on." I did as she asked. We talked for thirty minutes, and by then my obsession with the wine had dissipated. . . .

My last and most terrible compulsion to drink gripped me in September 1976. My newspaper sent me to a far corner of northern Maine for an interview with a family of authors. Helen and Jose Yglesias, their son Raphael, and Lewis Cole, Helen's son by a previous marriage, were all writing books in various corners of an old farmhouse near Brooklin. The interview proceeded smoothly with this lively, articulate and amusing family. I stayed for lunch, and Helen brought out the white wine to accompany it. Without warning, I began to come apart. I wanted to drink that wine, with the kind of sickening urgency only an addict knows. My concentration was going; I could not sustain the conversation. I abruptly terminated the interview.

I drove like a madwoman, heading for the Bangor airport an hour and a half away, where I had reserved a room at the airport hotel for that night. By this time, the obsession to drink had seized me and was shaking me like some great dog. I could barely see the road. Every bar along the way seemed to be beckoning me. I wanted to drink, but I could not drink. I had been taking a little white Antabuse pill every morning for several months, prescribed by a doctor who worked with alcoholics. With Antabuse in me, one ounce of liquor—or less—would make me dangerously ill.

I pulled up to the Bangor airport sweating with fear. I telephoned my A.A. sponsor, Anna L., in New York. She was not there. I called another close A.A. friend in New York. Jerry said, instantly, "Don't stay there overnight. Take the next plane here." He told me to come straight from La Guardia to his apartment and to stay and talk with him until I felt better. "Stay overnight with me and my wife if you need to," Jerry said. "We'd love to have you."

Jerry's calm assurance, the unhesitating willingness to help that is typical in A.A., catapulted me onto the next plane to New York and through the hours that followed. After an hour or so with Jerry, I went serenely home to bed. I am convinced that without Antabuse in me, I would have pulled in at one of the bars on the road to the Bangor airport. In those early months and years of sobriety, I was deeply grateful to the drug, because it protected me from even the most overwhelming urge to drink.

I had begun taking a daily dose of Antabuse several months before the Bangor episode under the supervision of Dr. Ruth Fox, an elderly psychiatrist who had introduced the drug into the United States from Denmark in 1950 and who had been doing research and treatment in the field of alcoholism since the 1930's. My psychiatrist, a friend of Dr. Fox's, had suggested I join her small therapy group for alcoholics, which met every Wednesday night at her office-apartment in midtown Manhattan. I loved the group, which had a nucleus of about eight regulars, all in A.A. I immediately took to Dr. Fox and her accepting ways. She was utterly unlike my own psychiatrist, a tall, weedy and self-satisfied man who patronized me. That doctor had lectured me about how I managed my money. He had suggested I assuage my grief over Stan's death by picking up men at concerts. I sensed he did not respect women. He made me angry, although I was too intimidated by his intelligence and the air of command he exuded to say so. But he did send me to Dr. Fox. She was then in her early eighties, twisted with arthritis but never complaining of her pain. She would sit crumpled in a deep chair in her living room, nodding benignly as her circle of tortured patients struggled their way toward recovery. She prescribed Antabuse for most of us.

Antabuse meant that I made one decision a day not to drink, instead of dozens. Some people call it a crutch, but I call it blessed insurance that strengthened my determination to stay sober a day at a time. Is insulin a crutch for a diabetic?

Dr. Fox, the world authority on the drug, told me that when you are saturated with Antabuse, you know you cannot drink safely after the last dose for the next four or five days, or even longer. If you do drink on Antabuse, you become violently ill. She called it "a time bomb that will never go off unless you trigger it with alcohol." It was dispensed by prescription in a white, 250-milligram tablet the size of an aspirin. "The drug makes you sick if you drink on it," Dr. Fox said, "because it blocks a vital enzyme that helps the body to metabolize the alcohol." Since 1950, she had treated thousands of alcoholics with a combination of psychotherapy and advice to stick with A.A. I came to her therapy group as a supplement to my A.A. meetings and while continuing individual sessions with my male psychiatrist.

She warned me to avoid cough medicines, fruit compotes in wine, and desserts such as rum cake containing uncooked alcohol, but she said I need not avoid dishes in which wine or other alcohol had been evaporated through boiling, baking or simmering. She told me that I should suffer no side effects as long as I stayed off alcohol. Then she told me what would happen if I did drink on Antabuse: shocklike symptoms including a drop in blood pressure, rapid heartbeat, flushing, vomiting and fainting, and the necessity to be rushed to a hospital for emergency care. She gave me a card to carry in my purse, saying I was on Antabuse and giving instructions for treatment. I was suitably frightened. She told me that the medicine would really be a comfort and a support to me in my resolve. "You know that, from now on, alcohol can't make you feel better; it can only make you feel very ill," she said. "You will find something else to do, the impulse will pass, you will feel relieved." She said that as the weeks and months went by, in therapy and in A.A., I would find that my urges to drink would come less often and not as insistently. "Eventually, and it may take several years," she said, "you will feel strong enough in your sobriety to do without Antabuse altogether."

I had one close call with Antabuse. I was dining out one night with a friend who knew I was on the drug and what its side effects could be. He ordered a Bloody Mary, so I ordered a Virgin Mary. I was bored with the endless succession of plain tonics I had been drinking and thought, "Why not a spicy tomato juice for a change?" I gulped it down (like most alcoholics, I was a gulper, not a sipper). Within ten minutes, my face began to flush, my heart was pounding madly and I felt woozy. Bob said, "My God, they must have put some vodka in your drink by mistake." He rushed me to the restaurant bathroom, taking Dr. Fox's telephone number from me as I lurched through the door.

"Yes, she is having a mild toxic reaction," Dr. Fox told Bob. "There was probably not much vodka in her drink, so she won't have to be hospitalized." She instructed Bob to take me home at once, put me to bed, and stay with me until I fell asleep. "She will sleep peacefully for about eight hours and then awake refreshed and feeling normal," she said. That is what happened.

At Dr. Fox's, I found Anna L. A clinical psychologist, Anna was co-leader of the doctor's Wednesday night therapy group. She became my sponsor. A sponsor in A.A. is not someone who recommends you for entrance; it is a big sister or big brother who has a longer experience of sobriety and, under the best of circumstances, becomes your closest friend and adviser. Some people call their sponsors every day, if only to say hello. I called and saw mine frequently. We loved each other.

Response and Analysis

1. How did Alcoholics Anonymous help Nan Robertson avoid using alcohol? Describe one incident in which Alcoholics Anonymous helped her when she wanted a drink.

2. What does Robertson's essay reveal about the power of addictive drugs? About the challenges of quitting physiologically and psychologically addictive drugs?

3. Some people believe that people who abuse alcohol and other drugs could quit on their own if they wanted to badly enough. Do you share this view? Why or why not?

4. How did Antabuse help Robertson quit drinking? What would happen if she had a drink while taking Antabuse? What learning principle explains why it is effective?

Research

Suppose you want to conduct a study at your college or university to determine the percentage of students who are abusing drugs. Because you do not have the time to interview every student, you ask a small group of students to participate. How would you select the students to participate? How can you be fairly sure that the information you gather will generalize to the entire student body?

DYING TO BE BIGGER

D. H.

Psychological Concept
steroid abuse

What motivates a person to achieve a goal even at the risk of endangering his or her health? At fifteen years of age, D. H. is so determined to be a football star that he uses steroids to increase his size and prowess. Ignoring the prescribed dosage, he swallows five pills a day. Within weeks, D. H. notices unpleasant physical and emotional changes; he eventually becomes overly aggressive and, as his condition worsens, almost sterile. With the help of his parents, D. H. quits using steroids for a year. But what happens when he enters college and has as his roommate a six-foot-three, 250-pound linebacker? What adjustment problems does he experience after he quits taking steroids?

I was only fifteen years old when I first started maiming my body with the abuse of anabolic steroids. I was always trying to fit in with the "cool" crowd in junior high and high school. Willingly smoking or buying pot when offered, socially drinking in excess, displaying a macho image—and, of course, the infamous "kiss and tell" were essentials in completing my insecure mentality.

Being an immature, cocky kid from a somewhat wealthy family, I wasn't very well liked in general. In light of this, I got beat up a lot, especially in my first year of public high school.

I was one of only three sophomores to get a varsity letter in football. At five-foot-nine and 174 pounds, I was muscularly inferior to the guys on the same athletic level and quite conscious of the fact. So when I heard about this wonderful drug called steroids from a teammate, I didn't think twice about asking to buy some. I could hardly wait to take them and start getting bigger.

I bought three months' worth of Dianobol (an oral form of steroids and one of the most harmful). I paid fifty-five dollars. I was told to take maybe two or three per day. I totally ignored the directions and warnings and immediately started taking five per day. This is how eager I was to be bigger and possibly "cooler."

Within only a week, everything about me started to change. I was transforming mentally and physically. My attention span became almost nonexistent. Along with becoming extremely aggressive, I began to abandon nearly all academic and family responsibilities. In almost no time, I became flustered and agitated with simple everyday activities. My narcissistic ways brought me to engage in verbal as well as physical fights with family, friends, teachers, but mostly strangers.

My bodily transformations were clearly visible. In less than a month, I took the entire three-month supply. I gained nearly thirty pounds. Most of my weight was from water retention, although at the time I believed it to be muscle. Instead of having pimples like the average teenager, my acne took the form of grotesque, cystlike blood clots that would occasionally burst while I was lifting weights. My nipples became the size of grapes and hurt severely, which is common among male steroid users. My hormonal level was completely out of whack.

At first I had such an overload of testosterone that I would have to masturbate daily, at minimum, in order to prevent having "wet dreams." Obviously these factors enhanced my lust, which eventually led to acute perversion. My then almost-horrifying physique prevented me from having any sexual encounters.

All of these factors led to my classification as a wretched menace. My parents grew sick and tired of all the trouble I began to get in. They were scared of me, it seemed. They cared so much about my welfare, education, and state of mind that they sent me to a boarding school that summer.

I could not obtain any more steroids there, and for a couple of months it seemed I had subtle withdrawal symptoms and severe side effects. Most of the time that summer I was either depressed or filled with intense anger, both of which were uncontrollable unless I was in a state of intoxication from any mind-altering drug.

After a year of being steroid-free, things started to look promising for me, and I eventually gained control over myself. Just when I started getting letters from big-name colleges to play football for them, I suffered a herniated disc. I was unable to participate in any form of physical activity the entire school year.

In the fall, I attended a university in the Northeast, where I was on the football team but did not play due to my injury. I lifted weights with the team every day. I wasn't very big at the time, even after many weeks of working out. Once again I found myself to be physically inferior and insecure about my physique. And again came into contact with many teammates using steroids.

My roommate was a six-foot-three, 250-pound linebacker who played on the varsity squad as a freshman. As the weeks passed, I learned of my roommate's heavy steroid use. I was exposed to dozens of different steroids I had never even heard of. Living in the same room with him, I watched his almost daily injections. After months of enduring his drug offerings, I gave in.

By the spring of my freshman year, I had become drastically far from normal in every way. My body had stopped producing hormones due to the amount of synthetic testosterone I injected into my system. At five-foot-eleven, 225 pounds, disproportionately huge, acne-infested, outrageously aggressive, and nearing complete sterility, I was in a terrible state of body and mind. Normal thoughts of my future (not pertaining to football), friends, family, reputation, moral status, etc., were entirely beyond me. My whole entire essence had become one of a primitive barbarian. This was when I was taking something called Sustunon (prepackaged in a syringe labeled "For equine use only") containing four types of testosterone. I was "stacking" (a term used by steroid users which means mixing different types) to get well-cut definition along with mass.

It was around this time when I was arrested for threatening a security guard.

When the campus police came to arrest me, they saw how aggressive and large my roommate and I were. So they searched our room and found dozens of bottles and hundreds of dollars' worth of steroids and syringes. We had a trial, and the outcome was that I could only return the next year if I got drug-tested on a monthly basis. I certainly had no will power or desire to quit my steroid abuse, so I transferred schools.

After a summer of even more heavy-duty abuse, I decided to attend a school that would cater to my instinctively backward ways. That fall I entered a large university in the South. Once again I simply lifted weights without being involved in competition or football. It was there that I finally realized how out of hand I'd become with my steroid problem.

Gradually I started to taper down my dosages. Accompanying my reduction, I began to drink more and more. My grades plummeted again. I began going to bars and keg parties on a nightly basis.

My celibacy, mental state, aggressiveness, lack of athletic competition, and alcohol problem brought me to enjoy passing my pain onto others by means of physical aggression. I got into a fight almost every time I drank. In the midst of my insane state, I was arrested for assault. I was in really deep this time. Finally I realized how different from everybody else I'd become, and I decided not to taper off but to quit completely.

The average person seems to think that steroids just make you bigger. But they are a drug, and an addictive one at that. This drug does not put you in a stupor or in a hallucinogenic state but rather gives you an up, all-around "bad-ass" mentality that far exceeds that of either normal life or any other narcotic I've tried when not taking steroids. Only lately are scientists and researchers discovering how addictive steroids are—only now, after hundreds of thousands may have done such extreme damage to their lives, bodies, and minds.

One of the main components of steroid addiction is how unsatisfied the user is with his overall appearance. Although I was massive and had dramatic muscular definition, I was never content with my body, despite frequent compliments. I was always changing types of steroids, places of injection, workouts, diet, etc. I always found myself saying, "This one oughta do it" or "I'll quit when I hit 230 pounds."

When someone is using steroids, he has psychological disorders that increase when usage stops. One disorder is anxiety from the loss of the superior feeling you get from the drug. Losing the muscle mass, high energy level, and superhuman sensation that you're so accustomed to is terrifying.

Another ramification of taking artificial testosterone over time is the effect on the natural testosterone level (thus the male sex drive). As a result of my steroid use, my natural testosterone level was ultimately depleted to the point where my sex drive was drastically reduced in comparison to the average twenty-one-year-old male. My testicles shriveled up, causing physical pain as well as extreme mental anguish. Thus I desired girls less. This however did lead me to treat them as people, not as objects of my desires. It was a beginning step on the way to a more sane and civil mentality.

The worst symptoms of my withdrawal after many months of drug abuse were emotional. My emotions fluctuated dramatically, and I rapidly became more sensitive. My hope is that this feeling of being trailed by isolation and aloneness will diminish and leave me free of its constant haunting.

Response and Analysis

1. Why did D. H. begin and then continue using anabolic steroids even when he knew they were harmful for him? D. H. writes that he was in a "terrible state of mind and body" when using steroids. What psychological problems did he experience? What physical problems?

2. How did excessive use of steroids affect D. H.'s sexual interest and behavior? Why?

3. What signs of being addicted to steroids did D. H. exhibit?

Research

Suppose you want to know if people who use steroids have low self-esteem and tend to be depressed. You must decide whether you want to develop a questionnaire to assess self-esteem and depression or to use existing questionnaires whose reliability and validity are known. What are the advantages and disadvantages of using existing questionnaires or of developing your own questionnaire?

COCAINE: HELEN'S STORY

John C. Flynn

Psychological Concept
cocaine dependence

Cocaine is a drug that can induce feelings of euphoria and confidence, but users can become addicted to it after only a short period of time. With continued use, they may experience insomnia, paranoia, sexual dysfunction, and seizures. Helen was a twenty-six-year-old computer systems analyst with an upscale lifestyle when she had a toxic reaction to cocaine. After using the drug for an extended period of time, Helen suffered a seizure, was hospitalized, and had some irreparable loss of memory. Why is cocaine so addictive? What influences in Helen's life led her to try and then use cocaine regularly? How did the drug affect her emotionally, socially, and professionally?

Let me tell you about Helen.

You'd like her. Everybody does. She's warm, outgoing and easy to know, the kind of person who makes friends readily. Her effortless smile and infectious laugh suggest an openness that draws people to her. She is a bright, ambitious, hard-working, young professional whose career is definitely upward bound. . . .

"Helen." White Coat was speaking. "Helen, I'm Doctor Walsh. Can you hear me? Helen, can you tell me what the trouble is?" . . .

Locating the voice required an inordinate amount of concentration, more than she could muster, and the whole process was made more difficult by the rushing sound of wind in her head. The blowing and whistling noises, varying suddenly and without warning in amplitude and pitch, sprang out of a constant, dull background roar to assault her with wave after wave of uncontrollable fury. And flashing lights, like the rushing wind, were creating a disturbance inside her head. They had started as a minor annoyance that distracted her and made concentration difficult; now they were terrifying. They popped and crackled in a multicolored display of reds, blues, purples, oranges and the brightest, most dazzling bolts of lightning she had ever seen. So dazzling were they that she thought they might blind her. Sometimes the lights seemed to explode out of her head and into the room, where they illuminated the entire scene with shafts of ricocheting light. At other times they raced toward her, into the very interior of her brain, threatening to explode her head into a thousand pieces.

"Stop the lights!" she screamed, pounding on her temples with her fists. "Please! Please, stop the lights!"

"Helen." It was White Coat again, speaking more urgently now and holding each of her hands in order to restrain her from hitting herself again. "Helen," he said more firmly now, "tell me what the lights are like."

Without warning, Helen's body straightened on the edge of the table, her eyes rolled back in their sockets, she expelled air forcefully from her lungs in a kind of muted cry, and before anyone could prevent it, she catapulted off the examination table and crashed to the floor, where she lay thrashing in a paroxysm of violent contractions.

"Grand mal! Grand mal!"

"Seizure!"

"Somebody get her tongue!"

Helen was not able to hear these cries of the emergency room personnel. The convulsion had rendered her unconscious. The violent and chaotic firestorm in her brain, the synchronous discharge of millions of brain cells running riot, had overwhelmed her awareness of the world around her. Mercifully, she would have no memory of lying, as she now was, on the cold, tile floor, her body trembling with the residual muscular tremors that marked the effort of her brain to reestablish some sense of normal control over its own function. . . .

The paramedics had found Helen sitting alone on the floor in a corner of the kitchen. Her legs were pulled up under her chin and her arms were wrapped tightly around her knees. A miniature ceramic pipe lay at her feet. Her eyes darted rapidly back and forth around the room, never seeming to focus on anything in particular. They did not focus on the paramedics as they attempted to question her. She was agitated and appeared to be fearful. She responded to their questions only obliquely, seeming to be much more interested in whatever it was that her eyes were following around the room. She complained of head pain and of being bothered by flashing lights. She was too agitated and disoriented to comply with their request that she lie down on the gurney. The two paramedics half carried her between them to the ambulance and took her directly to the hospital emergency room.

[Dr. Walsh's] examination, begun once the convulsions had subsided, indicated that Helen was a young woman (her driver's license said that she was twenty-six years old), well-dressed and well-nourished. Upon admittance to the emergency room, her blood pressure was elevated to an alarming level, her pupils were dilated, she had a fever of 102 degrees, her heart rate was 125 beats per minute and the electrocardiogram (ECG) revealed irregular cardiac rhythms. Her skin was noticeably red, and she was sweating profusely. The nasal septum, the cartilage dividing the two nostrils, was perforated. She remained quite agitated and confused throughout the examination.

After about thirty minutes, most of Helen's physical symptoms had declined in severity. Her blood pressure had returned to near normal limits; the fever had declined to 100 degrees; her heart rate was down to 95 beats per minute; sweating had ceased; her pupils had returned to normal size. Helen's mental status showed gradual improvement during this period. She was considerably less agitated, although she remained quite confused and disoriented.

Dr. Walsh was fairly confident that he knew what had precipitated Helen's crisis. While a definitive diagnosis would have to wait until the completion of a history and the results of various laboratory tests, his tentative diagnosis was quite clear in his mind: his patient was suffering from a toxic reaction to cocaine.

Why Didn't Anybody Tell Me?

Helen didn't know what she was getting into. She had no idea when she began using cocaine that she could end up as a crisis case in the emergency room of a hospital. She did not use other drugs, not even marijuana—it made her sick. She drank alcohol on the weekends, but rarely drank to excess. Alcohol was, as she put it, "a way of mellowing out."

Certainly she had no inkling that the drug she tried so casually, at the urging of her friends, could have long-run consequences that were so different from the immediate feelings of pleasure that she experienced when she first tried it. Listen to her description, given several weeks following her release from the hospital, of that first exposure to cocaine.

"I was at a party with some new people and I was feeling pretty mellow and laid back. Charley, my fiancé, had already tried a hit. They kinda coaxed me and teased me, and Charley was telling me what a blast it was, so I went along. This friend of Charley's put a couple of lines on the table and showed me what to do. He told me that I should first rub a little coke on my gums with my finger. Then he gave me a rolled up dollar bill and showed me how to snort it up my nose. And I did.

"It was unbelievable. There's no other way to put it. I didn't know it was possible to feel so good! I mean, not in any specific way. Just good. The party had been going on for some time and I was pretty mellowed out. When I snorted the coke, nothing happened for a while, like for maybe three or four minutes. Then, it was like the whole world opened up to me. Everything seemed great. I felt kinda wired, but not in a bad way. Like, I just had a lot of energy. I felt like I could do anything I wanted to." . . .

At the time of this experience, Helen was a responsible, upwardly mobile young professional. She was dedicated to her career in computer applications in the business world. Her current position was that of a highly paid systems analyst. Charley, her fiancé, was a certified public accountant with a large firm. His future was as bright as hers. Helen had a new car that she traded every other year, a tastefully furnished apartment and a man that she deeply loved. She had no way of knowing what was to come.

What was to come was an increasing involvement with cocaine, an involvement that would jeopardize everything that she valued in her life. As this involvement intensified, she would see her job performance slip to the point of endangering her promising career. Her relationship with Charley would be strained to the breaking point. She would end up in the hospital with her life at risk.

The basic fact is that Helen, and Charley as well, came to like cocaine more than they ever would have imagined possible. Perhaps "like" is not a strong enough word to describe the attraction that they felt. They were drawn to it in a way that was new to them. Unlike drinking alcohol, which for them was merely one of many related activities that constituted a relaxing evening, cocaine soon became center stage, a star, the stand-out, one-of-a-kind activity that provided the whole reason for having the evening.

They began doing the drug at parties with friends. As the cocaine use increased, these parties would last all weekend. There was a lot of alcohol and plenty of cocaine. There was also sex. Cocaine seemed to make sex better, and during these marathon weekends when nobody slept, it made sex much more likely. Helen's recollection of those times tells the story.

"Jeeze, the whole thing is hard to believe. We didn't know what was happening. Neither of us.

"We really both got into the high. At first, Charley more than I did. . . . But, hey, I don't mean to lay it all off on Charley. It's as much my fault as his. But once we started concentrating on the drug, once it became our thing, a thing that we did by ourselves, not just at parties, then we were screwed. We couldn't turn it off.

"At first, a lot of the push did come from Charley . . . but no way am I blaming him. I should have been able to handle it. But it became such a sexual turn-on for him that he didn't want to go out any more. He wanted to stay home a lot, get high and make love. There was a lot of that kind of stuff at the parties, you know, but we could never get into it. . . . You know, swapping partners and all that stuff. So we stayed home more and more and did coke."

Helen found herself increasingly withdrawn from her relationships with friends. The world that she inhabited with Charley became progressively restricted. Just as their outside interests decreased, so did their interest in their work. They worked at their jobs during the day, each of them with mounting ineffectiveness, all the while looking forward to the evening when they could return home and do more cocaine. With hindsight, Helen was able to see the way the events unfolded.

"The damn drug took us away from other people and finally ended up by taking us away from each other. After a while the only thing that was important was cocaine. *We* didn't even count anymore.

"See . . . what happens is that when you're doing enough coke the downside gets to be unbearable. So you do more. And more. And when you do enough of it, you get to the point that the only thing that matters, the only thing that can pick you up, the only thing that gives you any pleasure at all, is the goddam cocaine.

"It's unbelievable, in a way. We started out doing coke to get high and have fabulous sex. At least that kept us close, kept us holding on to each other. But toward the end we didn't even have sex anymore. It wasn't as good as the cocaine. All we wanted to do was stay high, and finally we didn't even care about what the other person was feeling, or what the other person was all about.

"We became like the proverbial ships that pass in the night. We floated by each other on a sea of cocaine. Each one of us was intent on steering his own course. We were aware of one another only to the extent of trying to avoid a collision in the dark."

Does Anybody Know What's Going On?

The fact that Helen was so ignorant of what lay in store for her represents one of the real ironies of the present day. *This is a drug-intoxicated culture that understands almost nothing about drugs*. Drugs in the United States are dealt with mostly by catchwords and slogans: "addict," "dope-head," "just say no," "zero tolerance," "restrict supply," "reduce demand," and so on.

The trouble with catchwords and slogans is that they too often make very complicated problems seem simpler than they really are. Catchwords conceal the complexity of a problem under a superficial layer of apparent understanding. Helen's lack of knowledge of the possible consequences of her cocaine use is due, in large part, to her willingness to accept this kind of sloganeering as a substitute for knowledge.

Not that she didn't think that she had a lot of information. She ran with a hip crowd, a switched-on, get-it-while-you-can crowd. And they all "knew a lot about cocaine." What they knew was revealed in their conversation.

"Hey! This is a real mindblower!"

"If you're hung over, a little snort will fix you right up."

"Don't lick up the leavings with your tongue. It's bitter as hell. Better to rub it on your gums."

"When you have sex while you're on this stuff, it's like it's never gonna end."

Helen never took the time to inform herself about the drug that she so casually accepted from her friends. It did not occur to her to ask questions about what the drug did to her mind. She was even less inclined to wonder about how cocaine affected her brain in order to do these things to her mind. Furthermore, even if she had thought to ask such questions, it is unlikely that she would have found any answers close at hand. Certainly not from her fellow drug users. None of these people had any real information about cocaine. Their knowledge was concerned largely with the folklore of the drug, most of which had little to do with the descent into addiction that Helen experienced.

Response and Analysis

1. Why did Helen try cocaine? How aware was Helen that cocaine is one of the most addictive drugs? What were her reasons for continuing to use cocaine?

2. How was Helen physiologically addicted to cocaine? Psychologically addicted? How did her addiction influence her self-concept, interpersonal relationships, and performance at work?

3. Why was Helen unable to control her use of cocaine? Discuss both environmental and physiological influences.

Research

Helen's story highlights the importance of drug education because she was not knowledgeable about the addictive power of cocaine. Suppose the members of a committee whose mission is to educate students at your campus about drugs ask you to help them design a program to inform students about the psychological and physiological effects of drugs. Your first task is to get information about the psychological and physiological effects of drugs. Where might you go on campus to get this information? What types of information do you think would be most effective in educating students about the dangers of drugs? Why?

chapter 10

SEXUAL DYSFUNCTIONS AND DISORDERS

*I lose my respect for the man who can make
the mystery of sex the subject of a coarse
jest, yet, when you speak earnestly and seriously on the subject, is silent.*

HENRY DAVID THOREAU, *Journal*, 1852

Sexuality is a fundamental part of human experience. It helps define who we are. The term itself contains many meanings for individuals and for social relations. Gender identity, sexual desire, the ability to procreate, and an expression of love for another all fall under this broad term. Sexuality can also involve disorders, psychological distress, interpersonal conflict, and legal sanctions.

In this chapter, we consider three areas of abnormal sexual behavior: sexual dysfunction, paraphilias, and sexual aggression. Sexual dysfunction includes several problems related to sexual desire (e.g., diminished desire, aversion to sex) or functioning (e.g., difficulties during arousal or orgasm, or pain during sex). Problems in this area are distressing to the individuals involved and often negatively affect relationships.

Paraphilias involve sexual urges or behavior toward inappropriate objects or persons. Among the paraphilias are exhibitionism (flashing), fetishism (attraction to nonsexual objects such as shoes or rubber), masochism (urges or behavior involving humiliation, pain, or suffering), and sadism (urges or behavior involving inflicting pain or suffering). Also included are pedophilia (urges directed toward or behavior with a child) and other less common paraphilias. Many of the paraphilias, when acted out, are classified as criminal behavior.

Sexual assault is criminal behavior, not a psychological disorder (although some perpetrators might exhibit psychological disorders). Sexual assault combines psychological elements of power and aggression with sexuality, and is defined as sexual activity that occurs under actual or implied force. We include it in this chapter because sexual assault has profound psychological consequences for victims and remains a troubling social problem.

The first selection in this chapter presents a case of male sexual dysfunction. Lloyd Van Brunt developed sexual impotence because of medication he took for a prostate condition. This temporary condition of impotency frightened him, and he learned more not only about his own attitude toward sexuality but about those of other males as well.

Pedophilia can be intrafamilial (involving family members) or extrafamilial (involving nonfamily members), although many researchers distinguish between incest (which might or might not involve minors) and pedophilia. In the second selection, Michael Ryan tells of being sexually molested by a neighbor when he was five years old. What first appeared as an adult taking an interest in him was really an adult acting on his strong sexual attraction to children.

In the last selection, Migael Scherer describes her assault and its aftermath. Scherer's story illustrates one victim's struggles with recovery, but it indirectly raises important questions about the causes of sexual aggression and the appropriate social or legal responses to such behavior.

A FEAR OF IMPOTENCY

Lloyd Van Brunt

Psychological Concept
sexual dysfunction caused by a medical condition

The phrase "impotent man," Lloyd Van Brunt so aptly says, is perceived by many as an oxymoron, a contradiction of terms. Yet that is what he found himself to be, albeit temporarily, when he was diagnosed with benign prostate hyperplasia. It was the medication, not the disease, that affected him sexually. Van Brunt discovers the vulnerability men may feel when they become impotent, and he shares his reactions to the ways both men and women respond to him. Van Brunt wants to talk about his condition with other men, but finds it difficult, not only because of his embarrassment and pain, but because others sometimes fall into a light banter when the issue is mentioned. Why might some men and women find impotency difficult to discuss?

An image of Priapus, the Greek god of procreation, functioned as a scarecrow in ancient gardens. Whether a figure with an enlarged phallus worked better to scare off larcenous birds than a straw man with outstretched arms is questionable—but I found myself intrigued by this and other images of Aphrodite's rogue son after a second visit to a urologist's office a few months ago.

I did not have prostate cancer—the scourge of men my age—the doctor told me cheerfully. The P.S.A. (prostate-specific antigen) levels fell within the normal range. However, I did have a disease: benign prostate hyperplasia, or B.P.H.—also a problem quite common in the men of my 50- and 60-something generation. In my case, the cystoscopy test showed the enlarged gland to be almost completely blocking the urethra. So that was why I had to get up several times a night to urinate.

I was so relieved that I did not have cancer, I scarcely listened to the doctor telling me about some new drugs designed to shrink the prostate gland. However, one of the side effects of the medication he was going to prescribe for me was that it sometimes caused sexual impotence. In my new-lease-on-life euphoria that prospect flew by my head like a foul ball.

I laughed off my first failure as a lover and so did the lady I live with. I knew that temporary impotence happened to all men at one time or another, and so did she. Not to worry, I was told, but right now we were both tired so let's stop fumbling around and get some sleep.

A few evenings later, however, her tone changed. After repeated failures, I began to feel panicky and tried explaining what the urologist had told me about the drug I was taking. My impotence was *temporary*, I almost shouted. When she replied tartly, "I hope so," I grabbed a pillow and made my way to the living room couch. Rationally, I knew it wasn't her fault—but, emotionally, I felt it wasn't all mine either.

In that encounter it seemed that I had been displaced to some sexually neutral zone. Neither my mind nor body had been charged with eroticism. Having been on automatic pilot over this terrain of lovemaking for decades, I wondered whether at 58 I was to be retired permanently and—almost as worrisome—whether the loss of self-confidence I felt now would be lasting.

I had been brought up in the macho tradition of the Southwest, where potency was the cornerstone of a man's stature. According to the prevailing ethos of the time, "impotent man" was oxymoronic.

To have talked about such an intimate thing would have been considered very bad form. Of course, there were the usual barroom and locker room jokes, "Did you hear the one about the guy who couldn't . . ." but they were really a way of fending off fear of the real thing. A man kept things like that to himself, if he didn't want to end up the butt of women's gossip. And women could be unmerciful about a man that way. A man's dignity was all-important.

I didn't feel very dignified at the moment. I felt weak—not macho at all. I felt very much like talking about my problem with someone who could understand it. I considered the person in the bedroom. After all, she hadn't told me to leave. Perhaps my irritable reaction to one offhand remark had been inappropriate. Very probably, my dear love would have taken me into the comfort of her sleep-warm arms.

My reluctance to return to the bedroom as the world woke around me was prompted not so much by any anticipated lack of sympathy in my partner but by the persistent feeling that I would be trying to explain myself to the wrong sex. A woman—any woman, I felt—could not truly understand what impotence might mean to a man.

I needed to confess and be understood by a man. Adolescent conditioning had, of course, made me leery of trusting another male with intimate details of my life.

In conversation with another male, it would be up to me to let down my guard first. Too, once started on the subject, there would be no holding back, no clumsy ducking behind a glass partition of pretense. I would be talking about *me*, my inability as a man to function sexually.

Watching a trusted friend, a man I had known for 30 years, make his way to the restaurant men's room a second time the next evening at dinner, I thought sure that owning up to him and discussing my problem would now be easy. Already we had joked about our prostate gland conditions, how both of us were summoned by the ridiculous and humbling commands of our aging bodies.

Upon his return, though, whenever I tried steering the conversation to my troubles in the bedroom, my old friend insistently turned these fumbling attempts at intimacy into the kind of bantering humor we had grown comfortable with over the years. It was as if he might be thinking that I was trying to work up the nerve to ask for a large personal loan. It was clear to me that a dead-serious conversation would now be impossibly awkward, completely out of context.

As we were leaving I couldn't help noticing some of the younger men in this old hangout of a restaurant looking at the attractive women they were with—as though they would remain young forever—and hoping their generation might learn to talk more easily of intimate things. For me, for my generation, impotence and other forbidden subjects would continue to be viewed as assassins—about whom it was best to keep the witness of oneself silent. *Omertà.*

Of course, my true love finally convinced me, this code of male reticence did not extend to doctors.

The son of Aphrodite was indeed a rogue god, I thought a week or so later, taking two medications now, the first to shrink the prostate gland, the second reassuringly prescribed by the urologist to counter the effects of the first. And like all the gods, Priapus enjoyed a good jest. Perhaps I would use an image of him as a scarecrow if I ever got that place in the country I was always talking about.

In the meantime I can tell him a few things about good jests. A really funny joke is usually at somebody else's expense. And the problem with that, dear old Priapus, is that in this life "somebody else" has a way of shift-shaping into a personal pronoun. A me, for instance—or a you.

Response and Analysis

1. How did Lloyd Van Brunt's sexual dysfunction affect his view of himself as a man? How did societal influences affect his reaction?

2. Van Brunt says that he felt no woman could fully understand his problem. Do you agree? Do you think that men and women have fundamentally different ways of looking at and experiencing sexuality? Why or why not?

3. Why was it difficult for Van Brunt to communicate his concerns to a male friend? What behaviors does he say were used to deflect communication about intimate sexual problems?

Research

Some feminists maintain that the research and treatment of sexual dysfunctions has historically emphasized a mechanistic view of sexual behavior, focusing more on the mechanics of the sexual response cycle and not enough on interpersonal relationships. Suppose you want to review professional books on sexual dysfunction published in the last twenty years to see if there have been any changes in their emphasis. How would you identify which were the most popular books? How would you determine the degree to which they emphasized mechanics or interpersonal aspects? What conclusions could you make?

SECRET LIFE

Michael Ryan

Psychological Concept
pedophilia

Pedophilia is a serious disorder in which an adult experiences urges for, or may seek sexual contact with, pre-adolescents. In this excerpt from Michael Ryan's autobiography, we learn of Ryan's first experiences with pedophilia, the shame he has lived with, and the silence in his family that allowed the molestations to continue. When he was a young boy, Ryan was assaulted by a man who lived nearby. These assaults affected him into adulthood: he became obsessed with sexual conquests that focused on young girls and female college students. Because of these involvements, he was dismissed from the faculty at an eastern university. Suffering from public humiliation and the break-up of two marriages, Ryan resolved to change. Some readers may find portions of Ryan's article disturbing because of the abusive ordeals he presents.

I was sexually molested when I was five years old, probably for about a year (I can remember the change of seasons), probably from one spring through the next winter, 1951–1952, during the last part of the Korean War. I was sitting in our backyard playing in the dirt when a man appeared in front of me with a camera and took my picture. He was young and handsome—but I believe that was what I thought later, after I was under his spell. He was an adult—they all seemed the same age except for the grandmothers and grandfathers who were old (*old* was a different species of adult). This one was interested in me. When I looked up and saw him snap my picture, I was startled but not frightened. He came over and squatted in front of me. I hadn't moved. His hair was dark brown and slicked straight back like my father's. I was sitting in the dirt with my knees akimbo pushing miniature metal trucks around inside the circle my legs made. He asked me if I liked him taking my picture. I liked it okay. He asked if my mother was home, and when I told her she was, he knocked on the screen door.

His name was Bob Stoller, he explained to my mother. He was our neighbor's son just back from Korea, our neighbor who lived up the block (I wasn't allowed to go off the block or cross the street by myself). He was just back from Korea and was trying to get started as a professional photographer, and would my mother mind if he took my picture? He could do this one right here in the yard (did he tell her he'd already taken one without her permission?) and we'd see how it turned out.

It turned out great. The Professional-Quality eight-by-ten glossy of me in my favorite gray-and-black Hopalong Cassidy sweater is still among the family albums in the bottom drawer of the secretary in my mother's living room. He brought our copy to us the next day—everyone liked it—and asked if I could come up to his studio so he could take a few in Kodacolor. In 1951, color was a very exotic medium. Only a Professional could take color photographs, and then mostly in a studio where the lighting was strictly controlled. My mother supposed it would be all right, did I want to do it? I did want to do it. I liked the picture, I liked Bob Stoller, and he had mentioned that he had brought back some guns from Korea that he would show me (no, they wouldn't shoot, the Army won't let you take them home that way). And he also owned an accordion. I loved the buttons on accordions. I was ready to go that minute. . . .

The appointment was made, and the day came. . . .

His studio was set up in the attic, where he also kept his guns. . . .

The stairway to the attic was narrow and steep and unfinished and smelled like a cedar chest. It was like the rabbit hole in *Alice in Wonderland*, only climbing not falling through the passage to another world. Before long it would be exactly that. Knowing what would happen there, I would feel a new emotion as he followed me up the stairs, a blend of wonder and dread. Even this first time the passage seemed mysterious and secret. At the top was a daybed, a rug, a chair, a bathroom, a kind of living space set off from the rest of the attic where he had established his box camera and a little pedestal surrounded by quartz lights. It was cold. Bob Stoller switched on an electric heater, and it whirred, the exposed coils turning from black to orange to red. I sat on the bed and he brought over the guns, their muzzles stuffed with dirty hard cotton, M-1's and dummy grenades and strange pistols with three-bullet barrels, even a German Luger that was not likely ever to have been in Korea. I guess he bought them somewhere. Maybe he had never been in Korea himself, but that didn't occur to me or to anyone else, as far as I know.

This is when he first touched me—not between the legs. He put his arm around me while we looked at the guns. He had piled them by the bed and on the bed, and he pulled them across our laps as we sat with our backs against the wall. I stroked the polished wood stocks and blue steel barrels of the rifles. He helped me aim across the attic at the box camera and bathroom doorknob. He helped me cock the hammers and pull the triggers. We did it for a long time. He didn't get impatient. It was a physical closeness I liked very much. The attention was all on me now, on whatever I wanted. I had never had a better time. His body was big and warm, the guns were fascinating. I was five years old.

Then it came time to take my picture. I had to put on a costume, which he showed to me: a red cape, a pair of stubby wooden horns glued to a circle of black elastic that went under my chin, and a tiny diaphanous red jockstrap. . . .

When I had all my clothes off—it was freezing—Bob Stoller suddenly pulled the curtain back. I felt terror—I'll never forget it—I was naked and he loomed over me. Standing straight up, I didn't reach his waist. He seemed twice as big now as before, and the light behind him made him into a dark hulk. It was so sudden. I was going to put the costume on myself—what was he doing?

"I want to make sure you get it on right," he said. He pulled the jockstrap up, and kept adjusting it around me, touching me. I felt like a bar of iron was being shoved up into my stomach. I felt nauseated and dizzy, my legs wouldn't work. I pushed his hands away and said I could do it myself. I was about to cry.

Then he changed again. I think if he would have gotten mad, I might have run away. No one had ever talked to me about being touched, but he was still a stranger and I was upset. But then he was nice, wonderfully nice, just as he had been while we looked at the guns, the way he had been in the yard and playing the polka on the accordion. He helped me with the cape, which was like Superman's; he adjusted the horns, kidding me about their not being straight (this insane costume he must have spent hours making—how many little boys had worn it?). He rubbed my head with his palm the way my uncles did.

He calmed me down. Maybe he apologized. I got up on the pedestal, surrounded by the quartz lights, and he took my picture, talking to me the whole time in a soothing voice, saying nice things, telling me I was handsome. . . .

How much time passed it's impossible now to say. It may have been a couple of hours, with this man's attention focused exclusively on me, courting me, making me feel special. I was handsome, I had good muscles, I was big for my age, I was smart, my hair was soft, I would probably become a good baseball player. We would be friends. I thought this would be wonderful. Since I was cold, why didn't I take a warm bath now and we would take more pictures next time, in a couple of days. . . .

He drew the bath and left the bathroom again before I took off my underpants and got in. A minute later he knocked lightly on the door and poked his head in (the door was behind me) and asked how I was doing and if he could come in, making a little joke about not wanting to surprise me again. He sat down on the toilet with the lid down and talked to me a little about who knows what (how many hours of childish *talk* in a year? how could he not be bored senseless with it?), talked to me about taking baths by myself, which I said I did, figuring the more grown-up I was the more likely it was he'd want to be my friend. He asked me if, when I took a bath by myself and nobody else was around, did I ever play with it? Did I ever make it stiff so it stood out straight? I said I did, looking down shyly. It was true, I did, not often but sometimes, and I was astonished anyone else could know about this or guess it. I was also a little embarrassed, and also pleased to be sharing this secret, which Bob Stoller said he'd never tell anyone ever, it would be just between us two. It was our secret. He was still sitting on the toilet. Then he asked if I would touch myself and show him how I did it. He asked me to play with it so he could see.

The water was warm, the steam rising gently and making the air warm, too. Bob said to use both hands, to just put my fingers underneath it and tickle it and make it feel good. I started to do what he said and the familiar feeling came back as it stiffened, a dream feeling that before I had had only by myself; it never occurred to me that anyone else ever had it, it seemed naughty, but here was my friend sharing it with me and he didn't think it was bad and we were in this nice secret place together. I don't know how long I did it for him, not long probably. When it was still stiff, he brought over a towel and said to stand up in the tub and he would dry me off. I did stand up and he took the plug out and began rubbing me with the towel all over and now it felt good and dreamy and warm not like when he touched me before in the dressing stall and he told me to put my arms around his neck to steady myself while he did it and I did, in a swoon, the classic gesture of surrender and embrace.

If at that moment I had been able to scream and run away, or evaporate into the steamy air, I believe my whole life would have been different. But I was already gone. He had me and he knew it. He carried me in his arms into the other room. The heater was already reset by the bed, aimed at the spot where he knew he would lay me down, talking to me the whole time the way a lover does. Was he kissing me? I think he was, but not on the mouth. Somehow he explained an even better secret we could share, that he could play with it in his mouth the way I had with my fingers, and still inside the dream feeling he was kneeling in front of me and tickling it with his tongue and lips.

Of course, I couldn't climax, and straddling his big head and steadying myself on it with his mouth on me was like the disappointing slow last moments of the ride on the mechanical bucking horse in front of the grocery store. I started to come out of the dream feeling. It felt so strange, and too frightening to be pleasant. I may have said something, I don't know, but the spell was broken by the time he stopped and asked me to do the same thing to him. . . .

[Years later] I told my mother about being molested. My father has been dead for more than thirty years. My mother has lived alone all this time, half a mile from my sister's home. My sister's family is the new family, a very different one than the one I grew up in, and my mother has been a part of it, helping to raise my sister's children, who are now in their early twenties and about to start their own new families. They are big fans of my mother's, and I can see why: I look at her through their eyes and see the caring, spirited, good-humored old woman they see, whereas for my whole adult life I have seen her through a plastic shield of resentment for her inability to protect me from Bob Stoller and my father and for giving me her guilt and shame. . . .

I don't know if [my family] needed to know the truth about me, but I needed them to know. . . .

I believed my mother knew it already somewhere in her heart.

I sat down across from her at her dining-room table as soon as I had carried my bags in. My mother is a small, sturdy woman in excellent health; at eighty she walks a couple of miles a day and does double acrostics. . . .

I told her I had something I had to tell her, then told her that I had been sexually molested by Bob Stoller for about a year when I was five years old. She cried and said, "I'm so sorry." . . .

She said almost wistfully, "He seemed like such a nice guy."

I said that he had probably made himself seem like a nice guy so that he could molest children.

"It seemed okay," my mother said, referring to his taking my picture. . . .

I said, "Mother, Mother, a twenty-three-year-old man and a five-year-old boy. Think about it. Let it sink in. Didn't that seem strange?"

She said she didn't know I was going to his house. I know she knew I went to his house, although she surely didn't know how often I went there. But this was turning into a cross-examination, with me as the prosecutor, and I didn't want it to. She cried some more, yet what I had told her didn't seem to register. Apropos of nothing, she started talking about her father, about being her daddy's little girl (where was this coming from?); then with no transition she switched to asking me where I thought she should be buried—she owned the plot next to my father in Milwaukee, but it seemed ridiculous to send her body all the way back there, didn't it? What did I think?

I thought, I'd better go upstairs by myself, and I did. I was pretty upset. I said a prayer. The important thing was to tell the secret and just let it go. I wasn't doing this for my mother, I was doing it for me.

Response and Analysis

1. To what extent was Stoller's behavior typical of persons with pedophilia? Why was it confusing for the child Michael Ryan?

2. How might learning approaches, in general, explain how persons develop strong and persistent sexual urges toward children?

3. What are common treatment approaches for pedophilia? How do psychologists determine whether the treatment is effective?

4. What can parents do to help protect their children from sexual abuse?

Research

Researchers sometimes recruit prisoners to participate in their studies. Suppose a researcher sought volunteers for an experimental treatment program of pedophilia. Some persons who were convicted of pedophilia refuse to participate, but others agree. One motivation for them to agree is that they might be looked at more favorably by the parole board if they seek treatment. Suppose further that the treatment program is conducted and the prisoners soon finish serving their sentences. One year after the participants are released, the researcher finds lower recidivism rates for offenders who participated in the experimental treatment program than for non-treated offenders. What problems might complicate interpretation of these results?

SURVIVING A SEXUAL ATTACK

Migael Scherer

Psychological Concept
sexual assault

Sexual assault can leave physical injuries and overwhelming emotional scars. Migael Scherer is a survivor of sexual violence. Grabbed by a stranger and held at knife point in a laundromat, she was taken to a small room in the back and was attacked. Scherer describes the incident and the ongoing terror and anxiety that made for a difficult recovery. Some readers may find portions of the article disturbing because of the abusive attack she details.

I woke this morning confused, hurt, and exhausted. In an attempt to help myself, I called the mental health clinic at Group Health. The pamphlet I had been given in the emergency room said they had specially trained therapists. Hoping that the certainty of an appointment would steady me, I dialed the number. The woman who answered took my name. "What is this concerning?" she asked. I tried to keep my voice even as I explained, but my spirits plunged when I was transferred and then put on hold. Alarmed at the sudden panic that rose to the surface, I hung up. Someone called me back, patiently talked me through my tears, and arranged an appointment early next week. I am weak, weaker than I thought. And I am afraid. . . .

Friday, March 25

I am almost immobilized by fear today. My breathing is shallow, my heart constricted. I am obsessed with entrapment fantasies in which I am the predator and the sandy-haired innocuous-looking rapist is the unwitting prey. In those fantasies—they are almost dreams—I cannot convince anyone to help me because he looks so harmless. The only way I can get help is when he turns back into the predator and I am under attack again, sometimes under his hands, sometimes under his knife, which stabs rather than slices.

And yesterday was so good. Who knows what turned it around, or will turn it around again? . . .

Wednesday, March 30

Ha! I'd clearly forgotten what it really felt like to be afraid until this morning.

What was intended to be a simple breakfast at Lambert's with Paul,[1] who will be gone on business overnight to San Francisco, was instead thirty minutes of high tension. All because of a man who vaguely resembled "my" rapist.

Probably what triggered it was that he was reading a newspaper. The set of his shoulders and the part of his hair, his short nose and his cheekbones and even his forehead were almost the same. The effect was so overwhelming I could barely sip my coffee.

But he was not the same man. His hair was too thin and too receding. His eyes were brown and a little too small for his face, which was a little too full. And his complexion was too coarse, as though he'd had acne when he was young. Despite these very clear differences, when he put on his blue-gray jacket and walked toward us at the counter to pay his bill I could hear my heart's roar. And I could not resist watching him walk across the street and drive off in his silver-colored car.

Tuesday, April 12

I find myself these days avoiding something I feel compelled to do in order to move on: to write the physical and emotional details of February 9. I feel that if I do so, for myself alone, I will be able to control the flashbacks a little better, to let go of that day. If I cannot loosen its grip on me, at least I can loosen my grip on it.

Ever since my conversations with Chris and Teri[2] last week, I had been thinking about calling Seattle Rape Relief. The yellow piece of paper given to me in the police station described it as a source of free counseling and information. Judy Burns, the therapist I had seen last month at Group Health, had suggested I give them a try. But for some reason I couldn't bring myself to dial the number. . . .

I was immediately relieved that I made the call. "Would you like to speak to a counselor?" the woman asked, not waiting for me to phrase my need. And once again I was lucky. Connie Tipton is forty-five, lived on a boat for six years in California, seemed to pick up on the kind of person I am. She did a lot of the talking, reassuring me that I'd done splendidly so far, congratulating me on making the call, assuring me that all my hesitations and confusion, the stalled feelings and grief were not only normal but should be acute at this stage. "After all," she said, "it's only been two months."

"The memories are so vivid," I said. "Are they always going to be like this? In technicolor and full stereo?"

"I know it's hard to believe now," she said, "but they'll fade, with time. That doesn't mean you need to stop talking about what happened, or your feelings. Talking like this is one of the best things you can do to heal." . . .

Wednesday, April 13

OK. Here goes. The events of that Tuesday, February 9, 1988:

---

[1] Scherer's husband
[2] Friends of Scherer

There was a parking spot immediately in front of the Kwik-Kleen, so I turned around at the dumpster behind the laundromat, glancing at the blank, barred windows there. I parked, grabbed my basket from the back of the car, and hefted it through the door.

Two men were there that morning, and both were in the aisle of washers and dryers that begins at the door. . . .

He was sitting in the far corner, just to the left of the two utility doors, in right profile. What caught my eye was the white metal chair he was sitting in. I had not seen one of those chairs in months, and had missed them. I had grown accustomed to sitting on the bench next to the laundry table, but it was awkward. Good, I thought, it will be more comfortable this time if that chair is empty when I return.

His legs were crossed (left over right, I think) and he was reading. His hair was brownish blond, straight, full, combed from a part on his left. A pretty nice haircut. He was slender and what I consider average height. At least so he seemed in his seated position. He did not look up.

I took my laundry to the two front-load washing machines closest to the door, which face the second aisle.

The front-load washers always clunk when their cycle is over, so I looked up almost as soon as the red light went off. . . .

Depositing my coat and purse on the table next to the dryers, I proceeded to load my wet laundry into three of them. I followed my usual procedure: two for jeans, towels, underwear, and T-shirts; one for light shirts and easy-to-dry stuff. I set aside the painter line that I did not want to dry. I thought about our vacation as I tossed in shorts and Paul's white pants, which I had bought the day before.

The smell of a freshly lit cigarette caused me to look quickly over my left shoulder. It is not a smell that belongs with laundered clothes, and it jarred me from my routine. Two or three dryers down the sandy-haired man was staring into a dryer, his right hand on its open door, a filtered cigarette hanging in his mouth. I had not heard him move from the bench, but I hadn't been listening either. I noted his hair, his short, slightly upturned nose, his clean chin line, his well-shaped hand, the color of his jacket. And I noticed that his face had hardened or tensed slightly, as if the cigarette had toughened him. . . .

It was then that he struck: a tight grip around my ribs, another at my right shoulder and across my neck. Both my hands instantly reached for my throat to pull his hand away. I thought and said, "Jesus, I don't believe this." I felt a cool, sharp hardness pressing across the left side of my neck and thought, Oh, god, a knife. Every alarm inside me was screaming escape. I pulled at his arm, struggled and twisted. I made no sound.

Either as a result of our struggles or his deliberate move we were both on the floor. It was during this controlled fall that I saw the knife, a large black-handled jackknife with a straight, tapering, blackened blade. My left side was pressed against the linoleum floor. He was on top, still behind me, still gripping fiercely. For the first time, he spoke.

"Don't scream," he said in a low monotone. "If you scream I'll cut your throat I swear to god I will."

"OK," I breathed. "OK." I noticed a sharp pain and stickiness in my left hand and realized I was pulling at his knife and cutting myself. But I couldn't keep my hands away. The pressure of the blade was so firm that, for the moment, it was my only focus, my only perceived danger.

He pulled me up with him and pushed me toward the corner utility-room door. It was at this point that my brain began to engage and that time slowed down. "Open the door," he said.

Immediately he pushed me ahead of him into the utility room, closing the door (presumably with his foot) behind us. With the sound of that closing door several things happened inside me simultaneously. I remembered, all in a single piece, a rape-prevention video seen while teaching high school twelve years ago. I remembered how I had broken up a fight between two boys in my classroom. I remembered a friend's escape from a rapist in Jamaica, when she distracted him with greed for her gold ring. Two messages sprang up: Stay calm. And: Use your wits; be clever. I forced myself to breathe more slowly. I forced my body to sag a bit against his. . . .

"Take your pants off," he said. With both hands I unbuttoned my Levi's, pushing them and my underpants down past my hips, squirming slightly. "Take your pants off."

"I want you to masturbate," he said. His voice had softened, lowered. I reached with my right hand between my legs and began rubbing myself. . . .

With his left hand gripping my right shoulder, he turned me around to face him. The point of the knife pricked into my neck, just below my left ear. I looked into his face. . . .

In an instant, both his hands clenched around my throat. I was on the floor, on my back, and he on top of me, tightening his grip. Immediately my hands grabbed at his, clawing desperately. My mind screamed: Oh no I got one of these guys, *oh no*!

My breath rasped and labored as his thumbs pressed deeper, each painful gasp desperate, animal-sounding. This is what it is like to die in terror, I realized. This is what other women have felt. Paul's face, and a white sand beach with palm trees, and a blue sky, flashed through my brain.

My body was weakening rapidly, each breath noisier, more gurgly and more difficult to take. I felt myself poised just above my head, poised to leap out the window, to get out of here. *I don't want to die!* I screamed inwardly, my fingers digging into his. Then I remembered: Exhale to relax and conserve energy. Hoping to gain strength and time, I willed myself to exhale and go limp.

At that exact instant his hands unclenched. "You're a very lucky woman," he said hoarsely into my left ear. Gratefully, greedily, I breathed and swallowed. I felt him get off me, heard him step away. I didn't move. . . .

I leaped from the door, scooped up my jacket, and ran out of the laundromat into the open protection of the boat shop across the street. I held up my bleeding left hand. I felt the sting of cuts on my neck. . . .

Monday, May 2

What is happening to me? Since Thursday night I have been increasingly remote and withdrawn. The lives around me are full and preoccupied. I am surrounded by an isolating membrane that only the strongest, most demonstrative love can penetrate. I want to cling, but sense that my fierceness will repel.

It has been three months now—one quarter of a year overlaid by fear, sorrow, pain, confusion, exhaustion, and terrifying memory. They darken even the brightest days. Where is the sharp joy of being alive? What am I doing with my "second chance" at life? With all the strength I can muster I am accomplishing so little.

It was a bad idea to entertain last week, two nights in a row, with friends who are unable to comfort me or even acknowledge my wounds. There I was, in the impossible position of reassuring others, pretending that everything is fine. Exhausted by the effort, I could only retreat into a corner of the couch and wait out the evening. It saddens me to realize that there are some friends I need to avoid for a while. Paul is right; it's best to keep our social life quiet. . . .

Wednesday, June 1

This morning it finally awoke: rage. As I was sanding drawer glides in the aft cabin, thinking about Helen, the image of my attacker sprang to mind. God *damn* you, I thought. You are the cause of all my pain. You have robbed me of so much energy and peace. You have crippled my ability to help my friends. See what you have done!

If I saw him now my impulse would be to attack. For an hour this morning I lay in bed fantasizing, not about how to catch him but how to entice and hurt him. It's about time I felt this emotion, so powerful it brings tears. Last week was such a hard lesson to me. I am broken so easily by the hardships of others, of myself. And why? Because one hateful, evil man collides with me, randomly selects me as the object of his violence. God *damn* him. . . .

Saturday, July 23

Breakthrough. Amid yesterday's sun and warmth, after a string of lucky events, I put my finger on Mugshot #4. *He* is in jail, under arrest for his actions on February 9. . . .

There he was: the short, slightly upturned nose, the height of his forehead, the spacing of his eyes, his cheekbones, and the way his ears lay against his head. Even his mouth, which I could never have described, I recognized instantly. Most horrible of all, that indifferent, distant gaze.

Recoiling, I pressed my hands together and lifted them to my lips. "I think he's on this page," I said softly through my fingers. Casually, as though he were surprised, O'Brien asked me which one.

"Number four." Bending over the montage, I traced my fingers around that face, imagined a cigarette hanging from the mouth in the right profile. Oh, yes. I backed into the counter, arms folded tight into my stomach.

Though my words were not definitive, my body language certainly was. Of course, they had been watching me intently. It must have been an electrifying moment for them, yet their faces remained composed, unimpressed. They admitted that this was the strongest emotional response they had observed in me. Peters asked me if I could identify the assailant in a lineup. "Absolutely," I replied.

Response and Analysis

1. Victims of sexual assault often experience a variety of psychological problems after the incident. What problems did Migael Scherer have? What are the most common problems that victims experience? What psychological disorder(s) is/are most consistent with these problems?

2. It is often difficult to think about the psychological processes of the offender, particularly when we are acutely aware of the suffering of the victim. But sexual offenders' behavior, in addition to being criminal, is also a concern of psychology. What types of motivations and cognitions often drive sexual offenders to attack others? How might learning and psychoanalytic theories explain those motivations and cognitions?

3. What are the most common treatments for sexual offenders? How successful are they at preventing further crimes?

4. What can be done to prevent sexual assault?

Research

A problem for courts, parole boards, and the public in general is predicting which sex offenders are most likely to commit further crimes if they are released from prison. Many states have passed laws allowing the public to be told if a convicted sex offender moves into their neighborhood. If you compare states that had such laws with states that did not, could you determine if such laws help prevent further crimes? What data would you collect? What factors would need to be controlled? Do you think that such laws would reduce rates of sex crime? Why or why not?

chapter *11*

COGNITIVE DISORDERS

My forgetter works very well.

NELLYE LEWIS, age 92,
personal communication

Cognitive disorders result from temporary or permanent alterations in and damage to the brain. There are many causes for these disorders, including aging, injury, infection, hormonal imbalances, loss of blood, or substance abuse. Not surprisingly, older persons are more often affected by cognitive disorders, especially the dementias. Persons who suffer with cognitive disorders can have problems in perception, attention, memory, consciousness, comprehension, expression of language, or behavior.

Cognitive disorders can cause severe stress for the sufferer and the family. June Lund Shiplett is one such family member. Her husband, Charlie, suffers from vascular dementia (formerly called multi-infarct dementia), which involves cerebrovascular disease. Patients often have lesions in specific areas of the brain, and those lesions can affect behavior. Charlie's behavior is erratic and unpredictable, varying considerably from one day to the next. Shiplett describes her husband's behavior and her attempts to cope with it.

Perhaps the most widely recognized dementia is Alzheimer's disease. Many people have family members or friends who have been touched by this disorder. Alzheimer's disease is characterized by a steadily progressive deterioration of intellectual function. Memory disturbance is often the primary feature, but other symptoms include language and visuospatial disturbances, and personality and mood changes (e.g., irritability, apathy, depression, impulsivity). The cause of Alzheimer's disease is not fully understood, but patients show atrophy of brain tissue. The course of the disease can vary from person to person, with some patients deteriorating rapidly while others deteriorate slowly. Larry Rose was fifty-four years old when he was diagnosed with Alzheimer's disease. Soon after, he began to write about his experiences with the aid of a close friend who recorded events. In his extraordinary and lucid account, he describes his struggles to resist the confusion that constantly threatens him.

Though cognitive disorders more often affect older persons, they are certainly not limited to older persons. Katherine Lipsitz experienced initial signs of epilepsy during her teenage years; by college, she was having seizures. Epilepsy refers to a set of disorders characterized by intermittent periods of excessive electrical activity in the brain. This activity leads to altered consciousness and often to seizures. Lipsitz describes her attempts to first ignore and then cope with this disorder through behavioral strategies and medication.

Parkinson's disease is a slowly progressive condition characterized by tremors, rigidity, and postural instability. Many, but not all, sufferers also experience a decline in cognitive performance similar to that seen with other dementias. As Sidney Dorros explains in his account of living with the disorder, the physical symptoms alone can have profound social effects—for example, people began to react differently to him because of his facial rigidity. Parkinson's remains one of the most puzzling of cognitive disorders.

A GLASS FULL OF TEARS

June Lund Shiplett

Psychological Concept
dementia

June Lund Shiplett's husband, Charlie, was diagnosed with vascular dementia (formerly called multi-infarct dementia), an illness that destroys brain cells. Dementia often turned Charlie Shiplett into an angry, irrational person who did not know where he was or whom he was with. He was unable to care for himself, his moods fluctuated, and he was frequently abusive. June Lund Shiplett kept a journal to record what was happening to her husband, and then, as a means of surviving, to record what she was experiencing. She was her husband's primary caregiver, and her story reveals patience, faithfulness, and determination as she continued to be fearful and upset by her husband's verbal abuse and threats. Her story raises important questions: How soon do we "let go" of a loved one who is so ill? When do we recognize that we are no longer able to care for the person at home?

July 21, 1993

Charlie had a grand mal seizure today. It was about 7:00 A.M., and he was standing in front of the dishwasher to unload it when the seizure began and he fell right on the dishwasher door. Immediately, I called 911.

When the rescue squad and police arrived, Charlie was convulsing so badly that it took four paramedics and two police officers to strap him down to the gurney to get him into the ambulance. When they got him to the hospital, the doctors ordered a CAT scan among other tests and started giving him Dilantin to control the seizures. By 2:00 P.M., he had stabilized and it was safe to take him home.

This evening I talked with Dr. Geldmacher who told me Charlie has had more bleeding, and that he has what is called multi-infarct dementia. He explained to me that little blood vessels in Charlie's brain break and cause damage. Charlie is depressed, yes, but he also has a great deal of brain damage. The symptoms of multi-infarct dementia are similar to Alzheimer's but multi-infarct dementia destroys the brain faster. He also said Charlie will get worse until eventually I won't be able to take care of him anymore and he'll have to go into a nursing home.

Thank God, Charlie has finally been diagnosed. At least now I know what I have to deal with, although it's not very encouraging.

July 30

The past few weeks have been like one big roller coaster ride. One moment calm and almost normal, the next like a nightmare from the *Twilight Zone*. I feel like I'm living with a madman!

August 28

We went to Charlie's niece's wedding reception today and he did pretty well. However, I did have to give him a Lorazepam to calm him while we were there because the loud music and everyone talking started to get to him.

It upsets me so much that his family sees him for a few minutes and they can't understand why I'm so concerned. He seems all right to them.

On the way home, Charlie looked over at me and asked, "What TV studio were we at?"

"We weren't at a TV studio," I answered. "We were at the wedding reception for your niece and it was at a party center."

"Oh no, we weren't," he said. "I don't know why you're always trying to lie to me. I know a TV studio when I see one. They even had an announcer there with a microphone."

"All right," I said. "If you want to think we were at a TV studio that's fine with me. I won't argue the point."

Then he said, "What am I going to do about it?"

"About what?" I asked.

"About the hose. Because when the cold weather comes our water pipes under the house are going to freeze and break."

"We don't have water pipes under the house," I said.

"I know," he answered. "We don't even have any water in the house."

Oh no, I thought, not again, but he went on.

"And since we don't have water in the house they're going to condemn it for sure."

"They're not going to condemn it," I said. "I told you that before."

"That's all you know about it. You're just dumb and stupid, that's all." He was ranting like a maniac. "I never saw anybody so ignorant."

He kept going on and on, but this time I managed to change the subject. It's so hard to contend with something like this, to keep loving someone who calls you names and treats you like an enemy.

I remember how nice it used to be to sit here in the evening and enjoy the TV together. And how Charlie used to laugh and joke around. I also remember how thoughtful he used to be. How warm, generous and loving, and how close we were. Now, he's so wrapped up in his own mixed up world and in his own thoughts, he hardly pays any attention to what's going on around him, or what I'm doing. He doesn't seem to have a grasp on reality, and yet, his family thinks he's just fine, that he's just a little forgetful.

Sometimes I see the old Charlie shining through, but most of the time it's like I'm living with a stranger. I've lost him and I wish I knew why. I wish I knew God's purpose for all this. Charlie seems so tormented and tonight when he went to bed, he prayed and asked God to let him die. . . .

September 9

It's so hard to explain what he does. You have to be with him to understand. Today we went shopping. When we got home, he complained that he needed a new flashlight. He had taken the one we had apart and couldn't get it back together. I think he lost one of the pieces. I couldn't get it to go back together either.

I told him we'd go buy a brand new one, so we left for the discount store. When we got there one of the clerks directed us to the sports department where there was a whole display wall full of flashlights.

"All right," I said to Charlie. "Pick one out."

He studied all the flashlights on the wall, then said, "They don't have the kind I need."

I frowned. "What do you mean they don't have the kind you need? They've got every kind of flashlight imaginable."

"No, they don't," he said. "They don't have one that blows dirt."

I flinched. "There's no such thing," I said.

"Oh yes there is," he insisted. "And I need one."

"Charlie," I tried to get through to him, "there is no such thing as a flashlight that blows dirt."

"Oh yes there is, and I'll just prove it to you." He headed for a sales clerk who was working on one of the displays. "Excuse me," Charlie said, interrupting him, "but could you tell me where you have the flashlights that blow dirt?"

I laugh every time I think of the astonished look on the clerk's face.

"We don't have any flashlights like that, sir," he said, trying to be polite.

Charlie started arguing with the clerk about it, so I got him out of there as quickly as I could. All the way home he kept saying he didn't know why no one had ever heard of a flashlight that blows dirt.

September 15

I don't know how much more I can take. He thinks he's right when he's wrong and he just won't listen. It's so hard to try to explain to people what we go through all the time, how unpredictable our lives are, how traumatic each day can be. I just hope I live long enough to see the end of it because I wouldn't want any of the children to try to cope with all of this. It wouldn't be fair to them.

It's 8:30 P.M. He's sitting on the sunporch and he's been crying for over an hour and I don't know what to do. I've tried everything I can think of to quiet him down, but he still just keeps right on crying. When I ask him why he's crying he says, "I don't know." It hurts to see him like this.

It's 9:30 P.M. and he finally went to bed. He is so tired and worn out and he says his head is hurting him. I wish things could be different.

September 17

We had a good day today. He was even laughing and joking around. It was almost like old times. His smile was there and his eyes were crinkling and full of love and mischief just like the old Charlie I've known and loved. Oh, how I wish it could always be like this. . . .

January 31, 1994

Charlie was in so many different moods today. There were frustrating times, then other times when he actually laughed and kidded around, just like old times.

The other day Yvonne compared living with Charlie like living with someone who has multiple personalities. She said there's no way to know from one minute to the next which one will appear.

I think it's a perfect description. Sometimes he's the stubborn little boy, pouting and refusing to talk and doing nasty little things as if to get back at me. Other times he's the grown up Charlie who thinks he can do anything. And sometimes he's the docile, contrite Charlie who thinks he's a terrible person and apologizes for everything. Then he's the soft-hearted Charlie who would do anything for anybody and would never think of calling me names. I never know what to expect. Today, I guess he's mostly the confused little boy, so I hugged him a lot and I tried to make him smile as much as I could. I think it helped us both because today I don't feel like crying all the time. . . .

February 21

I feel a little better tonight. I talked to Dr. Geldmacher this afternoon. He told me I could use the Haloperidol at my discretion, just so Charlie didn't have more than four pills in an eight hour period. He also told me not to hesitate to call him for help. When I told him that practically everything Charlie says is irrational, he said it's to be expected, because Charlie's brain is so badly damaged.

February 23

Today's the second day I gave Charlie extra medication and it seems to be helping. When I combed his hair this morning, he was playing peek-a-boo with me and giggling like a little kid. I hugged him a lot today because for the first time in a long time, I really felt like it.

Before Charlie and the neighbor went for their usual walk, I helped him get his coat on, then gave him some extra quarters for coffee at the drive-in. Charlie smiled at me and said, "Gee, I like it when you get me ready like this, it's fun." . . .

March 6

For some reason the Haloperidol doesn't seem to be working today. I don't know how much longer I can handle him. I try not to provoke him, but with Charlie I don't have to do anything except be there to provoke him.

I loved the Charlie he used to be, but I have to admit to myself that there are times I hate this Charlie. A person can be verbally abused just so much before it kills any love that was there. I know it's the disease and not him, but tell that to my heart. . . .

March 18

Another Friday has rolled around. I was supposed to go away tonight, but by the way Charlie was acting, I was afraid to leave him with Yvonne and Braxton. Am I glad I didn't!

He got up out of bed about 10:30 P.M., went into the bathroom, then stopped by the kitchen sink. I was in the living room sitting by the fireplace, but I knew where he was.

"While you're at the sink will you bring me a small glass of cold water?" I asked him.

Instead of bringing me the glass of water I wanted, he went into his bedroom, got the thermos of ice water that he keeps on his bedside stand and brought that over to me.

"I don't really want your thermos full of water," I explained to him. "All I want is a small glass of water."

"Okay," he said, and he took his thermos back into the bedroom, then went into the kitchen.

Well, I thought he was going to bring my drink of water any minute. Instead, I heard loud, weird noises coming from the kitchen. Jumping up from my chair, I hurried into the dinette area just in time to see Charlie raise his arm and throw a handful of ice cubes into one of my cooking pans.

Charlie had taken all of my pots and pans out of the cupboard, lined them up on the kitchen counter, had all the empty ice cube trays strewn around the counter, and was throwing water and ice cubes into all the pans. Water and ice cubes were everywhere.

"What are you doing?" I yelled.

"I have to," he shouted. "We're running out of water."

"We aren't running out of water," I yelled back. "Now, put everything down and leave it alone."

"Get away!" he threatened and he took a swing at me.

I ducked out of his way, then tried to get by him to grab some paper towels and wipe up the mess.

"No!" he shouted. "Get away," and he swung at me again, then pushed me toward the kitchen table. "If I don't get more water in these pans, we're going to be out of water by morning, and you know it," he insisted.

"Charlie, stop it," I pleaded.

By now I was frantic as he went back by the sink, grabbed a small pan that had some water in it and started tossing water all over the counter with the rest of the mess.

"*Please*," I begged. "Please, leave it alone and let me clean up this mess. We aren't running out of water, Charlie, there's plenty of water. Please!"

After throwing the pan with the water in it into one of the other pans that was there, he suddenly whirled around and came at me again with his arms flailing to keep me from getting into the kitchen.

Quickly backing up, I moved into the dinette area picked up the phone and called Yvonne. I kept her on the phone for the next half hour while Charlie kept going over to the kitchen sink, grabbing handfuls of ice cubes and throwing them all over the place. Then he'd get water from the tap and slop it into all the pans. Every time I tried to stop him, he'd come at me with fury in his eyes, clenched fists, arms swinging, yelling that we were running out of water.

Yvonne's said she's so afraid that one of these times he might connect when he tries to hit me like he did tonight, and so am I. So far, I've been able to stay out of his way, but I always worry, too, that someday I won't—it's frightening. . . .

Looking Back

I realize now that we all have burdens in life to either accept or reject. It's not the burdens we have that count, but how we face them. We can square our shoulders, stick out our chins and keep going, or we can sit down, give up and become a basket case ourselves. It's whatever way we choose. And I think the best way is to stick out your chin, keep your faith, and a heart full of love. I learned that I'm stronger than I thought I was and that love is one of the strongest emotions we have as human beings. Love is not just wanting to be with someone all the time, and it isn't just the physical excitement and touching, it's sharing who and what you are with that other person. It's giving yourself unconditionally, without thought to reward. It's hanging on when you don't think you can possibly hang on any longer.

And yet that's where I made another mistake. I held onto Charlie too long and I hope anyone reading this journal will learn by my mistake. I should have let go of him much sooner than I did because by the time I finally let go, he wasn't really my Charlie anymore. Please, don't do what I did. If you have a loved one who has dementia, don't keep them at home with you until they begin to destroy you. And being a caregiver can destroy you if you let it.

As I look back, I realize that I made many mistakes. Some were the times when I doubted that God was with me, other times were when I thought what was happening to us was our fault because of something we might have done. I know now that God didn't do this to Charlie and me, and we didn't do it to ourselves either, it's just something that happened.

I think we all have a tendency to dislike failure, and I think that's what I was afraid of doing, failing. Failing Charlie when I felt he needed me the most. Now, I understand that letting go of him wasn't failing him. I had to let go of him in order to keep on loving him because the horror I was going through was slowly destroying that love. When every day becomes a battle just to survive, let go. When you realize you're losing your own identity, let go. When the doctors tell you that it's time, don't fight them, let go. I didn't fail Charlie, but I almost failed myself because I didn't want to accept life without him.

Response and Analysis

1. Imagine having to care for a spouse whose behavior is unpredictable and whose memory is rapidly deteriorating. What conflicts might you experience? How might your own health be affected? What were some of the hardships June Lund Shiplett faced when taking care of her husband? How did she deal with them?

2. How did dementia affect Charlie Shiplett's intellectual functioning? His memory?

3. How did dementia affect Charlie Shiplett's emotional functioning and moods, and contribute to his violent behavior?

Research

June Lund Shiplett's account vividly presents the challenges of taking care of her husband, who was living with dementia. Suppose you want to conduct a study to examine the experiences of those who are caregivers for someone living with dementia. One of your primary concerns in selecting participants is that the sample is representative of most caregivers. What might you do to obtain a representative sample? Is it important that the sample is representative? Why or why not?

SHOW ME THE WAY
TO GO HOME

Larry Rose

Psychological Concept
Alzheimer's disease

An electrical engineer working in Louisiana, Larry Rose began experiencing memory loss and realized that his mental abilities were declining. He thought that a vacation and vitamins would set him right. Gradually, however, his confusion increased—he made mistakes writing checks, friends' faces and names were harder to remember, thoughts became tangled, details were lost, and conversations became a challenge. He became sad and anxious about the seriousness of his condition, but his sense of humor and gratitude for a good life helped sustain him. With the support of a special friend, Rose kept notes and recorded his experiences in the early stages of Alzheimer's disease.

Stella became insistent that I see the doctor. She was working in her office one morning and asked me to make her a cup of instant coffee. I went into the kitchen and looked around for a few minutes. Then I went back to her office and asked, "What is instant coffee?" She finally quit laughing when she saw that I was serious. It was then that she came unglued like a two-dollar umbrella.

"I'm going to make an appointment with Dr. Trahan right now. Something is terribly wrong with you, and I have had all of this absent-mindedness I can take."

"*You* have had all *you* can take? You should be looking at it through *my* eyes," I thought to myself. I knew I was in trouble, too, and I had no idea why. . . .

We got a call from Dr. Trahan a few days later, stating that all of the tests looked normal, but there were a few more tests he wanted to do, and he would schedule them later. . . .

The following month, Dr. Trahan called to tell Stella that I should see a neurologist. I had written him a check for six-hundred, seventy dollars to pay a balance of six dollars and seventy cents that the insurance had not paid. He said, "Not only is the check for the wrong amount and the date is wrong, but it looks like it was written by a ten-year-old. At this rate, Larry will be in a nursing home in less than two years!"

Stella made an appointment with the neurologist for a week later. I could hardly wait to see him. I just *knew* that it was nothing serious, and that he would prescribe a pill or something, and I would be all right in a few days.

The examination went well, or so I thought. He checked my reflexes, my vision, and my hearing. He had me read from a *Reader's Digest* and then tell him the gist of the story. I thought I had done well, but I lost the thread of the story several times, and could only get back on track by prompting. . . .

Slowly and painfully, I was becoming aware of the darkness in my mind. I realized that my mental abilities were fading and that I must work to overcome my fear of this loss. Everything that is important to me in life is slowly slipping away. Friends' faces, places and names are becoming harder and harder to remember. I am preoccupied with time and can never remember what time it is.

I try to face reality. Will I soon forget who I am? Is there a reason for all of this? Why am I living, if there is no purpose to life at all? Will I soon be leading an empty existence? No, I can't be thinking that. A life is never wasted. Even in this helpless state, there has to be a reason. I know that even in the most hopeless situations, there is still a possibility for growth. I must never lose sight of that.

I had tears in my eyes for the first time in years. Stella touched my arm. "Everything will be okay, Larry. We'll go through this thing together." Touch is so very important. It has become an art to Stella—how to touch and guide me. Will there be a day when touch is the only thing left?. . . .

The good days were not to last long, however. Stella had asked me to buy her some thin copper wire for a stained-glass project she was working on. Boy, did *that* request stick in my mind. I bought a roll of copper wire every time I went to town. I must have had ten rolls of wire on her workbench when she finally realized what I was doing. Although she told me she had enough wire to last her awhile, that didn't stop me. I still bought a roll every time I thought about it. She finally took all the extra rolls back to the hardware store and got my money back. Then she told the salespeople not to sell me any more copper wire. After that, when I'd try to purchase copper wire, they'd convince me that I didn't need any more. . . .

The weeks passed slowly. I had started carrying a notepad to remind me of important things. I read through it ten times a day and, so far, my notes showed I hadn't done anything stupid.

I found a paper in my pocket one day that read, "Don't forget to give Dr. Trahan back the key to his store." What in hell was I doing with a key to his store? Moreover, where *was* the key? "Maybe," I said to myself, "I just won't mention it, and he won't ask." So far, it's worked.

I am starting to have trouble finding the right words in conversation. Just today, I asked Stella, "Where is the sack of mushrooms?"

"What sack of mushrooms, Larry? We don't have any mushrooms, and anyway, I don't buy them in a sack."

"Sure we do, Stel. I saw them last night, the little, white, fluffy things in the sack."

"Oh, you mean *marshmallows*. They're up in the corner cabinet."

Poor Stella. She really has to stay on her toes when talking to me. Luckily, she is very adroit under pressing conditions. She has learned quickly how to figure out what I mean when I ask something like, "Where is my brown thing (my comb)?" or, "Where is the green stuff (mouthwash)?" Stella always knows.

One night, Stella asked me to sit down. "We need to talk." I hated it when she said that, because it usually meant that I was in trouble. "What do you want for Christmas?" she asked.

"A tombstone," I answered promptly.

"What? What in the world are you talking about? You're not going to be needing one of those for a long time."

"Yes I am. There is only one way to beat this thing in my head, and that is to die. I'm not going to lie in a nursing home with my mouth hanging open, like some Alzheimer's patients I've seen on TV. I just need to find a cool way to check out, like skateboarding down the side of the First National Bank building." . . .

The next morning, I went to Wal-Mart to pick up something or other . . . I forget what. I know it wasn't copper wire! I had taken Stella's Lincoln, because it was parked in front of my pickup. After 15 or 20 minutes, I came out of the store, but I couldn't find my pickup. I must have looked for over an hour, and walked past the Lincoln ten times. I was beside myself, and dreaded calling Stella to tell her that someone had stolen my pickup. I was walking back to the store to see if I could find a phone, when an old friend and coffee-drinking buddy walked up to me.

"Hi, Larry. How you doing? I see Stella let you drive her car today."

I looked at the keys in my hand. They had Lincoln written all over them. "Oh, yes, I better head for the gas station. She only lets me drive it when it's out of gas." I was thinking fast. I was *thinking*. I was also very relieved. Now I wouldn't have to tell Stella anything. . . .

If that is all Alzheimer's is—a little memory loss, I would be a happy camper. The fact is that Alzheimer's affects the brain, and the brain controls not only memory, but reasoning, walking, sight, and swallowing, as well as many other abilities. . . .

I am becoming more and more withdrawn. It is so much easier to stay in the safety of my home, where Stella treats me with love and respect, than to expose myself to people who don't understand, people who raise their eyebrows when I have trouble making the right change at the cash register, or when I'm unable to think of the right words when asked a question. Maybe it would be easier for them if I didn't look so healthy. . . .

I can feel myself sliding down that slippery slope. I have a sadness and an anxiety that I have never experienced before. It feels like I am the only person in the world with this disease. . . .

I feel that I am walking a precipice alone. No one understands the frustration in my thoughts. I must keep pushing myself to use the abilities I have left, pushing right to the end. How much further do I have to go? How long will it be before I reach that vast canyon of nothingness? . . .

The letter from Social Security came today. I was afraid to open it; Stella looked at it first. I had been approved for the maximum benefits. It was the saddest day of my life. I am sure most people would have been thrilled, and maybe I was too, in a way, but it also meant that this thing in my head is real. Social Security doesn't just give disability benefits for the asking. They really do an investigation; they have good doctors at their disposal, who check every tiny symptom before making their decision. The whole process took just over 90 days. (I must add that I was treated with kindness and respect from everyone at the Social Security offices.) . . .

I feel an anger, a rage inside my head. It is a defused anger, not localized to any substrata—it cannot be narrowed down to any one thing. Mostly, the anger is with myself.

My thoughts are tangled, not in any order. This is hard to bear, since my memory has always been excellent. I can recall when I could read a page in a book, any book, then read it back, from memory, six months later, word for word. I have done it often.

I once told my boss that if he ever wanted me to remember anything, he should tell me that it's important, and tell it to me slowly, and I would remember it, word for word, for as long as I live. So far, I can still remember things that he told me ten years ago, but I can't remember what I did yesterday!

Will there be a day when I won't even know who I am? The things that make me Larry? Will it matter then? The anger goes as quickly as it comes.

I think anger can be justified, at times. It's normal to be angry with Alzheimer's. It's a thief, a murderer, a destroyer of minds. I try to channel my anger in practical ways. The best way for me to do this is to write down my thoughts. Stella's word processor must be jammed by now. I write down my thoughts and experiences almost every day. Some day, my kids, or their kids, might want to know. If the words that I write don't make any sense, I mow the grass. We have the best-groomed grass in the neighborhood. Between writing and mowing, I have neither the time nor the energy for anger.

I try hard not to think of my problems, or why this has happened to me. Carrying a load of resentment inside can only be destructive. . . .

Some time ago, we received an information package from the Alzheimer's Association. In one pamphlet, there was information about a new program called "Safe Return," a nationwide, community-based safety net that helps identify, locate and return individuals who are memory-impaired. The program provides an identity bracelet or necklace; clothing labels and wallet cards to identify the individual; registration in a national database, and a 24-hour, toll-free 800 number to contact when an individual is lost or found.

Although I have a wallet card and an identity necklace, Stella thought it would be a good idea to register in the new program. They provided an application, which asked for a lot of information, including addresses and phone numbers of friends and family. . . .

One afternoon when I wasn't doing much, I decided to fill in as much as I could. I worked on it for about an hour, then put it aside. A week or so later, I told Stella that maybe she should finish the application and send it off to the Association. She looked at what I had filled in. I have never heard her laugh so hard in all the years I have known her.

"Larry, what sex are you?"

"What a silly question, Stel," I answered.

"Where the application asks for 'Sex,' you put 'None,'" she said, still laughing.

"They want you to be truthful, don't they?"

"Yes, but you're going to give us a bad image by being *too* truthful!"

"You know, that reminds me of the employment applications I used to get. One lady who was applying for a secretary job wrote down under 'Sex,' 'Only one time, in Baton Rouge.' Another fellow wrote 'Yes' under the question 'Salary desired?' I hired him. He was the only employee I had who knew exactly what he wanted."

We laughed until I could hardly catch my breath.

"Well, I am going to change your answer to 'Male.'"

"Sure. I don't even remember that question," I said, truthfully. . . .

Alzheimer's is not a word you hear every day (unlike AIDS, which you hear about regularly, and which has its own constitution and civil rights). Alzheimer's, it appears, has no agenda in government. It has no "in-your-face" advocates. I'm not even sure it is a disease. It's just a *thing*, a word. It's not caused by a virus or a bacteria. It just is. It's an enigma; and it keeps the afflicted from exerting any control over their own destiny. . . .

I understand that there are 19 different drug studies going on all over the world right now, aimed at relieving the symptoms of Alzheimer's. I'm participating in one of them—along with a thousand others like me. We are on the cutting edge of research. There are dangers, but it is also dangerous to do nothing. I have been a mover and a shaker all my life. I can't just sit and do nothing. . . .

Although I feel good about myself at times, I strive to remember that, merely because I sometimes feel more at ease, I should not make the mistake of supposing that the danger is over. It comes back soon enough. My thoughts become jumbled, progressing to complete disorientation and confusion, and my speech becomes garbled or slow. The words that once came so fluently must now be thought about for some time. I avoid conversation when I'm in this state of confusion. Past events, as well as recent ones, are often forgotten, and my ability to do everyday tasks is gravely impaired. I work my mind harder now than ever before. . . .

My thoughts drift back to the Alzheimer's patients I have seen in nursing homes, just lying there, gone, for all intents and purposes. Can they still think? What are their thoughts? Are they closer to God than we will ever know? Closer than you and I?

There is so much to do, so little time. My doctors tell me that I am on what is called a "plateau." I am no better, but no worse. I could stay on this plateau for ten years or ten minutes. There is no way of telling. I am going to live every minute like it was my last. If my condition should worsen, no one can say I didn't give life everything I had, that I didn't try everything possible.

There are many people in the world whom I still haven't met. I must get busy. If you are one of the people whom I haven't met, I'm sorry; it's my loss.

If, when you read this . . . you feel a certain sadness, as some have told me they did, let yourself be sad, but not for me. Let yourself feel for all sick people. I have had a good and prosperous life. I have done it all, and I have enjoyed it. If I die tonight, I won't be cheated out of anything. Most of all, I have had the love of some beautiful people . . . and I have loved them, too.

Response and Analysis

1. How does Alzheimer's disease affect Larry Rose's memory? His intellectual functioning? His emotional functioning?

2. Why is Rose sometimes angry with himself? Why does he begin to withdraw from social situations?

3. What are Rose's concerns about his ability to take care of himself? How does he deal with these concerns?

4. What accommodations have Rose and his companion Stella made that allow him to function more effectively?

5. What are several possible explanations for the etiology of Alzheimer's disease?

Research

Suppose you are part of a research team that is testing a new drug designed to minimize the mood fluctuations caused by Alzheimer's disease. Assume that your participants are fifty people diagnosed with the disease. You plan to give twenty-five people a new drug for six months and twenty-five people a placebo for six months. After six months, you will assess the frequency of mood fluctuations.

What is the independent variable? What are the two levels of the independent variable? What is the dependent variable? What is your hypothesis? Include the levels of the independent variable in your hypothesis.

I REFUSED TO BE SICK . . .
AND IT ALMOST KILLED ME

Katherine H. Lipsitz

Psychological Concepts
epilepsy, grand mal seizure

Katherine Lipsitz was a successful college student "struggling hard for perfection." She had the desires of most young women her age: to enjoy good times with friends, to be attractive, and to succeed in school. But she suffered from muscle spasms and seizures, which she kept secret from others as long as possible. When she was told she had epilepsy, she ignored her doctor's treatment program.

Epilepsy is a serious neurological disorder caused by continual firing of neurons in one area of the brain. The firing rapidly spreads to other areas of the brain; as a result, those with this illness not only have seizures but also may speak incoherently and even lose consciousness. Medication is available to control the disease, and most people with epilepsy are able to live reasonably normal lives.

At one point, Lipsitz decided "not to be an epileptic." What motivated this decision? What stages of acceptance did she experience?

This is what they say I do: First I lose consciousness. Then my knees buckle and I collapse. Where I am is important when I collapse: I've tumbled down a flight of stairs, fallen on the sidewalk and slipped under the water in a bath. Many times I go into convulsions. For me, convulsions last three to five minutes and cause a complete loss of muscle control, so that I writhe and shake and sometimes hurt my head. Occasionally, I'm told, I have vomited and lost continence. Afterward, I breathe heavily or snore; it takes a while until I know where I am.

I have never seen another person go through a grand mal epileptic seizure, and I don't remember my own: I black out. But my college roommate and others have described my seizures to me, and I know that they're not pretty.

I must have understood that epilepsy isn't pretty, because the first time a doctor told me I had it, during the summer after my sophomore year at Vassar College, I immediately and passionately denied the diagnosis. I couldn't have epilepsy, I told myself; epileptics are flawed, and I was struggling hard for perfection.

By the time I entered Vassar, I thought I had finally overcome a lifetime of imperfections. I grew up in New York City with a beautiful mother, a successful father—a music producer—and two very intelligent older brothers. For 12 years, I attended an Upper East Side private school. My childhood was privileged; but I was the youngest in my family, the tallest in class—and always overweight. This last flaw was unacceptable. When I was young, classmates called me names. Adults would murmur: "What a shame! She has such a pretty face."

At age 15 I became thin—by force of will combined with bouts of anorexia and bulimia. I started hanging out with a fast, popular crowd at Studio 54, Area, and Xenon. Yet I continued to feel awkward and out of place—like the fat, ugly kid I thought I'd been.

About this time, I also became dimly aware that something else was bothering me. I began to have muscle spasms, which I later learned were called myocolonus, a pre-epileptic condition. These spasms would happen in the early morning or in moments of stress. I hid them from family and friends. I spent a lot of time alone, dreaming of the day when some man who was smart, kind, and funny would come along and carry me away to happiness.

That first year at Vassar, I began to have full-fledged seizures, though I still didn't know what they were. Amazingly, nobody found out. I was very pleased about that. I also met and began to date a boy who wore a Rolex watch and Bally loafers and was strong-minded, quick-witted, and smart. I was not about to tell him of my seizures or my growing fears. I know I was afraid that he'd leave me, but I think I was even more afraid of admitting to myself that something was very wrong.

I spent the summer after my sophomore year in Spain. I had one seizure before I left home and another after I returned—the latter one I couldn't hide from my parents, who took me to a doctor. The doctor, a neurologist, ruled out a brain tumor and then, describing epilepsy as a mysterious disorder whose causes he couldn't be sure of, cautioned that I'd have to rest every day, abstain from alcohol, and take medicine that would prevent seizures but might also cause weight gain, raise my testosterone level, and promote growth of body hair.

That's when I decided not to be an epileptic. I had worked so hard to be like everybody else; I wasn't about to become the overweight male ape the doctor seemed to be describing. My attitude was: I would drink when I felt like it and sleep only if it didn't interfere with my social life; what the doctor didn't know wouldn't hurt him. I left his office. I never took the pills, and went on with my life as though nothing had changed.

When I returned to school junior year, things were different. The guy I dated had graduated from Vassar and from me. I stopped wearing makeup and caring how I dressed. As I revealed my condition to a few friends, I grew self-conscious about being the only kid I knew who spent quality time with her neurologist. Mostly, I was afraid—not so much of the seizures themselves as of hitting my head during convulsions. I was sure epilepsy would kill me. I believed I should make a will. I didn't think about getting better.

I woke up early one morning junior year facing three men I'd never seen before. "I don't know you," I said. My roommate, stepping forward, explained, "Kate, these men are paramedics. You had a seizure, and you have to go with them." The men took me to the emergency room of the county hospital, where I saw people in real pain, shouting for help. This scared me, but not enough to change. I told myself that all I wanted was to be a normal college kid and I would do it with willpower.

The second semester of my junior year, I met a different kind of guy—no Bally loafers or Rolexes, but I liked him—partly because he liked me. By now I'd gained 20 pounds; whenever I felt sorry for myself I ate, and I'd been feeling very sorry for myself. I was amazed that this boy found me attractive.

Then early one morning, after he and I had gone out drinking and fallen asleep in his dorm room, I woke up feeling strange. I tried to go back to sleep. When I awoke again, my friends the Emergency Medical Technicians were there. The boy had called them. They took me to the Vassar health clinic, where the boy sat with me for hours and held my hand—teaching me a lesson I've never forgotten in how to treat people. Later, he told me how scared he'd been that I would die. I didn't know how to reassure him, because his fears were exactly like my own. So I stopped dating him—stopped dating anyone for the next five years.

Now I know that people experience epilepsy at different times of life and for different reasons, and that it can be controlled. Some people are born with epilepsy; others have their first attack after a blow to the head or similar trauma. I seem to have what's called "idiopathic" epilepsy—literally meaning "cause unknown," but in my case associated with a genetic susceptibility. At the end of my junior year in college, however, I felt as though I were the only person on earth who had this illness, that nothing could be done to stop it, and that no one could accept me with it. The truth is, I couldn't accept myself.

I hit a low point: I wasn't like other college kids. They were experimenting with alcohol while I was experimenting with different combinations of medication. Hard alcohol was poison. And every time I drank, trying to prove I couldn't be something I knew I was, I had a seizure. My friends drove back and forth to New York City; I couldn't even apply for a driver's license until I could prove I'd been seizure free for 18 months. So I went to classes, watched TV, and ate anything I could get my hands on. I became more isolated. Food took the place of a best friend. Then a new neurologist finally convinced me to give up drinking.

This doctor, whom I still see, saved my life. Highly regarded in his field, and also kind and gentle, he was the first person I met whom I couldn't manipulate or make feel sorry for me. By taking a firm stand, he showed me that the only thing keeping me from getting my epilepsy under control was me.

Under his care, I began to take all my medicine. I graduated from Vassar—60 pounds heavier than when I'd entered, but also changed in other, more positive ways. I wasn't so arrogant or insistent on perfection; I'd stopped being a spoiled brat. I moved back to New York City and gathered a group of close friends whose idea of a wild night was dinner out. I didn't drink. I rested. And, for the first time since I was 15, my seizures stopped.

I got a job as a secretary in a large advertising agency—where I wanted to be. Six months later, two weeks before my 23rd birthday, I was promoted to junior copywriter. I had lost a few pounds in spite of my medication, and hadn't had a seizure in a year. I felt I had epilepsy beaten.

To prove it, I went to a party on my birthday and drank everything in sight—margaritas, alcohol punch, beer. The next morning I woke early and took my dog for a walk. Out on the street, I suddenly didn't feel well. My knees buckled and I fell to the ground. As in previous days, I woke up in the hospital. I had a blood-stained face, and a doctor was putting stitches in my chin. My mother was there, crying, and my roommate from Vassar, with whom I now shared an apartment, was there asking me if I was okay. That's when it hit me—I wasn't okay, and I knew it. Both these women had always been there for me, putting my welfare above their own concerns, never blaming me or losing patience. And how had I repaid them? By being selfish—never once thinking what effect my careless behavior had on them. For the first time, it was clear to me that I'd have to change—not for a month or a year but for life.

That's how I arrived where I am today—26 years old and free of seizures for the last two years. Some days I still feel shaky, but I take my medicine and know how to manage my illness. I eat fruits and vegetables and brown rice instead of junk food, and I work out five days a week. I've lost 45 of the 60 pounds I gained in college. I have a driver's license that I don't use much but that makes me feel free. For a year, I went out with a guy who loved me as I am; now I believe that's in the cards for me.

I have joined the Epilepsy Society of New York City, where I do volunteer work. I've learned a lot there. For one thing, many people find the hardest part of epilepsy is living not with the illness but with the stigma attached to it. This was true of me, and has been true through the ages. In medieval Portugal, epilepsy was considered divine punishment for acts of bestiality committed by a person's ancestors. The Catholic Church once prohibited epileptics from becoming priests, fearing they were possessed by the devil. Until the 1980s, a law barred epileptics from marrying in Missouri. Other myths hold epilepsy a mark of genius. I am neither a possessed person nor a genius, but I am better for having learned to live with epilepsy. It's taught me to be kinder and more empathetic. A few months ago at the Epilepsy Society I met a beautiful, blonde-haired 15-year-old girl. We were talking about her boyfriend. "Does he know you have epilepsy?" I asked. "Oh, no. I could never tell him *that*," she said. So I asked her how she would feel if *he* were the one with epilepsy. "I'd keep dating him and love him anyway," she said, a slow smile spreading across her lovely face.

It was the right answer. Though the road is rocky, I hope she learns to love herself as well.

Response and Analysis

1. Katherine Lipsitz writes that "many people find the hardest part of epilepsy is living not with the illness but with the stigma attached to it." What stigmas might be associated with epilepsy? How might stereotypes and social pressures make life difficult for someone living with epilepsy?

2. What were Lipsitz's physical symptoms during the grand mal epileptic seizure? What changes in consciousness did she experience?

3. In what ways has living with epilepsy taught Lipsitz to be "kinder and more empathetic?"

4. What stages of acceptance did Lipsitz experience? How did she modify her lifestyle to accommodate living with epilepsy?

Research

Suppose you wish to conduct an experiment to investigate stereotypes and stigmas that might be associated with epilepsy. You decide to ask a random sample of college students to participate. You have to decide which of two assessment procedures to use. One procedure involves asking the participants to list as many words as they can think of that they associate with epilepsy. The other procedure involves presenting a list of one hundred traits to the participants and asking them to place a check next to each trait that they associate with epilepsy. List two advantages and two disadvantages of each approach. Which approach would you use? Why?

PARKINSON'S: A PATIENT'S VIEW

Sidney Dorros

Psychological Concept
Parkinson's disease

Sidney Dorros was in the prime of his life. He was director of the Publications Division of the National Education Association, was married, and had four children. One day he began to lose dexterity in his fingers. Over a period of several months, his muscles stiffened, his facial expression became somewhat frozen, and he often became restless or impatient. But not until two years after his first symptom would Dorros be diagnosed with Parkinson's, a progressive neurological disease in which cells in the substantia nigra that produce the neurotransmitter dopamine degenerate.

Dorros struggled with issues central to his life: How could he continue to work and provide for his family? What would happen to his relationship with his wife, children, and friends? What treatments could bring him relief? After living with Parkinson's for many years, Dorros learned, with the help of physicians, the love of his family, and his own courage and determination, to accommodate the illness.

Parkinsonism does not suddenly attack its victim. It sneaks up on one—slowly, quietly, but inexorably. Its initial signs are so subtle that Margaret Bourke-White, famous *Life* photographer, in writing about her heroic battle with parkinsonism, referred to the first evidence of the condition as a "wisp of a symptom."[1] In her case it was a slight dull ache in her left leg which she noticed when she climbed stairs.

In my case it was a slight ache in my left shoulder and then a hint of a tremor in my left arm while raking leaves on a beautiful Indian summer day in October. I attributed the ache to fatigue; my wife thought I wanted to avoid an unappealing task—and we both thought little of it. But the ache in the shoulder did not leave with the leaves of autumn. So I consulted a physician, an internist. He diagnosed the condition as bursitis and suggested a shot of cortisone.

"It only hurts when I do something like rake leaves," I told him. "I'd rather quit raking leaves than risk the possible ill-effects of a drug as strong as cortisone."

"Hmpf!" he snorted, "I can't do anything else for you."

When I told my wife about it, she too said, "Hmpf!" But she did do something to help my shoulder. She raked leaves.

That was the first of many burdens that she took on as the symptoms of parkinsonism gradually stooped and stiffened me. . . .

When my fingers began to lose their nimble touch-typing pace, I thought it was due to typist's cramp. When my wife pointed out that my shoulders seemed to be more rounded than usual, I thought I was too tired to sit or stand up straight, or perhaps I wasn't getting enough exercise, or maybe I just had bad posture habits. I would often get impatient, nervous, restless, or irritable, which surprised my family and friends. This too was attributed to fatigue.

It was our family physician and friend, Bob Jones, who first recognized that I had symptoms of parkinsonism. Bob was an ideal general practitioner—broadly knowledgeable, considerate, and available. He lived in the community he served, and he even made house calls. He dealt with the patient and his or her idiosyncracies, not just the ailment. He had a zest for life that was infectious.

During a routine physical checkup, I told Bob of the slight ache and tremor in my left shoulder and arm. He noticed that I didn't swing my arms freely when I walked, that my movements were a bit slow, and that my facial expression was somewhat frozen; but he didn't announce these observations at the time.

"You may have a neurological problem," he said. "I'd like a neurologist to check you out." . . .

About a week after the initial examination, I got the diagnosis from Bob Jones. He took the time and exercised his skill to minimize the trauma when he broke the news that I had parkinsonian symptoms. He said that the ailment follows many different courses, and that some cases progress very slowly, or arrest themselves, or are limited in their symptoms. He told me that I didn't require any medication at the time but that there were medicines and exercises that could alleviate the symptoms considerably. . . .

Superficially, I went along with my designation as a parkinsonian, but deep inside of me a voice said, "It can't be!" And for nearly a year, I really didn't accept the diagnosis. . . .

---

[1] Margaret Bourke-White (1963). *Portrait of Myself,* p. 359. New York: Simon & Schuster.

As I returned home from Bob's office, I wondered why I still doubted the diagnosis of parkinsonism. I remembered that ever since early childhood, I had harbored a secret desire to accomplish something memorable in service to mankind. Suddenly I understood. I had been afraid that by accepting the diagnosis I would lose all hope of realizing this dream.

I've since come to believe that many other people, for reasons of their own, carry within them equally strong drives and aspirations. These strongly affect a person's reactions to a chronic ailment such as parkinsonism and need to be recognized, understood, and somehow accounted for by the patient and those who wish to help him. This is not easy when the motivations are well hidden. . . .

I began to get symptoms that were noticeable to others. Slight tremor in my left hand was the first perceptible sign, but this could usually be temporarily alleviated or obscured by moving my hand and arm about or by resting my hand on some surface at the appropriate angle and level. My handwriting also became noticeably smaller and uneven. Sometimes I would have difficulty walking, especially after standing or sitting still for a while. At other times I would be unable to lift either foot. I felt frozen to the spot. But I soon developed a strategy for breaking the ice. I would kneel down and pretend to tie one of my shoelaces. This movement usually loosened my muscles enough to enable me to step out when I stood up. After a while, though, friends began to wonder out loud why I had to tie my shoelaces so often.

Like many parkinsonians, I was reluctant to tell people that I had the ailment. However, when I thought that they were noticing and wondering about the symptoms I did try to tell them the cause as matter of factly as possible. I learned that people often misinterpret some of the symptoms if they don't know their origin. When I told them about my illness and its effects, it eased some of their concerns. For example, I remember one time while I was interviewing a candidate for a position in the Publications Division of NEA, I got the feeling she was becoming tense. I told her, "I have a chronic ailment of the nervous system called Parkinson's disease which affects my facial expression. So if I appear to be frowning at you or at your papers, please remember that I'm not really frowning. It's just tight muscles." . . .

Despite the tribulations I endured during the . . . years . . .when parkinsonism first became a serious problem and . . . when it became almost intolerable, I resisted accommodation to limitations imposed by the ailment. Instead, I tried desperately, in the words of Dr. Oliver Sacks, ". . . to transcend the possible, to deny its limits and to seek the impossible . . ."[2] That is, I tried to conduct my life as if I were not ill. My efforts to transcend the impossible resulted in a vicious cycle. The more I ignored my limitations, the greater those limitations became. . . .

I hit new lows: physically, mentally, and in key human relationships that eventually forced me to accommodate to reality—to adjust the style of my life to the conditions of my life.

I was pushed deeper into the valley of despair by pressures at home and at work. At home my wife's buoyant spirit and emotional support weakened as she herself became overwhelmed with problems. About that time her period of

---

[2] Oliver Sacks (1974). *Awakenings*, p. 226. New York: Doubleday & Company.

menopause began, bringing with it physical discomfort, emotional upset, and depression. I have known women to have been pushed into depression by any one of the problems Debbie faced: adjusting to four independent-minded, adult and teenage children; living with a husband whose frustrating, mysterious illness often made him seem a frightening stranger; and experiencing the trauma of a difficult menopause. Yet most of the time Debbie was able to cope with all three situations at once. Friends and relatives, and even her own children, hardly ever saw her lose her cool. . . .

But while Debbie appeared to be laughing on the outside, she was sometimes bitterly crying on the inside. . . .

It was during this period that we changed from sleeping together in a double bed to sleeping in separate beds. Perhaps it doesn't seem so serious for husband and wife to sleep in separate beds. Many spouses do it all their lives. But Debbie and I were lonely, isolated, and frightened by the separation. After nearly twenty-five years of togetherness, each of us came to feel rejected by the other. How then did it happen, and why didn't we remedy the situation when we became aware of its implications? Partly because the situation grew slowly and unplanned and partly because it was accompanied by emotional crises that were too strong to overcome.

I previously described the problem of restless nights. At first I used to return to bed, but as the problem continued I found it increasingly difficult to get back to sleep. I was plagued with fears and restlessness, especially in the dark. Debbie was a light sleeper and my tossing and turning disturbed her. We both sought the security of sleeping in each other's arms, but my compulsion to move was too frequent for her to be comfortable. . . .

I had become so emotionally unstable that I would fly into rages upon slight provocation. Despite my wife's tremendous patience and support over a period of years, as my frustrations grew I would blame her for not being sensitive enough. . . .

I found it increasingly difficult to concentrate for long periods of time or to make decisions. It was difficult to tell whether my illness, the side effects of the medication, or emotional reactions to life's problems were responsible.

At work, I found dealing with personnel problems and changing organizational and operational conditions increasingly difficult. When asked to draw up a reorganization plan for the publishing function of the organization, I reorganized myself, with the approval of my supervisor, into a consultative position entailing hardly any administrative responsibility. . . .

The most difficult part was getting to and from the office. The twelve-mile drive became too much for me, or too scary for my car pool associates, and so when my turn came someone else drove. But then a new problem arose. I would often have difficulty walking out to the car or getting from the parking garage to my office. I could sometimes make it only by running. A friend would go ahead of me to clear the way, or follow carrying my briefcase. I was fortunate to have such good and patient friends. Some days they would wait for me because I could not make it to the auto and had to rest or wait for my medication to work. When I had such a bad day that I felt I had to see the doctor on an emergency basis, or just couldn't bear to be at the office any longer, they would take me home early. . . .

"If you get a lemon, make lemonade."

As we learned to adjust to retirement we found some advantages in my relief from the pressures of time and responsibility. Retirement enabled us to enjoy our lives more, to cope more effectively with my ailment, to improve our relationships with our children, and to render increased service to others.

Like many other couples, Debbie and I had feared that too much togetherness might break our already strained marital relationship. However, within a year after retirement our love and respect for each other began to increase. After more than twenty-five years of frustration over differing attitudes and habits on a few crucial matters we began to accommodate to each other. My adjustment to retirement was aided also by the introduction of a new medication that increased my ability to function—not enough to resume remunerative work—but enough to improve my roles as husband and parent. . . .

I tried to arise, eat, move my bowels, exercise, and go to bed at regular times. I also tried to stick to my schedule for taking medication more rigidly than in the past. Instead of taking emergency doses of medication when I felt unable to move, I took emergency rests. . . .

Norman Cousins has publicized the idea that if negative emotions produce negative chemical changes in the body, positive emotions may produce positive chemical changes. . . .

He asks, "Is it possible that love, hope, faith, laughter, confidence, and the will to live have therapeutic values?"[3]

I can attest that they have. I believe it's been love and the other positive emotions listed above that have sustained me as much as medicine since the loss of my wife. First, memories of our love and faithfulness to each other for thirty years helped counteract the grief I continued to feel and still feel over her death. Then, just as new medications have appeared to rescue me each time I have come near the bottom physically, new sources of emotional support came forth when my morale needed boosting.

In addition to the increased attention from my children, and other relatives and friends, members of the Parkinsonian Society provided an important source of emotional support. When the leader of a well-financed but differently organized local Parkinson program in another state came to visit PSGW, he observed: "You don't have as much money to work with as we do, but you have a much more important ingredient. You have love!"

But all the emotional supports mentioned above did not keep me from experiencing many hours of loneliness and depression.

---

[3] Norman Cousins (1979). *Anatomy of an Illness as Perceived by the Patient*, p. 35. New York: W. W. Norton & Company.

Response and Analysis

1. What were Sidney Dorros's fears when he learned that he had been diagnosed with Parkinson's disease?

2. What physical symptoms of Parkinson's disease did Dorros experience?

3. How might friends or acquaintances of someone with Parkinson's disease misinterpret some of the symptoms?

4. What lifestyle changes did Dorros make to accommodate living with Parkinson's disease?

5. What is known about the etiology of Parkinson's disease? What is the prognosis?

Research

Suppose you are interested in using the case study approach to understand how people accommodate living with Parkinson's disease. Assume that you have scheduled an appointment to interview someone who is living with the disease. Make a list of topics that you would want to discuss with the participant.

Briefly discuss two advantages and two disadvantages of the case study approach. What types of questions or issues cannot be answered with this approach?

chapter 12

DISORDERS OF CHILDHOOD AND ADOLESCENCE, MENTAL RETARDATION, AND EATING DISORDERS

> *If there is any gift I can give you, may it be for you not to allow yourself to be measured by numbers or outside things that don't matter.*
>
> CAROLYN COSTIN, *Your Dieting Daughter*

Psychological disorders among children are an important health concern. More than 10% of children in the United States have psychological problems severe enough to require treatment. But not all get treatment, and many of those who do not may go on to become troubled adults. The diagnostic category for disorders of infancy, childhood, and adolescence exists partly to help recognize the special needs of this population. However, a separate category for disorders of childhood is primarily a convenience. There is no clear distinction between disorders usually first recognized in infancy, childhood, or adolescence and those usually first recognized in adulthood. Some supposedly adult disorders (e.g., anxiety disorders, mood disorders, schizophrenia) can be first diagnosed in childhood, and some disorders that are usually first diagnosed in childhood (e.g., learning disorders) might not be diagnosed until the person has reached adulthood. The readings in this chapter represent a broad range of problems that share a common feature: symptoms usually reach clinical attention before the sufferer reaches adulthood.

Mental retardation is characterized by subaverage intellectual functioning, usually by intelligence quotient scores below seventy. It is also associated with limited social skills and onset before eighteen years of age. Most persons diagnosed with mental retardation are diagnosed with mild mental retardation, which means they can develop some academic and social skills, and, with support, lead successful and productive lives. David Dawson is one such person. In the first selection, Dawson describes his experiences with Down syndrome, a chromosomal abnormality that produces mental retardation and distinctive physical features. Despite his limited verbal skills, he conveys with disarming honesty the pleasures and frustrations of his life.

Autism is a pervasive developmental disorder typically diagnosed by three years of age. Many children with the disorder show aversion to social contact or affection, preferring instead the repetition of stereotyped behaviors. About 75% of people with autism also have mental retardation, with most of those functioning in the moderate mentally retarded range (IQ scores between thirty-five and fifty-five). However, some persons with autism, such as Temple Grandin, Ph.D., have extraordinary intellectual abilities. She tells of her creative ways to live a less isolated existence. Grandin's fascinating story recounts her childhood experiences and the ways in which she has come to deal with her autism.

Another disorder often encountered in childhood is attention-deficit/hyperactivity disorder (ADHD). In previous versions of the *Diagnostic and Statistical Manual*, hyperactivity and attention-deficit disorder were diagnosed separately; in the DSM-IV, however, they are combined, but provisions are made for diagnosing subtypes that are predominantly hyperactive, predominantly inattentive, or combined. Because the disorder is often (but not always) accompanied by disruptive behavior, it creates considerable problems for children, their families, and their schools. Ann Colin's son was diagnosed with the disorder. Like approximately one-third of children with ADHD, he did not respond positively to medication. Fortunately, he did respond to cognitive therapy, learning to modify some of his impulsive behaviors. Most researchers believe that therapy must be part of a treatment program to achieve long-term success.

Eating disorders are not listed under the disorders of infancy, childhood, and adolescence in the DSM-IV, but under a separate category. However, they are usually first diagnosed in adolescence or very early adulthood. Especially prevalent among young women in the United States, eating disorders appear to be on the increase. Many people believe that cultural pressures are largely responsible for the rise. Carolyn Costin shares this view. Long before she became a director of an eating disorders clinic, she suffered from anorexia nervosa. She describes the thoughts, feelings, and behaviors she had at the time.

MY FRIEND DAVID

Jean Edwards and David Dawson

Psychological Concepts
Down syndrome, mental retardation

Jean Edwards, who developed and implemented programs in the Pacific Northwest that assist children and adults with retardation, is optimistic about adults with Down syndrome living independently and creating their own life. David Dawson, a client in one of her programs, became a great friend. Edwards writes, "He has done much to teach me about friendship. . . . we cherished the differences and allowed each other to be ourselves, expressed honest feelings of endearment, and stood faithful." The following account is based on a series of interviews with Dawson who tells about his life as a person with mental retardation: his relationship with family members; what he is capable of learning; what others teach him by their attitudes and care; and of his dreams for the future. His accomplishments are impressive; his relationships with others are endearing.

My name is David Leonard Dawson and I am 46 years old. I live with my mother in Portland, Oregon. I am a person with Down's Syndrome. When I was born in 1936, Dr. Hendricks told my mother it would be best to put me in an institution but she said "No."

My mother says that when we were born (I am a twin—my brother Doug is 3 minutes younger than I) that we were both healthy. I weighed 5 lb. and 14 oz. And my brother Doug weighed 6 lbs. and 10 oz. When I was two weeks old mother did notice some differences. I had smaller ears than Doug and had some trouble nursing.

Doug seems more active. Later, Dr. Hendricks showed her some other differences: shortness of fingers, slant to my eyes, small ears, crease across the palm of my hand. That is when Dr. Hendricks said it would be best to put me in an institution. He didn't know anything about Down's. Mother didn't either. She was on her own. She said Dad was a good husband but he didn't know what to do either. So, Mother made up her mind to do everything she could. There were no special nurses, no special schools, no books. Just mother and my twin brother Doug as a model. As Doug developed Mother watched how he did things and taught me. When Doug rolled over, she rolled me over. When Doug sat up, she sat me up until I could do it myself. I was never really more than a couple of months behind Doug except in talking and here I lagged more than a year. Finally, Mother taught me to talk by repeating words very slowly and clearly in my ears. Of course, I don't remember this but Mother told me. Mother had help from my older sister and brother. My sister Jean was 18 years older, Peggy 10 years older. Mother said it was hard. She told Jean first. Jean pledged to help. She didn't feel it was a discredit and helped a lot. In fact, Mother got a lot of help from my brother and sisters and their friends who were old enough to enjoy playing with two cute twins.

I had a happy childhood. Enjoyed swimming, bike riding and playing with my brother Doug and friends. Some say that this early "normalization" with my brothers and sisters made up for a lot I missed by not going to public school. When I was 6, Mother took me to a private kindergarten but it didn't work out. After 2 months we quit that. They didn't understand. Mother said they were afraid of Down's Syndrome. But Mother didn't give up. She went to the school board asking for educational training for me. The school board sent her to the visiting nurses association. The visiting nurses association sent her to a psychologist to do more testing. That psychologist said the testing did not allow me to go to public school. He also told Mother about a lady who took "people like me" in a basement half-days.

That's when we met Mrs. Roecker who had a little school in her basement. She told Mother she had a quota of kids and couldn't take me. But when Mrs. Roecker met me she agreed to take me one day a week. After one day she told Mother, "He's got lots of potential. Bring him everyday." I was 8 years old then. That was my school for the next 10 years. At first I was a student but when Mother taught me to read Mrs. Roecker used me as an aide with the young children. Mrs. Roecker's methods of teaching are now written in books like Mother's infant stimulation methods are. But they didn't have any books then. They did what worked. Mrs. Roecker used books, music and talking about our own experience. Toys enriched our day. Mother was such a good teacher, Mrs. Roecker hired her to teach the little little kids. She toilet trained them, taught them to dress and talk just like she had me.

At home I had the same friends as my twin brother Doug. I was treated normal. I had chores. I made my bed, raked the leaves, weeded the garden, and helped in the kitchen. Mother helped me try new things. Mother wanted me to have a special way to achieve that was different than my twin, Doug, so she had me take tap dancing. I liked tap dancing a lot. It was a good experience too. I learned to swim without any trouble at all, but lots of people were afraid to let me try. My Dad died when I was 5 years old. That's why I owe so much to Mother. She did it on her own. When we were teenagers Doug and I were still friends. Mother says that this was the first time that Doug showed some sensitivity about me having Down Syndrome. Mother took him aside and had a long talk and ended it by telling Doug, "Just remember, Doug, but by the grace of God, it could have been you." She felt he understood after that. Mother says I was a normal teenager. I played basketball and baseball with the guys on the block. Mother says I was a little short on humor and took things too personally. At about age 14, I did learn to tease and joke around. I can be touchy. I have feelings. I can be hurt.

After I left the Roecker school at age 17, I spent a number of years in transition. I worked for a while at the double "O" workshop and then moved to my sister Jean's seventy-acre farm in Wilsonville. [After] her sudden death from a cerebral stroke two years later, Mother and I [moved] to our present apartment near Beaverton in 1968.

Then we learned about the Jean Edwards Activity Center, a pre-vocational and independent living training program for persons with retardation. They said "yes." Here I had a chance to learn job skills about bus riding and more. On June 12, 1974, I started job training at Portland State University in the vocational careers program.

After months of training, job explorations, bus riding training, job try-outs, I tried several jobs: mail room sorting, and mail room delivery, folding towels in a gym locker room. All these jobs were civil service jobs and required that I pass the Civil Service Exam. It didn't work out until July 17, 1976 when I went to work at the Hickory Stick Restaurant. I still work there. I love [my] job there. It's the most important thing in my life. My first boss Barbara Henderson gave me a chance. Dee Dee Cook, a fellow employee, helped me a lot. She was a friend. She understood. Wanted to understand. She wanted to help me learn because she believed I could if taught the right way. When we got a new manager Lynn C. Lewis, Dee Dee was a friend in helping him know about Down's persons. Now I have a new boss, Jack. We are just getting to know each other. I wanted to work hard for him and show him I can be one of his valuable employees. I respect him a lot. Things are not good in our country. Our economy is poor. Restaurant business is down too. I respect my boss for keeping me even if he had to shorten my hours.

It's so important for me to work every day. I've learned a lot since I got my own job. My brother Bob who lives in Albuquerque, New Mexico came to visit and he couldn't believe all the things I can do now. Ride the bus independently, handle money and make purchases, order from the menu in restaurants, use the telephone.

My mother is 87 years old. We are good friends. I owe everything to her. She has some bad days with arthritis but in most ways she is healthy. We live together. I am glad to help her now when she is old because she helped me so much when I was young. My brother Bob is 62 years old and lives with his wife Elaine in Albuquerque, New Mexico. They have one daughter, Susan. She is my favorite niece. My brother Bob is a retired military officer and has [his] own plane and a helium filled balloon. My sister Peggy is a widow and 56 years old. She lives just a few blocks from Mother and I with her two sons Keith and Bobby. My sister teaches swimming and directs two swimming pools. My twin brother Doug lives in Vancouver, Washington, with his wife Marsha and has two sons Scottie and Steven. Doug works in electronics. My sister Jean died in 1965 and my Dad died in 1941. My mother gave me a ring that was my Dad's. It has his initials on it. I wear it everyday.

Someday I might get married. I have a cute friend Mary. She is living in an apartment training program getting ready to be independent. Maybe we will get married. We've been friends for a long time. . . .

I like being me. I've been remarkably healthy. I don't smoke or drink heavily. I ride my exercycle most everyday. I still enjoy swimming but with my job I don't get to swim much. My family is proud of me today and I am proud of me, too. I have some fussy habits like washing my hands all the time, organizing things the way I like them and doing things the same way I was taught them. It took me a long time to learn some things so I am particular about the way I do them.

I am glad my family gave me the chance to be me. Glad they [let] me catch the cricket in the jar, fall off my bike, roll out of the car, ride the bus and get a job. All were risks. From risks I learned. From getting lost I found my way. Finding my way, I learned about my neighborhood and city.

Jean Edwards asked me what I will do when Mother is gone. I said, "I'll miss her!" But I will take care of myself. I'll water her plants, feed her birds and do the things she taught me. She's taught me to take care of myself. That's what mothers do. They teach you to take care of yourself.

Response and Analysis

1. Briefly discuss David Dawson's ability to communicate, perform tasks, work, and live on his own. What hardships might Dawson's mother and family have experienced while raising him?

2. Why did Dawson believe it important to share his experiences? What misconceptions might the general public have about mental retardation?

3. How does Dawson's development and success illustrate the principle of "least restrictive environment" in the treatment of mental retardation?

4. Dawson dreams of getting married. What factors are important for him to consider in deciding about marriage? In having a child?

Research

Suppose you develop a test to assess verbal skills (e.g., the ability to define words, the ability to understand and answer questions). You want to know if the test is reliable. You individually test twenty children who are six years old. Two weeks later, you readminister the same test to the same children. You find that the scores were higher for all of the children on the second test than on the first test. Why might this have occurred? How might it affect your judgment about the test's reliability?

EMERGENCE LABELED AUTISTIC

Temple Grandin and Margaret M. Scariano

Psychological Concept
autism

Temple Grandin was diagnosed with autism, yet she earned a Ph.D. in animal science and teaches at Colorado State University. Although she credits early intervention beginning when she was two-and-a-half years old for her recovery, Grandin still retains some symptoms. For example, she is apprehensive about being touched; to alleviate these feelings, she developed a squeeze or hug machine. The machine has sides that exert various degrees of pressure depending on how the controls are set. After lying for twenty minutes in this machine, Grandin feels refreshed and relaxed.

Here Grandin tells of her experiences as an autistic child—her sensitivity to sound and touch and her early frustrations communicating with others. How does she react to various stimuli? What anxieties does she have? What seems to comfort her?

I was six months old when Mother noticed that I was no longer cuddly and that I stiffened up when she held me. When I was a few months older, Mother tried to gather me into her arms, and I clawed at her like a trapped animal. She has said she didn't understand my behavior and felt hurt by my hostile actions. She'd seen other babies cuddling and cooing in their mother's arms. What was *she* doing wrong? But she figured she was young and inexperienced. Having an autistic child was scary for her because she didn't know how to respond towards a baby who rejected her. Maybe my seeming rejection was not unusual so she shoved her apprehension aside. After all, my health was good. I was alert, intelligent, and well-coordinated. Since I was the first-born, Mother thought my withdrawal was probably normal, part of maturing and becoming independent.

This withdrawal from touch, so typical of autistic children, was followed in the next years by standard autistic behaviors: my fixation on spinning objects, my preference to be alone, destructive behavior, temper tantrums, inability to speak, sensitivity to sudden noises, appearance of deafness, and my intense interest in odors.

I was a destructive child. I drew all over the walls—not once or twice—but any time I got my hands on a pencil or crayon. I remember really "catching" it for peeing on the carpet. So the next time I had to go, instead of using the carpet, I put the long drape between my legs. I thought it would dry quickly and Mother wouldn't notice. Normal children use clay for modeling; I used my feces and then spread my creations all over the room. I chewed up puzzles and spit the cardboard mush out on the floor. I had a violent temper, and when thwarted, I'd throw anything handy—a museum quality vase or leftover feces. I screamed continually, responded violently to noise and yet appeared deaf on some occasions.

At age three Mother took me to a neurologist to be examined because I did not act like the little girls next door. I was the first child in a family of four and none of my younger sisters or brothers behaved the way I did.

The EEG and hearing tests were normal. I was measured on the Rimland checklist where a score of +20 indicates classical autism (Kanner's syndrome). I scored +9. (Only about 10 percent of children described as autistic fit in the narrowly defined Kanner's syndrome because there are metabolic differences between Kanner's syndrome and other types of autism.) Although my behavior patterns were definitely autistic, the beginnings of basic, infantile but nonetheless meaningful sounds by age three and one half lowered my Rimland checklist score. But the frustration for both parent and child is evident in any degree of autism. After the evaluation, the doctor said there was no physical impairment. He suggested a speech therapist for my communication disability. . . .

Mother said at first I had a very limited vocabulary and stressed words heavily like "bah" for ball. I spoke in a one word pattern—"ice," "go," "mine," "no." My efforts must have sounded wonderful to Mother. What a step forward from humming, peeping, and squealing!

But it wasn't only my lack of speech that concerned Mother. My voice was flat with little inflection and no rhythm. That alone stamped me as different. Coupled with speech difficulty and lack of voice inflection, I was well into adulthood before I could look people in the eye. As a child I remember Mother asking me time and again, "Temple, are you listening to me? Look at me." Sometimes I wanted to, but couldn't. Darting eyes—so characteristic of many autistic children—was another symptom of my autistic behavior. There were other tell-tale signs. I had little interest in other children, preferring my own inner world. I could sit on the beach for hours dribbling sand through my fingers and fashioning miniature mountains. Each particle of sand intrigued me as though I were a scientist looking through a microscope. Other times I scrutinized each line in my finger, following one as if it were a road on a map.

Spinning was another favorite activity. I'd sit on the floor and twirl around. The room spun with me. This self-stimulatory behavior made me feel powerful, in control of things. After all, I could make a whole room turn around. Sometimes I made the world spin by twisting the swing in our backyard so that the chains would wind up. Then I'd sit there as the swing unwound, watching the sky and earth whirl. I realize that non-autistic children enjoy twirling around in a swing, too. The difference is the autistic child is obsessed with the act of spinning.

There is a mechanism in the inner ear that controls the body's balance and integrates visual and vestibular input. Through a series of nerve connections, the eyes, after some amount of spinning, will start jumping about (become nystagmatic) and the stomach queasy. Then, the child will stop twirling or spinning. Autistic children often have reduced nystagmus.[1] It is as if their bodies were demanding more spinning as a kind of corrective factor in an immature nervous system.

Whatever the reason, I enjoyed twirling myself around or spinning coins or lids round and round and round. Intensely preoccupied with the movement of the spinning coin or lid, I saw nothing or heard nothing. People around me were transparent. And no sound intruded on my fixation. It was as if I were deaf. Even a sudden loud noise didn't startle me from my world. . . .

Deborah Fein and her colleagues in Boston have an interesting concept of the cause of autism. "In animals autistic-like behavior may result from a lack of input, whereas in autistic children, it may result from failure to attend to input. Because of the very early onset, these children may be deprived of the perceptual experience that normally forms the building blocks of higher percepts, concepts and language." This ties in with earlier studies concerning the inability of autistics to handle simultaneous stimuli and being able to attend to only one aspect of a compound visual or auditory stimulus. Today, even as an adult while waiting in a busy airport, I find I can block out all the outside stimuli and read, but I still find it nearly impossible to screen out the airport background noise and converse on the phone. So it is with autistic children. They have to make a choice of either self-stimulating like spinning, mutilating themselves, or escape into their inner world to screen out outside stimuli. Otherwise, they become overwhelmed with many simultaneous stimuli and react with temper tantrums, screaming, or other unacceptable behavior. Self-stimulating behaviors help calm an over-aroused central nervous system. Some researchers believe that autistic children have a hyperactive nervous system, and some children with hyperactive behavior have a slow nervous system. The autistic child self-stimulates to calm himself and the hyperactive child is excessively active because he is trying to stimulate an under-aroused nervous system.

Miss Cray, our governess, took advantage of my distress at noise. She used sound as a means of punishment. If I daydreamed, my spoon in mid-air, while eating lunch, Miss Cray would say, "Temple, eat. If you don't finish your soup right now, I'll pop a paper bag at you." She kept a supply of paper sacks on top of the refrigerator so that she could burst them in my face if I misbehaved or drifted away from the world of people. This sensitivity to noise is common among adult autistics. Even today, sudden loud noises such as a car backfiring, will make me jump and a panicky feeling overwhelms me. Loud, high-pitched noises such as a motorcycle's sound, are still painful to me.

But as a child, the "people world" was often too stimulating to my senses. Ordinary days with a change in schedule or unexpected events threw me into a frenzy, but Thanksgiving or Christmas was even worse. At those times our home bulged with relatives. The clamor of many voices, the different smells—perfume, cigars, damp wool caps or gloves—people moving about at different speeds, going in different directions, the constant noise and confusion, the constant touching, were overwhelming. One very, very overweight aunt, who was generous and car-

---

[1] An involuntary, jerky movement of the eyes

ing, let me use her professional oil paints. I liked her. Still, when she hugged me, I was totally engulfed and I panicked. It was like being suffocated by a mountain of marshmallows. I withdrew because her abundant affection overwhelmed my nervous system.

But I survived those first five years—not always with grace, but invariably with gumption.

Response and Analysis

1. According to Temple Grandin, why do autistic children "have to make a choice of either self-stimulating like spinning, mutilating themselves, or escaping into their inner world to screen out outside stimuli"? How did Grandin screen out outside stimuli?

2. The DSM-IV identifies three key features of autism that must occur before the age of three: (a) impairment in social interaction; (b) severe impairments in communication; and (c) restricted, repetitive, and stereotyped patterns of behavior. List two behaviors reported by Grandin that show evidence of impaired social interaction. List one behavior that shows evidence of impaired communication and one behavior that shows restricted, repetitive, and stereotyped patterns of behavior.

Research

Suppose you develop a new technique that you believe may minimize the likelihood that autistic children will engage in self-injurious behavior, such as head banging, hair pulling, and self-biting. You want to assess the effectiveness of your new technique. One of your first tasks is to identify participants for your study. Because autism is a rare disorder, it might be difficult to locate a large number of autistic children who engage in self-injurious behavior. As a result, you decide to use a single-subject design and evaluate the behavior of only one individual. The child will participate in your program three times a week for six months.

How will you determine if your program has effectively reduced self-injurious behavior? How can you be sure that your program will work with other autistic children?

COPING WITH ATTENTION-DEFICIT/HYPERACTIVITY DISORDER

Ann Colin

Psychological Concept
attention-deficit/hyperactivity disorder

Children who suffer from attention-deficit/hyperactivity disorder are often easily distracted, have difficulty concentrating for a period of time, are often disorganized, and frequently react impulsively. Ann Colin experienced frustration with her four-year-old son, Willie, who suffers from this disorder. When prescription drugs did not sufficiently help, Colin found a cognitive therapist who was willing to work with her son in helping him reduce his level of frustration. Colin describes Willie's behavior before and after treatment, and she is now hopeful that the family will be better able to handle any difficulties that her son may have in the future.

Januray 30, 1994

It's another blustery Saturday, and Willie, our towheaded 4-year-old, is raging as if the winter storm outside has moved into his body. Unlike most children with attention-deficit disorder (ADD), Willie has not been helped by Ritalin, the medication commonly prescribed—perhaps because he's too young. For the past week he's been trying Dexedrine, a pharmaceutical cousin of Ritalin. Although the pills are supposed to help Willie feel less impulsive and emotional, as we're eating, he suddenly becomes furious.

"I wanted Aladdin, not Jasmine," he explodes, holding up the plastic princess that came from McDonald's.

"I'm sorry, sweetheart, they're not giving out Aladdin this week. Should we put it on the list?"

To help avoid temper tantrums when Willie wants something that we can't give him, Dr. Andersov, the psychologist we've been consulting, has suggested keeping a list of desired items he can earn with good behavior. If he still gets angry, she's told us that we should give him some time to cool down on his own.

"Come on, Willie," I say. "Let's cool down."

"No!" he shrieks. "I want Aladdin!" Willie howls, his face turning red. This is well beyond the scope of a typical preschooler's outbursts. My son's hands are balled into tight little fists. His back is rigid, a braid of anger and adrenaline.

When I try to stroke his hand, he swings around and scratches me. Two red marks well up on my wrist. I'm so astonished, all I can do is grab him and pull him into his room. So much for our cooldown. I'm white-hot and Willie is howling.

"No, no! I don't want to go," he's shouting.

"You scratched me," I say. "That's not okay."

I put him in his room, slamming the door behind me. "You can come out when you're ready to follow the rules of the house," I hear myself saying firmly. I'm mad—furious, really—but I don't want to raise the stakes by getting into a screaming match.

"I won't stay here," Willie shouts from inside his room. "I'm going to escape. I'm going to get a match and set the house on fire. . . ."

He pulls at the door, which I'm holding closed as hard as I can. We don't have an outside latch on this door—we had never thought we'd need one. After all these doctors and medicines and specialists, I fell like we're worse off than we were a year ago, when Willie first got the tentative ADD diagnosis at age 3. While some experts believe ADD can't be diagnosed until a child is age 5 or 6, Dr. Andersov felt Willie's symptoms showed all the markings of classic ADD . . . I can't believe how awful the scene is: Willie butting against the door like a caged bull, me the grimacing monster making him a prisoner.

Willie continues to hurl his body against the door. What's going to happen when he gets too big for me to handle? Already it's hard for me to carry him up the stairs.

The movement stops on his side of the door, and I pray that he has just worn himself out. I'm about to let go of the handle when I hear the huge crash of something against the door. Something solid and large—a chair, maybe.

"Willie!" I scream. "That is enough!"

"I'll teach you," Willie howls. "I'm going to kill myself. I'm going to run away and never come back, and then you'll be sad forever!"

I make a mental inventory of what's in his room, if there's anything sharp he could hurt himself with. I can't believe this is my own sweet child in there. I wish I could wake up and find this has all been a bad dream.

Clutching the door handle as if it were a safety raft, I'm in a panic. *Don't engage him; don't enrage him.* Dr. Andersov's words ring in my ears like a mantra. My own breathing sounds deafening to me, huge waves of oxygen that seem to bring no air.

A few minutes pass and I hear nothing from inside. After a few more, I release the doorknob. Willie seems to have calmed down, though I'm a nervous wreck.

I walk downstairs and am grateful to see my husband, Peter, who has just come home. "What are we going to do?" I ask him. "This medicine isn't working either."

Suddenly we hear the skittering of little feet on the stairs—Willie making his escape. "Mom," he says softly, "can I come out now?"

"Are you ready to follow the rules of the house?"

"Yes, Mommy. I'm sorry I scratched you." He hugs me and I pull him close.

I don't know if I can take any more scenes like this. What if Willie impulsively hurts himself or somebody else? Peter and I stare at each other helplessly. We know we've got to do something.

February 6, 1994

Since the drugs haven't helped and Willie's behavior has been so alarming, Dr. Andersov agrees that he's ready for cognitive therapy; we had held off on it until now because we were told he was too young. Willie will start seeing Dr. Andersov once a week, and I'll act as what she calls a "cotherapist." We'll mostly play with toys in her office in order to re-create some of the difficult situations he encounters at school.

It's a huge time commitment and means more hours for Jolie, our baby-sitter, who'll have to take care of our 2-year-old son, Nicholas, while Willie and I are at Dr. Andersov's. It's also expensive, given that my career as a freelance writer doesn't produce regular paychecks and our family's health insurance pays only half the cost of each office visit. What choice do we have, though? This is our only hope.

March 9, 1994

The director of Willie's nursery school is calling frequently, concerned about Willie's behavior. Peter and I spend as much time in the classroom as we can, trying to help Willie negotiate better with the other kids, but he is still easily frustrated and aggressive. In the block corner, for example, Willie might knock down another child's building or hit his classmates to get what he wants. He also can't stand to be teased, not even the mild, joking kind that's typical of the way many preschoolers communicate with each other. I keep reminding myself that this is a boy who thanks us repeatedly for giving him a bubble bath. Why can't his endearing side come out in school?

The director says she's hopeful that Willie can stay in the class, but he needs to have an extra adult with him each morning during free play, circle time, and gym—his hardest activities. She's recommending we hire a graduate student to be what she calls a "shadow," as it's not really practical or desirable for Peter and me to fill that role.

I suppose I should be grateful they're not kicking him out, but I'm worried about the expense of a shadow because it's not covered by our insurance. There are extra "floater" teachers on call, but the director says she needs to keep them free for emergencies. (If this isn't an emergency, I wonder, what is?)

April 11, 1994

The goal of our therapy is to stretch Willie's tolerance of frustration, so he'll be better able to play games according to other kids' rules. Dr. Andersov also wants to help him understand the difference between "mean" and simply silly teasing. If he can handle a little at a time with us in her office, he should be able to deal with more on his own at school.

Today he dumps about two dozen green plastic soldiers out of a plastic bag onto the sand table and starts lining them up, making two armies in a face-off. Willie usually insists that I be on his, the "good-guy," team.

"But I want to be on the bad-guy team," I say, arching my eyebrows like a cartoon villain. I make a face as if I've just smelled something awful. "Yuck," I say. "I'm stinky, like a dirty diaper."

Willie's eyes are wide with delight and shock. He seems to see that if I can tease myself, it must not be so bad to occasionally get called a name, especially if it's such a funny one.

"Now, it doesn't hurt your mom to be called a dirty diaper—right, Willie?" Dr. Andersov says.

"No. . . ." he acknowledges, cautiously. "It's just funny teasing."

"I'm so stinky," I say, pretending to sniff myself. "You better not be on my team."

"Okay," he says, gamely. "I'm on the other team and you're with the stinky, dirty diapers."

"Ughhh," Willie says, knocking over one of his men dramatically. "You killed me with your stinky smell." Score one for the dirty-diaper team. I guess.

August 24, 1994

We're on vacation in Massachusetts, and the boys are having a ball, catching frogs all day and eating ice-cream sandwiches on the porch after dinner. Willie begs me to take him swimming at a nearby lake.

Only a few kids are left on the beach when we arrive, digging long canals in the sand. Willie crouches down, watching them, trying to figure out their game and how he can be a part of it. The fact that Willie understands he needs to nego-tiate an invitation is a big step for him, the kind of specific skill building we had been working on all spring at Dr. Andersov's.

"Excuse me," Willie says to the oldest child. "Your game looks cool. Can I play with ya'?"

The boy turns and shrugs as if it's the most natural thing in the world that Willie would join them.

"Okay, get water," he says.

Willie grabs his bucket and is about to run to the lake when he wheels around and beams at me, giving me a giant thumbs-up.

September 13, 1994

Today is Willie's first day at his new school, and we're all so excited that we're ten minutes early for the bus. Though his preschool never formally asked him to leave, it was clear that they were unwilling to have him continue on to kindergarten without a shadow, and we wanted him to be in a class where he could manage on his own.

Picking a place for him was a real challenge. Peter and I looked at regular schools, but realized we needed to investigate programs designed for kids with learning or behavioral differences. The special-ed program in our local public school was overenrolled, so we chose a private school. The tuition is steep, but we'll be able to deduct it as a medical expense on our taxes.

The classes are small: eight students with two teachers. Behavior and reading specialists are also on staff. I have a good feeling about this. I think we're finally with a place that will appreciate Willie for who he is.

December 20, 1994

Remarkably, Willie's teacher, Mrs. Rose, has told us that he's a pleasure to have in class. There have been no tantrums or shouting, and we know from his busy calendar of playdates and birthday parties that he's made lots of friends. Yet I was still astonished when Dr. Andersov told us last month that we could start winding down Willie's therapy.

Today is his "graduation" day. Dr. Andersov looks almost as proud as I feel. I look at the sand table and soft maroon carpet where I've spent ten months of weekly visits with Willie. He's grinning from ear to ear at his going-away celebration. Dr. Andersov has bought cookies, and he munches away happily as he draws with her markers.

Although she's told me that her door is always open to us, it's almost unimaginable to me that we're not going to be spending this intense, revelatory time together every week. It's been such a privilege to see Willie through all the setbacks and breakthroughs. I've learned so much about the way he thinks.

I pick up one of the markers. "I love you," I write to Willie.

Dr. Andersov writes, "I'll miss you."

Willie reads her note out loud. I don't know what we would have done without her this year. I feel like she's saved Willie's life.

The doorbell rings outside, and Jolie and Nicky, who have come to meet us, enter the waiting room.

"Would you like your brother and baby-sitter to join your graduation party?" Dr. Andersov asks.

"Okay," Willie agrees.

We open the door, and suddenly it seems very crowded inside with Nicky dashing back and forth. "Don't run, Nicky," says Willie, the voice of authority. "I'll help you get the toys."

I glance at my watch, realizing it's almost time to go. Willie hugs Dr. Andersov at the door, and I do too. There's the smell of snow in the air, and the sky is a deep blue-purple. In less than two weeks, it will be a new year.

Willie wants to run ahead and promises me that he'll stop at the corner. I close my eyes and can picture his strong legs moving, a determined look on his face to go faster. Though I know we'll still have issues to deal with as he gets older, I feel confident now that we can work with Willie to handle any challenge. When I open my eyes, there he is, exactly where he promised—panting, exhilarated, waiting for the rest of us.

Response and Analysis

1. What behaviors did Willie exhibit that reflect attentional problems or hyperactivity? Were these behaviors present in two or more settings?

2. What challenges might a parent have who is raising a child with a disruptive behavior disorder? What negative feelings and stresses did Willie's mother, Ann Colin, report?

3. What cognitive therapy techniques did Willie's therapist implement? Why were they effective?

4. What factors should parents consider in deciding whether drug therapy should be used with a child diagnosed with a disruptive behavior disorder? What assessment techniques might be used to determine if a drug therapy is effective or has side effects?

Research

Suppose you are interested in designing a study to examine whether sugar is a causal factor in ADHD. In thinking about the study, you realize that you will have to rely on parents' reports to assess the child's behavior. You are concerned that the parents may have expectations about the effects of sugar and that these expectations may influence how they interpret their child's behavior. For example, parents may "see" more hyperactive behaviors in their child if they believe he or she has just eaten a food with high sugar content. Similarly, parents may "see" fewer hyperactive behaviors in their child if they believe he or she has just eaten a food with low sugar content. How might you design the study to (a) avoid these expectations and biases, and (b) have someone other than the parents rate the child's behavior?

YOUR DIETING DAUGHTER

Carolyn Costin

Psychological Concept
anorexia nervosa

Carolyn Costin, Director of the Eating Disorder Center of California, has recovered from anorexia nervosa and has been working for the past seventeen years with individuals suffering from eating disorders. Costin's story is representative of those of others, often women, who suffer from anorexia nervosa. Driven to be perfect, to be the best, to be thin, Costin was determined to lose weight and became obsessed with food. Her weight dropped drastically, her hair began to fall out, she became emotional, and her menstruation ceased. Why would an attractive, young woman starve herself? How does she break her obsession with food?

Sitting in biology class, 10:10 A.M., almost time for nutrition. I couldn't stop thinking about those big chocolate chip cookies that you could smell baking in the school cafeteria. As usual, Nancy and I were "on diets" and, as usual, I knew she would meet me at the snack line to see if we were going to let each other "off the hook." As usual, we did, and giggling we each got a cookie and some breakfast rolls to share. After all, why should we be miserable and deprive ourselves. I and all my friends tried one diet after another, but our favorite was ice cream sundaes after school or burritos during lunch. There were too many other problems to deal with, let alone trying "not to eat." It wasn't that any of us were obese or anything but we could have shed a few pounds to our advantage. At five feet, four inches, and 135 pounds, I was "getting up there," but no one else seemed to care as much as I did. My friend Nancy felt about the same. We were just becoming "sensitive" about life, learning about Kahlil Gibran, J.D. Salinger, evil people like Hitler, and love. I guess we were both pretty disillusioned about the mess of humanity. It was the time of our life when losing a boyfriend was the most miserable experience imaginable, and for our birthdays that year, which were only a few days apart, we bought a big two-layer chocolate cake and ate it all ourselves, teary eyed, but together.

I always knew there was something better out there for me. I knew I had a certain strength and willpower that would really show up somewhere. I was the girl who read her chemistry book with a flashlight on the school bus headed to and from the basketball game. I was the only teenager who preferred her mother to drive her certain places so she could read or study in the car. I had to be the "best." I was never a quitter. I always had to win. My brother refused to play chess with me because it took me so long to make my move. He said I took the game too seriously and that I should be willing to "lose to learn" or to "risk a few pieces in order for long-range advantage." He never understood that I couldn't lose, it didn't seem like an option to me. And he never grasped that to lose a pawn, even for the chance to get his queen, was traumatic because I couldn't count on the future, only on the moment, and each piece seemed so important.

This was the time in my life when I was beginning to realize, as most female adolescents do, that beauty would get you everywhere, and that, for some reason, I really needed to prove something. I felt tough and strong and smart on the inside and showed it, but plain, even ugly, and unnoticed, on the outside. I excelled academically, got into student government and drama, even became the school mascot, but none of that was enough.

I decided I was finally going to do it, I would be the one, among all my friends, who would lose weight. And so diet I did. I was proud of myself; my mother was proud of me. My friends asked, "How did you do it, what diet did you go on?" They said admiringly, "You look so good." These comments helped me continue and then something just snapped. It seemed easy. I felt determined. I had a goal to work toward, a tangible reward, a constant task to occupy me. In those adolescent days with few goals, confused values, and feelings of no purpose, dieting gave me a curious strength. I would always tell myself, "You don't need this tortilla chip or that cookie, or a bite of her candy bar." I reasoned, "These things will always be around, you can have them later if you want." Later took a long time to come.

My friends tried to get me to eat or break my diet: "Come on it's my birthday" or "Just this once for me." But if you had a lot of friends, this meant all the time. If one were going to be tough and strong and true, the rule had to be *never* break the rules. I almost lost some friends over it. In the beginning I think they were mostly jealous of my willpower, but eventually they were frightened and saddened by it.

I didn't see *it* coming. They didn't see *it* coming. Nobody saw *it* coming. At that time, only a handful even knew what *it* was. And so when I left for college, at around 115 pounds, I was 20 pounds lighter and 20 times more screwed up than I or anyone knew.

When I was introduced to Debbie, my assigned college roommate, my first thought was that she was thinner than me. She was nice and I decided I even liked her, but I would have liked her more if she were fatter. We were truly an odd couple. She was, by religion and since childhood, a vegetarian, almost unheard of back then. Debbie's vegetarianism made dieting easier for me. Although I didn't convert to vegetarianism immediately, our eating habits were quite peculiar, quite different, and yet very compatible. She didn't want a refrigerator in the room, and neither did I. We both watched our budgets, as well as our diets. In the dining hall, we'd both take salad and veggies and then she'd go for the potatoes and bread and beans—all the things I "couldn't eat." That's how it was, I couldn't. By this time, there was a self-defined mandate imprinted on my brain of "allowables," "watchouts," "rarelys," and "strictly forbidden" foods. But it didn't seem odd to me. In fact, I felt righteous about it. Debbie, having dealt all her life with comments, criticisms, and nagging about her "diet," was very conscientious and respectful about not bugging me about my eating habits. We got along great.

Soon my thoughts, day and night, became obsessed with weight and food and controlling them both. At first, Debbie didn't know of the inner torture I was going through, but slowly she began to understand.

"I'm so damn fat," I said, standing on the bed in the dorm room looking into our mirror. "I'm not going. Look at my legs. I can't believe this," and I started to cry.

"You are out of your mind. You're nuts," said Debbie. "Look at you. You're so damn skinny."

"These pants make me look fat. Look at this, no really come here. Look at this, don't you see, right here on my legs?"

"You are really full of it. Let's go. Wear something else then."

"I just got these."

"Well wear them then, they look good."

"I can't, damn it. I'm sorry, Debbie, just go, go ahead, leave me alone." I wept hysterically on the bed. How could I be fat? I weighed 90 pounds now. I was proud of that. How come I looked so fat?

The next morning I went upstairs, first thing, to borrow someone's scale. It registered 89 pounds, and I felt relieved. I had a better day that day.

I skipped breakfast, as I did most every morning, feeling guilty because it had been paid for in my room and board fees. I just couldn't fit the calories into my regimen. First of all, it was the easiest meal to skip entirely, lunch and dinner being too sociable, almost necessary for interaction and contact.

"I'm worried about you," people kept saying. I loved the comments. It all proved I was thin. I couldn't really see it myself. I can't remember ever really looking too thin—even at 79 pounds, with repeated warnings from my friends and my doctor, cessation of menstruation, and wearing size 1 pants.

Emotionally, I don't ever remember feeling thin enough to let go and eat a meal or even a piece of cake. I always "watched it." I was always on guard, constantly reprimanding myself for slight mishaps or an overextension of my allotted calorie intake. I once even tried to throw up after eating some *forbidden food.* Lucky for me, I couldn't do it.

It didn't matter to me that I couldn't take a bath because I was so bony it hurt to sit in the tub. It didn't bother me that when I slept on my side I had to put a pillow between my knees because the bones had no padding and hurt without it. It didn't make much difference that I was so cold all the time to the point of turning blue and that my hair was falling out. I was thin, and being thin seemed more important than anything else. Now I know it was much more than that.

I was very emotional that year. Someone could walk into my room and ask me how I was and I'd start to cry. I would go for a walk and cry watching the leaves falling from the trees. I called my mother constantly and cried. My mom took me to our family doctor. He told me that my weight was too low but all my blood tests were normal. He told me that even though he couldn't say there was anything wrong with me now, eventually problems would show up and I would pay for it later. I gloated about the "nothing was wrong now" part and ignored the "pay for it later" part—and no one knew what to do.

My mother became increasingly worried. I guess everyone was, but me. I thought they were all exaggerating. So what if I sometimes became depressed and tearful, it had nothing to do with my weight. As far as that was concerned, I actually felt fine. I jogged and exercised every day. I did 205 sit-ups every night. The extra five were in case I did a few sloppy ones along the way. Looking back to that time and at my clients now, I am amazed at the power of mind over matter and at what the human body can endure.

On visits home, I took comments like, "What do they feed you at school?" as compliments. I prided myself on eating less than anyone around me. I never wanted to be second best in anything, especially dieting. I was proving that losing weight was something I was good at, best at, admired for. People often asked me, "How did you do it?" or commented, "I'd like to follow you around and eat what you eat for a while." If they only knew. What they didn't see was my obsession with food. While everyone thought I was doing "without food" and had conquered our society's obsession with food, I was one of the worst offenders.

The truth was that I would wake up in the morning and worry about how I was going to avoid breakfast. I thought about what the dining hall was serving. I checked the menu every week and memorized it. I couldn't stand it when other people passed up food. I'd think, "What a waste, I'd eat if I could." I never thought I could. I felt so obsessed by food that I knew I could never let up on my control over my eating because I would never be able to stop. I would end up obese and disgusting.

At lunch I'd join everyone with my green salad sprinkled with vinegar and maybe half an apple or a little cottage cheese, if I felt a little daring. Then I had to fill my afternoon studying, if not in class, so that I could make it to 5:00 P.M., preferably 5:30, when I had to face dinner. After that, it was easier, with no more routine meals to be dealt with. I was fairly safe until morning, when it started over again. Beginning that year and for seven years after, I did not eat spaghetti, hamburgers, a sandwich, a piece of toast, pancakes, French toast, pizza, bacon, enchiladas, apple pie, lasagna, a chocolate bar, or a soft drink containing sugar. These were poison. There was no reason on earth to eat them. But, if I could have eaten them without the calories, I wouldn't have hesitated about eating every single one.

I was addicted to chewing gum (at times, exceeding more than 12 packs a day), sugarless only. I also, for some reason, always allowed some ice cream. I figured there was no substitute for it (frozen yogurt wasn't around yet) and so it was carefully incorporated into my daily diet. Since I only allowed minimal calories each day, around 600 (over 1,000 was taboo), ice cream sometimes took up a great portion. Therefore, on many occasions, aside from my usual salad, I would choose ice cream over the meat or fish or cheese or whatever else might have been infinitely better for me. I wanted that ice cream. It always seemed worth it. It was my treat or reward for being "so good."

I dreaded school parties or picnics. I dreaded visits from friends back home. I dreaded dealing with food when I went home. I dreaded going out to dinner. I dreaded birthday parties and holidays, all because I had to psyche myself up for "not eating" and for dealing with others who might pressure me to eat. They were all potential situations for my demise or a breakdown; that is, eating too much.

I had an inner voice. It was as if a little man were living inside my head. He plotted out the day's food allowance, he automatically calculated calories of any food that was before me or that was going into my mouth. He always told me I didn't need this or that food item, and if I ignored him, he punished me with guilt and stomachaches and tears and made me eat even less food for a while and do more exercise.

He made me put my bike on the highest gear so I had to strive hard for what could have been an easy ride. He made me swim laps whenever I got in a swimming pool; to merely play in the pool was to be lazy. He made me keep running until I reached the freeway or the lake or the dorm or whatever landmark he decided would be difficult enough for me. He made me say No, when I wanted to say Yes, study when I wanted to play, starve myself almost to death when all I really wanted was to eat, to live, and to be happy.

It took seven years, but I recovered. I am recovered from the desire to be thin at any cost, from the need to be perfect, and from the illusion that what I look like is more important than who I am. Recovery takes time; it is a process. There was never a point when I said, "Now I am recovered." It is more a sense of looking back and realizing that something very terrible is now gone and something more true to my real self has taken its place. It would be false and misleading to say that as a female in this society I do not have my share of body-image issues, wanting to wear size 5, wishing that 41 didn't mean wrinkles, and even feeling fat sometimes. And, often I order my salad dressing on the side, and drink my cappuccinos nonfat. I even exercise. But I also eat Häagen-Dazs in my bubble bath at night, share bags of M&Ms with my Labrador, Gonner, and I drink, instead of pass up, a glass of champagne. And if the dressing happens to come on the salad . . . oh well, no big deal. I will no longer sacrifice. I will no longer betray myself or my body in the pursuit of some cultural standard, or in the quest for acceptance or praise for my external qualities. I have found a balance. I have made peace with food, and with myself.

Response and Analysis

1. What factors does Carolyn Costin believe influenced her to develop an eating disorder?

2. What physical problems does Costin experience as a result of her eating style? Psychological problems? Relationship difficulties?

3. How are values concerning physical appearance conveyed to children, adolescents, and adults? What pressures do young men and women in American society experience if they do not conform to the idealized body image? How might these pressures affect self-esteem?

4. Why might eating disorders be more common in the United States than in Eastern cultures?

Research

Suppose you conduct a study to investigate the relationship between self-esteem and anorexia nervosa. You have one hundred female and male students at your college or university complete an eating disorders questionnaire and a self-esteem questionnaire. You find that there is a moderate positive correlation ($r = 0.22$) between anorexia nervosa and self-esteem. What are the three possible explanations for this relationship? Why is it not possible to determine which explanation is correct on the basis of your findings?

chapter 13

INDIVIDUAL AND GROUP THERAPY

Nothing can be changed until it is faced.

JAMES BALDWIN

Psychotherapy refers to any formal, systematic treatment designed to help persons who are experiencing psychological problems. For years, people have debated whether psychotherapy is a science or an art. Certainly, it is some of both. It normally involves dialogue between one or more clients and a therapist or team of therapists. Therapists must rely on a theoretical framework to understand and treat problems; that theoretical framework usually comes from years of training and supervised practice.

The techniques that therapists use vary and often depend on the therapist's theoretical orientation. For example, insight-oriented approaches such as psychoanalytic, humanistic, or existential therapy focus on emotional and relationship issues, often using the therapeutic relationship as the primary focus of attention. Behavioral and cognitive-behavioral approaches, which use conditioning techniques, modeling, hypothesis testing, and cognitive restructuring, center more on specific behaviors or the thoughts associated with specific behaviors. Other forms of treatment rely heavily on antipsychotic, antianxiety, and antidepressant medications or other biological treatments (often in conjunction with one of the approaches above). Treatment approaches must also be adapted to the special needs of the clients (e.g., children or less-verbal clients require different ways of interacting). Most therapists describe their approach as eclectic, meaning that they draw on techniques from different theoretical orientations.

Research into the effectiveness of different approaches for various disorders is critical and is ongoing. We do know that most forms of treatment are better than no treatment at all, that no one approach works best for all disorders, and that the quality of the relationship between the therapist and the client is very important for successful outcomes. Some research suggests that paraprofessionals with limited training can be effective. But few would doubt that broad-based understanding of disorders and specific interpersonal skills are critical for treatment effectiveness.

This chapter offers readings that present questions and issues that confront all treatment professionals, regardless of their theoretical approach. How does a therapist establish the groundwork for a good working relationship in therapy? How can lessons learned in therapy be generalized outside of the therapy setting? How should a therapist react when clients exhibit bizarre and irrational behavior? How might a therapist intervene when families or people from different cultures present novel ways of looking at an issue? How might cotherapists work together with a family?

In the first reading, therapist David D. Burns shows how the cognitive techniques he teaches clients can also assist him in coping with the stresses of being a therapist, which, at times, can be considerable. In the second selection, psychologist Lauren Slater describes her struggle to understand the world of her schizophrenic clients as she tries to help them connect with each other through group therapy. Next, psychologist Royal Alsup shows, through his work with a Native American adolescent girl, the importance of adapting the therapeutic work to one's understanding of a client's cultural context. Finally, family therapists Ivan B. Inger and Jeri Inger present their initial interview with a family whose twelve-year-old son Steve is being seen by a counselor at his school. In this session we see the advantages of doing therapy with a family and of the creative way a team of therapists work together. These selections show that providing treatment for people suffering from psychological disorders can be challenging and rewarding.

FEELING GOOD

David D. Burns

Psychological Concept
applying cognitive therapy techniques to work-related stress

Difficult clients can make unreasonable demands, show extreme hostility, and violate many of the social norms that lubricate most interactions. As a result, psychotherapists and other mental health workers may feel overwhelmed, unappreciated, and even abused. Some therapists may come to expect this—it is part of the job—but expecting it does not necessarily make it easy.

As a cognitive therapist, David Burns helps clients look at the way they think about their world, and especially at what they expect from themselves and others. Certain thoughts and expectations may lead to negative emotions and negative behavior. Using himself as an example, Burns shows that challenging one's thoughts and expectations can lead to more reasonable expectations for oneself and others and, in turn, to more positive emotions and behaviors.

A recent study of stress has indicated that one of the world's most demanding jobs—in terms of the emotional tension and the incidence of heart attacks—is that of an air-traffic controller in an airport tower. The work involves precision, and the traffic controller must be constantly alert—a blunder could result in tragedy. I wonder however if that job is more taxing than mine. After all, the pilots are cooperative and intend to take off or land safely. But the ships I guide are sometimes on an intentional crash course.

Here's what happened during one thirty-minute period last Thursday morning. At 10:25 I received the mail, and skimmed a long, rambling, angry letter from a patient named Felix just prior to the beginning of my 10:30 session. Felix announced his plans to carry out a "blood bath," in which he would murder three doctors, including two psychiatrists who had treated him in the past! In his letter Felix stated, "I'm just waiting until I get enough energy to drive to the store and purchase the pistol and the bullets." I was unable to reach Felix by phone, so I began my 10:30 session with Harry. Harry was emaciated and looked like a concentration camp victim. He was unwilling to eat because of a delusion that his bowels had "closed off," and he had lost seventy pounds. As I was discussing the unwelcome option of hospitalizing Harry for forced tube feeding to prevent his death from starvation, I received an emergency telephone call from a patient named Jerome, which interrupted the session. Jerome informed me he had placed a noose around his neck and was seriously considering hanging himself before his wife came home from work. He announced his unwillingness to continue outpatient treatment and insisted that hospitalization would be pointless.

I straightened out these three emergencies by the end of the day, and went home to unwind. At just about bedtime I received a call from a new referral—a well-known woman VIP referred by another patient of mine. She indicated she'd been depressed for several months, and that earlier in the evening she'd been standing in front of a mirror practicing slitting her throat with a razor blade. She explained she was calling me only to pacify the friend who referred her to me, but was unwilling to schedule an appointment because she was convinced her case was "hopeless."

Every day is not as nerve-racking as that one! But at times it does seem like I'm living in a pressure cooker. This gives me a wealth of opportunities to learn to cope with intense uncertainty, worry, frustration, irritation, disappointment, and guilt. It affords me the chance to put my cognitive techniques to work on myself and see firsthand if they're actually effective. There are many sublime and joyous moments too.

If you have ever gone to a psychotherapist or counselor, the chances are that the therapist did nearly all the listening and expected you to do most of the talking. This is because many therapists are trained to be relatively passive and nondirective—a kind of "human mirror" who simply reflects what you are saying.[1] This one-way style of communication may have seemed unproductive and frustrating to you. You may have wondered—"What is my psychiatrist really like? What kinds of feelings does he have? How does he deal with them? What pressures does he feel in dealing with me or with other patients?"

Many patients have asked me directly, "Dr. Burns, do you actually practice what you preach?" The fact is, I often do pull out a sheet of paper on the train ride home in the evening, and draw a line down the center from top to bottom so I can utilize the double-column technique to cope with any nagging emotional hangovers from the day. If you are curious to take a look behind the scenes, I'll be glad to share some of my self-help homework with you. This is your chance to sit back and listen while the *psychiatrist* does the talking! At the same time, you can get an idea of how the cognitive techniques [used] to overcome clinical depression can be applied to all sorts of daily frustrations and tensions that are an inevitable part of living for all of us.

Coping with Hostility: The Man Who Fired Twenty Doctors

One high-pressure situation I often face involves dealing with angry, demanding, unreasonable individuals. I suspect I have treated a few of the East Coast's top anger champions. These people often take their resentment out on the people who care the most about them, and sometimes this includes me.

---

[1] [According to David Burns] some of the newer forms of psychiatric treatment, such as cognitive therapy, allow for a natural fifty-fifty dialogue between the client and therapist, who work together as equal members of a team.

Hank was an angry young man. He had fired twenty doctors before he was referred to me. Hank complained of episodic back pain, and was convinced he suffered from some severe medical disorder. Because no evidence for any physical abnormality had ever surfaced, in spite of lengthy, elaborate medical evaluations, numerous physicians told him that his aches and pains were in all likelihood the result of emotional tension, much like a headache. Hank had difficulty accepting this, and he felt his doctors were writing him off and just didn't give a damn about him. Over and over he'd explode in a fury, fire his doctor, and seek out someone new. Finally, he consented to see a psychiatrist. He resented this referral, and, after making no progress for about a year, he fired his psychiatrist and sought treatment at our Mood Clinic.

Hank was quite depressed, and I began to train him in cognitive techniques. At night when his back pain flared up, Hank would work himself up into a frustrated rage and impulsively call me at home (he had persuaded me to give him my home number so he wouldn't have to go through the answering service). He would begin by swearing and accusing me of misdiagnosing his illness. He'd insist he had a medical, not a psychiatric problem. Then he'd deliver some unreasonable demand in the form of an ultimatum: "Dr. Burns, either you arrange for me to get shock treatments tomorrow or I'll go out and commit suicide tonight." It was usually difficult, if not impossible, for me to comply with most of his demands. For example, I don't give shock treatments, and furthermore I didn't feel this type of treatment was indicated for Hank. When I would try to explain this diplomatically, he would explode and threaten some impulsive destructive action.

During our psychotherapy sessions Hank had the habit of pointing out each of my imperfections (which are real enough). He'd often storm around the office, pound on the furniture, heaping insults and abuse on me. What used to get me in particular was Hank's accusation that I didn't care about him. He said that all I cared about was money and maintaining a high therapy success rate. This put me in a dilemma, because there was a grain of truth in his criticism—he was often several months behind in making payments for his therapy, and I was concerned that he might drop out of treatment prematurely and end up even more disillusioned. Furthermore, I *was* eager to add him to my list of successfully treated individuals. Because there was some truth in Hank's haranguing attacks, I felt guilty and defensive when he would zero in on me. He, of course, would sense this, and consequently the volume of his criticism would increase.

I sought some guidance from my associates at the Mood Clinic as to how I might handle Hank's outbursts and my own feelings of frustration more effectively. The advice I received from Dr. Beck was especially useful. First, he emphasized that I was "unusually fortunate" because Hank was giving me a golden opportunity to learn to cope with criticism and anger effectively. This came as a complete surprise to me; I hadn't realized what good fortune I had. In addition to urging me to use cognitive techniques to reduce and eliminate my own sense of irritation, Dr. Beck proposed I try out an unusual strategy for interacting with Hank when he was in an angry mood. The essence of this method was (1) Don't turn Hank off by defending yourself. Instead, do the opposite—urge him to say all the worst things he can say about you. (2) Try to find a grain of truth in all his criticisms and then agree with him. (3) After this, point out any areas of disagreement in a straightforward, tactful, nonargumentative manner. (4) Emphasize the importance of sticking together, in spite of these occasional disagreements. I could remind Hank that frustration and fighting might slow down our therapy at times, but this need not destroy the relationship or prevent our work from ultimately becoming fruitful.

I applied this strategy the next time Hank started storming around the office screaming at me. Just as I had planned, I urged Hank to keep it up and say all the worst things he could think of about me. The result was immediate and dramatic. Within a few moments, all the wind went out of his sails—all his vengeance seemed to melt away. He began communicating sensibly and calmly, and sat down. In fact, when I agreed with some of his criticisms, he suddenly began to defend me and say some nice things about me! I was so impressed with this result that I began using the same approach with other angry, explosive individuals, and I actually did begin to enjoy his hostile outbursts because I had an effective way to handle them.

I also used the double-column technique[2] for recording and talking back to my automatic thoughts after one of Hank's midnight calls (see Figure 1). As my associates suggested, I tried to see the world through Hank's eyes in order to gain a certain degree of empathy. This was a specific antidote that in part dissolved my own frustration and anger, and I felt much less defensive and upset. It helped me to see his outbursts more as a defense of his own self-esteem than as an attack on me, and I was able to comprehend his feelings of futility and desperation. I reminded myself that much of the time he was damn hard working and cooperative, and how foolish it was for me to demand he be totally cooperative at all times. As I began to feel more calm and confident in my work with Hank, our relationship continually improved.

Eventually, Hank's depression and pain subsided, and he terminated his work with me. I hadn't seen him for many months when I received a message from my answering service that Hank wanted me to call him. I suddenly felt apprehensive; memories of his turbulent tirades flooded my mind, and my stomach muscles tensed up. With some hesitation and mixed feelings, I dialed his number. It was a sunny Saturday afternoon, and I'd been looking forward to a much needed rest after an especially taxing week. Hank answered the phone: "Dr. Burns, this is Hank. Do you remember me? There's something I've been meaning to tell you for some time . . ." He paused, and I braced for the impending explosion. "I've been essentially free of pain and depression since we finished up a year ago. I went off disability and I've gotten a job. I'm also the leader of a self-help group in my own hometown."

This wasn't the Hank I remembered! I felt a wave of relief and delight as he went on to explain, "But that's not why I'm calling. What I want to say to you is . . ." There was another moment of silence—"I'm grateful for your efforts, and I now know you were right all along. There was nothing dreadfully wrong with me, I was

---

[2] A listing of negative self-statements on one side of a column and positive self-statements on the other side of the column

Figure 1.   Coping with Hostility

Automatic Thoughts	*Rational Responses*
1. I've put more energy into working with Hank than nearly anyone, and this is what I get—abuse!	1. Stop complaining. You sound like Hank! He's frightened and frustrated, and he's trapped in his resentment. Just because you work hard for someone, it doesn't necessarily follow that they'll feel appreciative. Maybe he will some day.
2. Why doesn't he trust me about his diagnosis and treatment?	2. Because he's in a panic, he's extremely uncomfortable and in pain, and he hasn't yet gotten any substantial results. He'll believe you once he starts getting well.
3. But in the meantime, he should at least treat me with respect!	3. Do you expect him to show respect *all* the time or *part* of the time? In general, he exerts tremendous effort in his self-help program and does treat you with respect. He's determined to get well—if you don't expect perfection, you won't have to feel frustrated.
4. But is it fair for him to call me so often at home at night? And does he have to be so abusive?	4. Talk it over with him when you're both feeling more relaxed. Suggest that he supplement his individual therapy by joining a self-help group in which the various patients call each other for moral support. This will make it easier for him to cut down on calls to you. But for now, remember that he doesn't *plan* these emergencies, and they are very terrifying and real to him.

just upsetting myself with my irrational thinking. I just couldn't admit it until I knew for sure. Now, I feel like a whole man, and I had to call you up and let you know where I stood . . . It was hard for me to do this, and I'm sorry it took so long for me to get around to telling you."

Thank you, Hank! I want you to know that some tears of joy and pride in you come to my eyes as I write this. It was worth the anguish we both went through a hundred times over!

Coping with Ingratitude: The Woman Who Couldn't Say Thank You

Did you ever go out of your way to do a favor for someone only to have the person respond to your efforts with indifference or nastiness? People *shouldn't* be so unappreciative, right? If you tell yourself this, you will probably stew for days as you mull the incident over and over. The more inflammatory your thoughts and fantasies become, the more disturbed and angry you will feel.

Let me tell you about Susan. After high-school graduation, Susan sought treatment for a recurrent depression. She was very skeptical that I could help her and continually reminded me that she was hopeless. She had been in a hysterical state for several weeks because she couldn't decide which of two colleges to attend. She acted as though the world would come to an end if she didn't make the "right" decision, and yet the choice was simply not clear-cut. Her insistence on eliminating all uncertainty was bound to cause her endless frustration because it simply couldn't be done.

She cried and sobbed excessively. She was insulting and abusive to her boyfriend and her family. One day she called me on the phone, pleading for help. She just had to make up her mind. She rejected every suggestion I made, and angrily demanded I come up with some better approach. She kept insisting, "Since I can't make this decision, it proves your cognitive therapy won't work for me. Your methods are no damn good. I'll never be able to decide, and I can't get better." Because she was so upset, I arranged my afternoon schedule so that I could have an emergency consultation with a colleague. He offered several outstanding suggestions; I called her right back and gave her some tips on how to resolve her indecisiveness. She was then able to come to a satisfactory decision within fifteen minutes, and felt an instantaneous wave of relief.

When she came in for her next regularly scheduled session, she reported she had been feeling relaxed since our talk, and had finalized the arrangements to attend the college that she chose. I anticipated waves of gratitude because of my strenuous efforts on her behalf, and I asked her if she was still convinced that cognitive techniques would be ineffective for her. She reported, "Yes, indeed! This just proves my point. My back was up against the wall, and I *had* to make a decision. The fact that I'm feeling good now doesn't count because it can't last. This stupid therapy can't help me. I'll be depressed for the rest of my life." My thought: "My God! How illogical can you get? I could turn mud into gold, and she wouldn't even notice!" My blood was boiling, so I decided to use the double-column technique later that day to try and calm my troubled and insulted spirits (see Figure 2).

After writing down my automatic thoughts, I was able to pinpoint the irrational assumption that caused me to get upset over her ingratitude. It was, "If I do something to help someone, they are duty-bound to feel grateful and reward me for it." It would be nice if things worked like this, but it's simply not the case. No one has a moral or legal obligation to credit me for my cleverness or praise my good efforts on their behalf. So why expect it or demand it? I decided to tune in to reality and adopt a more realistic attitude: "If I do something to help someone, the chances are the person *will* be appreciative, and that will feel good. But every now and then, someone will not respond the way I want. If the response is unreasonable, this is a reflection on that person, not me, so why get upset over it?" This attitude has made life much sweeter for me, and overall I have been blessed with as much gratitude from patients as I could desire. Incidentally, Susan gave me a call just the other day. She'd done well at college and was about to graduate. Her father had been depressed, and she wanted a referral to a good cognitive therapist! Maybe that was her way of saying thank you!

Figure 2.   Coping with Ingratitude

Automatic Thoughts	*Rational Responses*
1. How can such a brilliant girl be so illogical?	1. Easily! Her illogical thinking is the cause of her depression. If she didn't continually focus on negatives and disqualify positives, she wouldn't be depressed so often. It's your job to train her in how to get over this.
2. But I can't. She's determined to beat me down. She won't give me an ounce of satisfaction.	2. She doesn't have to give you any satisfaction. Only you can do this. Don't you recall that only *your* thoughts affect your moods? Why not credit yourself for what you did? Don't wait around for her. You just learned some exciting things about how to guide people in making decisions. Doesn't that count?
3. But she should admit I helped her! She should be grateful!	3. Why "should" she? That's a fairy tale. If she could she probably would, but she can't yet. In time she'll come around, but she'll have to reverse an ingrained pattern of illogical thinking that's been dominating her mind for over a decade. She may be *afraid* to admit she's getting help so she won't end up disillusioned again. Or she might be afraid you'll say, "I told you so." Be like Sherlock Holmes and see if you can figure out this puzzle. It's pointless to demand that she be different from the way she is.

Response and Analysis

1. How did David Burns come to understand and then respond to Hank's angry outbursts?

2. What cognitive therapy techniques does Burns use? What other situations might benefit from these techniques? Why?

3. Burns says that he seeks advice from colleagues on certain cases. What is your reaction? How does this affect your view of him as a therapist?

4. Burns's article raises an interesting question: What happens when therapists seek psychological treatment? What features do you think psychologists and psychiatrists look for in a therapist? Do you think most therapists seek treatment from therapists with the same orientation as themselves? Why or why not?

Research

Suppose you want to study the effectiveness of cognitive techniques for treating depression. Before beginning the study, you think about several variables that might influence the results: (a) therapists' years of practice; (b) severity of clients' symptoms; and (c) level of rapport between therapist and client. How might each of these variables affect the results?

WELCOME TO MY COUNTRY

Lauren Slater

Psychological Concept
group therapy with persons with schizophrenia

Psychologist Lauren Slater began her professional career working in an institution with persons diagnosed with schizophrenia. The patients were often lost in worlds of their own; they showed marked delusions, hallucinations, and bizarre associations. They often spoke in incoherent sentences. Slater's conception of her clients' problems emphasizes their isolation and their loss of meaningful connections to other human beings. In group therapy, she finds herself exhausted by constantly directing their attention to objective reality and to basic living skills. She decides to experiment and use unconventional therapeutic techniques. Her attempts to help clients overcome their isolation and make connections with each other show that creativity has a place in therapy.

My first group. Six men, all of whose charts I've read prior to actually meeting them. I watch as they file into the group room. They say their names one by one when I ask, and as they do I match up names and faces with the information I've gleaned from records.

There is Tran, nicknamed Moxi, a small, cocoa-colored Vietnamese who came to this country after the war, and who bows to invisible Buddhas all day in the corridors. There is Joseph, with a mangy beard, a green-and-khaki combat helmet he puts on the pillow next to him when he sleeps. Charles is forty-two years old and dying of AIDS. Lenny once stood naked in Harvard Yard and recited poetry. Robert believes fruits none of us can see are exploding all around him. And then there is Oscar, 366 pounds, and claiming constant blow jobs from such diverse females as the Queen of England and Chrissy, the Shih Tzu dog next door.

Oscar slogs into the group room, groans, lowers himself onto the floor, and lies there with his hairy belly bloating up.

"I am," I say, my voice cracking from fear (for I have never done this kind of work before; all my other patients have been violent or sad or scared but not . . . not . . . *this*), "your new group therapist. We'll be meeting once a week to talk things over, see how your lives are going, confront problems, think up solutions, play some games, even. How does that sound?"

Silence. Oscar, on the floor, appears to be asleep. Surprisingly delicate snores issue from his thick lips. The other men sit pressed against the walls or staring into their own squares of space as though they are strangers riding a train. And yet some of them have been living together in this institution for as long as seven years. As I get more acquainted with these people, I will come to understand how they almost always dwell in such silence. At mealtimes, or in the common room, they sit rocking, tracing imaginary figures in the air, lecturing on astrophysics to an invisible audience of esteemed colleagues, while in some place I cannot get to, comets explode and suns warp into white dwarves. The men's worlds are so far away from me and from one another that only occasionally will they reach out to filch a cigarette from someone next to them, moments later hunching back into themselves and collapsing into private giggles.

But I don't know any of this yet. I'm still brand new. I look around at my drooling patients. My mind charges over techniques, hovers, herds—how can I get them to interact? The silence thickens and I can hear, coming from outside, the dry gratings of insects in the summer heat.

Finally Joseph clears his throat, takes off his combat helmet, and stares deeply into its hollow. "What's in there, Joseph?" I ask. "What's in your helmet?"

"Blood be gone and hell swell saboooose," he says. "A girl curve feminine adventure."

I struggle to think of what to say. What part of this do I understand? What part can I, or any of the other group members, connect to? A girl curve? An adventure? I decide to let it go. "And, Charlie," I say, "can you tell me something about yourself?"

"Char*les*," he cries. "No not Charlie but Char*les* Char*les* Char*les*." He bites into his lip and swings his head so violently I am reminded of a long time ago, when I went to the aquarium and saw a shark with a fish in the barbs of its teeth, the shark's flat silver head whipping back and forth as its prey's body burst. "Charles Charles Charles," he keeps repeating.

"Charles," Lenny, a black man, sings from the other side of the room. Lenny has skin the color of deep coal, his limbs long with rippled muscles rooted in them. Lenny looks so healthy, his body speaking the bones and sinews that stretch inside it. Surely, I think, this man will make some sense.

"Oh, Charles," Lenny says, looking not at Charles but resolutely up at the ceiling, "you need a protegé like Henry Collins. I have my protegé, Henry Collins, and if I don't go to Chelsea he stays with me and helps me not to be a pimp. I was once a pimp but before that my name is Cuppy."

"Cuppy?" I say to Lenny, squinting. "Your name is Cuppy?"

"Sometimes," Lenny says. "That depends on the fog."

It is useless, I think to myself during the first few weeks of the group, to try to get these men to connect with one another or myself, because connections between human beings depend at least partly on words, and the words of the schizophrenic are terribly skewed. The schizophrenic speaks a mumbo-jumbo language psychologists call a "word salad," nouns and verbs, fragments from the past, snippets of dreams all tossed into the lush wet mess. Sometimes beautiful sparks of sense do fly out, and other times bizarre but poetic hallucinations—the man with the blue ears who sleeps on the ceiling, miraculous cures that curl from test tubes foaming inside someone's head. You look for these swaths of sense and rhythm and, as you would any good wave, you try to ride it, but too often it fizzles into foam and you find yourself washed up in a tangle of mental kelp. . . .

It is late August now, and I've been leading the group for two months. . . .

I am tired of the bizarreness of my patients, more tired still of trying to ignore their hallucinations and to focus, instead, on money and meds and keeping the shirt stain-free. When Lenny tells me in group he is communing with a woman who is also a paintbrush, I say to him, as I've been trained, "No, Lenny. There are no women who are also paintbrushes in this group. Why don't you tell all of us what you actually mean? Why don't you stop slumping, sit up, and button your shirt?" When Joseph tells the group he has shot seven soldiers in World War One, I say, "You have never been in World War One. You are here in this room. With all of us now. Tell us what your plans for the weekend are and why you have overslept three days in a row." Doing this work is like being the goalie in a soccer game; over and over again the swift kicks of craziness come at you, and over and over again you try to deflect them, or better yet, take the air right out of the ball. . . .

And that may be why, when, a few days later, Oscar announces a spaceship has landed on his enormous belly, I break down. "All right," I say, looking around the room, eyeing the door and hoping it's closed so none of the other staff can hear, "why don't we go for a ride in it, then? Let's go."

"Let's go!" the irrepressible Lenny shouts, jumping up and down.

"Where?" I say, and indeed I mean it. I am thinking of the diced-up apples of desire, the green leaves of love. What about these things I hear in the schizo-phrenic's dream talk? . . .

Lenny strides across the room and eases down on the floor right next to Oscar. He takes his deep-black hand and lays it on top of Oscar's swollen white stomach. The hand sits there like a black star in a white sky, some sort of weird reversal.

"Move in," I say, looking around to the rest of my group members. "Charles," I say, "move in, right up next to Oscar. You too, Moxi," I say to the little man who, week after week, sits hunched and rocking in a corner, who won't move, won't speak, ever. Moxi is the most closed-off of all. He is missing three fingers and one testicle because the voice of Mother Mary told him to cut them off. The most he will do in group is mumble a yes or a no. "You too, Moxi," I say a little louder.

The men all eye me, something alert in their usually slack faces; they edge forward on their seats. I edge out of my own seat and sit on the floor, so close I can see the rise and fall of Oscar's belly, on his face the bubbles of sweat that seep from large red pores.

"A spaceship," I repeat to Oscar. "On your belly right now. To take us into your world." The rest of the men creep forward, sit Indian-style in a circle around him. It's the closest I've ever seen any of them get to one another. "We are going into the spaceship," I say, "and we're all riding up. What do we see, Oscar? Where are we?"

Lenny still has his hand on Oscar's belly, and now he is moving it back and forth, rubbing. Oscar, his voice flat and thick, begins to speak.

"Sheba," he says. "We are going to see Sheba. She lives up there, my girl does, in the sky. She is a star. She eats leg of lamb without the skin. And octopus."

"Octopus," Joseph says. "Freaky."

"Sheba is your girl," I say.

"I have hundreds of girls," Oscar replies, "all over the sky. Definitely they are albinos. They keep me company. They love me."

"They love you," I say and, thinking of the overweight unloved-by-girls Oscar, something sad rises up in me. I feel my own voice grow low, whispery. The room seems darker, even though the summer sun burns like an ember in the white sky outside. Shadows, sexy shadows, ripple and sway on the walls. . . .

One day, a week before Charles finally dies, I bring a rubber ball into group. "OK," I say. "Everyone up. Stand in a circle."

"Not unless Robert comes," Lenny mumbles.

"Robert can come," I say, looking over toward Robert, who has his hands jammed over his ears. "Take your hands away from your ears, Robert," I shout, "and join our circle."

We make a circle, even Moxi.

"Whoever has the ball," I explain, "cannot toss it to someone else unless he asks a question of that person first. And whoever receives the ball has to answer the question and cannot throw the ball without asking a new question. In this way, we will reestablish our friendships and continue to get to know one another better."

The men stare at me, flat-eyed. I throw the ball to Joseph. "Joseph," I say, "what are you most afraid of?"

Joseph catches the ball. "Chips," he says. "Chips the CIA have planted in my brain." He throws the ball to Oscar. "Oscar," he says, "are you—?" but then he splutters into panicked giggles and can't finish the question. Oscar doesn't even bother catching the ball. It bounces off his blubbery chest and dribbles into the center of the circle.

"OK!" I say, all fake enthusiasm. "Let's start again!" I trot into the center of the circle, pick the ball back up. But I feel ridiculous.

I bounce the ball, thinking. "Robert," I say, tossing it again. "Who do you most love?" Robert catches the ball, cradles it, and won't let go. "Throw the ball, Robert," I say. "Go on." He throws the ball then, but backward, over his head, so it swerves outside the circle, and we're all left looking at one another, looking at nothing.

I sigh. "It's hard for everyone," I say at last. "Maybe you are all too upset about Charles."

"Nuh-uh," says Oscar. He slinks back into his customary slump on the floor. "We're not upset about Charles. We're all like Charles. None of us can die, because we're already dead."

And then each member of the circle, as though on cue, slumps to the floor. Only Moxi is left standing.

Moxi's eyes tick around the room, tick back and forth over the fallen bodies. His little broom of a mustache quivers. "No," he says. It is maybe the first word he has ever said in group. "No!" he says again. "Not true! Not true!" His English is laden with a heavy Vietnamese accent. "No no no," he chants. "I come here all the way from Vietnam. I have family. Family!"

"Who's in your family?" I ask, thinking of the chart I read on Moxi, in which it was reported his father and three sisters were bombed to death in his village during the war.

"Here!" he says, his eyes still swinging around the room, lighting on me and then on the other slumped men. "Here, here. In America! My family is in this place, this room. Now!" he shouts. "Here!"

And then Moxi bursts forth. He splits his separate sphere. I don't know why Moxi once put a knife to his penis but perhaps it had to do as much with the imagined voice of Mother Mary as with the need to cut away the thick skin of madness and maleness that prevents unions from happening with any ease.

And Moxi bursts forth. He unzips his fly, and with his hips shrugs off his pants. . . .

And the little man, half-naked, begins to dance. The rest of the men come together, draw in. They hum and clap in time to a rhythm and we are all a part of it, some sacred strip dance of death and life and the links between bodies—my fingers, your toes, my cut, your crying. Moxi sways. He rolls up his shirt sleeve and, crooning, points to more charred spots on his skin. "Here," he says. "And here too." He points with precision, insists that we see his hurts, insists, yes, that we see *him*, and some love gets built around his bared body.

Still naked, Moxi kneels and begins to draw a female figure.

"Who is she?" Robert whispers.

"She is a lady," Moxi answers. "A lady from Vietnam who I want to marry but who is already married."

He looks like he is going to cry now as he scurries about the room rolling down his shirt sleeves, pulling back on his pants. Then he does cry, standing in the center of the group room. He puts his hand over his heart and starts to sing in Vietnamese. His voice and the ballad have a mournful, ancient feel, each word with some weeping inside.

"Moxi, that was beautiful," I say. "What does the song mean?"

"I love a lady who doesn't love me; I am lost, oh, so lost," Moxi says. "That's what the song means." And then he sings it again, louder, his voice lovely and quavering.

"You are so lonely, aren't you, Moxi," I say.

"Yes, and I am so sad because Oscar won't shake my hand."

Oscar, leaning back against the wall, hands folded on the bubble of his belly, opens one eye as slowly as a lizard in the sun. "Huh?" he says.

"You won't shake my hand," Moxi repeats, agitated now.

"Don't always feel like it, Moxi," Oscar says. "Sometimes I'm just too tired."

"But you want Oscar to shake your hand, Moxi," I say.

"Everyone to shake my hand," Moxi says.

"Can we shake Moxi's hand?" I ask the group.

"Yeah," says Lenny. "And then we go to a whorehouse."

"OK," I say to Moxi. "Go on. We want to shake your hand."

Moxi skips around the room, nimble, hopeful. He cavorts and bows. He shakes each man's hand with pride. "Welcome to my country," he says to each person as he clasps him in a handshake. "Welcome to my country."

"Welcome," each one of us says back.

What country does he mean? I wonder. For sure there is something a little crazy about all of this, but also so appropriate. I think of the empty skull Oscar once drew and how we are, in this group, trying to learn to go through bone and enter those private sockets where our separate brains sit. And I think, Dr. Maslow, no matter how sick we are, how strained we are, we never stop wanting such closeness. We never lose the language altogether.

Response and Analysis

1. As a group therapist, Lauren Slater uses some creative techniques to try to get the group members to interact with her and with each other. What techniques does she use? What benefits and risks might accompany the way she facilitates interactions among these clients?

2. Slater implies that she was taught to emphasize reality testing, self-help skills, and social skills with the clients. How effective is social-skills training in improving the functioning of schizophrenic clients? How does it compare with the effectiveness of insight-oriented or exploratory therapies such as cognitive, psychoanalytic, or humanistic psychotherapy?

3. Group therapy with persons with schizophrenia might have quite different goals than group therapy with people from other populations. How might the group goals and the therapist's behavior differ between this group and (a) a support group for victims of abuse, or (b) a group of juvenile delinquents?

Research

Imagine you want to compare three methods of treating schizophrenia: (a) medication alone; (b) group therapy alone; and (c) medication in conjunction with group therapy. The independent variable is type of treatment. The dependent variable is schizophrenic behavior. Which type of treatment do you think would be most effective? State your prediction as a hypothesis (include all three levels of the independent variable). How long would you conduct the study? Why? How would you measure the effectiveness of each treatment?

THERAPY WITH AN AMERICAN-INDIAN GIRL: A NATIVE AMERICAN PERSPECTIVE

Royal Alsup

Psychological Concept
culture and psychotherapy

When a client and a therapist come from different cultures, they often have different values, interactional styles, and worldviews. This can pose a significant problem for treatment. When the therapist fails to understand the influences of the client's culture, the client may feel misunderstood or pressured to abandon her or his cultural heritage. As a result, the client may feel that mental health services fail her or him, and might avoid using the services or leave treatment prematurely. As our country becomes increasingly ethnically diverse, this problem becomes more urgent. Many therapists now receive training for working with persons from specific cultures. Another approach is to have the therapist come from the same culture as the client.

Here therapist Royal Alsup describes his work with an adolescent Native American girl and notes how her cultural beliefs conflict with many traditional therapeutic techniques. He also shows how the use of alternative techniques, such as art and storytelling, can produce positive results when they are used in the context of the client's cultural background.

The psychology and worldview of the American Indian holds that it is in the silent solitude of the mind and heart, along with the ceremonial way, that one understands one's "limitations and freedom." When an American-Indian youth is pressured by the dominant culture's mental health professionals to speak about a death in the family, he or she becomes painfully caught in a clash of cultural values. The cultural conflict over how to process the experience of death brings about feelings of dread, despair, anxiety, isolation, and limitedness. American-Indian cultural norms prescribe that one can only speak with respect for the dead; and it is better not to speak at all than to risk drawing the spirit of the deceased back into the world. The therapist's ignorance of the importance of silence, words, rituals, and ancestors disrupts the dialogical healing process in the meeting of client and therapist. . . .

This study concerns a 15-year-old American-Indian girl who resisted treatment of substance abuse that was a symptom of unresolved grief from the loss of a family member. She had been to approximately five culturally insensitive therapists to whom the juvenile justice system had referred her. The reports from the therapists consistently labeled her as silent and resistant and concluded that she could not benefit from treatment and therefore that incarceration in a youth prison was the only solution.

Session One

The American-Indian girl entered the therapy session saying that she had seen me at a tribal ceremony and funeral and that she trusted me. Then she fell into silence for about ten minutes. I then told her a Coyote-Buffalo story that deals with tradition and one's role and function in tradition. In traditional Indian stories, Coyote-Buffalo are seen as both transpersonal and existential; and the stories teach moral development that balances the sacred and the profane. The Coyote-Buffalo story became a touchstone of reality for her to relate to instead of to the therapist. The story took her out of her silence, made her feel cared for, and brought about excitement and inspiration that helped her relate her own personal story to the mythic tale. At my suggestion, she used art materials with enthusiasm to make a collage to express herself symbolically.

By projecting her intimate feelings and the caring of her tribal traditions onto the symbols of the collage, she was able to integrate cognitively and affectively her tribal moral tradition as it was expressed in the story. The storytelling made her aware that the choices she was making had been taking her away from her "path of life," causing her to be psychologically and spiritually out of balance. She used alcohol and drugs to mask the pain of her feelings of disharmony, discomfort, and suffering.

Session Seven

In this session, I gave the Indian girl an assignment to do a collage of how she saw her tribe and what the tribe represented in her life. As she worked, her tribal story unfolded, and she expressed the feelings of safety, security, belonging, and love that she received from the experience of being known by the Creator. . . .

Her collage showed a landscape symbolizing her tribal land within certain boundaries. The symbols of rituals, the landscape, and the Creator expressed that these touchstones of reality talked to her personally to reassure her of her Indianness within the sacred cathedral of her tribal land. The symbols in her collage brought about a psychological transformation of her attitude from one of depression, constriction, and limitedness to one of joyfulness, expansiveness, and freedom.

By the end of this session, the girl was more "self-affirmed" and seemed to have more of a sense of how she fit within the boundaries of her daily life because she felt more "centered." She started talking about how she had been losing her sense of being and her sense of identity. Now she could see her limitedness within this mythological world, but she was also inspired and excited about claiming her freedom by not feeling driven to conform to the non-Indian youth at her high school. Now she saw that to follow her tribal ways and the morals of living nonindulgently would help free her from her addiction to methamphetamines. It gave her an experience of how the limitations of her Indian traditions also gave her meaning, purpose, and freedom.

Session Twelve

At this session, I suggested she do a collage about her family and the role or function her family members played in the tribal community. I also told her another Coyote story. In this one, Coyote reverses all the destruction caused by the loggers' greed. All the trees are returned to the forest by blue-shirted logger-shamans, who put the trees back in the ground, re-attach the boughs and limbs, and thus re-establish all the natural habitats of the animals. American-Indian stories unite consciousness with the unconscious, thereby giving the Indian a deep sense of direction and purpose. The structure that gives meaning in this psychological process is what existentialists call *intentionality*.

The girl enthusiastically started a new collage that showed her family members, who were loggers as well as dance people. Members of her family traditionally brought their dance regalia and dancers to help with the tribal renewal ceremony that puts the earth back in balance. This artistic moment was literally a renewal of her personality in that it gave her a real sense of her identity as an Indian person. The affective awareness of her family as loggers who were also dance people working for the earth's balance made her feel a deep I-and-Thou meeting with me. This dialogical presence was the true healing event because it made her feel her connectedness to a therapist who was truly interested in her family mythology and her tribal community. She felt proud of belonging to her family and tribe, and her sense of freedom sparkled through her joy and excitement.

There were several more sessions in which the girl further strengthened her sense of Indian identity. She started living according to her traditions; and the pride she took in her family's role in the tribal community as dancers and regalia makers helped her to abstain from using drugs. In a year, she was released from probation and became an honor student. Her new, stronger sense of identity as a tribal member helped her to confront the isolation that resulted when she lost her substance-abusing friends, and this gave her a context of greater freedom and potential.

The death-and-grief issues were addressed in psychotherapy through the indirect, symbolic processes of storytelling, art making, and dreamwork that honored her need for silence and her sense of being. During therapy, she had a dream that reassured her that her family member had survived the journey from ordinary life to the spirit land. The dream relieved her depression and her grief and put her back on her tribal path of life.

Conclusion

The mental health professional needs to be alert to the following for the healing dialogue to be created in the Between with American-Indian clients:

1. A mythological worldview that is based in the concrete, existential events of daily life and reflects a personalism of the transpersonal and immanent Creator.
2. The sacredness of all human personality.
3. The social existence of the Supreme Personality, who addresses the American Indian through various touchstones of reality—ritual, story, song, myth, dreams, visions, regalia, and the landscape that is more global than regional.
4. The independence, uniqueness, and wholeness of the American-Indian client in response to the address from the Supreme Personality.
5. The individuation process of the American Indian that helps maintain and develop a "we" psychology and brings about individuation through participation in community.
6. The importance of confirming American Indians' identity or sense of being, their tribal family, and their personal mythology as these unfold in the I-and-Thou moment within the therapeutic setting.
7. The need to practice indwelling by attending ceremonies, visiting families, working with tribal healers, and engaging in communicative social action. . . .

Finally, it is ontologically necessary in psychotherapy with American-Indian clients to draw upon silence, or the creative pause, and to use tribal symbol systems through storytelling and art making. Silence in the therapeutic milieu creates an environment where the internal conflict of opposites—death and life, meaninglessness and meaning, limitedness and freedom—can be creatively resolved. Silence allows the symbols to emerge and to integrate the troubled psyche. Through the use of tribal symbols in the therapy session, the therapist witnesses and confirms the integrity of the Indian person. In this manner, an I-and-Thou meeting is created that brings about the client's confrontation with his or her freedom. This shift in attitude brings about the existential healing.

Response and Analysis

1. Why does Royal Alsup suggest that an understanding of cultural issues is important for effective treatment?

2. Alsup describes this case from an existential perspective. What are the main assumptions of this approach? How do they fit with the cultural conflicts faced by the client?

3. What theoretical assumptions are behind the use of drawing and storytelling as therapeutic techniques? What assumptions do you think are behind the use of silence?

4. Alsup says that mental health professionals need to be aware of several factors when treating American-Indian clients. Which of his seven conclusions, or which parts of his conclusions, do you think generalize to any ethnic population? Why? To what extent might Alsup's conclusions be influenced by his theoretical orientation?

Research

Indwelling is the practice of therapists attending ceremonies, visiting families, and taking part in the cultural life of clients. Suppose you are interested in examining whether indwelling can improve therapeutic outcomes. You decide to send surveys to a random sample of therapists who do and do not practice indwelling. Your findings suggest that therapists who practice indwelling report more improved therapeutic outcomes than therapists who do not practice indwelling. What possible alternative explanations could account for your finding?

CREATING AN ETHICAL POSITION IN FAMILY THERAPY

Ivan B. Inger and Jeri Inger

Psychological Concepts
family therapy, collaboration by cotherapists

In this transcript, cotherapists Ivan and Jeri Inger work with Dan (the father), Rebecca (the mother), and their two sons, Steve, age twelve, and Tim, age ten. Steve has been labelled as severely emotionally disturbed, and his teachers and counselors at school want to learn what part the family might play in Steve's problems. Steve was described to them as being "a very strange boy . . . withdrawn . . . dishevelled . . .

confused, [and] very, very bright." He admits having terrible fights with his parents, being anxious, and being "the most picked-on kid in school."

The family agreed to let this session be recorded (and subsequently published) and was glad to contribute to the education of others. In this selection, the initial interview has already begun and some time has been spent getting acquainted and making the family feel comfortable. Note how the Ingers follow important principles of family therapy: giving each member the freedom to speak, focusing on the way the family deals with their problems (the process) rather than exclusively on the problems themselves (the content), and exploring whether the family's problems might be broader than the troubled behavior of Steve, the identified client. In italicized passages, the Ingers reflect on what is taking place during this session.

Note: This portion of the interview takes place after the therapists, Ivan and Jeri Inger, have acknowledged that all of the family members are nervous and have helped put them at ease. The therapists want to learn about the family and ask questions about the activities they enjoy doing together. The father, Dan, and his son Tim are building an addition to the house, but Steve, his other son, says that he does not work with them because he is not very good with his hands. The mother, Rebecca, then says that Steve is hard on himself, and this raises the question of whether anyone else in the family is hard on himself or herself.

Dan: Sometimes I find myself deciding to be hard on myself, and sometimes I find myself having it approach me, and I kind of realize that I'm in that situation. And sometimes there are different reactions. You can step back and think, gosh, I really need to lighten up here. Did that really count that much? Other times, you know . . .

Jeri: You actually think that way?

[Jeri disrupts Dan in genuine amazement. Dan has just told us about his ability to reflect upon his actions. In light of the information we were given about this father, we are truly amazed and impressed with his reflectivity, sensitivity, and ability to articulate both. Now we must let go of our stereotypic misconception of this man and his family. Our misconceptions could interfere with our ability to hear them in their own right. If we continue to invoke misperceptions, we will have a mis-meeting.]

Dan: Yeah . . .
Jeri: You can back away and observe it?
Dan: Sometimes. [Laughs] Sometimes.
Jeri: That's very impressive.
Dan: It's easier to do it the decision way than . . .
Ivan: You mean sometimes you decide, "I'm going to be hard on myself?"
Dan: Yeah, sometimes when you feel your performance demands that you be hard on yourself, then you decide to be hard on yourself.
Ivan: Do you think Steve knows how to do that? [To Steve] Do you know how

to do what your Dad just said he knows how to do? To step back, to say: "Why am I doing this?" And he makes a decision whether to be hard on himself or not?

   Steve: No. I don't really know how to do that.

[Ivan is looking to see if this is a shared attribute between father and son, furthering the question about shared attributes. It is also a question about Steve's ability to see his connectedness to his father.]

   Jeri: How do you think your Dad learned how to do that?

   Steve: Well he probably got . . . well he probably . . . probably just learned from, you know, what he was going through. He probably just learned from getting himself knocked down a few times.

   Ivan: Really? He had some hard knocks?

   Steve: I don't know, but probably.

   Ivan: [To Steve] Have you had some?

   Steve: Yeah.

[Ivan has made a calculated guess that since Steve was faltering, he was probably thinking about himself.]

   Ivan: Have you been knocked down?

   Steve: Mmm-huh [Yes].

   Ivan: Did you learn the same way he has learned?

   Steve: I don't learn very much.

   Ivan: You don't? You mean you're already set in the way you do things?

   Steve: No, I don't learn very quickly but, . . .

   Ivan: So you're careful about learning?

   Steve: [Sigh] Yeah.

[Steve says he does not learn very much, and he is a slow learner. Ivan introduces a positive alternative by suggesting that he is a careful learner. This offers Steve options to think about.]

   Rebecca: He approaches people very cautiously. 'Cause people tend to hurt him. He interprets, or it seems to me, he interprets a lot of actions in a different way than other people.

   Ivan: Tim, did your Mom say something that upset you?

[Ivan abruptly turns to Tim out of concern for his nonverbal reaction at that moment.]

   Tim: No. It's just that it seems my brother knows a lot, but he just wants to get bad grades. I don't know why, but he just likes to get bad grades.

   Ivan: Why do you think a guy would like to get bad grades?

   Tim: To get attention.

   Jeri: Wait! I've got to go slow because this is amazing. You think that he knows a lot, but he just gets bad grades in order to get attention?

[Jeri is amazed that Tim is aware of how smart Steve is, and that Tim has given so much thought to this dilemma that he has come up with his own hypothesis.]

    Tim: Well, it's just that I know he's really smart, and . . .
    Ivan: He's really smart?
    Tim: Yeah.
    Ivan: Does he know that?
    Tim: Yes!
    Jeri: Wow!
    Ivan: He knows that.
    Steve: I'm definitely top of the class!

[What a different response compared with Steve's previous self-effacing remarks. Tim has inadvertently brought out a side of Steve that is positive, self-confident, and may never have been seen in the school system.]

    Ivan: You're definitely top?
    Steve: Yeah. I should be.
    Tim: I think everybody makes fun of him because he's so smart.

[Tim offers us his very valuable hypothesis about why his brother is treated badly at school by his peers.]

    Ivan: Really? He's so smart that they make fun of him.
    Steve: I think I should be in a higher grade, but I'm just not motivated, 'cause, I mean, I've gone through review like this for the past four years. School's boring, you don't learn almost anything.

[This is Steve's hypothesis about why he does not produce in school. He believes he is bored and confined to reviewing subjects he already knows.]

    Ivan: Is that right? But they haven't caught onto this yet at school?
    Steve: I've tried to tell people.
    Ivan: Who have you tried to tell?
    Steve: I don't know. I've told my Mom and Dad. Actually they're the ones who got the idea.

[The hypothesis is a shared view with his parents. It is also a view known to Tim. They must talk about all this at home.]

    Ivan: So who did they tell?
    Steve: I don't know.
    Jeri: If Dad is similar to you by being hard on himself, is he also similar to you in being very, very smart?
    Steve: Um-huh. [Yes]

Ivan: So he's smart too?

Jeri: Does anyone know that Dad is smart?

Ivan: [To Tim] You must be smart, because you're the one who brought this whole thing up.

Jeri: Do people know that Dad is smart?

Tim: [Whispers] I'm smart too.

Jeri: [Also responding to Tim] You are too!

Ivan: You must have two smart parents because I think smart kids come from smart parents.

Rebecca: No.

Ivan: No?

Rebecca: No, I just come along for the ride.

Ivan: Wait a minute!

Jeri: Sounds like one more person is hard on themselves.

[We now get a glimpse of the possible origin of Steve's self-effacing attitude.]

Ivan: Yes. Not only that, but, that's where we started the conversation that Steve doesn't think a lot of himself. We now have a dilemma here.

[It is important that we have picked up on that earlier comment about people being hard on themselves. It turns out that being hard on oneself is part of a basic attitude held by the family. It is becoming clear to us that this whole family believes that being hard on oneself is an important attribute.]

Jeri: Yes.

Ivan: So we have a family that's hard on itself, but smart. [To Rebecca] Except, you won't accept being smart?

Rebecca: Well, I'm smart, but I'm not like him [Steve] or this one [Tim], or this one [Dad], in the sense that, you know, I'm bored.

Jeri: You're also the only woman in the family. . . .

Ivan: What about you, Tim? How close do you think Dad and Steve are?

Tim: I don't play with Steve much cause he likes to jump on me all the time.

Ivan: Is he too big to jump on you?

Tim: Yeah. Well, he . . . when it comes to smart . . . well, we're just alike, but . . .

Ivan: When it comes to smart you're alike?

Tim: Yeah. But he never thinks smart unless it's at school and he's learning.

Jeri: He doesn't think smart?

Ivan: I didn't quite get that.

Tim: He doesn't like to use his brain. Only when he wants to, only when he needs to.

Jeri: So, he doesn't use his brain in school?

Ivan: You think he has control of that?

Tim: Yeah.

Ivan: You do? [To Steve] You think you have control over when you think smart and when you don't?

Steve: I'm usually too busy trying to stay away from a fight or just save myself from getting beat up. I don't have any time to think of schoolwork.

Ivan: So it's pretty scary?

[We learn for the first time that Steve spends most of his time at school being scared and finding ways to avoid being beaten up by other boys. It seems that most of the time he is acting out of fear. This is very different from acting from a position of being emotionally disturbed. His worldview is that school is a dangerous place. Thus, his actions are syntonic with his worldview.]

Steve: Yeah. When I have to go out, I have to tie down all my things. I have to tie them in the classroom at my desk because people go through there and ransack my things.

Ivan: You mean they kick you out of the room?

Steve: Then I have to go out and I have to go out with the teachers into the halls where they watch the other guys. So, I always have to be right beside the teachers. Because if I'm left alone in a classroom, they'll kill me.

Ivan: They'll kill you?

Steve: Well, pretty close to it. They do some pretty gruesome things to me. I've been hit, punched, kicked, knocked over . . .

Ivan: Nobody there to protect you?

Steve: Huh, uhh.

Ivan: Do you tell anybody?

Steve: I tried once.

Ivan: . . . about how dangerous it is . . .

Steve: . . . but the bell rang and I had to go to the classroom.

Jeri: [To Steve] Can I interrupt you a minute?

Steve: Yeah.

Jeri: Dan, have you heard this before?

Dan: Yeah, I have.

Jeri: Okay. I wasn't sure if you had.

Dan: I think that for Steve that's a real thing. That's really how he feels. Kind of a spooky thing.

Ivan: Have you ever been picked on yourself, Dan?

Dan: No, I don't think so.

Ivan: You haven't had that experience, then?

Dan: Nah, I wouldn't say so.

Ivan: So you wouldn't know what it's like to be that scared?

Dan: I don't think I'd know what it's like to be that scared, but I think I'd know what it is to be, oh, kind of, what would I say, marginally popular, or something like that, or a little different, you know.

Ivan: A little different.

[By repeating one line of the dialogue we punctuate the idea we are repeating, and in addition we find that sometimes we can help clients stay with that thought or come back to it if their mind is going too fast. Again, it is a way of slowing things down so everyone can keep up with the thoughts, ideas, and feelings of everyone else. We hope the family will learn to do this and slow themselves down and, thus, communicate more clearly. . . .

We have some important threads to go back to. We feel that we have enough information now to be able to weave these threads about the pattern of the fabric of the family. We also feel that we have developed enough trust with Steve to elicit genuine feelings, different from the ones we might have elicited earlier in the process.]

Steve: [My mother has] known me since I was a little baby. Parents like to be protectors. She wants to try and fight my battles, and, right now, I'm going through adolescence. So, I'm trying to grow up, and I'm being restrained a little bit. Sometimes I just, I'm not sure what I think, I just kind of lose my head, and I kind of go wild, I just . . .

Jeri: . . . like a person being restrained from growing up.

Steve: Yeah, I don't think very clearly or rationally. I just kind of don't put my head on straight. You know, say things I would never even mean to say.

Ivan: Is that adolescence?

Steve: I don't know.

Jeri: Is that adolescence or is that being restrained from growing up?

[We are asking for such distinctions in the hope of learning about Steve's theory of what is going on with him. To what extent is he, as a 12-year-old male, beginning to struggle with issues of individualism, autonomy, and self-sufficiency?]

Steve: It might be a mixture. It's probably more adolescence than being restrained.

Ivan: So, Mom is protecting you?

Steve: Yeah.

Ivan: Does that mean that's part of restraint?

Steve: By some people's standard, they'd be calling me over-sheltered.

Jeri: Over-sheltered? Okay.

[Steve is demonstrating that he has thought about these ideas. He has an ability to reflect on the relative merits of his ideas about himself and his relationships. This does not seem to be subject matter that a seriously emotionally disturbed adolescent would be preoccupied with.]

Ivan: Maybe your Mother still thinks she has a 12-year-old that she's raising, and she doesn't realize she has an 18-year-old.

Steve: Well, I'm not emotionally ready.

Jeri: Not emotionally ready for what?

Steve: Well, for living on my own or anything.

Jeri: Oh, okay, oh good . . .

Steve: Well, what happened is, in grade school, you know, jumping from 6th grade to 7th grade, it's like trying to jump up a 40-foot wall. You've got to be really determined to go up it.

[Steve continues to impress us with his ability to be self-reflective and thoughtful about his own experiences and his own development. He is exceptionally articulate for a 12-year-old child.]

>Jeri: Yes.
>Steve: In grade school they just had mock fights and stuff, you know, nothing bad—they'll say things to you—it won't be that bad. And you think that alcohol and drugs are a real far-off thing, and then when you get into junior high you've always got this stuff around. You've got people actually wanting to throw you into walls.
>Jeri: Thrown into walls because . . .?
>Steve: Because they didn't like me. I mean, they don't really have any reason. They'll just go violent.
>Ivan: So who's there to protect you?
>Steve: Nobody.
>Ivan: Your Mom protects you at home. Can she protect you elsewhere?
>Steve: She hopes she can, but she can't.

[We have here a good example of what happens to a male child as he has experiences with other males away from home and away from the nurturing of his mother. It gets dangerous in the world, and his ability to cope with it is questionable. He seems to come from a home where there is no violence and where his being different is accepted. This is not the case in the unprotected world of school.]

>Rebecca: I wish I could.
>Ivan: Really, is that a tough job?
>Rebecca: [With tears in her eyes] Oh, yeah. It's hard to let him go.
>Ivan: To not be able to protect him in public?
>Rebecca: Oh, sure. I realize that's part of our struggle right now. Stevie used to be someone who was very easy to take care of, to fight his battles for him and stuff. I can share an incident with you. I'm beginning to recognize that part of that is just natural pulling away. He's growing up.

[Rebecca has let us know how hard letting-go is for her by using the diminutive, "Stevie." Here we have an example of a mother who is having to struggle with letting her 12-year-old male son separate from her. It is a self-effacing experience for the mother, and probably a premature experience for the son, who feels the cultural pressure to separate but does not have the emotional maturity to carry it off.]

>Jeri: Ouch!

[Jeri responds to Rebecca with compassion in a way that is open and sensitive and leaves room for humor.
We are now at a point in the interview where we are no longer struggling for under-

standing about this family because we are completely immersed with them in their experience. We are in that between *where the differentiation between who is inside and who is outside is not important. What is important is the genuineness of the contact of the moment and the confirmation derived from that feeling of being inclusive. It is a state of having reconciled the contraries so that we can accept them and they us in all our wholeness in the present.]*

Rebecca: He bought a little magnifying glass and took it to school. A kid took it away from him, and Stevie wasn't able to get it back. My natural inclination would be, let's get the boy on the phone, let's call the parents, let's get hysterical, let's get upset. What I did instead was I gave it back to Stevie. I said, Stevie, you're going to have to figure this one out.

Jeri: Is that right?

Rebecca: I thought that was really a big deal for me. Because it wasn't what I wanted to do.

Jeri: It was a big deal.

Rebecca: Yeah, it was.

Jeri: I'm impressed. But that must be hard for you as a mother.

Rebecca: Yes, because it's not normal for me to do that.

Jeri: Did anybody else know it was a big deal?

Rebecca: I think Stevie did, because the next day he processed what he was going to do about the situation. I was able to trust him enough to figure it out himself. He went up to the kid, and he gave him a couple of options. He can either give it back to me or he can give it to the vice-principal.

Steve: I said, either you give it to me, you let me look in your locker, or I'll have the vice-principal look through your locker. So you know, then he said that this was all a joke, and he gave it to me.

Rebecca: He was able to process it himself. I felt really good about it. I told him so, too.

Jeri: Do you think Dan knew what a big deal that was for you to be able to let go of Steve?

[We want to make sure that Rebecca is getting enough support to carry through with this difficult task of letting go of her first child.]

Rebecca: I think he knows that. He's the one who's been trying to tell me I should [laughing].

Jeri: I see.

Rebecca: It's very hard. It's real hard. I don't know, I've never had a teenager before. I don't know what I'm supposed to do. And I recognize that there's that pulling away, but there's still that wanting to nurture and wanting to be nurtured. And I don't know where the line is on that.

Jeri: That's tough.

Rebecca: Especially when kids pick on him.

Ivan: [To Steve] Did you know it was tough on Mom?

Steve: Yeah, it's probably extremely hard.

Ivan: More tough on her than on you?

Steve: I wouldn't say that. I'd say it's probably mixed. I mean I can be real cruel to people and I can be real cold. Okay, I can be real cold on the outside and kind of mean. Try to test me, and I'll bounce it right back at you. I don't let anybody mess with me, even though I can't do anything about it. I turn people away.

Ivan: You turn people away when you get cornered? Is it effective?

Steve: Mmm. Not always.

Jeri: [To Ivan] Are you as impressed as I am that he was aware that it was difficult for Mom? I usually don't come across 12-year-old kids who are striving for their independence and know it's difficult on their Moms.

Ivan: I was struck by that too. I'm wondering if other 12-year-olds don't understand him, if his parents also might not understand him, because he can take both sides.

Jeri: Yes.

Ivan: He's not acting like adolescents who take one side and fight to the death. Steve says: "Well, I understand that it's tough on you and it's tough on me." He understands all this. He says: "I'm not emotionally ready!"

Jeri: And he says: "She's restraining me, but I'm trying."

[This is an example of a spontaneous reflection between us about Steve and the dilemma of growing up and being different. We are discussing the self-reflectivity of this 12-year-old and we are confirming, but with a positive tone, how different he is.] . . .

Ivan: How are you doing, Tim? Are we paying too much attention to him?

Tim: Nooo.

Ivan: I remember you mentioned that he likes the attention.

Tim: Yeah.

Ivan: And you seem very quiet and mellow over there.

Tim: Yeah. I think he's just making up stories to get attention. And it makes me jealous.

[These two children continue to impress us with their grasp of their emotional reactions to one another. They are articulate about their feelings in ways many children, especially males, are not.]

Steve: The story I just told?

Jeri: [To Tim] And it makes you jealous?

Steve: What I said right here?

Tim: Yeah.

Ivan: He says he's jealous.

Tim: Well, most of it's true.

Ivan: Most of it.

Jeri: Do you think Steve ever gets jealous of you Tim?

Tim: Yeah. He gets jealous of me.

Jeri: When do you think he gets jealous of you?

Tim: Well, . . . I don't know. Well, . . . I know a lot of kids at school do.

Jeri: When do you think your brother feels jealous of you?

Tim: Well [long pause] . . . that I get to do a lot of things that Steve doesn't get to do.

Jeri: Like what? What do you get to do?

Tim: I get the mail. But he doesn't really care about that.

Ivan: What does he care about that you do that he's jealous of?

Tim: I don't know.

Steve: Well, okay . . .

Jeri: I think he wants to tell you.

Steve: Well, if I'm ever trying to do something with my Dad, I'll usually say something that I shouldn't, and that's it. Me and Dad will get in a yelling contest. Or not yelling actually, it's more like a discussion. Of course I go out of the house and I couldn't care less. But Tim, he seems to in-fight, he seems to worm his way in somehow.

Jeri: Worm his way in?

Steve: I guess I'm jealous of Tim because he knows what to say around Dad and when to say it. I'll open my mouth and say something really stupid. Most of the time I try to sell myself a lot on the idea that I don't care. I guess I really do care.

[Steve offers another amazing self-reflection about his feelings. He is able to articulate the internal struggle he has about a typical adolescent issue of caring and not appearing to care.

These children are being exceptionally candid. For our part, we are fully appreciating the conversation about similarities and differences and the reconciliation of and respect for differences.]

Ivan: So he [Tim] knows how to do things and stay in a good place with your Dad.

Steve: Uh huh.

Ivan: He has a very important skill.

Steve: Yeah. I'm not sure what you'd call it. You might call it deception, you might call it kind of lying [laughs]. He'll always find the solution, even if it's something there is one-in-a-million chance that it would work. He always finds his way into something.

Jeri: Do you think Dad is a little surprised at what you said, or very surprised?

Steve: I don't know. [Sigh] You'll have to ask him.

Dan: I am a little surprised, but not entirely surprised. I think it's part of what we were talking about earlier, about how you felt you were mostly like me. But I like to do things like pound nails, fix things, and your brother really likes that too. So that lends itself, doesn't it, to that earlier thing about jealousy?

Steve: Yeah.

Jeri: [To Steve] Do you like to do things that they like to do, the two of them?

Steve: Well, we talk. Sometimes I'll have a question and, the two of us, we'll have a talk.

Jeri: The two of you?

Steve: Yeah. We'll talk intellectual ideas. I'll ask him a question and it will come into a conversation. I'll tell him what I think on different theories.

Ivan: So you are both theory men?

Steve: Yeah. Sometimes we talk. Most of the time I usually think of the theories, and he usually just knows a lot of information. I usually judge on different things because I guess you could call me a budding poet.

Ivan: A budding poet!

Steve: Yeah. I like writing poems and stories.

Ivan: You do?

Steve: Yeah, I'm a pretty good author.

Jeri: You know I always think it's interesting the way that families work out. One kid gets a father that likes to do stuff, and one kid gets the father that likes to talk about stuff.

Ivan: This family has one father that likes to do both.

Jeri: Yes, and does both too.

Steve: I know, but he actually probably does more of the other things. Occasionally I can get him into a good discussion. We mainly agree on everything, so discussions are not real exciting.

Ivan: Is that right?

Steve: If you agree on things, discussions are not very exciting.

Ivan: Have you ever thought of writing poetry together?

Steve: I write better on my own, actually . . . .

Ivan: Can they cope with geniuses at your school?

Rebecca: Not unmotivated ones. Motivated ones they probably can because they plug them into the system that's already there. Ones that haven't been motivated don't get into the special programs. You gotta be motivated first.

Ivan: I'm getting the impression that Steve is protecting himself about some very important things. He's very motivated in this conversation, but you seem to be protecting yourself from the outside world.

Steve: I like discussing, especially with adults.

Ivan: I'm impressed that he needs a mentor. . . .

Rebecca: Can you remember one of your poems that you could tell them?

Steve: Oh yeah.

Tim: He has one about the turkeys being slaughtered.

Jeri: One about the turkeys being slaughtered.

Dan: It actually was an article instead of a poem that you published.

Steve: I was doing a project, and me and Randy, he's actually my best friend in school, wrote this article together about turkey slaughter on Thanksgiving. It was about Mr. Herbert McTurkey. He was protesting the turkey murders. He was out on the street protesting this ad for a turkey resort. This turkey resort would offer free rides on the train. What happened was they got the turkeys on the train, and cornered them, and they killed them.

Ivan: But they never returned.

Jeri: A resort is supposed to be a safe place.

[What an incredible metaphor Steve created about his school experience. He is promised an education, but that is not what he got. It is not a safe enough place to learn. It is clear that Steve has a deep sense of mistrust about school. It is very hard for him to trust the outside world. It does not seem, however, that he mistrusts his parents. In fact, he exhibits a good deal of compassion for them.]

Response and Analysis

1. How do the therapists help the family feel secure and unthreatened in this therapeutic setting?

2. What concerns besides helping the family feel unthreatened do these therapists have? What do they do to address these concerns?

3. What is reflection and what is its use in this interview?

4. What are the possible benefits of a male-female therapist team when working with families? What are the advantages of a two-person therapist team when working with families? The disadvantages? Do you believe the advantages outweigh the disadvantages? Why or why not?

5. What are the benefits of family therapy versus individual therapy?

Research

Suppose you are interested in assessing the effectiveness of family therapy. A critical issue that you need to address is how you can determine whether therapy has been effective. Would you ask the therapist or the client whether there has been a reduction of tension among the family members? Why? How else might you assess effectiveness? Would you hypothesize that clients and therapists understand or describe effectiveness differently? Why or why not?

Chapter 1 Anxiety Disorders

p. 3: "I Am Not Afraid" by Barbara Harrison. Copyright © 1996 by Barbara Harrison. Reprinted by permission of Georges Borchardt, Inc. for the author. Originally appeared in _Health_ magazine, May/June 1996. **p. 8:** From _The Sky Is Falling: Understanding and Coping with Phobias, Panic, and Obsessive-Compulsive Disorders_ by Raeann Dumont. Copyright © 1996 by Raeann Dumont. Reprinted by permission of W. W. Norton & Company, Inc. **p. 14:** "The Auto Accident That Never Was," from _The Boy Who Couldn't Stop Washing_ by Dr. Judith Rapoport. Copyright © 1989 by Judith L. Rapoport, M.D. Used by permission of Dutton Signet, a division of Penguin Books USA, Inc. **p. 20:** Reprinted with the permission of Scribner, a division of Simon & Schuster from _Achilles in Vietnam_ by Jonathan Shay. Copyright © 1994 by Jonathan Shay.

Chapter 2 Dissociative Disorders

p. 28: From _The Divided Woman_ by Sidney M. Katz, with the assistance of Lionel P. Solursh and Jane Loring (Don Mills, Ont.: General Pub. Co., 1973). Copyright © 1973 by Sidney Katz Enterprises Ltd. and Lionel Solursh. Reprinted by permission. **p. 34:** Copyright © 1994 by Dr. Elizabeth Loftus and Katherine Ketcham. From _The Myth of Repressed Memory_ by Dr. Elizabeth Loftus and Katherine Ketcham. Reprinted by permission of St. Martin's Press Incorporated. **p. 40:** Reprinted with permission of the author, Quiet Storm. Originally appeared in _First for Women_, November 1, 1993.

Chapter 3 Somataform Disorders and Factitious Disorders

p. 47: Excerpts from _Phantom Illness: Shattering the Myth of Hypochondria_. Copyright © 1996 by Carla Cantor. Reprinted by permission of Houghton Mifflin Company. All rights reserved. **p. 54:** From _The Broken Mirror_ by Katharine A. Phillips. Copyright © 1996 by Katharine A. Phillips, M.D. Used by permission of Oxford University Press, Inc. **p. 59:** From Marc D. Feldman and Charles V. Ford, _Patient or Pretender: Inside the Strange World of Factitious Disorders_. Copyright © 1994 by John Wiley & Sons, Inc. Reprinted by permission of John Wiley & Sons, Inc.

Chapter 4 Mood Disorders

p. 67: Excerpts from _Prozac Nation_. Copyright © 1994 by Elizabeth Wurtzel. Reprinted by permission of Houghton Mifflin Company. All rights reserved. **p. 74:** From _An Unquiet Mind_ by Kay Redfield Jamison. Copyright © 1995 by Kay Redfield Jamison. Reprinted by permission of Alfred A. Knopf, Inc.

Chapter 5   Suicide

p. 83: Excerpts from Chapter 2 and Chapter 27 in *A Time to Listen: Preventing Youth Suicide*. Copyright © 1987 by Patricia Hermes. Reprinted by permission of Harcourt Brace & Company. **p. 89:** From *Sunshowers* by Karen Kenyon. Copyright © 1981. Reprinted by permission. **p. 95:** From *Darkness Visible* by William Styron. Copyright © 1990 by William Styron. Reprinted by permission of Random House, Inc.

Chapter 6   Psychological Factors and Medical Conditions

p. 100: From *Is It Worth Dying For?* by Robert S. Eliot, M.D. and Dennis L. Breo. Copyright © 1984 by Robert S. Eliot, M.D. and Dennis L. Breo. Used by permission of Bantam Books, a division of Bantam Doubleday Dell Publishing Group, Inc. **p. 105:** "In Bed" from *The White Album* by Joan Didion. Copyright © 1979 by Joan Didion. Reprinted by permission of Farrar, Straus & Giroux, Inc. **p. 108:** From *Days of Grace* by Arthur Ashe and Arnold Rampersad. Copyright © 1993 by Jeanne Moutoussamy-Ashe and Arnold Rampersad. Reprinted by permission of Alfred A. Knopf, Inc. **p. 114:** Floyd Skloot, "Thorns into Feathers: Coping with Chronic Illness," *Commonweal*, February 10, 1995. Copyright © 1995 by Commonweal Foundation. Used by permission.

Chapter 7   Schizophrenia

p. 121: Carol S. North, *Welcome Silence: My Triumph over Schizophrenia*. (New York: Simon & Schuster.) Copyright © 1987 by Carol S. North. Reprinted by permission of the author. **p. 131:** From *Tell Me I'm Here* by Anne Deveson; foreword by E. Fuller Torrey. Copyright © 1991 by Anne Deveson. Used by permission of Viking Penguin, a division of Penguin Books USA, Inc. Also used by permission of Penguin Books Australia, Ltd. **p. 138:** Allan Davis, "I Feel Cheated by Having This Illness," from *Menninger Perspective*, 1996, #3. Reprinted by permission of the author and the Menninger Clinic.

Chapter 8   Personality Disorders and Impulse Control Disorders

p. 147: From *The Duke of Deception* by Geoffrey Wolff. Copyright © 1979 by Geoffrey Wolff. Reprinted by permission of Random House, Inc. **p. 151:** From *Girl, Interrupted* by Susanna Kaysen. Copyright © 1993 by Susanna Kaysen. Reprinted by permission of Random House, Inc. **p. 160:** From *Losing Your Shirt: Recovery for Compulsive Gamblers and Their Families* by Mary Heineman, C.S.W., C.A.C. Copyright © 1992 by Mary Heineman. Reprinted by permission of Hazelden Foundation, Center City, MN.

Chapter 9   Substance-Related Disorders

p. 167: From *Drinking: A Love Story* by Caroline Knapp. Copyright © 1995 by Caroline Knapp. Used by permission of The Dial Press/Dell Publishing, a division of Bantam Doubleday Dell Publishing Group, Inc. **p. 172:** Text, pp. 237–239, 241–244, from *Getting Better: Inside Alcoholics Anonymous* by Nan Robertson. Copyright © 1988 by Nan Robertson. Used by permission of William Morrow & Company, Inc. **p. 177:** D. H. was a sophomore in college majoring in psychology when this was written. Currently, he is working on his doctorate in clinical psychology at the California School of Professional Psychology in San Diego. Reprinted by permission of the author. **p. 180:** From *Cocaine: An In-Depth Look at the Facts, Science, History and Future of the World's Most Addictive Drug* by John C. Flynn. Copyright © 1991 by John C. Flynn. Published by arrangement with Carol Publishing Group. A Birch Lane Press Book.

Name Index

Subject Index